NOTE

GENERAL BONNAL'S "Vie Militaire du Maréchal Ney," an elaborate work, which reproduces a large number of hitherto unpublished documents from the archives of the French War Office, is the chief authority for the earlier chapters of this life of Ney. So far only two volumes of General Bonnal's work have appeared. They bring the story down to the summer of 1807. Use has also been made of the so-called "Memoirs of Marshal Ney," published by his family; of the memoirs of his aides-de-camp De Fezensac, De Léoncourt and Heymès; of the Count de la Bédoyère's collection of notes on the Marshal's life and family; of M. Henri Houssaye's works on 1814 and 1815; and of M. Weil's very complete study of the trial and execution, with the wealth of documents it contains.

A. H. A.

CONTENTS

CHAPTER I

PAGE

First Years (1769-1794) 1

Ney born in a year of great men—Family and birthplace—Education—Legal studies—Employed in the iron industry—Enlists in the hussars—First promotion to non-commissioned rank—A duel—Beginning of the Revolutionary Wars—Serves in campaign of Valmy—Promoted sub-lieutenant—Serves in Belgium—Jemappes—Aide-de-camp to General Lamarche—Treason of Dumouriez—Ney rejoins the hussars—Aide-de-camp to General Colaud—Promoted captain, Ney returns to his regiment—Serves under Kléber in Belgium—Selected as his staff officer.

CHAPTER II

In Belgium and the Rhineland—Ney a Brigadier-General (1794-1795) 12

Promoted major for brilliant conduct in the field—Generous treatment of Royalist prisoners—Siege of Maestricht—Capture of Austrian convoys—Promoted "chef-de-brigade" (colonel)—Partisan warfare—Surprise of Werneck's convoys—Siege of Mayence—Ney wounded—Refuses promotion to rank of brigadier-general—Sent home to recover from wound—Serves on Kléber's staff—Leads Jourdan's vanguard in the advance beyond the Rhine—Capture of Forcheim—Promoted to rank of brigadier-general—Retreat of the French armies—Ney with Jourdan's rear-guard—Under Hoche in campaign of 1797—Action at Giessen—Ney taken prisoner—Armistice—Ney exchanged—Peace of Leoben—Appointed to command a brigade of the "Army of England" at Amiens.

CHAPTER III

Ney General of Division (1798-1799) 36

"Army of England" broken up—Command at Abbeville—Command at Homburg—War with Austria—Capture of Mannheim—Promoted to rank of General of Division—Siege of Philippsburg—Given command of Masséna's cavalry—Ney's instructions to his officers—Command under Lecourbe in Switzerland—Transferred to Northern

PAGE

Switzerland—Defeat of Winterthur—Wounded in the battle—Convalescence in France—Rejoins and takes command of a division on Masséna's left—Battle on the Aar—Sent to command a division of the Army of the Rhine under Müller—March on Heilbronn—Incompetence of Müller—Ney's difficulties.

CHAPTER IV

COMMANDER-IN-CHIEF ON THE RHINE (1799) 58

Defeats of the Republican Armies—Ney's operations—Weak policy of Müller—Retirement of the Army of the Rhine—Loss of Mannheim—Müller recalled—Ney appointed to the temporary Command-in-Chief of the Army of the Rhine—Reorganizes the army—Recrosses the river—Action at Heidelberg—Recapture of Mannheim—Lecourbe appointed Commander-in-chief of the Army of the Rhine.

CHAPTER V

THE BEGINNING OF THE YEARS OF VICTORY (1799-1800) 73

Return of Bonaparte from Egypt—News of the *coup d'état* of Brumaire—Lecourbe gives Ney the command of his advanced guard division—Ney's march on the Neckar—The Austrians reinforced—Lecourbe retires again across the Rhine—Ney's leave of absence—La Petite Malgrange—Campaign of 1800—Ney recalled to the Army of the Rhine, now under Moreau—Plans for the campaign—Ney commands a division—Crossing of the Rhine—March on Ulm—Battle of Möeskirch—Fighting near Sigmaringen and Biberach.

CHAPTER VI

MOREAU'S DANUBE CAMPAIGN—HOHENLINDEN (1800-1801) 86

Connexion of Moreau's operations with Bonaparte's Italian campaign—Ney's victory on the Iller—News of Marengo—Austrian retreat from Ulm—Fighting along the Danube—Blockade of Ingoldstadt—Ney against Ney—Armistice—Ney returns to La Petite Malgrange on leave of absence—Winter campaign of 1800—Advance of the Austrians under the Archduke John—First fight with the Austrians—Moreau retires on the Hohenlinden position covering Munich—Battle of Hohenlinden—Ney's part in the decisive victory—Advance into Austria—Armistice—Ney returns to La Petite Malgrange.

CHAPTER VII

NEY MEETS BONAPARTE—MARRIAGE—MISSION TO SWITZERLAND (1801-1804) 105

A long holiday—Visit to Paris—Presented to the First Consul Bonaparte—Appointed Inspector-General of Cavalry—Project of serving in San Domingo—Gives up the idea—Courtship and marriage—Mission to Switzerland—Directs the French intervention—Disarms

PAGE

the Confederates—New constitution—Bonaparte's Act of Mediation—Mutiny of Swiss troops—Madame Ney in Switzerland—Arrangements with the new Swiss Government—End of Ney's mission—Recalled to take command of an Army Corps in the Camp of Boulogne.

CHAPTER VIII

THE CAMP OF BOULOGNE—THE COMING OF THE EMPIRE (1804-1805) . 124

Ney's last meeting with Moreau—The Camp of Boulogne—Ney in command of the 6th Corps at Montreuil—Life in the camps—Madame Ney at Montreuil—A scare—Royalist conspiracies—Proclamation of the Empire—Ney a Marshal of France—Napoleon at Boulogne—Ney in Paris for the Coronation—Embarkation practices—Failure of the Emperor's plans for obtaining the command of the Channel—A new coalition—The "Army of England" becomes the "Grand Army" and marches against Austria.

CHAPTER IX

THE CAMPAIGN OF ULM AND AUSTERLITZ (1805) 137

The new coalition—Mack's advance to Ulm—Napoleon's plans—March of the Grand Army across the Rhine—Details of Ney's corps—Advance on Ulm—Ney's victory at Gunzburg—Dispute with Murat—Mack's success at Haslach—Ney's victory at Elchingen—Given the title of Duke of Elchingen—Austrians driven into Ulm—Negotiations for the surrender—Ney's corps occupies Ulm—His campaign in the Tyrol during the Emperor's advance to Austerlitz—The peace of Pressburg.

CHAPTER X

JENA, EYLAU, AND FRIEDLAND (1806-1807) 152

War with Prussia—Details of Ney's command—Outline of the campaign—March of Ney's corps—His characteristics as a commander—Loose methods of staff service in the Grand Army—Jena—Ney sent to support Murat in the pursuit—Capture of Erfurt—Siege and surrender of Magdeburg—Ney and the 6th Corps at Berlin—Advance to the Vistula—Capture of Thorn—March into Poland—Sufferings of the army—Ney advances towards Königsberg without orders from Napoleon—The Emperor's censure—The Russians enter East Prussia—Ney's retreat—Operations against Lestocq—Battle of Eylau—Winter quarters on the Passarge—Guttstadt—Campaign of 1807—Ney covers the concentration of the Grand Army against the Russian advance—Friedland—Treaty of Tilsit.

CHAPTER XI

SERVICE IN THE SPANISH PENINSULA (1807-1811) 180

Stay in France—The château of Coudreaux—Spain—The rising against Joseph Bonaparte—Ney and the 6th Corps sent to Spain—Campaign

PAGE

in the north—Ney at Madrid—Pursuit of Moore—Ney at Lugo—Government of Galicia—Visitation of the Convents—Campaign in the Asturias—Soult driven into Galicia from Portugal—Ney evacuates Galicia—Visit to Paris—Attached with his corps to the "Army of Portugal" under Masséna—Siege of Ciudad Rodrigo—Quarrel with Masséna—Almeida—Busaco—Torres Vedras—Retreat of the French—Ney commands the rear-guard—Refusal to obey orders of Masséna—Ney deprived of his command.

CHAPTER XII

THE MARCH ON MOSCOW (1812) 195

Ney returns to France—Danger of an end of his military career—But Napoleon cannot do without him—Given command of the 3rd Corps of the Grand Army in the war with Russia—Concentration of the army—March to the Niemen—Invasion of Russia—Wilna—Halt at Witebsk—Advance on Smolensk—Ney's victory at Krasnoi—Ney at Smolensk—Capture of the city—Battle of Valutina—Russians offer battle at Borodino—Ney's part in the great battle—He is given the title of Prince of the Moskowa.

CHAPTER XIII

THE REAR-GUARD OF THE GRAND ARMY (1812) 210

Occupation of Moscow—Burning and plundering of the city—Privations of the army—Murat's defeat at Inkowo—Orders for the retreat—March out of Ney and the 3rd Corps—Sufferings and losses—March over battlefield of Borodino—Rear-guard action at Viasma—The Russian winter—Smolensk—Ney cut off from the army at Krasnoi—How he saved the remnant of the 3rd Corps—The "Bravest of the Brave"—The Beresina—Ney's intervention in the last day's fighting—The Emperor leaves the army—Horrors of the last stage of the retreat—Wilna—Ney's defence of the suburbs—Retreat to the Niemen—Ney and Wrede abandoned by their men in the bivouac near Kovno—Disorder at Kovno—Ney improvises a rear-guard to cover the crossing of the Niemen—The fight at Kovno—Legends and realities—Ney saves the remnant of the 3rd Corps on the Gumbinnen road—March to Königsberg.

CHAPTER XIV

THE CAMPAIGNS OF DRESDEN AND LEIPZIG (1813) 243

Ney returns to France—Napoleon raises a new army to meet the coming uprising of Europe against him—Ney rejoins the 3rd Corps in South Germany—Advance on Leipzig—His victories at Weissenfels and on the Rippach—Attack on Leipzig—Ney at the Battle of Lützen—Occupation of Dresden—Ney given command of an army of three corps at Torgau—Battle of Bautzen—Armistice and abortive peace negotiations during the summer—Austria joins the coalition—Blücher defeated—Schwartzenberg's move on Dresden—Battle of

PAGE

Dresden—Ney and the Guard—Vandamme's defeat—Ney sent to command the French northern army—Difficulties with his corps commanders—Defeated at Dennewitz—Discouragement and indiscipline in the army—Concentration on Leipzig—Ney's part in the battle—Wounded on the third day—Retreat to the Rhine.

CHAPTER XV

THE CAMPAIGN OF FRANCE AND THE ABDICATION (1814) 269

Situation at the opening of 1814—Ney in the east of France—Retreat before the Allied invasion—Napoleon takes the field—His first victories over Blücher—Schwartzenberg's march stopped—Napoleon's second march against Blücher—Craonne and Laon—The victory at Rheims—Ney's raid on Châlons—Napoleon's march against the communications of the Allies—Ney's splendid defence at Arcis-sur-Aube—St. Dizier—March of the Allies on Paris—Napoleon marches back towards Paris—Hears of fall of the capital—Concentration at Fontainebleau—Napoleon wishes to continue the struggle—Ney takes the lead in declaring further resistance hopeless—Presses for abdication of the Emperor—Mission to Paris—Napoleon abdicates.

CHAPTER XVI

THE RESTORATION—NAPOLEON'S RETURN—NEY DECLARES FOR HIM (1814-1815) 292

Honours paid to Ney by Louis XVIII—Peer of France—Errors of the reactionary Royalists—Ney offended at the treatment of his wife at court—Retires to Coudreaux—Suddenly ordered in March, 1815, to go to Besançon and take command there—Arrives in Paris—Hears of Napoleon's return from Elba—Interview with the King—The "iron cage"—Goes to Besançon—Difficulties of his position—At first zealous for the King and hostile to Napoleon—March to Lons-le-Saulnier—News of Napoleon's progress—Arrival of messengers from the Emperor—Ney regards further resistance to him as hopeless—Conference with Lecourbe and De Bourmont—The parade at Lons-le-Saulnier—Ney declares for Napoleon amid the enthusiasm of the troops—Meeting with Napoleon.

CHAPTER XVII

THE HUNDRED DAYS—QUATRE BRAS AND WATERLOO (1815) . . . 306

Ney "no longer the same man"—Napoleon's distrust—Tour of inspection—Return to Paris—Unfortunate speech to Napoleon—Left unemployed—Retires to Coudreaux—Present at the Champ de Mai—Made a member of the Chamber of Peers—Discouraging meeting with the Emperor—On eve of going to the army Napoleon invites him to his head-quarters—Ney at Avesnes—Crosses the frontier as a mere spectator—Given command of the left wing—Slackness of his operations—Quatre Bras—Conflict of orders between the Emperor and Ney—March on Brussels—Meeting with Napoleon on the

PAGE

morning of Waterloo—Ney leads the attacks on the English centre—The cavalry charges—Failure of the attack by the Guard—End of the battle.

CHAPTER XVIII

AFTER WATERLOO—THE COURT MARTIAL AND THE TRIAL BEFORE THE PEERS (1815) 329

Flight from Waterloo—Reaches Paris—Interview with Fouché—Speech in the Chamber of Peers—Menacing proclamation of Louis XVIII—The Convention of Paris—Preparations for flight to New Orleans—Goes to Lyons—Then St. Alban—Ney on the list of the proscribed—Takes refuge at Bessonis—Discovered and arrested—Efforts of his wife on his behalf—Ney imprisoned in the Conciergerie—Court Martial convened—Moncey refuses to serve on it—Preparations for Ney's defence—The Court Martial declares it is not competent to judge the case—The Government decides to arraign Ney before the Peers—Madame Ney's appeal to the Allies—First meeting of the Peers for the trial—The Indictment—The witnesses—Ney and De Bourmont—Deposition of Lecourbe—Sitting of December 5—Evidence of Davoût and the envoys who signed the Convention of Paris—Ney's defenders argue that the Convention and Treaty of Paris are in effect an amnesty covering Ney's case—Sitting of 6 December—Berryer's defence opened—Berryer resumes and raises the question of the Convention—The President of the Chamber rules that the Convention must not be pleaded—Ney forbids his counsel to continue to defend him in the face of this unfair ruling—The case closed—Ney found guilty of treason and condemned to death.

CHAPTER XIX

THE TRAGEDY OF THE LUXEMBOURG (1815) 361

Ney and his counsel in his prison room in the Luxembourg—Farewells—How Ney spent his last evening—News of the judgment spreads through Paris about midnight—Madame Ney hears of it—Efforts to see her husband—Ney awakened in the night to hear his sentence—Arrangements made for a hurried execution—General de Rochechouart and Ney—Permission for last interviews in the early morning of the 7th—Ney and M. Batardy—Last meeting with his children and wife—She goes to the Tuileries to plead for mercy—Ney and the Abbé de St. Pierre—The execution—How Madame Ney heard the news—Funeral of Ney—The national "act of reparation" to his memory.

LIST OF ILLUSTRATIONS

LIST OF MAPS

"THE BRAVEST OF THE BRAVE" MICHEL NEY

CHAPTER I

FIRST YEARS (1769-1794)

THE year 1769 was fruitful in famous men. In that year were born Napoleon, Wellington, the younger Pitt, Humboldt, and Cuvier, Marceau, Lannes, Soult and Ney.

Michel Ney, whom Napoleon hailed as "the bravest of the brave," came of a soldier race. He was a son of that eastern borderland, which had been for centuries a debatable ground between France and Germany and repeatedly the scene of war. Every town had its traditions of siege and battle and the people had a kind of hereditary disposition for the life of a soldier.

Ney's birthplace, the town of Saarlouis, has now been German for nearly a century. In 1769 it was a French frontier fortress. It had been fortified for Louis XIV by Vauban some eighty years before that date, and the townsfolk, though a mixed race, many of them German in blood and speech, were thoroughly French in sentiment. It says something for the patriotic and military spirit of the place that, though its population numbered only four thousand, it gave nearly two hundred officers to the armies of the Republic and the Empire between the years 1792 and 1815, including, besides Marshal Ney, eleven generals.

Ney's family belonged to the lower rank of the bourgeoisie. When he had fought his way to a dukedom in the new military aristocracy of the Empire Napoleon's heralds invented an elaborate coat of arms for the Marshal Duke of Elchingen, but they could not find for him any historic link with the old feudal nobility of Lorraine and the Palatinate. In the first stages of his career under the Republic it was a gain for him that no one could question that he was "a son of the people".[1]

There had been soldiers among his ancestors. They were not knights and generals, but mere common pikemen and musketeers, and later privates and sergeants in royal regiments that fought under officers whose first claim to command was noble blood. His father, Pierre Ney, born at Ensdorf in 1738, had been a soldier, had fought in the campaigns of the Seven Years' War, and been an obscure unit in the ranks of the French Army that Frederick the Great routed at Rossbach.

He had been apprenticed to a cooper before he joined the Army. After his years of military service he set to work again at his old trade and settled at Saarlouis, where he married Margaret Grœvelinger. Her famous son always spoke of her with deep affection. After his marriage Pierre Ney was fairly prosperous but never well off. Popular tradition calls him a blacksmith perhaps because a forge was part of the equipment of his small cooperage. He earned enough to give his children a good education. German was the language of their home. They learned French at school.

There were four of them, three sons and a daughter. Jean, the eldest was born in 1767. He joined the first battalion of the National Volunteers of the Department of the Moselle, when the regiment was formed in 1791, and on 19 September of that year he was elected to the rank of sergeant by his comrades. He served for two years in the Army of the North and for two more in the Army of the Sambre and Meuse. In August, 1792, he was promoted to sergeant-major, and in April, 1794, he received his commission as sub-lieutenant. On 15 August he was promoted to lieutenant, transferred to the 55th demi-brigade of the infantry of the line, and sent to serve with it under Bonaparte in the Army of Italy. He was killed on 19 June, 1799, in Macdonald's disastrous battle against the Austrians on the Trebbia.

[1] There were several branches of the family, and its name is variously spelt in registers of the eighteenth century, among its forms being Nau, Naye, New, Neu, Neuen, Nei, and Ney.

The second son was Michel, the future Marshal of the Empire. The third, Jacques, born on 7 March, 1771, died in childhood. The daughter, Marguerite Ney, was born on 7 October, 1772. She was twice married. Her second husband, Jean Claude Monnier, held lucrative posts in the Civil Service of the Empire, and was a wealthy man when he was forced to retire by the Bourbon Government in 1815. Madame Monnier died in 1819.

The house where Michel Ney was born and spent his first years is still standing at Saarlouis. It is a small, old-fashioned building, with one upper story, and three little dormer windows in the tiled roof. Three steps lead up to the door that opens directly on the street. A horseshoe is fixed above the lintel of the door, and over it, between two windows of the upper story, there is a large tablet of marble with the inscription:—

"ICI EST NÉ

LE MARÉCHAL NEY."[1]

The tablet was placed there in 1815 after the cession of Saarlouis to Prussia.

Pierre Ney's idea was that his eldest son, Jean, should carry on the business of the cooperage. He destined Michel for a professional career. It was through some branch of the legal profession that a bourgeois had the best chance of rising in the world, for it opened the way to employment by the Crown. Michel was therefore sent to the Collège des Augustins, a high-class day school at Saarlouis, directed by the Augustinian Fathers. But in those days the start in the work of life came earlier than it does now. Michel's college course ended in the summer of 1782, when he was only thirteen. Then as a boy clerk he entered the office of Maître Valette, the chief notary of Saarlouis.

It was not his choice, but his father's plans for him, that sent him to copy long-winded documents at a desk, and to learn the routine business of a notary. Michel had already other ideas. The sight of the military movements of a garri-

[1] "Here Marshal Ney was born."

son town, the stories he had heard from his father by the winter fireside of the campaigns of Frederick the Great, the news of the war with England and of victories beyond the Atlantic that more than compensated for failure at Gibraltar, had turned young Michel Ney's thoughts to a career like his father's. He could not hope to rise to high command, but he could dream of horse and sword, camp and march and battlefield, activity and adventure, instead of the endless task of handling dusty papers in the corner of an office.

For two years, however, he plodded on at his ungrateful occupation. Then, when he was fifteen, there came a change to a branch of the profession that offered more variety of interest. Pierre Ney obtained for his son an appointment as junior clerk in the office of the Procureur du Roi, the King's attorney, at Saarlouis. But Michel cared no more for serving summonses on defaulters in the payment of taxes, or copying the indictments of prisoners at the assizes, than he had cared for drawing up inventories of property, probates of wills, marriage settlements, and records of sales. He stayed only a few months with the Procureur du Roi. Then he begged his father to find him some more active employment, something that would take him away from the slavery of the desk. And Pierre Ney yielded to his son's wishes.

In the autumn of 1784 he left Saarlouis to be employed at the mines and ironworks of Appenweiler. He had still to spend part of his time in an office, but he was also employed at the works, and learned the processes of handling the ore, and turning it into cast and malleable iron. He proved such an apt pupil that next year he was attached to the staff of the superintendent at the ironworks of Saleck, where he had the opportunity of learning the further processes used in the manufacture of iron into machinery and goods for the market.

He worked at Saleck for three years, till the late autumn of 1788. Then at last the longing for a soldier's life tore him away from the forge and the workshop. Resigning his post at Saleck he tramped back to Saarlouis to pay a visit to his parents. Then he went on to Metz, where, on 6 December, 1788, he enlisted as a private in a regiment of hussars.

The first hussars in the French, or in any west European

Army, were Hungarian deserters, who in 1692 left the Austrian flag for that of Louis XIV and were formed into a regiment. Until 1776 the French Hussars were bodies of irregular light horsemen, wearing an imitation of a Hungarian costume, the regiments being raised in time of war and usually disbanded at the peace that followed it. But a Royal Ordinance dated 25 March, 1776, gave the four regiments of hussars then in existence a permanent position in the French regular cavalry, under the names of the Regiment de Bercheny (No. 1), Regiment de Chamborant (No. 2), Regiment de Nassau (No. 3), and Regiment d'Esterhazy (No. 4). Three years later the boy Duke of Chartres was appointed "Colonel-General of the Hussars," and a fifth regiment was formed in his honour, of which he was to be titular commander. It was known as the "Regiment Colonel-Général," and it was in its ranks that Michel Ney enlisted.

The uniform of the regiment was a dark-blue tunic, frogged with yellow braid, with a red cloth pelisse lined with white sheepskin. The cloak was blue. The sabretache red, embroidered with arms of the Duc de Chartres. The saddle cloth was a white sheepskin bordered with red cloth. The shako was black with a red pendant and a white aigrette. The sword was brass hilted, with a leather scabbard mounted with the same metal. The new recruit had an attractive uniform.

He was above the middle stature, five feet eight inches in height, with the body rather short and the legs long, not a bad build for a hussar. He had a wide forehead and blue eyes set well apart, a short nose and a full chin. His complexion was ruddy, and his hair, which the hussars wore plaited into a queue, was the colour that might be called auburn or red, accordingly as the speaker wished to be more or less complimentary. His comrades nicknamed him "*le rougeot*". "Carrots" or "foxy" would be the English trooper's equivalent.

He was kindly humoured though liable to sudden fits of temper; a hard-working fellow and a good soldier. He rode well and soon became one of the champion fencers of the regiment. But he had to wait three years for promotion. It was not till the New Year's Day of 1791 that he had his first step up the long ladder. That day he was made "brigadier" or corporal. When he enlisted the most he could have hoped for would be perhaps a lieutenancy on the eve of retirement, for the son of a working cooper could not be received among counts and marquises. But since then the epoch-making year 1789 had come and now all things were possible. Not a few privates and non-commissioned officers in the Royal Army (soon to be Republican and before long Imperial) were to use the proverbial phrase "carrying a marshal's baton in the knapsack".

His mother died at Saarlouis on 4 November in this year. Ney does not appear to have been with her at the last. Probably he had had some short leaves of absence from Metz to enable him to visit his home in the three years since his enlistment. His elder brother, Jean Ney, had joined the "National Volunteers" of his district, a few weeks before his mother's death, but was at Saarlouis for some months later, until the outbreak of war took the volunteers into the field. Then the old soldier, Pierre Ney, was alone with his daughter.

To the year *1791*, when Michel Ney was still "brigadier," belongs the story of his only recorded duel. The fencing-master of the Chasseurs de Vintimille, who were also in garrison at Metz, had challenged the fencing-master of the Hussars Colonel-Général, and wounded him badly. After this the victor behaved in an insulting and provoking way whenever he met the hussars. The non-commissioned officers of the regiment held a meeting and decided that a stop must be put to his insolence, and Ney was chosen as the champion who was to fight him. The challenge was accepted and the two swordsmen met in the presence of deputations of their comrades. They had just crossed swords when Ney felt himself pulled backwards by some one who had taken a firm grip of his plaited pig-tail. Turning he saw that it was his Colonel, who had thus unceremoniously interrupted the duel. The military code of the day made it a serious offence and Ney was marched off to prison. But a petition of his comrades led to his being set free with a caution in a few days.

Then another meeting was arranged with more precaution as to secrecy, and after a sharp encounter Ney wounded the fencing-master of the Chasseurs so badly in the wrist that he could never teach fencing again. Years after, in the days of his prosperity, the victor sought out the vanquished and found that he was living in poverty. He provided him with a pension at his own expense that made him comfortable for the rest of his days.

On 1 February, 1792, Ney was promoted to the rank of *maréchal de logis*, or sergeant-of-horse. Three months later he was made *maréchal de logis chef*, or sergeant-major. The promotion came in May, 1792, the month that brought the declaration of war against Austria, and opened the long period of the Wars of the Revolution and the Empire. Ney's chance had come and he made good use of it.

In July the Regiment Colonel-Général, now renamed the 5th Hussars, had marched from Metz three squadrons, nearly six hundred sabres strong, under the command of Colonel Lamarche. Ney had just been promoted again on 14 July—the anniversary of the Bastille, when promotions were to be expected. He was now "adjutant," not a commissioned rank in the French Army, but the highest among the non-commissioned grades. It meant much orderly-room work and much routine handling of papers, orders, and accounts, wherein Michel Ney's dull apprenticeship to the notary may have been useful to him. But it had the advantage of bringing him into close relations with his Colonel, and Lamarche was soon to be a general, with solid gain to Ney.

The 5th Hussars were for a while at the Camp of Carignan under General Lafayette. Then Dumouriez concentrated all available forces to bar the march of the invaders, for Austria was now the centre of a coalition, and Brunswick's army of Austrians, Prussians, and Germans generally, was across the eastern frontier and marching for Paris, threatening by proclamation a terrible vengeance for the deeds of the Revolution. The enemy was in Saarlouis. Before they came the 1st Volunteers of the Department had marched away to join the field army, so that Ney may have had some chance meeting with his elder brother. Thionville was besieged, Metz blockaded. The enemy was before Verdun sixty thousand strong at the end of August, and then Verdun surrendered and the only barrier between Paris and Brunswick's vengeance was the army of Dumouriez.

He took up a position holding the hill roads through the woods of the Argonne. The 5th Hussars were with General Dillon's brigade at Les Islettes among the hills and woods where the sharpest fighting took place, though it was nothing more than skirmishing, for Brunswick's main advance had broken down under stress of three weeks of steady rain that made the roads into morasses, so that Austrians and Prussians were starving, with supply trains sunk to the axles far behind them; and short rations, and wet bivouacks were spreading dysentery among the troops. Then failing to force the passes of the Argonne in front Brunswick marched round the French line of defence only to find Dumouriez in his way at Valmy. There, on 20 September, Michel Ney saw his first pitched battle, mostly an artillery action, hence called the "Cannonade of Valmy," for Brunswick's attack was not pressed home, when he found that the French line, supposed to be composed largely of new levies and mere volunteers, instead of breaking before his artillery fire, answered it back and stood fast, even showing presently a disposition to come to close quarters. After this failure Brunswick—with an army that had lost a hundred by disease for every man that had fallen in action—retreated to the Rhine. By this time Ney was an officer, promoted to the rank of sub-lieutenant during his first campaign.

After Valmy, Dumouriez marched against the Austrians in Belgium. Three armies were formed for the conquest of this outlying province of the Emperor Francis. On the left the Army of the North under General Miranda marched on Antwerp. With Miranda went Jean Ney and his comrades of the Saarlouis Volunteers. In the centre Dumouriez himself led the "Army of Belgium," afterwards famous as the "Army of the Sambre and Meuse". To this column the 5th Hussars were attached. On the right the Army of the Ardennes under General Valence marched to besiege Namur.

On 6 November Ney was with his regiment at the victory of Jemappes. On the 14th Dumouriez marched into Brussels. The Austrians fell back to the line of the Meuse.

In the following March (1793) the Austrians, with Coburg in command, advanced from the Meuse to retake Brussels. Dumouriez went to meet them with 45,000 men. Colonel Lamarche of the 5th Hussars was now a general in command of Dumouriez's advanced guard of 6000 men, and he had chosen Sub-Lieutenant Michel Ney to act as his aide-de-camp. The first fighting took place at Tirlemont on 15 March. Next day General Lamarche and the French vanguard had a fight with the Austrians at the village of Gossoncourt. The enemy failed in an attempt to storm the hedge-surrounded enclosures of the village, and as they fell back Lamarche, with Ney riding beside him, put himself at the head of his old regiment the 5th Hussars, and charged the retiring enemy, making many prisoners. But the first stage of the campaign ended with the French defeat of Neerwinden on 28 March.

It was after this failure that Dumouriez, cited to defend himself at the Bar of the Convention, arrested the War Minister and the Republican Commissioners, who had brought the summons to his head-quarters, and, failing to obtain the support of his army generally, deserted to the Austrian lines with his staff (including the Duc de Chartres afterwards King Louis Philippe) and about a thousand men. Among these were the greater number of the 1st Hussars, formerly known as the Régiment de Bercheny.

When General Dampierre took over the command and reorganized the army, what were left of the 1st Hussars were incorporated in the 2nd. The Hussar regiments were then renumbered, the 2nd became the 1st; the 3rd, the 2nd; the 4th, the 3rd; and the 5th was henceforth known as the 4th Hussars. This is how it comes that some biographers of Ney say that he enlisted in the 4th Hussars.

On 1 May Dampierre was mortally wounded in the defence of the entrenched camp of Famars near Valenciennes. He handed over the command to Lamarche, who held it during the operations on the frontier till 30 July when he was superseded and recalled. This deprived Ney of his staff appointment, and he had to return to regimental duty with the 4th Hussars. On parting with his aide-de-camp the General gave him the following testimonial:—

"I, General Lamarche, Commander-in-Chief of the Army of the Ardennes hereby certify that Lieutenant Ney of the 4th Regiment of Hussars has been employed by me as my aide-de-camp from 19 October, 1792 to 3 July, 1793, and that he has fulfilled the duties of his position with all the intelligence, intrepidity, activity, and courage for which such a post gives occasion, and that in all circumstances in which he has been employed even in the midst of danger he has displayed a discernment and a tactical insight that is seldom found."

From 1 August to 20 December, 1793, Ney was serving on the frontier as a regimental officer in Captain Boyé's company of the 4th Hussars. On 13 October he received his commission as lieutenant. In December General Colaud who was in command of a brigade of mounted troops watching the line of the Marne, while the Army of the North was in winter quarters, asked for and obtained him as his aide-de-camp. On leaving his regiment he received another testimonial, this time in the form of a certificate signed—in the democratic fashion of the time—by the officers and representatives of the non-commissioned officers and men. This is what his comrades said of him:—

"We, officers, non-commissioned officers, and hussars of the 4th Regiment, certify that the Citizen Michel Ney, Lieutenant in De Boyé's company of the said regiment, has, in every grade in which we have known him, acted as a brave soldier and a true Republican, and has at all times served with zeal for the interests and the welfare of the Republic, and that it is only according to what we know of his way of thinking and of his conduct that we have signed these presents for his use and for the information of all whom it may concern."

Ney served as aide-de-camp to General Colaud until 21 April, 1794, when, having been promoted to the rank of captain, he returned to the 4th Hussars to take command of a company.[1] General Colaud sent him a letter stating that while acting as his staff officer he "had fulfilled his duties with zeal and activity, and displayed in his service all the intelligence and patriotism of a pronounced Republican".

The early summer witnessed the advance of the new Army of the Sambre and Meuse into Belgium under Jourdan. Ney's regiment was attached to the left wing commanded by General

[1] The squadrons of the French cavalry were then organized each in two "companies," which were the right and left half-squadrons.

Kléber. The battle of Fleurus was won. Kléber drove the Austrians from Mons, and when they fell back on the line of the river Dyle he stormed their positions near Louvain on 15 July. It was on the day after this success that Ney attracted Kléber's attention. By chance he had been sent with his company of hussars to act as the General's escort in reconnoitring the position taken up by the Austrian rear-guard. During the operation Kléber was so struck by Ney's tactical judgment, his rapid appreciation of the situation, his clear concise replies to every question, and his handling of the escort, that later in the day he sent his aide-de-camp, Pajol, to him to ask him to serve on his staff. Ney at first expressed his reluctance to be again separated from his regiment, but finally yielded, and thus began a friendship that had a marked influence on his career.

CHAPTER II

IN BELGIUM AND THE RHINELAND—NEY A BRIGADIER-GENERAL (1794-1798)

KLÉBER was one of the great soldiers of the Republic. To serve even for a while under such a man and in close communication with him was for young Ney to obtain a practical training in the higher leadership of armies. Kléber gave him the temporary rank of adjutant-general, and, placing him in command of a picked body of cavalry, entrusted him with the task of preserving local order while the army advanced, breaking up hostile gatherings of the Flemish peasants, and protecting the movement of the supply columns. It meant continual activity, long hours in the saddle each day, and an unceasing vigilance.

On 30 July, while Kléber's advanced guard was marching on Pelenberg from Louvain, Ney performed an exploit which won him another step of promotion. He had been out on the flank of the advance with a party of thirty dragoons and a few chasseurs. They had had a long ride and were returning to the column, when the sound of cannon told them it was attacked by the Austrians. Ney made all speed and arrived in sight of the engagement, just at the moment when a squadron of the enemy's hussars had successfully charged and scattered the cavalry detachment of the French vanguard. Without a moment's hesitation Ney, with his handful of horsemen, rode at the victorious cavalry, and, striking in amongst them while they were disordered by their own success, broke them up and drove them back in confusion.

Kléber, who witnessed this gallant exploit, formally reported it to Citizen Gillet, the Representative of the People, or Permanent Envoy of the Government with the Army, in these terms:—

"Captain Ney, who is doing duty as adjutant-general, has performed prodigies of valour. With thirty of the 7th Dragoons and a few chasseurs acting as orderlies, he charged two hundred of Blankenstein's Hussars, and threw them into the greatest disorder."

Gillet, using the powers entrusted to him, at once promoted Ney to the rank of *adjutant-général chef de bataillon*, or major on the staff, in recognition of "his military talents and his patriotism".

During these operations on more than one occasion Ney had found among his prisoners *émigré* Royalists. At considerable risk to himself he always took steps to have them mixed up with the foreign prisoners, taking care to avoid anything that would call attention to their identity and so sacrifice their lives. One night his scouts brought him as prisoners two French priests, "half dead with fright, hunger, and fatigue". Fugitives from France, after refusing the Constitutional oath, they would have been sent to the guillotine if he had not taken steps to save them. Before their captors he spoke sternly to them, reminding them of the penalty they had incurred; then he sent away the soldiers on the pretext that he wished to interrogate the prisoners privately. As soon as he was alone with them he reassured them, provided them with food and money, put them in charge of an officer he could trust, gave them directions how to get away from the towns that would be traversed by the French advance, and arranged that they should have a disguise and escape during the night. Next day he pretended to be very angry at the prisoners having been so badly guarded. There were some awkward rumours of his having connived at their escape, but the Commissary Gillet turned a deaf ear to them, and said to Kléber: "Your friend Ney knows how to spare the blood of his countrymen".

During August there was a lull in the operations. Kléber was preparing to advance to besiege Maestricht, and the Austrians were watching him from the other side of the Meuse near the menaced fortress. In the last week of the month Ney was sent with a small body of cavalry to work round the right of the enemy, and make a raid on the convoys of supplies coming up in their rear. The expedition meant that for some days he would be isolated and dependent entirely on his own resources. He marched with his party from Diest on the 26th. That day he swept round the Austrian right without being discovered, captured a convoy of twenty-three wagons and sent it back to Diest. In the night one of his men deserted from the bivouac. This caused him some anxiety, but he decided to push on, and next morning secured another convoy, and had just started it off on the road to Diest, when his scouts brought word that a strong body of Austrian cavalry was on his right flank. A few minutes later news came that a second body of the enemy was on his left. He then realized that the deserter must have warned the Austrains of his raid, and that an effort was being made to surround him. The captured convoy was abandoned, and he rode towards Diest. Presently his advanced scouts brought a report that the way was barred by cavalry in his front. He was now between three bodies of the enemy and in imminent danger of capture. But though outnumbered and surrounded he was determined not to be taken. Riding rapidly forward he charged the enemy in front, cut his way through them, made their commander Count Hompesch prisoner, and brought him in to Kléber's head-quarters. For this new deed of arms Gillet promoted him, on Kléber's report, to be *chef de brigade*, a rank corresponding to that of colonel. He had had to serve for more than three years to gain the grade of corporal, but he had risen from sub-lieutenant to colonel in two. He was only twenty-five years of age, and might now count on a career.

The victory known to the French as the Battle of Ourthe was won on September. Jourdan, following up the beaten Austrians, left Kléber to besiege Maestricht, and himself occupied Aix-la-Chapelle. Finding strong forces in his front, he ordered Kléber to leave only a division before Maestricht and come to his aid.

Bernadotte commanded Kléber's advanced guard with Colonel Ney's flying column of horsemen on his flank following the line of the Meuse. Ney's men are spoken of in contemporary despatches as his "partisans". We would now use as the popular equivalent for the same idea the word "guerrillas". On 28 September they made an important capture. Ney's scouts discovered a convoy of barges coming down the river. It was laden with artillery ammunition for the garrison of Maestricht. On his approach the escort scuttled the barges, and, leaving them to sink, escaped by the further bank of the river. An hour later another convoy of barges was sighted. This was captured, some of Ney's chasseurs swimming out to secure the boats. They were found to be laden with provisions.

Next day Ney scouted far in front of the column. In the afternoon he was in touch with a body of Austrians retiring eastwards. Bernadotte directed him to attempt a night surprise of their bivouac near the village of Gangelt, but he found the enemy on the alert and in greater force than he anticipated, and asked for reinforcements. On the morning of the 30th Bernadotte sent the 2nd Hussars and a detachment of infantry. The Austrians had marched off at daybreak. Ney followed them closely, harassing them with frequent attacks. At last they halted at the town of Heinsberg, where they barricaded the entrances of the streets. Without waiting for Bernadotte, Ney led his infantry to the attack and drove the Austrians out of the place.

On 1 October Kléber was in touch with Jourdan. Next day the Battle of the Roer was fought, the passage of the river was forced, and the Austrians abandoned all the country up to the left bank of the Rhine. Ney was with Bernadotte during the action, and, in his report addressed to Kléber, the General wrote :—

> "I owe great praise to the brave Ney. He has assisted me with the intelligence you know so well in him; and I must say, to speak the exact truth, that he counts for much in the success we have obtained."

On the day after the victory the army of the Sambre and Meuse was marching towards the Rhine on a broad front, the right column being directed towards Coblentz, the centre towards Cologne, and the left (Kléber) towards Dusseldorf.

On the evening of 3 October, Bernadotte, who still commanded Kléber's advanced guard, halted for the night at the village of Geerath, and took up his quarters in the inn which Werneck, the commander of the Austrian right, had quitted only a few hours before. On the table of his room he found a paper which proved to be a duplicate copy of Werneck's orders, forgotten by the Austrian in the haste of his departure. The orders clearly described the route that Werneck's supply trains were to follow in order to reach the crossing of the Rhine at Dusseldorf. Bernadotte at once saw that this information gave an opening for his enterprising leader of "partisans," and he sent it on to Ney, with a reinforcement of two cavalry regiments, some infantry, and a couple of guns. Ney marched early on 4 October, intending to stop the convoy at Neuss, a town surrounded by old walls. When he approached the convoy with an infantry escort, was close up to Neuss, and 1200 Austrian cavalry, drawn up under the walls, were covering its movements. Ney showed only part of his force and tried to lure the enemy's cavalry into attacking, hoping to destroy them if they did so by a charge of the two regiments he held in reserve. But the Austrians contented themselves with protecting the march of the convoy through Neuss. Ney attacked with his artillery, infantry, and dismounted cavalry, as soon as the enemy were in the streets of Neuss. Their was a sudden panic among the Austrians. Setting fire to some of the wagons, they tried to escape with the rest. Sweeping through and round the town, Ney persistently attacked them along the Dusseldorf road, and in a few hours had captured all the wagons. Next morning he followed the enemy up to the ramparts of Dusseldorf, and only drew off and began his homeward march when he was fired on by the artillery of the place.

After this success he was employed with his flying column in protecting the establishment of Republican authorities in the district between the Rhine and the Meuse. Passing near Maestricht during one of his expeditions he was ordered by Citizen Gillet, as Representative of the People, to join the besieging force. Kléber had taken command of the attack, the heavy artillery for the siege was arriving, batteries were being prepared, and the approaches pushed steadily forward. The siege batteries opened fire on 26 October. On 4 November the place surrendered. Ney helped to secure this result, by an interview he had with the civil authorities of Maestricht, when he went in with a flag of truce and a message from his general to the military governor.

Kléber's troops, after the fall of Maestricht, were sent by

Jourdan to assist in the siege of Mayence. Jourdan was anxious to obtain for his own staff the services of Ney and other officers who had been with Kléber before Maestricht. The latter appealed to Gillet to overrule the Commander-in-Chief's proposal, and leave him his trusted colleagues. Gillet allowed Kléber to keep Ney with him till the matter was definitely decided by the Committee of Public Safety to whom the Representative referred it, in a letter in which he said :—

"I know them all well. I have seen them at work. They are in a good and vigorous school, and they have profited by it. They are full of zeal and I recommend them to you most heartily. It is an act of justice that I must do these brave young men. As for Ney, you will decide if he is to be left with Kléber. For my part, I think he would be more useful with the field army than before Mayence. He is a distinguished officer. His services are necessary with our large force of cavalry. Men of his stamp are not common."

Before the reply of the Committee could arrive Ney had been wounded before Mayence in a gallant attempt to carry one of the Austrian outworks by a *coup de main*. There was on the left bank an advanced lunette the fire of which greatly incommoded the workers in the trenches. A lunette is an earthwork with two faces meeting at an obtuse angle, but open at the rear or "gorge". Ney volunteered to surprise it, and was given a detachment of infantry and a party of dragoons to carry out his plan. At daybreak on 10 December he made a false attack on the front of the work with his infantry who opened fire from the advanced trench. When the attention of the Austrians was fixed on this threatened attack in front, he dashed out of the French works at the head of his dragoons, galloped round to the rear of the entrenchment, and rode for its open "gorge". But there was a wide ditch across the rear of the work. Ney, fine horseman that he was, jumped it, only to find himself alone among the Austrians for not one of the dragoons had attempted the leap. With his good swordsmanship he kept at bay the Austrians who rushed upon him, reached the edge of the ditch, leapt it again, and rode away after his retreating men, followed by a shower of bullets, one of which wounded him severely in the arm.

He reached the French lines suffering great pain, and depressed with the sense of failure and the fear that he would

2

lose his arm and so end his military career. He was consoled by Kléber's praise, and the report of the surgeons that his arm could be saved. Merlin de Thionville, the Representative of the People with the besieging army, came and told him that he was about to propose his promotion to the rank of brigadier-general in recognition of his gallantry. But Ney replied that he could not accept promotion after having failed in his enterprise.

He made a slow recovery. As soon as he could be safely moved from the field hospital Kléber proposed that he should be sent for a while to his old home to complete his convalescence there. On 7 January Merlin de Thionville announced this arrangement to Ney in the following letter:—

> "You are to go to complete your cure at home at Sarrelibre: I have given orders to Surgeon Bonaventure to detail one of his pupils to accompany you. Come back soon to give us your help against the enemies of the Fatherland."

Under the care of the young surgeon Ney was taken in a carriage over the snowy hill roads to Saarlouis, now known for awhile by its French Republican name of Sarrelibre, "Louis" being an unpatriotic element even in a local name, and "liberty" being in fashion. At home he had his sister Margaret to take care of him. His father, now a grey beard of over sixty, but still hale and hearty and able to direct his business, must have been proud of the soldier son, who could exchange with him impressions of the Prussians that Pierre Ney had seen victorious at Rossbach, and Michel had helped to pursue after Valmy.

Old scores were being paid off, and, better still, instead of serving for years in the ranks and coming home to put hoops on beer and wine barrels, a good soldier of the Republic could fight his way up the ladder and be colonel and general, at an age when in old times he would have been proud to be a sergeant.

Michel regained his health rapidly in those happy winter days at "Sarrelibre". There came from the Army letters to him that he must have shown proudly to old Pierre. General Bourcier, Jourdan's chief of the staff, wrote that Merlin de Thionville persisted in his recommendation of his promotion to the rank of Général de Brigade. If he still objected to take it, he must write to the Government at Paris. Ney remained obstinate, and the promotion did not come for more than a year later. There was a letter, too, from his chief Kléber, addressing him as "Mon camarade," telling him that as soon as he was well Jourdan would attach him to the head-quarter's staff of the Army of the Sambre and Meuse, and enclosing one more certificate of good service to add to his collection:—

"From the head-quarters at Ober-Ingelheim, the 22nd Nivôse, IIIrd Year of the Republic, Kléber, General of Division, commanding the Army corps before Mayence, certifies that Citizen Ney, adjutant-general, chef-de-brigade, has commanded with distinction a corps of cavalry partisans, during the whole of the campaign of the Army of the Sambre and Meuse; that in all the operations entrusted to him he has shown an intrepid courage and a consummate intelligence, especially at the siege of Maestricht, where his valour rendered great services to the Republic; and that having come as a volunteer to the siege of Mayence to assist in the capture of the place, he has received a bullet wound which interrupts his active service until the re-establishment of his health."

This came quickly. He had been less than a month at home when on 14 February, 1795, he rejoined the Army, reporting himself for duty at Jourdan's head-quarters.

In April Prussia, in order to have a free hand against Poland, abandoned the Coalition, and made peace with France by the Treaty of Basel. Several of the minor German States followed her example. Then Spain, Portugal, and Naples made peace, and England, Austria, and her ally the King of Sardinia, were all that remained in arms against France. For the summer campaign on the Rhine two French armies were formed, each between eighty and a hundred thousand strong. The Army of the Rhine and the Moselle was besieging Mayence, and had detachments watching the line of the Rhine as far south as Strasburg. It was under the command of Pichegru, the conqueror of Holland. The other army, known as the Army of the Sambre and Meuse, was watching the line of the river northwards from Mayence by Coblentz and Cologne as far as Emmerich. Jourdan was still commander-in-chief, and Kléber commanded the left.

When the latter handed over the command of the siege operations against Mayence to Pichegru, and went away to take command of the left wing of Jourdan's army, Ney had been directed to remain before Mayence, and was to serve on

Pichegru's staff. But Kléber was reluctant to part with the young colonel, whom he now regarded not only as a valuable assistant but also as a personal friend. He appealed to the Committee of Public Safety in a letter dated from Crefeld on 13 July, 1795:—

"The Adjutant-General Ney," he wrote, "served all the last campaign; his military talents have been of service to me as well as to the Republic, and in this respect I have complete confidence in him. I ask you most urgently, Citizens, to leave this officer with me, and to change accordingly the orders given attaching him to the Army of the Rhine. The good of the service alone leads me to make this request."

His petition was granted, and Ney went north with his chief, who was given the command of four divisions of the Army of the Sambre and Meuse, stationed along the Rhine from Cologne to Dusseldorf.

The right or eastern bank of the great river was held by the Austrian Army under Clerfait, and the French could only carry on their siege operations against the western face of Mayence. On the river-side the Austrians had complete access to it, and could send in all the supplies and reinforcements needed for its defence. This campaign of 1795 on the Rhine is historically interesting as marking the close of a period in the art of war. For two centuries armies had fought for the possession of fortresses. A campaign turned on the efforts of one side to maintain the siege of a fortified city, and those of the other to relieve it. It had not yet been realized that the important thing was not to occupy positions, and capture walled cities, but to attack and destroy the main fighting force of the enemy, wherever it might be found, and for this end to concentrate in one striking force every available man, horse, and gun. Bonaparte's campaign in Italy in the following year marked the coming of the new methods of war, but as General Horsetzky[1] remarks there was something of the same spirit in Clerfait's operations in the second stage of the campaign of 1795.

At its outset the two armies, French and Austrian, were both acting on the same principles that the generals of the seventeenth and eighteenth centuries held to be almost sacred. The opposing forces were strung out in long lines of detachments

[1] "Feldzüge der Letzten Hundert Jahre," p. 30.

along opposite banks of the Rhine on a front of 250 miles. There was dispersion of force and division of command. On the French side Pichegru in the south was practically independent of Jourdan in the north. The only way in which an attempt was given to impart unity to their operations was by means of a plan of campaign and subsequent detailed orders sent to them by Carnot from Paris. The transmission of these orders depended on the speed with which horses could travel over hundreds of miles of road, and it was a risky thing for a commander to diverge from the directions thus received, even in the presence of a locally changed situation, without referring his proposed change of plans to Paris, and awaiting the reply dictated by Carnot.

There is a letter of Jourdan's, which brings out all the disadvantages of this way of carrying on a great war. Writing to his colleague in command on the upper Rhine, and suggesting a change in the plans sent from Paris, he concludes his letter thus:—

"I wrote yesterday to the Executive Directory, explaining my ideas. I do not know if they will approve of them, but I think that, being nearer the theatre of war than they are, we are in a better position to judge what special movements we ought to make to attain the object they have in view. And we cannot shut our eyes to the fact that if we are obliged to write to Paris every time that we think we ought to change something in the instructions sent to us, we shall pass our time in writing letters and in being beaten."

This was very much what happened. Carnot, the "organizer of victory," who at his desk in Paris raised armies and provided their generals with plans of campaign that had so far been successful, owed part of his renown to the fact that the Austrian generals had so far slavishly followed the traditions of the time, and allowed themselves to be beaten in detail. Nor had Carnot entirely emancipated himself from the old methods. They still played a large part in his beautifully complex plans, and the plan of 1795 was one which would have been difficult to carry to success even with modern methods of intercommunication. It was doomed to failure once Clerfait grasped the opportunities it gave him, and declined to make his own movements correspond to those of his adversaries in the old-fashioned way of opposing corps to corps along a line of hundreds of miles, instead of concentrating his strength on one section of the enemy.

In the first place Carnot's plan—as usual at the time—had not for its direct object the destruction of the Austrian field army. What it aimed at was to establish the French armies on the right bank of the middle Rhine in order to complete the blockade of Mayence on the east side, and so ensure its capture. With this object, instead of concentrating the Republican armies to cross the Rhine at any one point, and place a strong fighting force in the hands of one leader on the right bank above or below Mayence, there was to be a series of crossings. First Kléber, on Jourdan's extreme left, was to cross near Dusseldorf. He was then to march southward along the right bank driving in the Austrian right, and facilitating the crossing of Jourdan, with the centre of the Army of the Sambre and Meuse near Cologne. Then while the left and centre moved up the Rhine, Marceau with the right was to cross at Neuwied, with the help of a bridge of boats put together on the Moselle and floated down to the shelter of the island at Neuwied, running the gauntlet of the distant fire from the river batteries of Ehrenbreitstein as it passed Coblentz. Pichegru was to make a diversion in Jourdan's favour by throwing his right across the river above Mayence.

That such a plan could be adopted, and should actually have for a while seemed to promise success, shows how feeble had been the Austrian leadership till now, how slavishly the generals of the coalition had made their own operations depend on the initiative of their opponents. Clerfait, massing his forces, beat his divided opponents in detail, and on 29 October attacked the French on the right bank of the Rhine before Mayence, drove them across the river, captured all their siege train, and inflicted on them a loss of 3000 men. On both banks the besiegers hurriedly retreated.

Clerfait had not only relieved Mayence, he also separated the Army of the Rhine and Moselle under Pichegru, from the Army of the Sambre and Meuse under Jourdan. He made good use of his central position, first striking at Pichegru, defeating him and driving him southwards on Landau, joining hands with Wurmser during the operation. Jourdan after his failure had withdrawn to the left bank of the Rhine. Clerfait leaving part of Wurmser's force to watch Pichegru, swung round against Jourdan's right under Marceau, and forced the French back towards the Moselle. Then exhausted by his own energetic efforts, on 21 December to the utter surprise and the great relief of the two French commanders, he proposed an armistice to enable both sides to go into winter quarters, now that the weather was broken and the roads were deep in snow. The proposal was gladly accepted.

During this unsuccessful campaign of 1795, we hear little of Ney. He was doing duty as a staff officer under Kléber, and carried out a number of enterprising reconnaissances. But there were no brilliant exploits to add to his record. He was learning in the latter stage of the campaign the lessons of defeat, and had more than one opportunity of showing the cool courage required of a commander of a rear-guard.

In April, 1796, a new era in war began with Bonaparte's first victory in Italy. It is difficult for us to realize that when the young Republican General marched across the frontier and defeated the Austrians and Piedmontese in the Genoese Apennines the armistice concluded at the close of the campaign of 1795, was still in force on the Rhine. But it was not until May that the Paris Government ordered its generals on the Rhine to put an end to the long truce. No modern state would dream of being at peace on one of its frontiers and engaged in active operations on another, with the armies of the same enemy facing it simultaneously on both.

The best of the Austrian Generals, one of the great leaders of his time, the Archduke Charles, now commanded the army on the Rhine. Clerfait's failure to follow up his success had led to his supersession. Jourdan still commanded the left wing of the French forces in the Rhineland, the Army of the Sambre and Meuse. Pichegru had been superseded and the right, now known as the Army of the Rhine, was commanded by Moreau.

The Archduke Charles had proposed to open the campaign with an advance against the French positions, but, in consequence of the rapid progress of the French arms under

Bonaparte in Italy, he was ordered to send Wurmser with 25,000 men southwards through the Tyrol to assist in an attempt for the relief of Mantua. Thus weakened, the Archduke reluctantly decided to act on the defensive.

In Italy Bonaparte was left to carry out his own plans. Jourdan and Moreau on the Rhine were supplied with a plan of campaign by Carnot, and were still required to correspond with Paris as to any modifications they thought advisable.

Carnot's plan for 1796 had the disadvantage of his plan for the year before. It contemplated a divided advance into South Germany, and offered the Archduke the opportunity of beating the Republicans in detail. By the end of May the French were in much the same positions they had occupied at the opening of the campaign of 1795.

Kléber crossed the river near Dusseldorf on 30 May, and, advancing on the very roads he had followed the year before, drove in the weak detachments of the Austrian extreme right. In the minor engagements during this advance Ney was in command of a column of cavalry, cutting in between the Austrians and the river, harrassing their flank, and securing a considerable quantity of the supplies they had collected in their cantonments along the Rhine. Jourdan crossed at Neuwied, joined hands with Kléber, and, following up the retiring Austrians, passed the river Lahn on a broad front, his main column directed on Frankfurt. Detachments were sent to besiege the eastern or land front of Ehrenbreitstein and to observe the garrison of Mayence.

By the middle of June the advance of the Archduke, who had concentrated a locally superior force on the Main, compelled Jourdan to suspend his forward movement. He took up an unnecessarily long line on the Lahn where the Austrians attacked him, driving in his outposts and cutting off Soult's division on his extreme left. When Jourdan found he could not hold his own he entrusted to Ney the dangerous mission of conveying the orders for the retreat to the isolated detachment under Soult. Escorted by half a squadron of hussars Ney made a daring ride through country that was traversed in every direction by the enemy's cavalry. He arrived just in time to warn Soult, and accompanied him in the perilous retreat by which his division, all but surrounded by the enemy, was saved from destruction. In the general retirement of Jourdan's army towards the crossings of the Lower Rhine, Ney, at the head of a column of 800 horsemen, was frequently engaged with the pursuing Austrian cavalry. While the retreat was in progress Carnot wrote to Jourdan a consoling letter, on 20 June, in which he told him that "to retire at the right moment in order to return later with greater advantage is to make a skilful application of the rules of war," provided always that the *morale* of the soldier did not suffer. Carnot's admirers praise the letter. It looks rather puerile, and reminds one of the story of the Federal general who, after Bull's Run, explained that the Northern Army had made a strategic concentration to the rear to protect Washington.

Moreau, like Pichegru in 1795, was slow in beginning. He did not cross the Rhine at Strasburg till 20 June, and as the main Austrian forces had been moved northwards he had not to face serious opposition. He drove before him the Austrian corps between the Rhine and the Black Forest. The Archduke Charles, when he heard the news, fell back from the Lower Rhine and reinforced his left to oppose Moreau. This enabled Jourdan to advance again to the Lahn in the first week of July.

The Archduke now retired towards the Danube valley, keeping between the two armies of Moreau and Jourdan, which were advancing eastwards into south Germany on parallel and widely separated lines. The Archduke left strong rearguards in front of each of the French columns, and waited his opportunity to fall with concentrated force on one or other of them.

In this march eastwards Ney was given the command of the advanced guard of Jourdan's army—three battalions, three regiments of cavalry, and two guns, detached from Colaud's division.

On 9 and 10 July there was hard fighting about Nieder-Merle and Friedberg, in which Ney's detachment was at first engaged alone, but was supported on the 10th by Colaud's and Lefèbvre's divisions. The Austrians lost three guns and a number of prisoners. On the 16th Jourdan occupied Frankfurt. The advance was continued next day and on the 29th Ney took the town of Lohr after a sharp engagement. On 3 August Jourdan was so ill that for some time he left the command of the Army of the Sambre and Meuse in the hands of Kléber. On 7 August Kléber found the Austrians under Wartensleben in battle array near the small fortress of Forcheim. In the fight that ensued Colaud's division broke through the enemy's centre, and Ney, after taking part in the victorious attack, followed up the retreating Austrians for some miles at the head of the cavalry. Returning from the pursuit he was sent by Kléber to summon the commandant of Forcheim to surrender, and spoke so forcibly to him that he agreed to hand over the place at once, though the French engineers thought it could have made a prolonged resistance.

On the evening of the victory Kléber announced to his friend that he would at once recognize his services by giving him the rank of *Général de Brigade*, which he had refused seventeen months before, when he was wounded at the siege of Mayence. The confirmation of this promotion arrived from Paris on 15 August. The official document set forth that Ney was promoted "in reward for his valiant conduct during this and the preceding campaign". Jourdan, who had recovered and resumed the command of the army, sent the decree to him with a covering letter in which he wrote :—

> "The Government has discharged a debt of gratitude to one of its worthiest and most zealous servants, and has only rendered justice to the talents and the valour of which you give new proofs each day."

Nuremberg had been occupied on 10 August, and next day Ney summoned and took possession of the fort of Rothenburg making its garrison of 300 men prisoners.

From Nuremberg, after a brief halt, Jourdan advanced with his divisions in parallel columns on a broad front, through hilly wooded country, with Wartensleben still retiring slowly before him. He was anxious at having no news of Moreau, and threw out Bernadotte's division to his right to try to gain touch with him. Moreau was on the Danube, equally without news of his colleague.

On 21 August Jourdan received within a few hours news that Bernadotte was being attacked by superior numbers, believed to be commanded by the Archduke, and from Moreau a despatch warning him that the Archduke was turning northwards to fall upon him. It seems not to have occurred to Moreau that, instead of pushing back the relatively small force left in his front, it was his business to attempt also a northward march to his comrade's help. But the operation was becoming every hour more difficult. The Austrian Commander-in-Chief was using his central position to throw every available man and gun against the northern French army.

On the morning of 23 August Jourdan, finding that hostile forces were accumulating against the heads of his widely separated columns in the hill country, decided on a retreat. General Ney was given the command of the rear-guard of a column formed by Colaud and Grenier's divisions. On the 24th he had a trying experience. He had with him two regiments of cavalry and a "demi-brigade" (two battalions) of infantry commanded by Colonel Dehée. Attacked by the whole of Wartensleben's corps, and with his line of retreat cut by a mass of Austrian cavalry, he found himself under the sad necessity of abandoning the infantry to their fate, and fighting his way through with his mounted troops. He extricated the two cavalry regiments by a desperate charge against heavy odds. Dehée's infantry, formed in two squares and surrounded on all sides, beat off several cavalry charges, but when infantry and artillery opened on them at close range and the cavalry charged again, their ranks were broken, and the survivors were made prisoners. Dehée had been killed and half his men had fallen.

Jourdan continued his retreat, at first in two columns, one under his own command, the other under Kléber, whose rear-guard was commanded by Ney. Kléber and Colaud's health broke down and they went back to France. There was general depression at the collapse of the campaign, and Jourdan wrote to the War Office that he felt he had lost the confidence of his subordinate generals, and was ready to resign the command. Beaten at Wurtzburg, but very slackly pursued, he retreated to the Lahn. His failure forced Moreau to retire towards the Rhine.

On 11 September Ney, who was covering Jourdan's positions on the Lahn with his rear-guard troops at Giessen found himself in danger of being surrounded and cut off by the main body of the Archduke's army. The town was encircled by an old wall, and while Ney was evacuating it, the citizens suddenly closed the gates on the north side and admitted an Austrian detachment on the south. The result was that some companies of French infantry, who had not yet marched out, found themselves in a trap. Ney placed his guns in position outside the town, and himself approached the gate under a white flag. He told the townsmen who held it, that if the men they had entrapped were not at once allowed to march out, he would bombard and burn the place. He spoke in such a determined and threatening way that he frightened them into submission. They entreated the town council and the Austrian commander to save them from destruction by letting the Frenchmen go, and strange to say the request was granted, and the prisoners liberated.[1] It was a successful piece of mere bluff, for at most Ney could only have thrown a few round shot into Giessen, and they would have done little harm. If he continued his cannonade for any length of time he would have had tenfold numbers upon him and compromised his own retreat.

The defence of the line of the Lahn collapsed on the 16th, and Jourdan, retiring still further northwards, took up a position along the rivers Sieg and Agger, with his right resting on the Rhine near Bonn. He wrote to Paris again asking to be allowed to resign his command. He said that he could not understand by what chance he had been put into such a high position, and that he felt himself quite unfit for it. On 28 September he was replaced by General Beurnonville, who remained inactive on the Sieg, content that the Austrians made no attempt to drive him from it, and apparently not realizing that his own inaction left the Archduke free to divert a considerable force southwards for the operations against Moreau, who was driven across the Rhine. In October, while fighting was still in progress on the upper Rhine, Beurnonville agreed to an armistice of indeterminate duration with General Werneck,

[1] General Bonnal (*Vie Militaire du Maréchal Ney*) rightly speaks of the success of Ney's threat as "something almost incredible," and adds: "Besides his valour in action General Ney had a talent for terrorising the governors and the inhabitants of strong places into the capitulation he demanded".

whom the Archduke had left in command of the corps that observed the French positions along the Sieg and Agger—one more instance of this strange practice of local peace in the midst of a general war.

Before the armistice was arranged, Ney was, in the last week of September, sent to the extreme left of the line to protect that flank. He had with him two regiments of cavalry (6th and 9th Chasseurs), and the 20th Demi-brigade of Light Infantry. He was later reinforced with three more battalions (two battalions of the 48th Demi-brigade of the line and the 2nd Battalion of the 105th Demi-brigade). On 30 September he established his head-quarters at the village of Huckeswagen, where he spent some weeks. He took advantage of the lull in the operations to address a long general order to the troops under his command, which showed his painstaking attention to practical detail. It was a series of brief instructions on outpost work, patrolling and reconnaissance, and the action of a rear-guard.

Another order warned officers that, for the sake of good discipline, they must not drink at the inns with non-commissioned officers and privates. This was a reaction against the democratic methods of the Republican armies, which were full of officers promoted from the ranks. Ney warned his officers that if anyone disregarded his order, he would send the offender to prison at Cologne for a first offence and on its repetition he would propose that the officer concerned should lose his commission. Times were changing. A little earlier such an order would have exposed the general who issued it to the risk of being denounced as an aristocrat and a bad Republican. Now it seems not to have in any way diminished Ney's popularity with his officers and men.

Even before the armistice was formally signed in December, there was a tacit truce, with a line of demarcation to define the limits of movement of both armies. A Prussian officer, Major Jeckner, was sent to the Huckeswagen district to see that the line of demarcation was respected, and we hear of him dining more than once with Ney and his staff. Once the French deliberately broke the arrangement. During the last stage of the retreat of Jourdan to the line of the Sieg and Agger, a tumbril, containing a considerable part of the military chest of the army, had been captured by armed peasants near Freudenberg. Ney received information that they had secured nearly a million and a half of francs in coined silver, and were fighting among themselves over the sharing of the spoil. One foggy November morning he sent a party of sixty chasseurs across the demarcation line to try to recapture some of the money. They raided the village of Attendorf, and brought back 15,000 francs. Major Jeckner complained of this invasion of the Austrian zone, and was put off with an explanation that the chasseurs had lost their way in the fog.

After the conclusion of the armistice, Ney marched northwards to Elberfeld, where he established his head-quarters and found better cantonments for his men. Their general good conduct is shown by the fact that, notwithstanding his strict ideas of discipline, the order book of his detachment from 1 October, 1796, to the middle of January records only one case of crime serious enough to be dealt with by the General. One of the chasseurs is found guilty of drunkenness and absence from duty, but only a light punishment is inflicted. Ney orders that his name shall be excluded from all lists for promotion, until he has by steady good conduct redeemed his character.

At the end of January, 1797, Ney's brigade was broken up. There had already been several changes in the list of generals of the Army of the Sambre and Meuse. Amongst others General Lefèbvre had had to resign the command of his division through ill-health. On 10 January, the Commander-in-Chief, Beurnonville, wrote to the Minister of War, proposing that Ney should be promoted to the rank of General of Division, and given the command of the advanced guard of the whole army in the next campaign. Of Ney's services Beurnonville wrote:—

> "This officer, intrepid in every engagement during the whole of the campaign, has covered himself with glory. He has always been in command of an advanced guard, and I know of no one but him who can perfectly command that of the Army of the Sambre and Meuse."

The proposed promotion was not granted, but on 13 February Ney, still a *Général de Brigade*, was directed to join General Grenier's division, and take command of a detachment, which was to act as the advanced guard of the right wing of the army during the next campaign. On 3 March he established his head-quarters at Birkenfeld. His command was made up as follows: Cavalry, 6th Chasseurs, and 2nd Hussars; Artillery, a light battery; Infantry, 20th Demi-brigade (three battalions). The last of his troops joined him on 15 March. He had then nearly 3000 men under his command.

At the end of February Hoche had replaced Beurnonville as Commander-in-Chief of the Army of the Sambre and Meuse for the campaign of 1797. According to the fashion of the time he organized it with a right, centre, and left wing, commanded respectively by Lefèbvre, Grenier, and Championnet, each corps composed of two divisions. A seventh division under General Watrin was to be at his own disposal as a reserve. The cavalry attached to the infantry was reduced to a single regiment of chasseurs for each division. The rest of the mounted troops were formed into a corps under General D'Hautpoul, afterwards famous as a commander of cuirassiers under the Empire.

On 7 March, while Ney was still at Birkenfeld organizing his mixed brigade of all arms, Hoche wrote to him, telling him that D'Hautpoul's cavalry was to be organized in four divisions—hussars, chasseurs, dragoons, and heavy cavalry, and that he was to command the Hussar Division, composed of the 2nd, 3rd, 4th, and 5th regiments. The 4th was the regiment in which Ney had so long served in the ranks and as an officer. The 5th was a unit of later formation. Ney was to proceed with the formation of his division, and until hostilities began to take every opportunity of training it by manœuvres. He was not to act under any of the commanders of the right, centre or left, but would receive all orders either from D'Hautpoul, or directly from the Commander-in-Chief. Hoche ended the letter by expressing the satisfaction he felt in serving with a General "whose military merits were so generally recognized and esteemed".

In acknowledging the receipt of these orders Ney wrote to Hoche on 15 March:—

"I most sincerely share, *mon général*, the satisfaction that all my comrades have felt at your arrival among us, and the confidence with which your presence has inspired the whole of the army is a sure guarantee of the success of your enterprises. I shall be only too happy to contribute according to my small powers to realize your wishes and merit your esteem."

The plan of campaign was that Hoche, with the Army of the Sambre and Meuse, should cross the river, as in the two preceding years, at Dusseldorf and Neuwied, picking up the detachments already on the right bank. Moreau, with the Army of the Rhine, would cross higher up about Strasburg. The two armies were to advance to the Danube, and join hands with the Army of Italy under Bonaparte operating through the Tyrol. The advance of the two Rhine armies would be facilitated by the fact that the Archduke Charles had been sent to oppose Bonaparte's progress in Venetia, and was weakening the Austrian Army in South Germany by drawing heavily upon it for reinforcements.

In January, 1797, Bonaparte had defeated the last Austrian effort to relieve Mantua, winning the victory of Rivoli amid the ice and snow of the mountain plateau above the Lake of Garda. On 3 February Mantua had surrendered. In the beginning of March, while there was still an armistice in the Rhineland, Bonaparte had detached a corps under Joubert to invade the Tyrol, and, with the main body of the Army of Italy, had left Verona to enter Venetia. He had conceived the plan of a bold single-handed advance through the hills of Carinthia and Styria directly upon Vienna. On 12 March his advanced guards drove the Austrian detachments from the line of the Piava. On the 16th and 17th he forced that of the Tagliamento. On the 23rd the French were across the Isonzo the last of the three river lines on which the Austrians had tried to bar their progress. The Archduke Charles, defeated in front, and with his line of retreat menaced by Joubert's advance through the Tyrol, was falling back through the mountainous country of the eastern Alps, anxious only to delay the march of the victors. On 30 March Bonaparte occupied Klagenfurt, the capital of Carinthia, where he stopped his advance in order to open unofficial communications with the Archduke to ascertain if Austria was inclined to make peace, of which he intended to dictate the terms.

It was only after receiving the news of these successes that the Paris Government at last ordered Hoche and Moreau to break off the armistice, and perform the relatively easy task of driving the weak Austrian Army of General Werneck from South Germany. On 16 April Hoche sent a flag of truce to Werneck to denounce the armistice, and the same day his left under Championnet began its advance from the neighbourhood of Dusseldorf to the Sieg, while the centre and right concentrated to cross the Rhine at Neuwied. Hoche had 70,000 men under his command, mostly veterans of several campaigns. Werneck could oppose to them at the most only 35,000.

On 17 April Championnet crossed the Sieg. On the same day Hoche with the centre and right was across the Rhine at Neuwied, and, issuing from the entrenchments that covered his floating bridges, he drove back the Austrians, and next day Championnet effected a junction with him. The united army now followed up the Austrian retreat, Ney with his hussars and a battery of horse artillery being well to the front. On the 20th he several times charged the cavalry of Werneck's rear-guard.

Next day he was again in action with them near Giessen. Towards evening he found himself attacked by superior numbers. A regiment of Austrian lancers charged his battery as it was retiring, and one of the guns was in imminent danger of capture. Ney put himself at the head of a squadron of his old comrades of the 4th Hussars, and rode to the rescue. His onset drove back the lancers and saved the gun, but, as he pressed the enemy back, his squadron was suddenly charged on the flank by a regiment of heavy dragoons. Everything gave way before the shock. Ney's horse was rolled over badly wounded and when he extricated himself, he found that he was alone with only a broken sword in his hand. He made an effort to seize another horse, but he was ridden down by the Austrian dragoons, and bruised and exhausted he became their prisoner. The Austrians continued their retreat during the night, taking Ney with them under a strong escort. Next day Hoche's advanced guard, under Lefèbvre, was before Frankfurt-on-the-Main, and he was preparing to occupy it, when an Austrian officer arrived with the news that preliminaries of peace had been signed at Leoben by the representatives of Bonaparte and the Archduke Charles, and the long war was at an end.

An armistice was arranged, and the River Nidda was chosen as the line of demarcation between the French and Austrian troops.

Hoche had heard of Ney's capture on occupying Giessen on the evening of the 21st. He at once wrote him the following letter:—

"HEAD-QUARTERS, GIESSEN, 2nd FLOREAL,
"*Fifth Year of the Republic* (21 *April*, 1797)

"THE GENERAL COMMANDING-IN-CHIEF THE ARMY OF THE SAMBRE AND MEUSE TO BRIGADIER-GENERAL NEY.

"You must know me well enough, my dear General, to understand how afflicted I am at the terrible event that has happened to you.

"I have sufficient confidence in the spirit of mutual courtesy with which the Austrian Generals act, to expect that they will treat you as we have dealt with such of their colleagues as we have made prisoners in Italy. I am asking Monsieur Elznitz[1] to release you on your parole, and I am looking forward impatiently to the moment when I shall again grasp your hand. Let me know if I can send you anything helpful. Adieu, my dear Ney. Believe in my sincere and constant friendship.

"HOCHE"

Ney had been suffering from deep depression and disappointment. The arrival of this generous letter from a soldier-chief like Lazare Hoche reassured him. It showed that in the esteem of such a good judge of men he had lost nothing of his reputation by his misfortune. Five days after the conclusion of the armistice he had a further consolation. A messenger arrived from Hoche bringing a *ceinture de commandement*—the broad silk tricolour sash, fringed with gold, worn by Republican Generals, with a letter from Hoche in which he said:—

"In sending you the sash, which will be handed to you by the bearer of this letter, I do not pretend, my dear General, to recompense either your successes or your merits. I ask you only to accept it as a poor testimony of my particular esteem and my unalterable friendship. Let me have news of your health."

Then there arrived from the Paris War Office an official letter giving the highest praise to Ney's conduct, and assuring

[1] General Elznitz of the Austrian Army, the commander of Werneck's rear-guard.

him that the accident of his capture on the eve of the peace would in no way damage his reputation and his prospects.

Werneck at first made difficulties about accepting Ney's parole, but Hoche wrote to the Archduke Charles on the subject, and the news of this appeal to his superior officer made Werneck give way. On 6 May Hoche welcomed Ney in the French lines at Giessen. He was to remain on parole there until he was exchanged for one of the captured Austrian Generals. The exchange was arranged only two days later at Basel by the French and Austrian commissioners, who met there to effect a mutual exchange of prisoners, but it was not till 24 May that Hoche received the official documents from Paris, and was able to write to his friend:—

"I send you, my dear Ney, the certificate of your exchange, which has just reached me from the Government. You will resume your command, and believe me if we begin again, I shall put you in a position to win the praises of both friends and enemies."

On 7 June Ney again took command of his Hussar division. But the armistice and the preliminaries of Leoben ended in the Peace of Campo Formio. After commanding his division in camp and quarters during the long negotiations, Ney went on 31 December to Mayence, which had been handed over to France by the Treaty, and where he was directed to organize the small cavalry force that was to form part of the permanent French garrison.

After spending a few days there he returned to the headquarters of his Cavalry division at Homburg. At the end of January, 1798, the Army of the Sambre and Meuse was being broken up. England was now the only power that remained at war with the Republic, and an army was being concentrated on the coasts of the Channel, under the name of the "Armée d'Angleterre," destined for the invasion of that country under Bonaparte's command. On 15 February Ney marched from Homburg with his detachment, now reduced to a brigade of two regiments, the 3rd and 5th Hussars. Their post during the concentration of the "Army of England" was to be at Amiens.

CHAPTER III

NEY, GENERAL OF DIVISION (1798-1799)

NEY reached Amiens on 4 March, 1798, and found there General Desaix, who was in command of the Army of England, pending Bonaparte's coming. He sent Ney to Abbeville to prepare for the quartering of his hussars in and about that town, where the two regiments arrived on the 11th. But he was only a few weeks in command of them. Bonaparte, now all powerful in the military councils of the Republic, had declared that the time was not yet ripe for an attempt to invade England. He was preparing for his enterprise in Egypt. The concentration in the northern departments was broken up. Some of the regiments were sent to Toulon to be embarked on the fleet of Brueys. With them went several of the more prominent officers, including Desaix himself. But Bonaparte had probably not yet even heard of the exploits of a mere brigadier-general like Michel Ney. It was much later in his career that the bold leader of the vanguards on the Rhine came into the inner circle of Napoleon's Paladins.

On 26 April he obtained a short leave of absence—three weeks—which he spent at Metz. Why he went there is not explained, and there is no record of his having visited Saarlouis, though he may have gone there before he returned to Abbeville at the beginning of June. On the 15th of that month he was sent to Lille to command a brigade of cavalry stationed there. It was all garrison work, official routine, and inspections, with some minor manœuvre training.

On 24 August he received another destination. He was ordered to join the army concentrated on the Rhine under Joubert, and known from its head-quarters as the "Army of Mayence". It was being reinforced in view of a possible renewal of hostilities with Austria. His new command was a brigade of Chasseurs-à-Cheval (10th, 20th, and 23rd Regiments) in cantonments about Weilburg on the banks of the Lahn, the scene of some of his recent war experiences. It was for him an uneventful time. In September his head-quarters were moved from Weilburg to Hachenburg. On 11 October the 8th Chasseurs joined him and raised his brigade to the strength of four regiments. On 4 November the three original regiments were taken from him and sent back to France. After having for a few days only the 8th Chasseurs with him, he was given also the 4th Hussars, and on 11 December he transferred his head-quarters and his two regiments to Homburg in the Duchy of Nassau. This was Ney's uneventful record for the greater part of 1798, the year that saw Napoleon's campaign in the East begun, Rome occupied and the Roman Republic proclaimed, Switzerland revolutionized and the Helvetian Republic founded under the protection of France, and attempts made to invade Ireland.

In the expectation of renewed war with Austria, the Directory had raised the Army of Mayence to six divisions of infantry and a Cavalry division. Jourdan was in command of it with head-quarters at Strasburg, whither Ney was called on 4 February and given the command of the light cavalry detailed to act as the advanced guard of a new organization, the Army of the Danube. He had a brigade formed of the 1st Chasseurs and 4th and 5th Hussars. The Army of the Danube was formed by taking two-thirds of its strength from the Army of Mayence. The remaining third was henceforth to be known as the "Army of the Rhine". In expectation of an outbreak of war in the spring, the Directory at Paris had in January drawn up an ambitious plan of operations, and decreed the organization of the following armies:—

Official title.	*Commander.*	*Strength.*
Army of the Rhine . .	Bernadotte	15,000 men.
" " Danube . .	Jourdan .	40,000 "
" " Switzerland .	Masséna .	30,000 "
" " Italy . . .	Schérer .	50,000 "
" " Naples . .	Macdonald	30,000 "
" " Holland . .	Brune .	10,000 "
	Total	175,000 men.

Jourdan, besides commanding the Army of the Danube,

was to give a general direction to the operations of Bernadotte on his left and Masséna on his right.

The plan of campaign had the defect of dissipating, instead of concentrating, the striking force of the Republican armies. It was further based on the false idea that Switzerland was like a citadel between the Italian and German theatres of war, where an army could manœuvre freely to place itself on the flank of the line of operations of the advancing Austrians, pouring down on them from the mountains like an avalanche. The difficulty of moving and supplying an army on the mountain roads, the restriction of its lines of operation by the few and narrow openings from them, and the enforced separation of this large body of men from the armies operating north and south of it, were all left out of account. Masséna's 30,000 men would have been of more value if they had been placed at the outset on the Rhine or in the plain of northern Italy.

According to the Paris plan the Army of the Danube was to advance from the Rhine into the Upper Danube valley, with the Army of the Rhine covering its left flank, and the Army of Switzerland ready to descend from the mountains on the enemy's flank and rear. Meanwhile the Army of Italy, supported by the Army of Naples, was to attack the Austrians in Venetia.

Carnot was no longer at the Paris War Office. He had opposed the extreme measures of Barras, and had been expelled from France as a suspected Royalist. The ambitious scheme for the campaign included all the defects of his war plans and none of their inspirations of genius. Bonaparte was in the East with some of the best of the coming generals. The superior direction of the French armies was at the mercy of mediocrities.

On the other side Austria was mobilizing a quarter of a million of men. The Archduke Charles was to command on the Danube, and Suvaroff was to bring 60,000 Russians to his assistance. Seeing that war was inevitable the Paris Directory sent an ultimatum to Vienna, summoning the Emperor Francis to disavow the Russian alliance and stop the march of Suvaroff's army into his states within eight days. On the rejection of this demand, Jourdan was ordered to cross the Rhine on 1 March, 1799. Then Masséna summoned the Austrians to evacuate eastern Switzerland, which they had entered on the invitation of the canton of the Grisons, now in revolt against the "Helvetian Republic".

On the eve of the outbreak of war Ney performed an exploit which gained for him the long-deferred promotion to the rank of General of Division. He had been at Strasburg since the beginning of February, occupied with the training of his light cavalry brigade, but on 24 February Bernadotte obtained his transference to the Army of the Rhine, and next day directed Ney to proceed to Mayence, and provisionally take command of a brigade of cavalry.

Ney then proposed to Bernadotte that he should be allowed at once to attempt an enterprise, which he had been thinking over for some time. After the Treaty of Campo Formio the arrangements with several of the minor German Princes, who had been in arms on the side of the Coalition, had not been completed, and negotiations had dragged on through the short-lived peace. Mannheim on the Rhine was to have been handed over to France under the treaty, in order to give the Republic a fortified bridge-head on the east bank of the river. During the French occupation of the place, before the Austrians recaptured it, there had been a bridge of boats connecting Mannheim with the west bank, but the Elector Palatine had persisted in retaining possession of the place after the treaty, and had removed the bridge. Ney suggested to Bernadotte a project for securing Mannheim by a *coup-de-main*, and re-establishing the crossing there before the opening of the campaign against Austria.

His proposal was accepted. He had asked for a mere handful of men. Two companies of infantry were to be sent to an old entrenchment opposite Mannheim on the French bank of the river, and three guns were to be brought up under cover of darkness to the same position and masked near it. The 8th Dragoons were to be sent him from his brigade. While the preparations were in progress he disguised himself as a civilian, and reached Mannheim by a round-about way. Using German, his mother tongue, he spent some hours in the town without exciting suspicion, then he returned to Frankenthal, whence he wrote to Bernadotte on 28 February:—

"At Mannheim they think themselves in complete security, and are in the greatest confidence that peace will be quickly arranged. This afternoon I myself went and saw the boats for the construction of the bridge; they are lying anchored in the branch of the Rhine above the town, to the number of thirty, with all the tackle and timber for the superstructure, and these boats, with the four lying near our earthworks on the left bank, will be enough to complete the crossing. The garrison is made up of 350 Palatine troops, including 40 Light Horse, some of them old pensioners. The rest are recruits belonging to five or six different corps. A verbal summons from myself will be enough to make them lay down their arms. Besides there is not even one cannon in the place."

The three guns escorted by a company had already arrived. On 1 March Ney with the dragoons and two companies of infantry, for whom he could not get any cartridges, arrived at the old entrenchments opposite Mannheim. The first warning the town received was the sudden opening of fire from Ney's battery, which threw a few solid shot and shells into the place, causing a general panic. The firing did not last more than ten minutes, then Ney, with a few companions, crossed the Rhine in a boat flying a flag of truce and met the commandant and the civil authorities. He told them that he was prepared to bombard and storm the town, which belonged to France under the Treaty of Campo Formio, and he asked them to spare him the unpleasant necessity of causing the bloodshed and destruction resulting from an attack, that they could not hope successfully to resist. The result was surrender at discretion. That night Ney was in possession of Mannheim, and next morning the bridge of boats was being reconstructed. The number of prisoners showed that Ney had been misinformed as to the strength of the garrison. It was nearly double his estimate and numbered 460 infantry and 200 cavalry of whom 105 were mounted.

Ney marched his cavalry brigade over the floating bridge, and taking also two companies of infantry he advanced upon Philippsburg, which was held by another detachment of the Elector's troops. He was not strong enough completely to invest the place but he found that the commandant and the officers of the garrison were not at all earnest in their loyalty to the Elector, or bent upon a desperate defence. He had hardly arrived before the place when he succeeded in arranging an understanding that the garrison and the investing force should take up a line of outposts, beyond which neither should advance without giving previous notice that it was intended to begin active hostilities. On 8 March he wrote to Bernadotte that he was convinced that a speedy surrender could be brought about by finding money for some of the enemy's officers, and he had requisitioned 50,000 francs from Heidelberg. Bernadotte wrote next day from Mayence a reply, which throws a curious light on some of the methods of conquest employed by Republican Generals in the Wars of the Revolution :—

"I have just received your letter of yesterday, my dear Ney. I approve all that you have done. In war when one is not strong, one must be a bit cunning. It is very trying that I cannot spare a body of troops sufficient to invest Philippsburg. Promise 500,000 francs, promise 600,000 and even more if necessary. I pledge my word of honour to have them paid down the same day that the fortress is handed over to us, or at latest within twenty-four hours.

"*We shall pay it all by levying contributions.* Be open handed in supplying your emissaries with money.

"Try to get into correspondence with the most influential officers. The man who is not brave, my dear Ney, will nearly always allow himself to be corrupted with gold ; to profit by this weakness is an art one must master, and it is not easy to find the opportunity again if one lets it slip.

"It is allowable, my dear Ney, to employ every means when it is a question of serving one's country, and contributing to the glory of its arms."

Bernadotte would perhaps have had some difficulty in explaining how the glory of the French arms could be increased by purchasing the surrender of a third-rate fortress. Ney's negotiations did not however produce the result he anticipated, and Bernadotte had to send him during the month of March a battalion of infantry and eight companies of grenadiers from various regiments to enable him to make the blockade of the place more effective. He was occupied with this routine-like warfare while further south the Archduke Charles forced Jourdan and the Army of the Danube to retire through the Black Forest to its original positions on the Upper Rhine.

On 28 March the Minister of War forwarded to Ney a

decree of the Directory promoting him to the rank of General of Division in reward for the capture of Mannheim. He replied on 4 April with a characteristic letter declining the promotion, as he had refused the first offer of promotion to the rank of General of Brigade:—

"WAGHAUSEL, *the 15th Germinal, Year VII.*
"(4 *April*, 1799)

"TO THE MINISTER OF WAR.

"I have received, Citizen Minister, your letter of the 8th of this month,[1] in which was enclosed the decree of the Executive Directory which has promoted me to the rank of General of Division. The Directory, in promoting me to these new functions, has probably only considered the favourable reports with reference to me which have reached it. I would have accepted a decision, which does me such honour, if my talents were likely to justify the kind action of the Government. I hope it will interpret my refusal as a certain pledge of the disinterested civic spirit which guides me in the discharge of my duties as General of Brigade, and I beg that you will assure the Government that my conduct will never have any other object than to deserve, more and more, its esteem.

"Consequently, I have the honour to return to you the decree concerning this promotion, and I beg of you to express to the Directory my attachment to the Republic."

Modest as he was in his estimate of his own military talents, Ney had good right to claim that he was thoroughly disinterested in his conduct, for not only had he twice refused promotion, the first ambition of most soldiers, but he was also unlike the majority of the Generals of the Revolution in the fact that he never tried to enrich himself at the public expense.

On the same day that he wrote to the Minister of War, Ney wrote to Bernadotte:—

"I have the honour to request you, *mon général*, to forward to the Minister of War, by the first available courier, my refusal of the rank of General of Division. This offer of promotion flatters me, and at the same time inspires me with a very lively sense of gratitude for him who, by his favourable reports, has induced the Government to confer this new rank upon me. I hope that while you approve my conduct in this matter, you will continue to manifest your good will towards me, and I shall always respond to it with the most sincere and lasting devotion."

The result of Ney's action was only to delay his promotion for a few weeks. On 4 May he received a letter from the

[1] 8th Germinal = 28 March.

Minister of War informing him that the Directory insisted on his acceptance of the new rank, and at the same time assured him that the Government saw in the modesty that had led him to decline it a new reason for seeing that he had the reward of his earlier services.

In the first week of April he was occupied with some unimportant operations, the direction of reconnoitring and foraging parties, and the reinforcement of the investing force around Philippsburg. Bernadotte, disgusted at the insignificant part assigned to him, and the impossibility of any effective action now that Jourdan's advance had collapsed, ordered Ney to remain in position to cover a general retirement to the Rhine, and then resigned his command, and on 10 April started for Paris. Before leaving the Army he wrote to Ney:—

> "Wherever I may be, my dear Ney, I shall always remember you and take an interest in you. Believe in the sincere attachment I have vowed to you, and be assured that nothing that is agreeable will ever happen to you without giving me the liveliest pleasure."

Jourdan had also resigned, and there was a new arrangement of the commands on the Rhine and in Switzerland. The Army of the Rhine ceased to have an independent existence and became the left wing of the "Army of the Danube and Switzerland" under the supreme command of Masséna, who was to direct all the operations from the Alps to the middle Rhine.

On 12 April Ney was called to Strasburg to see the Commander-in-Chief. When he arrived there he found that Masséna had gone up the river to Basel, and he followed him thither, reaching the place on 16 April. Here he learned that he was to have the command of Masséna's cavalry in northern Switzerland. But within a few days of his appointment the order of battle of Masséna's army was modified, and Ney's force was considerably reduced. He was to command only the light cavalry of the centre and right, five regiments in all, two of which had not yet joined.

But there was soon another change in the plans of the Directory. The collapse of the French left in south Germany was swiftly followed by news of failure after failure on the right in northern Italy. Suvaroff had reinforced the Austrians in Venetia with his Russians, and taking command of the combined forces was pressing the French steadily westward forcing one after another the lines of the rivers that run down from the Alps to the Po. The project of using Masséna's army in Switzerland as a central striking force ready to co-operate with a victorious advance in the plains to north or south of the mountains had to be abandoned. For the present his task would be to stand on the defensive, repress the hostile movements of the insurgent mountaineers, and check the advance of the Austrians through northern Switzerland, while on his immediate right a division under General Lecourbe held the passes and mountain roads from the Lake of Lucerne southwards to the Italian slope of the main Alpine chain in the canton of Ticino.

On 8 May Ney was directed by Masséna to proceed with all haste to Lecourbe's head-quarters, where he was given the command of a detachment, made up of two battalions and two companies of French infantry, and two weak battalions of Swiss Republican troops; no artillery and for cavalry a corporal and six hussars. He was sent with this handful of about 2000 men to hold the Val Mesocco, the narrow valley which branches off northwards from that by which the St. Gothard railway now descends to the Lago Maggiore. He had his head-quarters and reserve at Mesocco near the north end of the valley and established posts in the passes leading eastward into the Grisons. He also kept reconnoitring parties of lightly equipped infantry in movement northwards over the Splügen and the San Bernardino passes. The weather was bad, with showers of rain varied with snowstorms in the higher passes, and the nights were intensely cold. Supplies were short, and the men, badly fed, clad in ragged uniforms. and sheltered only in roughly constructed huts, suffered severely, Not a company could muster anything like its full strength for duty.

But this trying service did not last many days. On 17 May Lecourbe wrote to Ney that the enemy had occupied Chur, stormed the fortifications at Luziensteig, and obtained complete command of the Grisons. To hold on any longer in the Ticino region would be to expose the whole division to the imminent risk of being cut off. There must be a prompt retirement northwards over the St. Gothard. Soult's division held Schwytz where he had broken up armed gatherings of peasants. His position there would cover and make the retreat possible. Ney's detachment formed the rear-guard in this march by the St. Gothard and the Andermatt valley to the Lake of Uri. While the movement was in progress Lecourbe received a letter from Masséna ordering him to send Ney back to rejoin the "Army of the Danube" in northern Switzerland, where he was to take command of the advanced guard of its central column at Winterthur. Lecourbe forwarded the order to him with a covering letter in which he said, "I am sorry not to have the advantage of keeping you longer with me, and I assure you of my esteem and of the friendship I feel for you".

Ney had just received the letter of the Directory dated 4 May insisting on his accepting the rank of General of Division, and Masséna, in recalling him to his head-quarters, intended to give him a command more befitting his new position than the direction of an outpost detachment in Lecourbe's division.

Ney reached Winterthur late on the evening of 24 May. It had been expected that he would take a rest at Zurich, but he passed through the town without stopping there and without reporting himself to the local commandant. He thus failed to receive a "letter of service" from Masséna's chief of the staff, General Chérin, which was waiting for him at Zurich, and which formally empowered and directed him to take command at Winterthur.

The place, now a busy industrial centre and an important railway junction, was in 1799 surrounded by a crumbling rampart that gave it the dignity of a fortified town, but was unarmed and useless for defence. Its military importance arose from the fact that it stands at the junction of a number of roads about midway between the Lakes of Zurich and Constance. The little River Toss, a tributary of the Rhine, runs past it. Masséna's army was in position to the westward along the line of the River Limmat, its right about Zurich its left towards the Rhine. In front of the Limmat positions three "advanced guards" had been pushed forward, to cover the right, centre, and left. This advanced outpost line was under the command of General Tharreau. The central detachment at Winterthur was the most important.

Two Austrian columns were advancing between the Lakes of Constance and Zurich, under Generals Naundorff and Hotze. Naundorff's advanced posts had been pushed forward to the west of the River Thur, by the roads from Constance towards Winterthur. The Archduke Charles had ordered him to occupy the latter place, and hold it to cover the crossing of the Rhine below Constance by the main body of his army from South Germany.

The troops at Winterthur were a brigade of four battalions under General Gazan, a brigade of two battalions under General Roger, and a cavalry brigade of three regiments under General Walther. General Oudinot was in command of the whole force. When Ney reached the place on the evening of 24 May, he declined to take over the command for two reasons; first he had not received his "letters of service" and secondly Oudinot had been ordered by Tharreau to attack the Austrian outposts in the direction of the Thur early next morning, and had made all his arrangements, and Ney, who neither knew the ground nor the troops he was to command, thought it better to leave the direction of the operation in his comrade's hands. He assisted Oudinot by riding out with Walther's cavalry and giving the brigadier some useful advice.

Naundorff's light troops held a line of villages along the Thur. Oudinot attacked in two columns, supported by detachments from the advanced guards of the right and left, and drove the Austrians across the river. But Tharreau had ordered that the affair should be a mere demonstration, and that the troops were to return at once to their positions about Winterthur. This retirement immediately after the morning fight on the 25th, gave the men an impression that something was wrong, and as Ney reported to Masséna "depressed the *morale* of the soldiers".

On the 26th Ney received his "letters of service" and instructions, and took over the command at Winterthur. He was disappointed at finding that he was to report to and receive the orders of Tharreau, instead of being in direct communication with his chief Masséna. He had not much confidence in Tharreau's powers of command, and he saw that delays and difficulties might arise from his communications with head-quarters having to pass by a round-about way. He wrote to Masséna expressing strongly his opinion that the commander of an advanced guard in touch with the enemy ought to be in the most direct communication with the Commander-in-Chief and responsible only to him. But until he received a reply to this letter he had to obey Tharreau's instructions.

Late on the 26th he received a message from the latter informing him that the troops about Winterthur would probably be attacked next day, and telling him that Soult on his right and Oudinot now in command of the nearest detachments on his left had been warned and would support him. Hotze was coming up to reinforce Naundorff and the latter had reoccupied the positions taken in the attack of the 25th.

Ney took these orders to mean that a stand was to be made all along the outpost line, and that he would not be isolated. At sunrise on the 27th he rode out to reconnoitre the ground in front of Winterthur and select positions on which to bar the expected advance of the enemy. Walther's cavalry he sent out in the direction of Frauenfeld to gain touch with the Austrians.

He moved out his small force of infantry, between 3000 and 4000 men, to the line of low hills about four miles north of Winterthur. The country to his front in the direction of the enemy did not allow of any extended view, except where the long trough of the valley leading towards Frauenfeld made an opening in the wooded hills. He ordered Gazan with his four battalions to advance up the valley, sending Roger with the two other battalions forward over the hills on his left to fall on the flank of any Austrian detachment that might try to bar Gazan's way. He did not know that the enemy were in force in his front. He expected to be in touch before long with supporting columns to left and right of his advance and to repeat the easy victory of three days before and drive the Austrian outpost detachments across the Thur.

There was a dangerous contempt for the "white coats" in

the whole proceeding. It was the first time Ney had commanded so considerable an infantry force in action, and he was taking very serious risks in not waiting for the reports of his cavalry before committing his two weak brigades to a further advance. But as a cavalry commander he had been used to taking risks, and finding that the bold game was the winning one. Suddenly the stillness of the early summer morning was broken by the dull reports of musketry volleys. Then among the clumps of pine woods on the slopes to the right of the Frauenfeld hollow Walther's troops were seen retiring. Gazan's column was forming up for battle across the road, and over the heights in front came the white-coated Austrian infantry. Roger's brigade had disappeared for the moment beyond the woods to the left.

Ney had ridden to the front with Gazan's brigade. The enemy was now advancing in force and the battle began. One strong Austrian column deployed into line, and attacked Ney and Gazan in front. Away to the left the sound of heavy firing told that Roger was also attacked. On the right another column pushed Walther back, and threatened to take Gazan's brigade in flank. Ney realized at once that he was heavily outnumbered. The fact was that Naundorff had sent 15,000 men to attack less than 4000 of the Republican troops. There was no sign of the reinforcements promised by Tharreau. There was nothing for it but to retreat. So Ney fell back upon Winterthur, making a dogged fight, and hoping against hope that at any moment the arrival of a French column to right or left would change the adverse conditions of the day.

Slowly the French gave way, but there was never a moment of unsteadiness. It was a well-fought rear-guard action, the men retiring by alternate detachments and in turn facing about to meet the enemy with bullet and bayonet. A last stand was being made at the gates of Winterthur, when Ney, who was riding on the flank of one of his battalions, suddenly went down, horse and man, before an Austrian volley. His horse was dead, but he rose at once with the blood running down from one of his knees, which had been wounded by a bullet.

He quietly told Gazan to direct the retreat through Winterthur and across the Toss while he had his wounded knee bound up and sent for another horse.

In a few minutes he had mounted again and resumed the command. The river was passed and for an hour and a half he defended its crossings against the enemy. But Naundorff's numbers enabled him to extend his line and cross the river at points above and below those held by the French. Ney then fell back to the margin of the pine woods on the heights south of the river and there for a while continued to defend himself against the Austrian attacks. Here his second horse was killed under him and he received another bullet wound, this time in the left hand. He now found himself "absolutely unable to continue in action" and definitely relinquished the command to Gazan. The fighting soon came to an end. The Austrians, satisfied with the capture of Winterthur, ceased to press their attacks and Gazan made an unmolested retreat towards the Limmat, after being rejoined by Roger. Walther's cavalry protected the retirement.

Wounded as he was Ney wrote the same night a full report to Masséna. He estimated the losses of his division at from 600 to 800 killed and wounded and about a hundred prisoners —one-fourth of his effective force. He blamed Tharreau for having committed him to the offensive and left him unsupported, but he did not write in any bitter terms though he must have felt deeply the disappointment that his first engagement as a General of Division had ended in defeat. He asked permission to go to Colmar to recover from his wounds and to take with him his staff officer, Adjutant-General Lorcet "who had been with him during the whole course of the action, and behaved in the most distinguished way, and had had the misfortune to have one of his ribs broken by a bullet".

Without waiting for a reply he left Gazan in command of the army and set off for Colmar on 28 May in a travelling carriage with Lorcet. On the way he received the desired permission, accompanied by a kind letter from the chief of the staff, in which, writing in the name of the Commander-in-Chief, Chérin assured him that it would be always a pleasure to do all that was possible to meet his wishes and that every one desired his speedy recovery and his return to the army. This showed that at head-quarters he was not blamed for the defeat of Winterthur.

Ney remained at Colmar for the greater part of the month of June and then went to Plombières to complete his recovery. In the third week of July he found himself well enough to return to the front. On 22 July he arrived at Basel, whence he wrote to Masséna reporting himself fit for duty and asking to be given some work to do. Next day he was directed to take command of the 6th Infantry Division, forming part of the left wing of the Army of the Danube under the orders of General Ferino.

In the eight weeks during which Ney had been disabled by his wounds great events had happened, and the fortune of war had been adverse to the Republican armies. In the first days of June the Archduke Charles had attacked Masséna's positions along the Limmat, and driven the French from the line of the river winning the engagement known as the first Battle of Zurich. Masséna, however, only fell back a few miles and established himself in a new line with his left on the Rhine above Basel. This was the position of the "Army of the Danube" when Ney rejoined it.

In Italy there had been a serious disaster, the prelude of worse defeats. In the middle of June Suvaroff had defeated Macdonald on the Trebbia. It was in this battle of the Trebbia that Ney's elder brother Jean met his death, while fighting as a lieutenant of the 55th Infantry.

On 8 July the Archduke had made an unsuccessful attack on the French lines. After this he detached from his army a considerable force which was sent over the Alps to assist in the operations in Italy. There was a lull in the operations in northern Switzerland, almost a tacit truce, during which Masséna received larger reinforcements than those that reached the Archduke from Austria. The balance of advantage was thus being restored to the French. This was the result of the operations of the allied armies being controlled not by Suvaroff and the Archduke Charles, the skilled commanders in the field, but by the theorists who composed the Aulic Council at Vienna. They insisted on directing the campaign from a board-room table at the Austrian War Office, and inspired only with old-fashioned theories of war they did not realize the simple truth that it was the business of the leaders in the field to follow up the advantages won on the Limmat and the Trebbia, and do their best to destroy the armies of Masséna in Switzerland and Macdonald and Moreau in Italy. Instead of this they ordered that the next step should be the reduction of the north Italian fortresses of Mantua and Alessandria, and it was to strengthen the Austro-Russians in Italy for this work that the Archduke was directed to cease his advance and weaken his fighting force by sending large reinforcements away over the Alps to Suvaroff.

When Ney rejoined on 22 July, the Army of the Danube had its extreme right near the Lake of Zug; its centre on the heights that form the left bank of the lower Reuss, and its left thrown back along the Rhine from the confluence of the Aar westward towards Basel. Though officially known as the 6th Infantry Division, Ney's command was a force of all arms. Its organization was:—

1st or Right Brigade. General Goullus. Head-quarters, Lauffenberg. 1st Demi-brigade Light Infantry, 2nd Demi-brigade Auxiliary Swiss Infantry, 8th Chasseurs-à-cheval and 17th Dragoons.

2nd or Left Brigade. General Barbier. Head-quarters, Rheinfelden. 103rd Demi-brigade of the Line, 1st Chasseurs-à-cheval.

Divisional troops. Some companies of light artillery and a company of engineers.

The troops were watching the river line, holding a number of posts along the bank, connected by cavalry patrols, with reserves in readiness to move to any threatened point. Ney inspected the various detachments, collected supplies, and generally saw that his command was fit for work whenever the tacit truce with the Austrians would be ended by the renewal of active operations.

Ney's official correspondence during this lull in the war shows how careful both sides were to avoid giving any unnecessary alarm that might accidentally lead to a sudden outbreak of hostilities. At the end of July Alessandria and Mantua had fallen. The Austrian commandant on the Bavarian bank of the Rhine sent a flag of truce to Ney's outposts at Bernau near the mouth of the Aar on 3 August to inform the French that if they heard a cannonade next day it would be only the firing of salutes with blank cartridge, when the news from Italy was announced to the troops in the Austrian camps. On 8 August General Oudinot, now chief of the staff to Masséna, returned the compliment, directing Ney to inform by flag of truce the Austrian commander on the other side of the Rhine that salvoes of artillery would be fired in the French camps on the 10th in honour of the Republican commemoration of the day.

On the 13th Ney was warned that the time of inactivity was coming to an end, and that movements had been ordered on the right and centre which would probably lead to a general engagement. Masséna was anxious to have a soldier like Ney employed at a point in his line where there would be more serious work than the mere watching of the Rhine on his left rear. So on the 15th he informed him that he was to hand over the command of the 6th Division to General Goullus, and take over that of the 5th Division, forming the left centre of the army.

It was not till late on the evening of 16 August that Ney received the formal order to proceed to Brugg, near the confluence of the Aar and the Reuss, and take over from General Heudelet the command of the 5th Division. He prepared to start next morning, but in the night there came a despatch from Goullus informing him that the enemy were attacking his right, and under cover of a heavy fire of artillery were trying to throw a bridge of boats across the Aar. Ney was not the man to relinquish the command of troops while they were going into action. He rode off in the darkness to Bernau, near the mouth of the Aar, and hurried all available reinforcements to the line of the river. Here he learned that the attempted crossing was a little higher up, at Klein Dettingen. A despatch from General Heudelet of the 5th Division informed him that the Austrians were constructing two boat bridges there, and the troops of the 5th were being moved to oppose them. Ney marched in the same direction with all the French and Auxiliary Swiss troops he had available, and after a sharp fight along the river banks about Klein Dettingen the Austrians were repulsed. He was preparing to make a counter attack, with a view to seizing and burning the boats and material they had collected for their bridges, when the enemy sent across a flag of truce with a request that hostilities should cease, and the informal truce be resumed. This was agreed to, and the boats were collected on the Austrian side of the Aar.

Ney then went on to Brugg, but once more there was a sudden change in his destination. Masséna had just received and transmitted to him an order from the Paris Directory removing him from the "Army of the Danube" and telling him to join the head-quarters of the "Army of the Rhine" at Mannheim. With the official letters Masséna sent him a personal request that he would delay his departure for a few days, as he anticipated further fighting would take place immediately, and he was anxious to have the advantage of his services. To this flattering request from his Commander-in-Chief Ney replied that he would remain until the 22nd.

Nothing, however, happened during these last days in Switzerland, and on the 22nd Ney started for Mannheim. He had asked to be allowed to take with him one of his staff, the Adjutant-General Ruffin. Masséna wrote to him that he was sorry to lose Ruffin and granted the request with regret. "It is a sacrifice," he wrote, "that I would not make for anyone else, but I cannot refuse you anything."

Ney's removal from the Army of the Danube to that of the Rhine was a piece of bad luck. Had he stayed in Switzerland, he would have taken part in Masséna's advance and the victory of Zurich—the one great success of a year of disasters. With the new Army of the Rhine he was thrown back into the days of small things, and condemned to serve under a sluggish incompetent commander, whose name is remembered only by specialists in the history of the time. Not military talents or services, but political interests, had placed General Leonard Müller in command of the Army of the Rhine. It had been formed to protect France against a possible raid across the upper river from southern Germany. The danger was not, however, serious so long as Masséna held his own and kept the Archduke Charles occupied in Switzerland, for the Austrians had in Bavaria only relatively small detachments of infantry. Their forces in South Germany were chiefly cavalry.

Müller, with his head-quarters at Mannheim, had at his disposal an army of three weak Infantry divisions and a division of cavalry. His right division under General Lewal was investing the Elector Palatine's fortress of Philippsburg, against which Ney had operated in an earlier campaign when he was under the command of Bernadotte (now Minister of War at Paris). The two other divisions were thrown forward into the hills on the east bank of the Rhine to cover the siege. They lay along the line of the little river Elsenz, a tributary of the Neckar. The extreme right was at Sinsheim, the left at Neckargemünde, where the Elsenz joins the Neckar. The division on the right of the line was commanded by General Colaud, an old friend of Ney and his chief in the days of the Army of the Sambre and Meuse. The left division was under General Dalaroche. The Cavalry division was under D'Hautpoul was stationed behind the line at Wiesloch.

Müller welcomed Ney to his head-quarters, found horses for him, and gave him at once some work to do. But congenial as his task was, the force placed at his disposal was so small that it would have been more befitting for a brigadier than a general of division. It was not quite 2000 strong. There were two battalions of the 29th Demi-brigade of the line, each mustering about 700 bayonets, two squadrons of the 3rd Hussars, each about a hundred strong, and for artillery three light guns. This little force was assembled at Steinsfurth near Sinsheim, on the extreme right of the advanced line on the evening of 27 August. Ney arrived there soon after midnight and took command of the detachment at 2 a.m. on the 28th.

The operation which he was to undertake was part of a plan of action which the Directory had sent to Müller. Korsakoff, with 30,000 Russians, was on the point of joining the Archduke, and Bernadotte, as Minister of War, had just directed Müller to use the Army of the Rhine for a demonstration in the upper valley of the Neckar, in order to give the Archduke the impression that a serious French invasion of South Germany was intended, and thus lead him to divert some of his forces to the country between the Rhine and Danube, and so render Masséna's task somewhat easier. The idea was sound but Müller carried it out in a very incomplete and half-hearted way. The only one of his subordinates who effected anything was Ney. This, however, was not the fault of his colleagues. They were held back by Müller's incompetence.

Ney's first object was the seizure of the town of Heilbronn on the upper Neckar. He was to turn out the Austrian detachment that held it, and levy contributions on the place and collect supplies there for the army. He marched early on the 28th and was before Heilbronn on the 29th. At 1 p.m. he was in possession of the place. In his report to Müller he noted that he had to act "with much circumspection" as there was plenty of open ground along the Neckar and the enemy was strong in cavalry. The Austrians had 1500 dragoons, hussars, and carbineers in the place, but only 400 infantry and no artillery, so Ney's three guns gave him a solid advantage. Probably the Austrian commander thought he had to deal with the vanguard of a much stronger force, for he made a poor show of resistance, and the capture of Heilbronn cost Ney only two men wounded. He thought the Austrians must have lost a good many men.

He reported that he had sent detachments to occupy Wimpfenn, on the Neckar about twelve miles below the town, and Lauffen some ten miles above it. He asked that six companies of the 3rd Battalion of the 29th Demi-brigade should be sent to reinforce him, and he ended his despatch with some important information, and a useful suggestion based upon it:—

> "The enemy is in small force everywhere on the right bank of the Neckar. It is my opinion that a bold and well-directed stroke would be successful, aiming at Ulm, to destroy the Austrian magazines there, and force Prince Charles to make a diversion even against his will. This might be accomplished with a corps of 12,000 men, and I could protect its left flank."

This was perfectly sound advice and if acted upon Ney's suggestion would have secured the result the Directory had in view when it ordered a movement on the Neckar. But Müller had no enterprise.

The same evening Ney wrote to him to report that

Wimpfenn had been occupied, but the attempt on Lauffen had failed. He asked for some more cavalry. Müller promised to send him the 6th Chasseurs-à-cheval.

On the 30th Müller wrote to Ney telling him that he was about to concentrate his efforts on the reduction of Philippsburg. He hinted that in taking this decision he had been overruled by the Government, but he was evidently seeking a pretext for abandoning the forward movement though it was hardly begun. He reminded Ney that a contribution was to be levied on Heilbronn and suggested 50,000 francs as the amount. He told him to send out reconnoitring parties as far as possible in order to find out what truth there was in current rumours that the Archduke Charles had sent strong reinforcements towards the Neckar and had himself arrived at Freudenstadt (forty-seven miles east of Strasburg).

The contribution had already been levied on Heilbronn, and not without considerable difficulty 100,000 francs had been obtained from the municipal authorities. On 29 August Ney had sent off one of his staff to convey the money to Müller's head-quarters. Müller had expected only half the amount, but when the money arrived he wrote to Ney that he ought to try to levy another 100,000. This suggestion was not adopted, for Müller, alarmed at reports that there was a large concentration of the enemy behind the northern hills of the Black Forest, did not wait for the result of Ney's reconnaissances, but sent him a hasty order to abandon Heilbronn and his posts on the Neckar, and withdraw to his starting-point at Steinsfurth near Sinsheim.

Ney reluctantly obeyed the order, and collected his force at Steinsfurth on 1 September. But that same day he was surprised to hear that Colaud's division was evacuating Sinsheim and falling back towards the Rhine, leaving his small detachment unsupported. He wrote a very outspoken letter to Müller, in which he told him that he could not understand why Colaud's force should be thus withdrawn without even being threatened by the enemy. He himself, he said, would now have to take care that the peasantry did not drive him out with pitchforks, such was the impression produced by this unnecessary retirement. If only one of Colaud's battalions had been left at Sinsheim, he could have held on at Steinsfurth and pushed reconnoitring parties up to and beyond the Neckar, but if he was left unsupported he would run the risk of being charged with reckless imprudence if he ventured on any such enterprise.

It was a new experience for Ney to have to act under a commander whose caution verged on cowardice, and how keenly he felt his position is proved by his having transgressed the rules of military discipline to the extent of writing such an outspoken censure on Müller's proceedings.

CHAPTER IV

COMMANDER-IN-CHIEF ON THE RHINE (1799)

THERE had been bad news from Italy. On 15 August the allies had completely defeated the French Army of Italy under Joubert, and the old veteran of the Rhine was among the dead. After this victory Suvaroff with the Russians was marching into Switzerland, leaving Melas and the Austrians to press the remnant of the French armies back upon Genoa. It was one of the darkest hours of the Republic.

Bonaparte, with some of the best of the younger French Generals, had been isolated in Egypt since Nelson's victory and the destruction of the fleet of Brueys in Aboukir Bay. Very little information as to what was happening there had reached France, and there was an impression, except among the most optimist of men, that the "Army of the East" and its commanders were hopelessly lost to the Republic. But the future master of France was already on his homeward way to change the whole face of the situation. On 22 August Bonaparte had run the blockade off Alexandria, and was making a venturous voyage through the Mediterranean accompanied by some of his most trusted officers. He was returning to seize upon the government of the Republic and to wrest victory out of the midst of disaster.

These coming events cast no shadows before. Even if the Republican Generals on the Rhine had known that Bonaparte was returning, they would probably have treated the news as a matter of no great importance. Most of them, like Ney himself, had never met the young Corsican soldier. They had seen comrades of theirs depart to share his triumphs in Italy and his wild venture in the East, but most of those who had remained in the northern theatre of war looked rather jealously on the soldiers of Italy, who had formed a kind of group of satellites for Bonaparte. And the soldiers who had followed him had the same kind of feeling for the men of the armies of the Rhine and Danube.

Ney had for years been doing his duty as a soldier in a quiet methodical way. He had never been in Paris. He had frankly given his adhesion to the Republic, but he had held aloof from politics. His correspondence is never disfigured by the rhetorical platitudes that came so readily from the pen of many of his comrades. He had never tried to push his fortunes except by hard service in the field. So far from being ambitious he had more than once refused well-merited promotion. A certain stolid self-possession and calm good sense was perhaps due to the fact that he had in him more of the German than the Frenchman, and so he remained untouched by the political excitement of the time.

In these autumn days of 1799 he was probably less affected by the bad news of disaster in Italy and new dangers in the central European theatre of war, than by the fact that he was himself under the orders of an incompetent and timid leader, whose hesitations and blunders would perhaps involve himself in the general discredit, that was only too likely to fall upon the unfortunate Army of the Rhine.

He held on at Steinsfurth till 5 September, sending out scouting parties towards the Neckar. One of these had a successful skirmish with a party of Austrian cavalry on the 3rd, and brought in some prisoners. By questioning these Ney ascertained that the enemy's force on the Neckar in his immediate front was about 1800 horse and 3000 foot (twelve squadrons and four battalions) with eight guns. They were strung out in a line of detachments along the river. He considered that, unsupported as he was, his best plan for imposing on the enemy was to resume active operations, and accordingly he marched on the village of Wimpfenn on the 6th. The Austrian detachment there retired on his approach, and he occupied the place without firing a shot.

Learning that Heilbronn was not strongly held he marched on that place next day, but here the Austrians made a stand, and were driven out only after some hard fighting. Ney reported to Müller on 7 September:—

"The enemy made a stubborn defence. He had cannon, infantry, and as many cavalry as I have. I reckon his force about equal to my own. He has just fallen back on Lauffen, where I intend to go to-morrow."

Next day he was able to write to Müller :—

"I have just got possession of Lauffen, my dear General. As I expected the enemy defended the position with a good deal of stubbornness. He is now in full retreat on Stuttgart, but I shall take care not to follow him in that direction, for his forces will continually increase as he falls back, especially his cavalry, and the slightest reverse would make it an infinitely difficult business for me to effect my retreat. I shall occupy the position of Eppingen to-morrow."

The march to Eppingen was a retirement. Ney rested there during the 10th, and that day received orders to act as the rear-guard of the Army of the Rhine, which was now falling back everywhere to the line of the river, Müller having received information that the Austrians under Schwarzenberg were advancing in superior force from behind the hills of the Black Forest. Ney retired by Wiesloch and Heidelberg, being reinforced on the march with four squadrons of cavalry and a battalion of light infantry. He was nowhere molested by the enemy.

General Müller was now preparing to act strictly on the defensive, holding the left bank of the Rhine from Strasburg to Coblentz, abandoning the blockade of Philippsburg, and evacuating all the right or eastern bank of the river except at Mannheim, where he held the town, in order to keep possession of the crossing there. Ney's detachment was now to rank as a division. The other divisional commanders were La Roche, Colaud, and Lewal. La Roche was to hold Mannheim, where there was a bridge of boats across the river, and Neckarau on the bend of the Rhine a couple of miles higher up. The other three divisions were strung out along the left bank. Lewal on the left from Coblentz to near Worms, Ney from Worms to Speyer, with La Roche in his front on the other bank about Mannheim; Colaud's division continued the line to near Strasburg. A force of some 30,000 men was thus guarding a front of about 300 miles. It was necessarily everywhere weak. The only show of strength was in the centre, but there La Roche was in a position that positively invited attack. Ney was to support him.

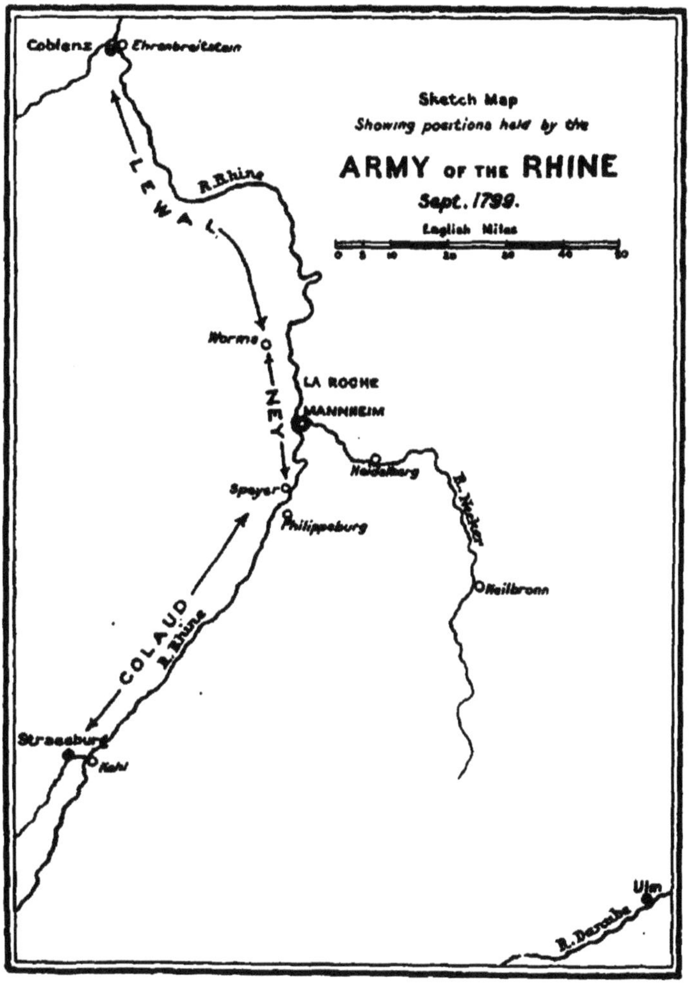
Sketch Map
Showing positions held by the
ARMY OF THE RHINE
Sept. 1799.
English Miles
0 5 10 20 30 40 50
Coblenz
Ehrenbreitstein
R. Rhine
LEWAL
Worms
NEY
LA ROCHE
MANNHEIM
Heidelberg
R. Neckar
Speyer
Philippsburg
Heilbronn
COLAUD
R. Rhine
Strassburg
Kehl
Ulm
R. Danube

For the front of more than thirty miles assigned to him Ney had at his disposal only three battalions and nine companies of infantry, three regiments of cavalry and six guns. He organized his division on 13 September in two mixed brigades of all arms and a reserve. His former staff officer, Lorcet, now a brigadier-general, had been sent to him. Ney put him in command of the right brigade at Speyer (two battalions of the 16th Demi-brigade of Infantry, three squadrons 3rd Hussars and two guns). The left brigade was posted at Worms under the command of Laffont, the Colonel of the 6th Chasseurs-à-cheval (a battalion of the 16th Infantry, the 6th Chasseurs, four squadrons strong, and two guns). Ney had his head-quarters and the reserve at Frankenthal, the force available being three companies of light infantry, six of grenadiers, the 17th Cavalry of the line, and two guns.

To sum up the whole situation, the Army of the Rhine was a mere line of river outposts with nothing behind it. The generals themselves realized the hopelessness of their position. On 16 September La Roche wrote from Mannheim to Ney that Prince Schwartzenberg's advanced guard was approaching and he expected soon to be attacked in force at Neckarau and Mannheim. And he went on to say:—

"You know both these places. You are aware that the former is naturally strong for defence, but with no bridge behind it, at a considerable distance from that of Mannheim, and having only two battalions to hold it, it cannot resist a well-directed attack made by very superior forces. The position of Mannheim is hardly worth mentioning, and if I were free to abandon it and establish myself at Neckarau I would not hesitate for a moment. What is to be done, my dear General, in this state of affairs? All one can do is to make a glorious resistance, and without really hoping to succeed, try to bring to naught the attack and the designs of the enemy. I shall make every effort for this end, but these efforts will have a better chance if you unite your forces to mine and come and help me with your valour and experience. I will let you know when it is time."

Ney replied to La Roche the same day:—

"Your position, my dear General, is certainly anything but satisfactory. I think that it is imperative to shift our bridge at once to the bend of the Rhine at Neckarau, and leave only small outpost parties to watch Mannheim and the left bank of the Neckar. In my opinion this is the only way to save the troops under your command and enable you to offer an organized resistance. The approaches to Neckarau are difficult, while those to

Mannheim are quite open. All this should induce you to transfer your bridge to the place where your main force can act, and should act, in the event of anything happening."

Ney sent a copy of this letter to General Müller with a covering note, in which he urged the Commander-in-Chief to direct La Roche to act upon it. It was curious that a divisional general should thus have to try to teach the chief of the Army of the Rhine his business. But the effort came too late. While Müller was still thinking over the proposal, Ney, early on the 18th, heard heavy firing in the direction of Mannheim, and was getting together all his available force for a rapid march to the help of his colleague, when he received this hastily written note from La Roche:—

"I had a presentiment that I would be attacked at daybreak this morning. I am attacked and very sharply. I can't tell you how it will end. Come to my help, and believe in my friendship.

"La Roche"

A little more than six months ago Ney had conquered Mannheim for the Republic. He was now to witness its loss. Hurrying to the point of danger with what force he had in hand, he could only delay the capture of the town for a while. The French were driven across the Rhine leaving Mannheim in the hands of the Austrians. Ney and La Roche tried to burn the bridge of boats but could only partly destroy it. The losses of the day were heavy. Two of La Roche's brigadiers, Generals Lefol and Vandermassen, were taken prisoners. Ney himself had more than one narrow escape. His left leg was bruised by a grazing cannon shot, and a bullet hit him full in the chest but it was spent and failed to penetrate. His horse was badly wounded. But the same night he wrote to Müller from Ogersheim (four miles west of the Rhine) that his injuries would not prevent him retaining the command of his division, which he had concentrated opposite Mannheim. He told his chief that he did not think the Austrians meant to cross the river just then, but added that, if they did, there was nothing to prevent them.

Müller had fairly lost his head and sent no orders. Ney took it on himself to meet the emergency. Sending some instructions, disguised as suggestions, to General La Roche, he ends by saying: "All this is really the business of the Commander-in-Chief, but as he is a bit slow in his decisions, the safety of the army demands that we should point the way for him". He reported to Müller, not asking for orders, but telling him what arrangements he had made.

But next day Müller recovered from the shock of the bad news from Mannheim and asserted his authority by sending orders that completely upset the common-sense arrangements made by Ney for opposing the enemy if he tried to cross the river. Müller directed Ney to keep his force in observation of the river line about Mannheim, but La Roche was to go further south and take post on the line of the Speyerbach (the little river that joins the Rhine at Speyer) facing northwards. Both were to be ready to retreat into the Palatinate on receiving a further order to that effect, Ney to retire on Kaiserslautern, La Roche on Landau. The latter expressed his feelings in a note to Ney in which he said: "I confess that it requires a strong supply of patriotism and devotion to enable one to serve under such circumstances. No doubt we shall have other orders this evening, once more changing everything we have to do. Alas, alas!" To which Ney replied: "Yes, my dear General, it is a sorry business to have to serve in this way. The orders as to the posting of the various divisions of the army are arranged in such a way that one can make nothing of them."

The weather had now broken and there were days and nights of rain. Ney took advantage of the rise in the river to inundate, by opening the sluices of the Frankenthal canal, the low ground of the left bank below Mannheim, thus restricting the points at which the enemy could cross. He obtained some useful information from correspondents at various places along the river and was able, on 22 September, to send Müller a reassuring report. He told him that although 5000 Austrians had been moved into Mannheim he believed this was only with a view of housing the men during the wet weather. He did not expect any attempt to cross in his immediate front. It seemed more likely that the enemy were moving towards the lower Rhine. Ehrenbreitstein would probably be summoned, and Dusseldorf taken, for the latter place could not make any prolonged defence. The Austrians had shown no disposition to follow up their success at Mannheim, and there was a general slackness in their movements. Ney suggested that probably the Archduke was being kept so busy by Masséna in Switzerland, that he was hesitating about detaching any more troops towards the Rhine. The conjecture did credit to Ney's judgment, for at that moment Masséna had begun the advance which ended in the great victory of Zurich.

During this stay at Frankenthal one finds in the letters of Ney's intimate friends messages to "Madame". During the last months of 1799 he had living with him at his head-quarters a German girl, named in one of the letters, but sometimes alluded to as "your wife". They were not married, however, and she soon disappears from his life.

General Müller, during his inglorious campaign, had never been near enough to the front to see an enemy. He was preparing to fall back from the Rhine and had withdrawn his head-quarters to Landau. On 24 September he sent a brief note to Ney asking him to come to see him there, as he had a communication from the Government to make to him. Ney reached Landau the same day and there heard to his surprise that the Directory had deprived Leonard Müller of his command and that, until further arrangements were made, he himself was to be Commander-in-Chief of the Army of the Rhine. He at once wrote to the Directory the following characteristic letter:—

"LANDAU, *the 3rd Vendémiaire, Year VIII.*
"(24 *Sept.*, 1799)

"TO THE EXECUTIVE DIRECTORY

"The Commander-in-Chief, General Müller, has sent for me to hand me the commission of provisional Commander-in-Chief of the Army of the Rhine.

"Have you considered well, Citizen Directors, how insufficient my military talents are for me to hold so important a post in these critical circumstances.

"I declare to you, Citizen Directors, that I can accept this position only for a period of ten days, and it is only due to my having been so strongly urged to do so by General Müller that I have decided to be, if necessary, a victim to the interests of the Republic. My devotion to the Republic is well known to you, Citizen Directors, and I swear to consecrate my last breath to its preservation."

The same evening he addressed the following circular letter to the divisional commanders :—

"The Executive Directory, has forced me, my dear comrade, to accept provisionally the command-in-chief of the Army in the place of General Müller, who is recalled to Paris. You know how insufficient are my military talents for this position, especially in such critical circumstances. I shall perhaps be the victim of my devotion, but I cannot avoid taking this step. I rely on your care for the safety of the troops confided to your charge, and on your special good will towards myself. I must also inform you my dear comrade, that I have formally declared to the Executive Directory that I will only retain the command of the army for ten days."

Ney's earlier refusals of promotion are some proof that he was sincere in his protestations, and we may assume that he was really anxious to hand over the command to other hands as soon as possible. At the same time it must be admitted that, for a man who expected to be superseded in ten days, he displayed a remarkable energy in introducing sweeping changes into the Army of the Rhine. It seemed as if he was determined that during his brief command the impress of his personal ideas should be set upon its future.

That very day he issued several orders and proceeded to alter its whole organization. Within a few days he made further changes. As Commander-in-Chief he had to provide for the defence of the frontier fortresses of the lower and middle Rhine, as well as for the army in the field. He proceeded to divide all the forces of his district into local and active divisions. The local divisions were the garrisons of the strong places. There were six of these commands, three on the river line, three in rear of it, the former being Strasburg, Mayence, and Coblentz (with Ehrenbreitstein); the latter Colmar, Landau, and Luxembourg. The active divisions were to form the mobile striking force at his disposal. There were more Cavalry than infantry units available after providing for the fortresses, and Ney, himself a cavalry officer, proceeded to recast the list of divisional commanders so that it became a list of generals belonging to the mounted arm of the service. The new organization of the Army of the Rhine was this:—

Divisions.	Generals.	Infantry. Battalions.	Cavalry. Regiments.	Artillery. Companies.	Head-quarters.
Advanced Guard	Lorcet	1	2	1	Lauterbourg
1st Division	Espagne	1	4	2	Rheinzabern
2nd "	Nansouty	1	4	1	Lambsheim
Reserve Division	D'Hautpoul	2	3	2	Wissemburg
Total . . .		5	13	6	

The head-quarters were nominally at Strasburg, where Ney left Müller's chief of the staff, Baraguay d'Hilliers, and the administrative staff of the Army. This was officially described as the "*Grand quartier général*". But at his own head-quarters at Hagenau he had with him his personal staff under Adjutant-General Ruffin, described in orders as the "*Petit quartier-général*". It was however the real centre of command.

Ney's appointment as Commander-in-Chief had been hailed with enthusiasm by the Army of the Rhine. Officers and men felt that the disappearance of General Müller was the end of a period of incompetence that was only too likely to end in disaster and disgrace. But his sweeping changes led to some friction. Baraguay d'Hilliers and his colleagues of the *Grand quartier* protested against being shelved in the bureaux of a frontier fortress. A divisional general complained bitterly of a cavalry officer being sent to take out of his hands a command he had held even before Ney himself arrived on the Rhine. He succeeded in soothing the feelings of some of the aggrieved officers. But he had made some enemies.

The idea on which his reorganization of his command was based was to leave to the garrison troops the general guard of the river line and to keep in hand a small striking force of mobile troops to oppose the enemy wherever he might attempt a crossing. He posted his active divisions on and near the river opposite Mannheim, Carlsruhe, and Rastatt, because his information was that the Archduke Charles, leaving Hotze in command in Switzerland, had come to Durlach near Carlsruhe, where he was concentrating a considerable force, and there were signs of a preparation to bridge the river at Seltz near Rastatt. Lorcet, with the advanced guard division at Lauterbourg, was opposite Carlsruhe, and his outposts along the Rhine watched every possible crossing-point to beyond Seltz. Behind him at Wissemburg was D'Hautpoul with the reserve, and Espagne with the 1st Division was on his left rear. Nansouty with the 2nd Division was on the extreme left and observed the river towards Mannheim. On the 26th Ney reported to Masséna the news he had obtained of the enemy and the arrangements he had made. That day he received encouraging news from Holland. Brune had completely defeated the Anglo-Russian Army under the Duke of York. Next day (27 September) he wrote to the Minister of War at Paris:—

"Reports which have just come to hand assure me that the enemy is marching up the right bank of the Rhine to reach Helvetia (Switzerland). Perhaps this movement has been forced upon him by General Masséna's attack which was to have taken place on the 2nd of this month of Vendémiaire (23 September) according to the information given to me."

On the 28th he wrote that he had further reports confirming the enemy's withdrawal and that he had a "telegraphic message" from Masséna announcing a great victory. The telegraphic message was of course sent by a line of semaphores. Masséna was thus in communication with Basel and Strasburg, and another line of semaphores on hill-tops and church towers linked Strasburg with Paris.

Two days later Ney received the following confirmatory despatch from Masséna, dated from Zurich on the 28th:—

"I write to you in haste, my dear General, to inform you of the success won by the Army of the Danube. We have completely beaten the two armies—Russians and Austrians. The Russians have already repassed the Thur. We are pursuing the remnants of the Austrian corps. The Commander-in-Chief, Hotze, was killed on the field of battle. Baggage and camp equipment, six standards and more than a hundred guns, are in our hands. The loss of the enemy's two armies in killed, wounded, and prisoners is over 20,000 men. Three Russian Generals are our prisoners. We crossed the Limmat on the 3rd of this month (25 September) at Dietikon, and the Linth between the Lakes of Zurich and Wallenstad. Next day at 4 p.m. we fought our way into Zurich."

The news from Zurich confirmed the view of the situation which Ney's keen military insight had, one may almost say, divined. He wrote to Masséna that he regretted that the loss of the footing on the further bank of the Rhine, afforded by

Mannheim, made it difficult to engage in an operation in force against the Austrian right in South Germany. But even so he meant to do something to delay the Archduke's obvious attempt to draw reinforcements from that side towards Switzerland.

During the next week Ney was preparing to take the offensive. It was not to be an attempt to invade South Germany in force. He had not the numbers for such an operation. His plan was limited to a series of simultaneous demonstrations all along the river from Strasburg and Kehl on the right to Mayence on the left. He handed over the command of the advanced guard at Lauterbourg to Brigadier-General Roussel, and sent General Lorcet to Hocheim near Mayence to take command of a new 3rd Division (really a mixed brigade of three cavalry regiments, a battery and six companies of grenadiers). The preparations were completed on 3 October and next day attacks were made all along the front against the Austrian posts, the garrisons making sorties across the Rhine, the divisions in the centre threatening a crossing of the river at various points opposite Carlsruhe, while on the left Lorcet, supported by a detachment from the Mayence garrison, advanced from Hocheim to Hochst at the confluence of the Nidda and the Main, menacing Frankfurt.

There were several minor engagements in all of which the French were victorious, the Austrians everywhere falling back, under the impression that the vigorous advance of the Republican troops must have serious forces in support of it. Ney himself joined the left column, which drove the Austrians from an entrenched position near Hochst and broke up a great gathering of armed peasants that had joined the enemy. Ney's report to the Minister of War on this affair is interesting. He won an easy victory, and the despatch proposes the promotion of a young soldier, who was to be one of the famous cavalry generals of the Empire and to meet a hero's death in the great battle of thirteen years later that gave Ney his princely title:—

"All the enemy's positions," wrote Ney, "and several entrenchments were stormed. The enemy's losses in this affair have been serious. More than 3000 peasants—a part of the 20,000 who had joined him—threw away their muskets, but notwithstanding their precipitate flight left a good many dead on the ground. We have to regret only a few brave men killed besides some sixty wounded.

"I request, Citizen Minister, that you will confirm the promotion I have made of Citizen Montbrun, Captain in the 1st Regiment of Chasseurs, to the rank of *chef d'escadron* (major of cavalry).

"I am assured by certain information that the diversion has completely attained its object. Already all the Austrian reserve troops are on the march for Frankfurt, followed by Generalc Shwartzenberg with a corps of 10,000 men in the direction of Mannheim."

Having sufficiently alarmed the enemy Ney ordered Lorcet to retire on Hocheim, and himself went to Landau, where on 8 October he received a letter from his former chief Lecourbe, informing him that he was on the way to Strasburg to take over the command of the Army of the Rhine, and ending with the words, "It is a real pleasure to me to have you with me". Lecourbe evidently had formed a good opinion of Ney during the short time in which the young general had served under him in the Ticinese Alps. But although Lecourbe reached Strasburg on the 10th he did not take over the actual command for some days and meanwhile left Ney a free hand.

It seemed as if the knowledge that his command was so soon to end inspired him with a determination to accomplish something important before he fell back into his old position of a mere divisional commander. From Landau he hurried back to Mayence, and, after making some changes in the organization of his active divisions, he concentrated a force of nearly 18,000 men immediately south of Mayence and on the left bank of the Rhine between that fortress and Frankenthal, a little to the north of Mannheim. His object was the recapture of that place. The information he had collected showed that it was not strongly held. The Austrian troops that had marched northwards, when he made his attack on Hochst and his feints along the river, were again retiring towards Switzerland. Prince Schwartzenberg had a strong rear-guard on the Neckar. But Ney considered the force he had in hand was sufficient to deal with any that might be opposed to it, especially now that the Republican soldiers were in good heart after their successes of a few days before.

On the 12th the movement began. General Lorcet occupied Trebur and Gross Gerau, on the right bank of the Rhine. Reinforcements were moved across through Mayence, and two divisions (mixed brigades) at Oppenheim and Frankenthal on the left bank were collecting boats for crossing at these points. Lorcet and Roussel, who immediately followed him, drove back two Austrian detachments. The fighting was not serious, but it gave the men the impression of success from the outset. On the 13th Ney had his head-quarters at Gross Gerau, and by that evening all the troops destined for the advance between the river and the hills on the east bank were through Mayence and across the Main.

On the 14th the advance continued. Ney's head-quarters were at Heppenheim. During the day the French drove an Austrian force out of the village of Zwingenberg. The men got out of hand and sacked the place. Ney was indignant at the news. He at once ordered General Lorcet to convoke a court martial to try and execute the leaders in the sack of the village, and at the same time requested the local authorities to draw up an account of the losses incurred by the villagers, which he promised should be paid in full.

The column from Oppenheim had crossed the Rhine and was moving up its right bank. On the 15th General Sabatier, with the newly formed 4th Division, crossed at Sandofen opposite Frankenthal. Schwartzenberg was reported to be holding Heidelberg on the Neckar in force. Lorcet, with the vanguard of the main column, pushed forward in that direction.

The orders for the 16th were that Lorcet with the main advance should drive the Austrians out of Heidelberg and cross the Neckar there, while Sabatier with the right column moved directly on Mannheim. If the Austrians held on there Lorcet would co-operate with Sabatier by moving from Heidelberg against the east side of Mannheim.

There was hard fighting at Heidelberg on 16 October from ten in the morning till long after dark. The Austrians met the French advance in the villages north of the town, and when driven from these made an obstinate defence of the bridge over the Neckar. When Lorcet sent this report to Ney at nine in the evening, the battle was still undecided. His hurriedly written message ran thus:—

"Mon Général,

"I have the honour to inform you that I came in contact with the enemy at Ziegler. His advanced parties grew in strength as they fell back from village to village as far as Dosenheim, where they were in considerable force; at this point they showed themselves in large numbers with infantry and artillery. I attacked them and they were beaten. There were about 1500 cavalry and a battalion of Croats. I pursued them as far as the bridge of Heidelberg. *Six times* I tried to carry it by assault. General Rouyer, the Adjutant-General Marconnier, and I myself, in turn led the attacks, but we could none of us obtain a success. Twice we got into the town, but each time the fire of the townspeople drove us out. The troops under my orders are now holding one end of the bridge, and the Austrians the other. The bearer of this despatch will tell you the rest."

Lorcet was reinforced during the night, and early on the 17th fought his way into Heidelberg without meeting with a serious resistance. The Austrians were retiring. Sabatier, marching from Sandhofen on Mannheim at the head of three battalions and a cavalry regiment, occupied the place at 5 a.m., without firing a shot. The garrison had been withdrawn before sunrise. In the afternoon of the 17th Ney sent Masséna a despatch, in which he thus reported his success:—

"I have to inform you, my dear General, that the troops of the Army of the Rhine have taken possession of Mannheim as well as of all the country on the left bank of the Neckar from Heidelberg to beyond Schwetzingen.

"This morning at 5 o'clock the enemy was beaten all along the front. We have taken from him a howitzer, some hundreds of hussars, uhlans, and infantry, as well as the Count Esterhazy, Colonel of the Westchay Hussar regiment and several officers. Prince Lichtenstein was mortally wounded in the defence of Heidelberg. Prince Schwartzenberg, who commanded the corps on the lower Rhine, is in full retreat. He is directing his march on Stuttgart."

Having secured Mannheim, Ney at once sent a force under General Thuring to renew the investment of Philippsburg. He had thus in a few days won back all that Müller's incompetence had lost, and could hand over his command to Lecourbe with the satisfaction of feeling that his brief tenure of it had been marked by a solid success. He had assumed the command of the Army of the Rhine at a moment when all seemed lost.

He had made the best use of the scanty resources at his disposal, and though compared to the great battles of coming years his engagements on the right bank of the Rhine were small affairs, the reoccupation of Mannheim was a serious gain, and still more important was the fact that under his leadership the soldiers of the Republic had regained confidence in themselves and in their chiefs.

CHAPTER V

THE BEGINNING OF THE YEARS OF VICTORY

ON 24 October Lecourbe took command of the Army of the Rhine. France was on the verge of great events. In September Bonaparte had suddenly arrived from Egypt, bringing news of victory; for on the eve of his departure from Alexandria a Turkish army, landed on the shore of Aboukir Bay, had been driven into the sea by the Republican troops. He had left Kléber in command of the "Colony of Egypt" and he could pose as a victor returning to claim his reward. He came at the critical moment when France was tired of the failures of the Directory, and the army was eager to see a soldier take the control of public affairs out of the hands of the lawyers and talkers. When he reached Paris he found that there was already a conspiracy in progress for effecting a change of Government. Sieyès, the constitution maker, was at the bottom of it, and Bonaparte's brothers Joseph and Lucien were deep in it. Naturally he took the lead in the execution of the plan and made it his own, for he alone could secure the co-operation of army, and this fact again gave him the control of events after the success of the *coup d'état* of Brumaire.

After the recapture of Mannheim one of Ney's soldier friends, General Boye, had written to him congratulating him on his exploits, and adding that "the return of General Bounaparde [*sic*] would rejoice the hearts of all good Republicans". This was the feeling of the army.

The news of the revolution in Paris only reached the Rhine three or four days after the event, although Paris and Strasburg were connected by a line of semaphore telegraph stations. The news was evidently held back until full instructions could be sent to the military and civil authorities in the provinces. Ney heard of it on 13 November by a letter from the commandant of Strasburg, his old comrade General Colaud, dated the evening before. The letter ran thus:—

"My dear General,

"The director of the telegraph has just communicated to me the two following despatches:—

"First despatch, dated 18th Brumaire (9 November): 'The Corps Législatif has been transferred to St. Cloud. Bonaparte has been appointed commandant of Paris. All is quiet and peaceful.'

"Second despatch, dated noon, the 19th (10 November): 'The Directory has resigned. General Moreau is in command at the Palace of the Directory. Everything . . .'

"*Note.*—This last word indicates some further news."

This scanty intelligence, suddenly breaking off with the first word of a new sentence, was not very enlightening. But enough was told to show that the Directory had fallen, and that the two men in whom the army trusted—Bonaparte and Moreau—were in control of the capital. Some days passed before any detailed news was available. Then there was general rejoicing in the army at Bonaparte's having made himself master of the government. A letter of Ney's written during this anxious time conveys to Colaud the warning that he had discovered that their correspondence was opened and examined while passing through the post.

Before the *coup d'état* of Brumaire Lecourbe had reorganized the Army of the Rhine, and some important military operations had taken place. The field army had been organized in four infantry divisions, each with a detachment of cavalry and artillery, and a reserve cavalry division. The arrangement was:—

1st Division. General Laborde. Blockading Philippsburg.

2nd Division. General Legrand. On the right about Bruchsal.

3rd Division. General Ney. Advanced guard. On the line of the Elsenz, east of Philippsburg.

4th Division. General Sabatier. On the left, holding Mannheim and Heidelberg.

Reserve division. The cavalry under General D'Hautpoul.

Ney's division was composed as follows:—

1st or Right Brigade. General Lorcet. Two battalions, 1st Chasseurs-à-cheval, 1 company (battery) light artillery.

2nd or Left Brigade. General Rouyer. Two battalions, 6th Chasseurs-à-cheval, 1 company light artillery.

Reserve. General Bonet. Six companies of grenadiers. Two heavy guns. The ammunition and supply train of the division.

Keeping to old-fashioned methods of war Lecourbe made the siege of Philippsburg the central point of his plan of campaign. One division blockaded the place. The other three were placed north, east, and south of it to cover the siege. Ney with the 3rd Division found himself again in much the same position, in which he had been when he first served with the Army of the Rhine under Müller. His troops were on the little river Elsenz about Sinsheim. The orders he received from Lecourbe on 28 October were almost identical with those Müller had sent him months before. He was directed to march on the 30th in two columns and occupy next day the towns of Heilbronn and Lauffen.

From Lauffen he was, if possible, to push an advanced party up the Neckar valley as far as Belsigheim. On his left Sabatier was to send a column to Nackarelz, lower down the river to protect him on that side. On the right Legrand with the 2nd Division would advance by Bretten to the important junction of roads at Pforzheim, in the direction of Stuttgart. Ney was ordered to levy contributions to the total amount of 300,000 francs on the district occupied, and to collect by requisition 150 horses.

The movement to the line of the Neckar began well. Ney's columns occupied Lauffen on 1 November, and Heilbronn on the 2nd, meeting with only a trifling resistance. The only hostile troops that showed themselves were small parties of Austrian cavalry. At the same time Legrand advanced to Pforzheim.

The enemy's horsemen in Ney's front had fallen back along the river towards Belsigheim, and he issued orders for the occupation of that place on 3 November. He knew it was held by an Austrian force of all arms, but it is clear that the reports he received underrated the enemy's strength. Lorcet's brigade was to attack in front, while a detachment, drawn from the second brigade (nine companies, two guns, and a squadron of cavalry) under Adjutant-General Ruffin, was to make a detour by the right bank of the Neckar and fall on the enemy's flank.

The action of Belsigheim was a disaster for Ney's division. Lorcet was attacked on the line of march by the enemy in very superior numbers and driven back with heavy loss. Lorcet himself was badly wounded. Threatened by the victorious Austrians, Ney had to abandon Lauffen the same evening and Heilbronn next day, and retreated on Sinsheim. In his report to Lecourbe he wrote that Lorcet's two battalions of the 8th Demi-brigade "had behaved very badly in the action of the 3rd". Lecourbe, who was with Legrand near Pforzheim, sent him a reassuring reply: "You have been unlucky," he said, "but I am quite satisfied as to your position".

Having driven in Ney, the Austrians turned on Legrand. On 6 November they attacked him at Pforzheim with a force estimated at 10,000 men, and he had to retire through the wooded hills towards Bruchsal. They followed him up and again attacked him on the 8th. He retired northwards towards Wiesloch. This left Laborde unprotected and he had to raise the siege of Philippsburg, and retreat to Hockenheim.

Lecourbe was discouraged by this series of failures. On the 8th he wrote to Ney:—

> "I am sorry to see that the troops do not make a good stand. There are too many non-combatants, hangers-on of the divisions, who spread panic, and so many others who are gorged with booty and only long for a retreat in the hope of being able to put their plunder in a safe place."

This is not a flattering picture of the Republican soldier. From other despatches of the time we gather that the men had suffered a good deal during this early winter campaign. They were ill-fed and in ragged uniforms and broken boots. This may have had something to do with the falling off in discipline and fighting spirit.

Lecourbe now received reports that strong reinforcements were on the way to join the enemy. Partial attacks were made on Ney's position on the 9th and on Legrand on the 10th. In both cases the enemy was repulsed. On the 10th Lecourbe ordered that all the heavy baggage trains should be sent back across the Rhine. This indicated an intention to abandon the right bank of the river at an early date.

During the following days there was some skirmishing along the front, but there was no sign that the enemy had been reinforced. It was now that the news of the *coup d'état* of Brumaire reached the army. Lecourbe was anxious to do something, and on the 16th he made a counter attack on the enemy's outposts in front of the 2nd and 3rd Divisions. Ney led the attack of the former in person. The day was a success. Ney reported that he had driven the Austrians from the villages round Sinsheim, and added that the troops of his division "had done their duty perfectly, all displaying an unheard-of courage".

Some days of inactivity followed. On 30 November Lecourbe wrote to Ney that he had been promised a reinforcement of eighteen fresh battalions in the next three weeks. The Army of the Rhine must therefore try to hold out on the right bank until this help arrived. But next day the Austrians attacked in force and drove in the 2nd Division on the right. On 2 December they attacked in the same way on the left. The 4th Division could barely hold its ground. In the centre there was skirmishing along the front of Ney's division. This activity of the enemy along the whole line, and the attacks in force on both flanks, seemed to indicate that he was now in great strength. On the 3rd Lecourbe issued orders for a general retirement across the Rhine. In order to secure an undisturbed retreat he sent a flag of truce to the head-quarters of the Austrian General, Sztarray, and concluded an armistice of undetermined duration. It was an undisguised acknowledgment of failure.

The last troops of the Army of the Rhine crossed the river on 7 December and went into winter quarters on the left bank. Lecourbe left the army and General Baraguay d'Hilliers was given the temporary command.

Napoleon Bonaparte, now First Consul, and in fact, though not in name, the absolute ruler of France, was planning already the military arrangements for the coming year. There was to be an end of the frittering away of the forces of France in half a dozen armies, with the consequent series of disconnected and indecisive operations. The Austrians held the right bank of the Rhine and all northern Italy except part of the territory of Genoa. They threatened a double invasion of France in the spring, over the Rhine and by the Alpine passes. Bonaparte intended to deal in person with the danger from Italy, and was planning a new campaign on the scene of his earliest victories.

He confided to Moreau the task of dealing with the danger from Germany.

Masséna had been sent to Italy where he was to win new laurels in the defence of Genoa. What was left of his "Army of the Danube" was handed over to Lecourbe, and became the right wing of Moreau's army. The centre in upper Alsace was to be commanded by Gouvion St. Cyr. The old "Army of the Rhine" was to form the left wing and during the winter was to watch the river from Strasburg to Mayence.

After the retreat across the Rhine there was no prospect of active operations until the spring of 1800. Ney had lately purchased out of his savings a small estate and country house near Nancy, known as La Petite Malgrange. He was anxious to take possession of it and spend a short holiday there. His health had suffered during the recent campaign and an old wound was giving some trouble. On 17 December he wrote to the Minister of War asking for leave for three months. It took some time for this permission to reach him, and it was only in the last week of January that he handed over the temporary command of his division to General Sahuc, and started for his country house near Nancy. Before going there he spent a few days at Basel in order to see the new Commander-in-Chief, Moreau, and exchange impressions with him.

There was still a fortnight of his leave remaining when on 12 March, 1800, Ney received at La Petite Malgrange a letter from General Gouvion St. Cyr, commanding the centre of the Army, with head-quarters at Basel, requesting him to rejoin there on the 22nd, as active operations were to be resumed at once. This was confirmed two days later by a letter from Moreau informing him that he was immediately to take command of one of St. Cyr's divisions.

Leaving Nancy on the 14th, Ney reached Basel on the 20th. He was disappointed at finding that his colleagues appointed to the command of the two other divisions of St. Cyr's corps were men in whom he had no confidence, and one of whom he believed to bear personal ill will to him—Baraguay d'Hilliers, whom he had offended, and Tharreau, whose blundering arrangements were responsible for the defeat at Winterthur.

His recall to the Army proved to be premature. There was no sign of any hostile movement, and on 30 March Moreau allowed him to return for a short time to La Petite Malgrange. He rejoined the head-quarters of the centre at Neuf Brisach on 22 April. He found everything ready for the crossing of the Rhine and the advance into Germany to begin in a few days. He was about to command a leading division of the largest army that France had placed upon the Rhine frontier since the war began, and it was the year that was destined to see Marengo and Hohenlinden fought and won.

Before relating Ney's part in Moreau's victorious campaign of 1800 we must see what was the general situation at its outset, and on what lines it was to be conducted.

Kray, who commanded the Austrians in South Germany, had been promised an army of 100,000 men, but he had not more than 60,000 when operations began again on the Rhine in the middle of April, 1800. These, too, he had broken up into a number of separate corps, which he had strung out along the river from the Swiss frontier above Basel down to Rastatt and the neighbourhood of Carlsruhe. He had his head-quarters at Donaueschingen. On the left Nauendorff was at Schaffhausen. In the centre Gyulai was at Freiburg, opposite Brisach. On the right Kienmayer was posted to watch Kehl and Strasburg, with Sztarray's corps to the north of him about Rastatt.

Moreau had double the numbers of the Austrians—an army of 200,000 men, organized in four corps—right, centre, left, and reserve, and spread out like Kray's army on a front of more than 120 miles. The left, at Strasburg and Kehl, was commanded by General Ste Suzanne; the centre, about New Brisach, by General St. Cyr; and the right, on the Rhine, above Basel, and in the border districts of Switzerland, by Lecourbe. Moreau had his head-quarters and the reserve corps at Basel. His scheme for the campaign was based on the traditional French plan for an invasion of southern Germany—a crossing of the Rhine at several points, an advance through the wooded hills of the Black Forest, the various columns uniting in the upper Danube Valley and then pressing on by the line of that river towards Vienna.

The First Consul was planning for his own campaign in Italy a new departure that broke with all tradition. He proposed to Moreau also a new plan of campaign for the Army of the Rhine, which would give the promise of decisive results at an early date—not the mere pushing back of Kray's army towards Vienna. Bonaparte was so anxious to persuade Moreau to adopt his plan that he called to Paris, General Desolles, the Chief of the Staff of the Army of the Rhine, and fully explained to him not merely the general idea but also the proposed details of its mission.

In the light of Napoleon's own subsequent campaigns the plan looks fairly obvious, but to the veterans of routine, even among the soldiers of the Republic, there was a clinging to old-fashioned ways that absolutely blinded them to other possibilities. The First Consul's proposal was that Moreau should leave only a mere screen of detachments along the Rhine from Basel to Strasburg. These with the garrison troops would make feints of preparations to cross the river. Meanwhile every man that could be spared from the centre and left would be rapidly concentrated on the Swiss bank of the Rhine above Basel; the river would be crossed at or near Schaffhausen, the line of advance being directed on Ulm, the place where Kray had his main supply depots, and on which he would try to concentrate. Bonaparte held that if Moreau adopted this plan he would drive in the Austrian left, compel a general retirement from the Rhine, and destroy the enemy's columns in detail.

Desolles conveyed Bonaparte's ideas and arguments to Moreau, but he could not be persuaded to adopt a plan that seemed to him far too daring. Bonaparte, as First Consul, might have imposed it on him, as Carnot and the War Ministers of the Directory used to send cut-and-dried plans of campaign to the generals in the field. But he showed a higher wisdom in refusing to force upon Moreau a plan that he did not like or appreciate, and which he would only have carried out half-heartedly. He allowed the Commander-in-Chief of the Army of the Rhine to act on his own ideas. The results would not be so brilliant or decisive, but Moreau was so strong in comparison to Kray that in the first stage of the

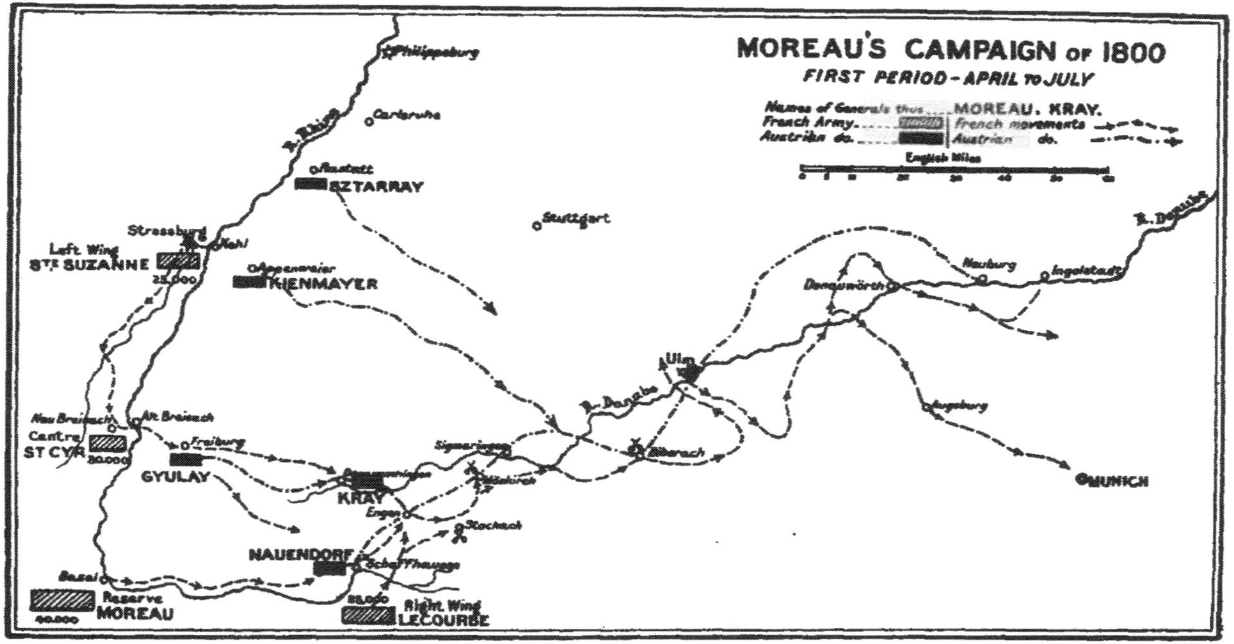
MOREAU'S CAMPAIGN OF 1800
FIRST PERIOD - APRIL TO JULY
Names of Generals thus ... MOREAU. KRAY.
French Army
Austrian do.
French movements
Austrian do.
English Miles
Philippsburg
Carlsruhe
R. Rhine
Rastatt
SZTARRAY
Stuttgart
Strassburg
Kehl
Left Wing
STE SUZANNE
22,000
Appenweier
KIENMAYER
Neu Breisach
Alt Breisach
Centre
ST CYR
30,000
Freiburg
GYULAY
KRAY
Engen
Stockach
Sigmaringen
NAUENDORF
Schaffhausen
Basel
Reserve
MOREAU
40,000
25,000
Right Wing
LECOURBE
R. Danube
Ulm
Biberach
Augsburg
MUNICH
Donauwörth
Neuburg
Ingolstadt

campaign the French must be successful, if any reasonable plan were followed.

When Ney rejoined, almost on the eve of the advance across the Rhine, he found Gouvion St. Cyr's three divisions forming the centre of the Army about Neuf Brisach. His division, which was numbered as the First, and was destined to act as the advanced guard of St. Cyr's command, was made up of ten battalions of infantry, two regiments of cavalry, two batteries, and a company of engineers in all about 10,000 men, organized in three brigades.[1] The 2nd of St. Cyr's divisions was commanded by Baraguay d'Hilliers and the 3rd by Tharreau.

On 25 April the troops of the centre began to cross the Rhine at Alt Breisach. Ney's division led the way, with Joba's brigade acting as its advanced guard. The crossing began in the darkness of the morning about 4 a.m. The division found in its immediate front only some weak detachments of Austrian cavalry, which fell back after a trifling skirmish or two. Ney then bore away to the left and occupied Eichstetten to the north-west of Freiburg. St. Cyr with the two other divisions crossed as soon as he had cleared the river bank, and marched directly on Freiburg. Gyulai evacuated the place after a sharply fought rear-guard action.

On the same day on the French left Ste Suzanne made a false attack from Kehl against Kienmayer's positions between Offenburg and Appenweier. This was only to keep the Austrian right occupied, for the same day the French left wing began to march southwards by Schlestadt to Neu Breisach, where it was to cross the river and follow the eastward march

[1] The Demi-brigades of the earlier Republican armies had been abolished in name under the Consulate, and each "Demi-brigade" became a line regiment of three battalions. The Light Infantry were organized as single battalion regiments. Ney's division was made up of the 12th Light Infantry, and the 54th, 76th, and 103rd of the Line; the 8th Chasseurs-à-cheval and 25th Heavy Cavalry; two companies (batteries) of light artillery and one of sappers. The brigades were:—

1st or Right Brigade. General Joba. 12th Legère, and 54th of the Line.
2nd or Left Brigade. General Bonet. 76th of the Line. 8th Chasseurs-à-cheval.
Reserve Brigade. General Bonamy. 103rd of the Line. 25th (Heavy) Cavalry.

of St. Cyr and the centre. At Basel Moreau began to cross the river with the reserve, and Lecourbe with the right wing was preparing to pass the Rhine between Schaffhausen and the Lake of Constance. On the 26th there was no further movement in the centre. Moreau continued the crossing of the river at Basel by the reserve, 40,000 strong, and encumbered with a huge wagon train.

Kray, the Austrian Commander-in-Chief, had now realized that the French were crossing the Rhine at several points, and he knew that they were in greatly superior force. He was a typical eighteenth-century soldier, and it never occurred to him that his central position gave him a chance of concentrating against one or other of the widely separated columns of Moreau's army. His only idea was to fall back everywhere towards the upper Danube valley, and concentrate on Ulm. On the 26th his two right detachments under Sztarray and Kienmayer were ordered to fall back on Ulm, their lines of march being so directed that Kray could not receive the least help from them till he himself was near that place. Gyulai with the Austrians retired back from Freiburg by the Hollenthal valley. St. Cyr did not directly follow him up, but marched from Freiburg on the 27th with Ney's division as his advanced guard, the line of march being selected so as to draw nearer to Moreau and the reserve or main body. The road was that which runs through the wooded hills of the Black Forest by Todtnau and St. Blasien, separated from Gyulai's line of retreat by the great central mass of the Feldberg. The march through the hills took three days. On the 29th the three divisions of the centre were in position on the little river Alb, which runs down to the Rhine past St. Blasien. The heads of Moreau's columns had reached the same river nearer the Rhine. Lecourbe was still on the south bank in Swiss territory, and Ste Suzanne with the left was at Freiburg.

On 30 April the centre remained halted. On 1 May Moreau with the reserve advanced further eastward to the line of the River Wutach. This move threatened the Austrians at Schaffhausen, and Nauendorf retreated towards Stockach. This cleared the way for Lecourbe to cross the Rhine east of Schaffhausen. St. Cyr's three divisions were moved forward to prolong the line on Moreau's left. There were now more than 80,000 French troops between the south-eastern slopes of the Black Forest and the western bays of the Lake of Constance. Kray had been rejoined by Gyulai and had moved across the Danube to the neighbourhood of Engen, between the river and the Lake.

Here the first serious fighting of the campaign took place on 3 May. Moreau, with his 40,000 men, attacked Kray, who had 45,000 in line at Engen. At the same time Lecourbe with 25,000 men marched on Stockach where the Austrians had important magazines of supplies. Stockach was defended only by some 9000 men of Nauendorf's corps. Lecourbe drove them out, and was then in position to march upon the left rear of the enemy's main position at Engen. But Kray had early news of his colleague's defeat and after holding his ground until the afternoon against Moreau he abandoned Engen and retired towards the Danube at Sigmaringen.

During the battle St. Cyr had been pushing forward on Moreau's left, but Ney's division was never near the scene of the fighting, and the only troops of the centre corps that were engaged were a brigade of Baraguay d'Hilliers' division that came into action just before the Austrians gave way.

There was no movement of importance on the day after the battle of Engen. Some of the divisions, Ney's among them, marched a few miles in order to be in position for the general advance on the 5th. General Bonnal in his study of the campaign remarks upon the slowness with which Moreau conducted his operations: "In the ten days that followed the crossing of the river," he says, "the Army of the Rhine had marched on five (25, 27, 28, and 29 April, and 1 May), had fought on one (3 May), and had rested four times (26 and 30 April and 2 and 4 May)". Kray and the Austrian Generals adopted the same leisurely methods. The vigorous leadership of Napoleon was soon to change the face of war.

On the 5th there was another battle. Ney heard the distant cannon thunder, but was never seriously engaged. Lecourbe was marching on Mosskirch where he would strike in upon the Austrian line of retreat. Moreau was following him with the reserve. Ney, with the rest of St. Cyr's corps, was moving on the left of the general advance. About Mosskirch, Kray fought a rear-guard action against Lecourbe, holding him back for some hours, but continuing his retreat when Moreau and the reserve came into line. Ney's advanced guard was in touch with an Austrian detachment covering Kray's right, but the rest of St. Cyr's corps was too far to the rear for them to reach the scene of the fighting till near nightfall, and Ney did not consider it worth while to do more than steadily press back the small force opposed to him. He kept strictly to his task of clearing the way for the onward march of St. Cyr's divisions. General Bonnal makes some remarks on the conduct of St. Cyr on this occasion, which are worth quoting for the sake of the light they throw on the contrast between the old and the coming methods of warfare:—

"He has been reproached," he says, "for having done nothing on the day of Mosskirch, and especially for not having marched to the sound of the cannon. Assuredly he might have shown more energy and initiative, but we must not forget that the methods of war then in use in the armies commanded by others than Bonaparte did not recognize 'marching to the cannon' and required that all movements should be ordered by the Commander-in-Chief, the sole judge of all the so-called 'scientific' manœuvres that were to be carried out in order to procure the retreat of the enemy, with or without fighting, and preferably without it."

On 6 May Ney at last found himself in a position that gave him some chance of a serious fight with the enemy. The so-called "centre" was now the left of the army on the actual scene of the pursuit of the retreating Austrians. The original left corps, that of General Ste Suzanne, was coming up from Freiburg by the Hollenthal to reach the Danube at Donaueschingen and would be close in on Moreau's left rear in the next day or two. But for the moment St. Cyr's divisions were nearest to the enemy's intended point of crossing on the Danube about Sigmaringen. Ney's division led the advance along the high ground on the south bank of the river. Early in the day he came upon a strong Austrian rear-guard and at once attacked vigorously. He drove the enemy in and made 1800 prisoners. But then he came on a second position bristling with artillery. He was not strong enough to force this second line and did not commit his troops to any close attack. He was waiting for St. Cyr to come to his aid with the other two divisions. But these did not arrive till late in the day, and meanwhile, under the protection of his strongly posted rear-guard, Kray was passing his army over to the left bank. Next day the last of the enemy were across the Danube, and Ney occupied Sigmaringen with a detachment, which served as a flank guard to the general advance eastward by the right bank of the river.

There was another action on the 9th at Biberach. Kray had recrossed the river at Riedlingen and threw himself across the line of Moreau's advance having in his own rear a safe line of retreat to Ulm. Ney took no part in the fighting. St. Cyr's other two divisions and two of Moreau's reserve were engaged. It was reckoned as a French victory, though Kray had not seriously disputed the ground and fought only to delay Moreau's march. Kray then fell back upon Ulm. He had been rejoined by his right wing and found reinforcements awaiting him, bringing up his total force to some 90,000 men. With this increase of strength, and the protection of the fortress with bridge heads on both banks of the Danube, he felt himself at last able to make a determined stand against the Republican armies.

CHAPTER VI

MOREAU'S DANUBE CAMPAIGN—HOHENLINDEN (1800-1801)

BONAPARTE'S plans for the campaigns of 1800 included both the German and the Italian theatres of war, and the time was now approaching for his personal intervention in the struggle. Melas, the Austrian commander in northern Italy, had driven Masséna into Genoa. The place was closely invested, on the land side by an Austrian corps under General Ott, on the sea side by a British squadron. Masséna held out doggedly, while Suchet held the coast road and the neighbouring passes against an attempt of Melas to penetrate into France by the Riviera.

The Austrians expected Bonaparte would come to the help of Suchet. But he had conceived a bolder plan. On 6 May he had left Paris to take command of the reserve army at Dijon, now to be known as the Army of Italy. He would then move it over the snowy passes of the western Alps which the Austrians considered to be impracticable for anything more than a small detachment. He would descend into the plain of North Italy on the rear of the enemy, cutting him off from his communications, and forcing him to fight under conditions in which defeat would be destruction.

Moncey, who commanded the troops in Switzerland, was to be reinforced by detachments from Moreau's Army of the Rhine, and descend into Italy by passes further to the eastward. Moreau's progress had secured the Rhine frontier, and he had advanced so far into South Germany that Bonaparte considered he could safely spare 15,000 or 20,000 men to co-operate in the Italian campaign.

Accordingly on 15 May a corps of 15,000 men, taken chiefly from Lecourbe's command, was ordered to march away through central Switzerland. This left the Army of the Rhine not quite 100,000 men for the operations against Kray.

Moreau was not strong enough with these numbers to besiege an army of 90,000 men at Ulm. His immediate object therefore was to manœuvre with a view to induce Kray to quit the fortress and fight in the open. For this purpose he first tried to tempt Kray into attacking him and then made a show of advancing towards the Austrian frontiers, in order to make his adversary anxious about his communications with Vienna. One can see how different the position would have been if Moreau had adopted Bonaparte's plan of a rapid march on Ulm from the Swiss Rhine. If this had been done there might well have been another "campaign of Marengo" in Germany.

The first stage of the operations nearly led to a disaster. The Army of the Rhine was moved up to the line of the Iller with the left under Ste Suzanne on the north bank of the Danube near Ulm. On 16 May Kray threw a superior force against Ste Suzanne, and was driving him back at every point when the Austrian advance was checked and the fortune of the day saved by Ney's prompt intervention. He hurried up all his artillery to the south bank of the Danube and brought an enfilading fire to bear on the Austrian flank, at the same time sending some of his infantry to reinforce his hard-pressed colleague. The Austrians, satisfied with their partial victory, retired upon Ulm.

Moreau then sent the whole of St. Cyr's corps across to the north bank of the Danube. But he soon became uneasy about his position, with his army thus divided by a broad river. On the 19th Ste Suzanne and St. Cyr were both recalled to the south bank of the Danube and a period of danger was over.

But Moreau proceeded at once to invite new perils. The Iller was crossed by the right, centre, and reserve divisions. and the army was spread out over a front of nearly sixty miles, The line formed an obtuse angle, with the salient pointing towards at Ulm, at Weissenhorn on the eastern side of the Iller. At this place, the nearest to the enemy, Ney's division was posted. The left was thrown back along the south side of the Danube, the rest of the line (centre and right) stretched away to the south eastward from Weissenhorn, on a front of thirty miles. From the right Lecourbe was ordered to send a column to seize Augsburg, and threaten the Austrian communications.

The whole arrangement was a piece of feeble folly, and once more Moreau owed the safety of his army to the inaction of Kray. Lecourbe occupied Augsburg on 28 May, but he had hardly entered the city when Moreau became anxious about this further dispersion of his forces and recalled him.

Bonaparte was by this time over the Alps into northern Italy, where events were moving with a decisive swiftness that contrasted with the deadlock of Moreau's operations on the upper Danube. A new army was organized at Strasburg, to be known as the "Army of the Lower Rhine," and destined to co-operate with Moreau if the war were prolonged through the summer. The troops were drawn from the French inland garrisons and the depots, and Moreau was directed to send General Ste Suzanne to command them. St. Cyr's health had temporarily broken down and he was at the same time given leave to return to France. In consequence of the departure of two of his lieutenants Moreau decided to reorganize his army and redistribute the commands. The huge reserve corps was broken up and the Army of the Rhine was now divided into three corps, right, left, and centre, with a right and left "flank-brigade". The new organization and distribution of the Army was as follows:—

Left flank brigade (observing Ulm). General Richepanse (12 battalions, and 25 squadrons).
Left Wing. General Grenier. 1st Division. Baraguay d'Hilliers.
2nd Division. Ney.
3rd Division. Legrand.
Reserve. Fauconnet.
Centre. General Moreau. 1st Division. Grandjean.
2nd Division. Leclerc.
3rd Division. Decaen.
Cavalry reserve. D'Hautpoul.
Right Wing. General Lecourbe. 1st Division. Gudin.
2nd Division. Montrichard.
Reserve. Nansouty.
Right flank brigade (to watch the roads towards the Tyrol). General Molitor (8 battalions, 4 squadrons).

Ney's division was reduced to two brigades, under General Bonet (54th of the line and 8th Chasseurs) and General Joba (76th and 103rd of the line).

The reorganization had hardly been completed when, on the night of 4 June, Kray passed 40,000 men across to the south bank of the Danube, and early on the 5th fell upon Richepanse's "left flank brigade" along the line of the Iller. Grenier came to the rescue with the left wing of the army. Ney's division was nearest the flank and came first into action. With one of Richepanse's regiments (the 48th) and Bonet's brigade he made a splendid bayonet attack on an Austrian column, scattered it and secured as trophies of his victory 300 prisoners, two guns, and seven wagon loads of ammunition. The Austrians fell back on their fortified lines as further French reinforcements were thrown into the battle. Kray had numbers on his side, but it is clear that the French were the better fighting men.

Some French officers had been taken prisoners in the first stage of the engagement. On 9 June Ney sent a flag of truce into the enemy's lines in order to convey a supply of money to the prisoners. The staff officer entrusted with this mission brought back important news. Some of the Austrian officers had told him that Kray had just received despatches from Italy according to which Genoa had surrendered. They said also that the First Consul was at Milan and had obtained "some slight successes," but they made light of these, and told the French officer that they expected the fall of Genoa would be the prelude to other victories for the Imperial arms.

The same day Moreau himself received a letter from Bonaparte dated from Milan, which gave a confident forecast of the Italian campaign and urged him to take more active steps to deal with Kray's army. Ney had already suggested, through his immediate chief Grenier, a march on the Danube above Ulm. This was the plan which Moreau adopted.

Richepanse was left to observe Ulm, and till the general movement had made some progress Ney's division remained at Weissenhorn in touch with him. The first advance was made by Lecourbe and the right. On 12 June he re-occupied Augsburg, placed a garrison there, and then moved westward on the 15th to Zusmarshausen to close on the centre under Moreau which was marching to cross the Danube near Dillingen. On the 17th Legrand's division of Grenier's corps moved up on

Moreau's left and occupied Gunzburg on the Danube. The bridge was found to be destroyed by the enemy who held the north bank of the river. They had burned or broken up the bridges for many miles above Ulm, and brought all the boats they could find across to the north bank.

Nearer Ulm they still had some force on the south side. Ney had been reinforced with two cavalry regiments (2nd Hussars and 19th Cavalry of the line). Early on the 17th he was ordered to send out a reconnaissance towards Leipheim, on the south bank of the Danube above Ulm. He entrusted the operation to Major Charpentier commanding the 8th Chasseurs-à-cheval, who took with him 200 of his chasseurs and 150 men of the 54th Infantry. The same evening Ney had the mortification of having to report that the reconnaissance had ended in a disaster. Charpentier had fallen into an ambuscade and been routed with the loss of many prisoners. After this success the Austrians abandoned Leipheim and withdrew to the north bank. When next day Ney moved up closer to the river with the whole of his division his march was unopposed.

On the night of the 18th parties of volunteers from Lecourbe's corps swam the Danube, surprised the Austrian posts near the bank, secured some boats, and made it possible for the right wing to begin the crossing of the river. Lecourbe was in action with a considerable force of the enemy on the morning of the 19th. He secured and repaired the bridge of Greimheim, Moreau brought the divisions of the centre to his help, and the Austrians, hurrying up to attack the French on the north bank, were beaten in detail. The fighting which went on along some miles of the river bank is known as the Battle of Hochstädt, and the day's success was all the more welcome to the French because some of the sharpest encounters took place on the very ground of Marlborough's victory and Tallard's defeat at the battle of Blenheim.[1]

On the 20th Grenier's divisions closed on the centre. Ney sent out a party of the 17th Dragoons to reconnoitre to the east of Ulm, and ascertained that Kray was withdrawing his

[1] Blindheim—the "Blenheim" of our English histories—is a village on the north side of the Danube close to Hochstädt.

army from the place. This information was confirmed by Richepanse. Grenier, acknowledging Ney's report, made the conjecture, verified by the events of the next few days, that the Austrian Army after leaving Ulm would retire to Nordlingen. On the 21st Ney marched to the bridge of Lauingen to cross the river there. He was all eagerness to pursue the Austrians, drive in their rear-guard, and capture guns, baggage, and prisoners. But Moreau having secured the crossing of the Danube had another fit of indecision, that gave a useful respite to his opponent. Beyond the closing up of the divisions of the left wing on the centre, the Army of the Rhine did little during the 20th, 21st and 22nd, and part of the 23rd.

On the 22nd Grenier had by order of Moreau directed Ney to send out a reconnaissance to ascertain the movements of the enemy. Ney, in his eagerness for action, had anticipated the order. Before Grenier's message reached him he had marched with a strong detachment of his cavalry towards Stotzingen on the north side of the river. He came upon what he took to be part of an Austrian rear-guard, drove it in by a vigorous attack, and only withdrew when the enemy brought five guns into action protected by a mass of cavalry. He was able to report that all the movements of the Austrians indicated a march on Nordlingen. He had taken some prisoners in the fight with the rear-guard. They told him that all that was left at Ulm was a small garrison of 3000 men, chiefly Bavarians. At the end of his report his impatience at Moreau's inaction led him to say that if there was any further delay Kray would escape. He suggested that the best way to stop him was to throw all the available mounted troops upon his rear-guard and force him thus to turn back in order to save it from destruction.

Patrols sent out by Ney early on the 23rd found the villages of Stetten and Bissingen completely clear of the enemy, who had now got a good start on their march to the north eastward.

That day orders arrived for Grenier's division to move up the north bank. Next morning Ney had again patrols out to the north-east in touch with the Austrians, and reported that an attack in force must inevitably result in the capture of a considerable part of their baggage convoy. But already

Moreau had pushed forward his right under Lecourbe against Nordlingen, following up with the centre. Lecourbe was driving in the Austrians upon Nordlingen late on the 23rd, when Kray evacuated the place.

Early on the 24th he sent Moreau a flag of truce with a proposal for an armistice. He informed the French General that he had news from Italy according to which Melas, after being defeated by the First Consul at Marengo on 14 June, arranged for a suspension of military operations with a view to peace. Moreau declined to accept Kray's proposal.

The Austrian Army now retired eastward from Nordlingen directing its march so as to reach the line of the Danube again at Neuburg, Kray intending to follow the river from that point, continuing his retreat by Ingolstadt on Ratisbon. On the 25th Ney, following up the Austrian retirement, fell upon a rear-guard escorting a large convoy at Œttingen: after a sharp fight he captured 60 wagons and 300 horses.

In reporting this success to Grenier he expressed the opinion that if the army would only make a two days' march Kray would be forced to fight and would fare as badly as, or even worse than, Melas had done at Marengo. Grenier, in acknowledging the report, wrote to Ney that he had been doing all he could to urge Moreau to more energetic action. But the Commander-in-Chief of the Army of the Rhine did not regard the situation from the same point of view as his more intelligent subordinates. They had grasped what is now an elementary idea in the conduct of armies, namely the maxim that the object of military operations is not the mere occupation of territory, but the destruction of the enemy's main fighting force. Moreau was inspired only with the old idea that it was enough to force the enemy to abandon this or that fortress, river line, or province. So now he was quite satisfied with having "manœuvred" Kray out of Ulm, and chiefly anxious to take possession of the capital of Bavaria. On the 25th he had directed General Decaen's division to march on Munich. Decaen occupied the city on the 28th after defeating an Austrian detachment under General Meerfeld. Lecourbe's corps occupied Donauwörth on the Danube, and Richepanse invested Ulm.

Kray, moving round by the north of Donauwörth, sent a strong corps across the Danube at Neuburg on the 26th. Moreau had anticipated this movement and feared it might be the prelude of a stroke against Decaen at Munich. He had transferred Lecourbe's corps to the south bank of the river and followed him up with two divisions of the centre. On the 27th Lecourbe headed off the Austrian advance near Neuburg, and though at first repulsed he succeeded in inflicting a defeat on the enemy. Kray retreated across the river by Ingolstadt, left a garrison there, and continued his retreat along the left bank of the Danube towards Ratisbon.

In this eastward march of the Army of the Rhine the left wing had become the rear corps and Ney had no share in the fighting. On the day of Lecourbe's victory Ney's division was near Monheim, north of Donauwörth, acting as a flank guard to the general advance. He was then moved forward to Eichstadt to levy contributions on the town and the neighbouring district. On 1 July he was reinforced with the 13th Dragoons, and ordered to invest Ingolstadt on the north side. That day his outposts were close up to the place. Next day it was invested by Ney's division on the north bank of the Danube and Legrand's on the south. The Austrian commandant of the place was a General Neu, and the soldiers joked about it being an affair of a close struggle "nez contre nez" ("Ney contre Neu"), "nose to nose".[1]

But no active operations were undertaken against Ingolstadt. The siege was a mere blockade. Moreau held the country southward by Augsburg to Munich while Lecourbe kept in touch with the Austrian retreat. On 10 July Kray proposed an armistice on the ground that peace negotiations were about to be begun between Vienna and Paris. The armistice was actually signed at Paarsdorf on the evening of the 15th. But the news had not reached Ney or his opponent Neu on the night between the 16th and 17th, when the garrison of Ingolstadt made a determined attempt to break out on the north side. The sortie was repulsed after some hard fighting in the

[1] The Austrian officer was perhaps a distant cousin of his French opponent. Ney came from the German borderland of France, and, among the various ways in which the family name was spelt, we find "Neu". See p. 2.

early hours of the 17th. Bonet's infantry brigade was hard pressed by the Austrians, when Ney came to the rescue with some of his cavalry and led in person a charge that broke up the enemy's attack. Four guns and 600 prisoners were taken in this action. It was not till the morning of the 18th that news of the armistice arrived.

It had been agreed that the troops on both sides should maintain their positions, and the three fortresses, held by the Austrians and blockaded by the French, should be revictualled every ten days, the besiegers holding a line of posts around them at a distance of two and a half miles (2000 toises = 4000 metres). Ney had some trouble at the outset in arranging the details of the positions during the armistice with General Neu. The commandant of Ingolstadt wanted to bring his garrison out of the town and billet them in the surrounding villages. Ney insisted that this must not be done, on the ground that the Austrians would thus be able to collect supplies from the country round and accumulate a store of provisions in case the siege was resumed. He carried his point, and Neu kept his troops in the town where he had to depend entirely on the supplies passed in through the French outposts every ten days, and strictly supervised by Ney's commissioners.

When this matter had been arranged he asked Moreau for leave of absence. His health had suffered during the campaign, and the doctors advised a visit to the waters of Plombières. Moreau had to refuse the request, for there were rumours that the armistice might be broken off at any time. During August and September there were some minor movements of troops, Moreau reducing the force round Ingolstadt, and using part of Ney's division to reinforce the main army about Munich and along the River Isar in view of an expected resumption of hostilities. But at the end of September a convention was arranged between France and Austria as a basis of what it was hoped would be definite peace negotiations, and under this convention the fortress of Ingolstadt was to be surrendered to the Army of the Rhine. Ney took possession of the place on 6 October.

There seemed to be now no reason why his long-deferred

leave of absence should be refused. Every one thought the war was over. He therefore again wrote to Moreau asking this time to be allowed to go for a while to rest at his country house near Nancy—La Petite Malgrange. Moreau granted the request, all the more readily because he himself was leaving the army for a while. He was on his way to Paris. Ney travelled with him to Strasburg. Then he went on to Nancy, looking forward to a well-earned rest after these long years of campaigning in the Rhineland.

But the general hope of an immediate peace was doomed to disappointment. Austria refused to accept the terms imposed by the First Consul, and determined to make one more effort to reverse the verdict of Marengo. In Italy the Austrian Army under Bellegarde held the line of the Mincio, the frontier of Venetia, and was opposed to the Army of Italy under Brune. But here the Imperialists intended to act only on the defensive. Their chief efforts were to be directed to the operations against the Army of the Rhine, of which Moreau had resumed the command, with his head-quarters at Munich. The French had by the middle of November some 90,000 men about Munich. Ingolstadt was held by Ste Suzanne's newly formed corps 18,000 strong. The Austrians had concentrated on the line of the river Inn in the neighbourhood of its junction with the Danube at Passau 90,000 men under the Archduke John, with an advanced corps under the Archduke Ferdinand thrown forward to Landshut. Twenty-five thousand men under the Elector of Bavaria and General Klenau held Ratisbon on the right, and on the left General Auffenberg with 20,000 more guarded the approaches to the Tyrol. The first object of the main army under the Archduke John would be the recapture of Munich.

Ney had not been long at La Petite Malgrange when he received a letter from Moreau's chief of the staff, dated 12 November, informing him that a fortnight's notice of the termination of the armistice would be given next day and hostilities would recommence on the 28th. He was directed to rejoin, as quickly as possible, Grenier's corps, which was to be assembled about Freising on the Isar, between Munich and Landshut, on the 22nd. A postscript was added to the official letter: "Travel day and night. Your presence was never more necessary".

Ney reached Freising on the 24th and resumed the command of his division. Its composition was as follows:—

Bonet's brigade. 15th and 23rd of the Line and 19th Cavalry.
Joba's brigade. 76th and 103rd of the Line and 13th Dragoons.

The 8th Chasseurs were under orders to join the division. Its total strength would be twelve battalions of infantry and three regiments of cavalry.[1]

Moreau had very defective information as to the forces, positions, and plans of the enemy. But he felt certain that their first movement would be against Munich, and for its defence he took up a line of positions running north and south through the great Forest of Ebersberg, a large tract of hilly and wooded country to the east of the city. The weather had been very bad for some days. There were heavy showers of rain followed by snow and though there was frost in the nights, there was a partial thaw in the daytime, with the result that all the roads were in a bad state and many of them almost impassable. This limited the possible lines of advance of the enemy, and enabled Moreau to reckon with all but certainty that the main attack would be made along the well-paved high road that crosses the River Inn at Muhldorf and runs nearly due west to Munich, traversing the forest from end to end. He concentrated his main force for the defence of this road, placing its centre near the village of Hohenlinden the meeting point of many of the cross roads of the Ebersberg woods.

On the extreme right Montrichard's division of Lecourbe's corps was posted at Helfendorf, on the edge of the woods, holding the road that runs south-east from Munich to the

[1] The distribution of commands in the Army of the Rhine about Munich at the opening of the winter campaign of 1800 was:—

Left Wing. General Grenier. Divisional Commanders: Legrand, Ney, Bastoul.

Centre. General Moreau. Divisional Commanders: Richepanse, Decaen, Grandjean, and D'Hautpoul (cavalry).

Right Wing. General Lecourbe. Divisional Commanders: Gudin, Montrichard, and Molitor.

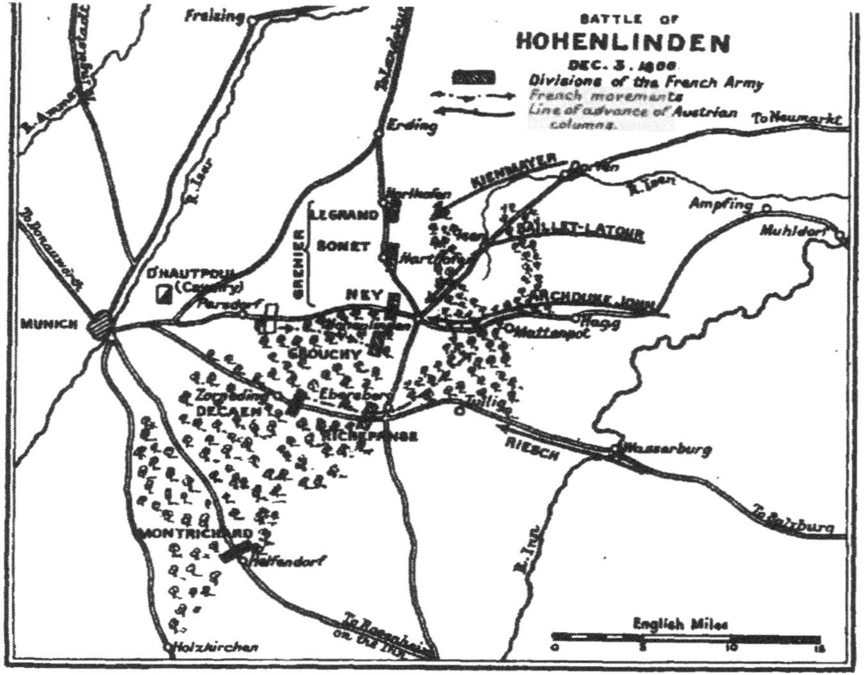
BATTLE OF
HOHENLINDEN
DEC. 3. 1800
Divisions of the French Army
French movements
Line of advance of Austrian columns.
To Neumarkt
Freising
Erding
R. Isar
To Donauwörth
MUNICH
D'HAUTPOUL (Cavalry)
Parsdorf
GRENIER
LEGRAND
BONET
NEY
GROUCHY
Zorneding
DECAEN
Ebersberg
RICHEPANSE
MONTRICHARD
Helfendorf
Holzkirchen
To Rosenheim on the Inn
KIENMAYER
Dorfen
R. Isen
Ampfing
Muhldorf
BAILLET-LATOUR
ARCHDUKE JOHN
Haag
Mattenpot
RIESCH
Wasserburg
To Salzburg
R. Inn
English Miles
0
5
10
15

crossing of the Inn at Rosenheim. In the centre Ney's division was assigned the post of honour, holding a position in the woods immediately to the west of Hohenlinden across and barring the main road to Munich. To Ney's left, the other two divisions of Grenier's corps prolonged the line to the northward. Behind him Grandjean's division of Moreau's own corps was in reserve at Parsdorf, with D'Hautpoul's cavalry on the same road still nearer to Munich. To the right of Ney, Richepanse's division held Ebersberg and watched the road running to the crossing of the Inn at Wasserburg. In the second line behind Richepanse was Decaen's division, about the village of Zorneding.[1]

On the 27th—the eve of the resumption of hostilities—the troops were in these positions. Next day Moreau occupied the eastern outlets of the forest, Richepanse advancing to Tullig on the road to Wasserburg, and Ney establishing an advanced post at Haag on the main road to Muhldorf, with a brigade in support at Mattenpot where the road ran through a defile formed by two wooded ridges. The army remained in these positions until the morning of 30 November.

Meanwhile the Archduke John had crossed the Inn a little above Passau. His plan of campaign was to move by Neumarkt to Landshut, join the Archduke Ferdinand's corps there, cross the Isar, and advance along its western bank by Freising on Munich turning the left of Moreau's positions. But the bad weather and the miserable state of the roads seriously delayed his march. On the evening of the 29th the main column had only reached Neumarkt. He then changed his plan, abandoned the idea of the wide sweeping flank march by Landshut, and decided to advance directly on Munich through the Ebersberg woods, marching by the main Muhldorf road and attacking Moreau in front.

The French Commander-in-Chief was still without any complete information as to the Austrian movements. He had heard of the enemy's presence about Neumarkt, but did not know that the Austrian main army was in this direction and

[1] See the annexed plan of the Battle of Hohenlinden. On this plan the dotted oblong near Parsdorf shows the original position of Grandjean's division, which was commanded by Grouchy on the day of the battle.

he expected the appearance of another force from across the Inn in his immediate front. On 30 November he moved forward towards the river in the hope of making the Archduke show his hand and thus "clear up the situation". Montrichard's division on the extreme right was sent forward to the neighbourhood of the Inn opposite Rosenheim. Richepanse advanced to watch the crossing at Wasserburg. Decaen's division was in support of him near Ebersberg. Grenier's three divisions were sent forward to watch the country towards Neumarkt. Ney was posted on the main road west of Ampfing, with another division on his left on the River Isen, and the third in reserve as a second line.

Patrols sent to the front by Ney obtained early information showing that the enemy were approaching. After dark a long line of watchfires, extending northwards from Muhldorf, showed that they were in considerable force. Ney's division lay along the eastern crest of a plateau which divides the valley of the Isen from that of the Inn, a rising ground dotted with clumps of wood and covered with half-frozen snow. He visited his outpost line at 6 a.m. on 1 December. It was still dark night, an hour and a half before sunrise. He remarked that the enemy's watchfires were burning low. He at once concluded that the men were no longer bivouacked around them. If they had been they would have been keeping up their fires, in a cold night like this and in a country where there was abundance of wood. They were therefore falling in for a movement of some kind—advance or retreat, probably the former. He got his division under arms. The men had their biscuit and coffee and formed up for battle.

It was well that he was on the alert. In the twilight a rush of cavalry drove in his advanced posts, and as the sun rose strong columns of infantry were seen to be advancing, and battery after battery galloped out and opened fire. Away to his left a similar attack developed against the division in the hollow of the Isen valley.[1] The French held their own against the first onset. Legrand's division was brought up by Grenier

[1] This was the division originally commanded by Bastoul. He had had to resign his command through illness and it was under the orders of General Hardy

to reinforce the fighting line, and Moreau himself, hearing the firing, rode on to the battlefield.

Ney now made a successful counter attack, and captured an Austrian gun and more than 800 prisoners. So far the day had been a success for Moreau thanks to the perfect steadiness and splendid fighting qualities of his veteran troops. But the enemy was being rapidly reinforced. The three divisions of Grenier's corps had in front of them the main Austrian Army, nearly 80,000 strong. Moreau, as soon as he recognized this, decided to break off the fight and retire upon his original positions in the Ebersberg Forest. He himself personally directed the retreat, which was made by alternate divisions. The Austrians soon ceased to press upon the retiring troops, and by noon the French were marching back through the snowy woodlands, in no way discouraged by what they regarded as only an unimportant check. Hardy had been wounded, and Ney's brigadier, Bonet, was given the command of his division, handing over his brigade to General Heudelet.

The Archduke John of course counted the battle a victory, an auspicious opening for the campaign. His officers and men were in high spirits at their success and he was resolved to follow up the French and drive them back to Munich. During the next day (2 December) his main army advanced towards the woods in three columns, and orders were issued for a general attack on the French positions 3 December.

Moreau had placed his seven divisions in much the same array as that in which they had stood on 27 November. Montrichard was withdrawn to Helfendorf. Richepanse to Ebersberg. Ney held the ground in the woods west of Hohenlinden, guarding the main Muhldorf-Munich road, with Grandjean's division now commanded by Grouchy on his right, and Bonet on his left at Harthofen, and Legrand at Horlkofen. Moreau had noted during the engagement of 1 December that the enemy were moving in three columns, the left column on the Muhldorf road. He was not of the first rank as a strategist in the direction of a campaign, but there was no better soldier than Moreau as a battle leader, and on the eve of Hohenlinden his forecast of the fight and his plans for it were a stroke of genius.

He concluded that with the country covered with half-melted snow and mud, the Archduke would mass the largest column of attack on his left where it could march by the paved main road. The two other columns, moving over more difficult ground to the north of it, would not be so strong in numbers and would probably make much slower progress. The head of the left column would therefore be the first to come into action, and it would have a long line of battalions and batteries strung out behind along the road by which it advanced. His plan was that Ney should attack the head of the main column about Hohenlinden, supported by Grouchy. Meanwhile Richepanse supported by Decaen was to swing round to his left, march through the woods, and fall on the flank of the Austrian advance between Hohenlinden and the Mattenpot defile. Bonet and Legrand were to delay the advance of the other two Austrian columns until the main column had been broken up.

With one minor exception Moreau had absolutely divined the Archduke's plan for the battle. The Austrians moved before sunrise on the 3rd. On the extreme right Kienmayer with 20,000 men started from Dorfen, marched up the Isen valley, and then advanced towards Horlkofen. The central column, 20,000 more, commanded by an Austrian General of Belgian descent, Count Baillet-Latour, marched on the village of Isen with orders to turn to the left after passing it and attack Hohenlinden from the north-east. The Archduke himself led the main or left column nearly 40,000 strong through Haag by the Munich road directly upon Hohenlinden. But there was a fourth column, the presence of which Moreau did not suspect—12,000 men under General Riesch, who crossed the Inn at Wasserburg, with orders to march on Ebersberg, and protect the flank of the general advance.

Ney's patrols had reported the presence of the enemy at the eastern outlets of the woods on the evening of the 2nd, and reports from the outposts during the night told that the Austrian watchfires near the road were on a very narrow front, not more than that of a regiment. This seemed to indicate that they had halted in column of march. There was some firing along the borders of the forest towards midnight. Then all was quiet until, in the darkness at five a.m., the Austrian advance began.

Richepanse had made an early start, followed by Decaen's division. As he marched through the woods to the northwest of Tullig he was attacked by the head of Riesch's column. He now acted in a way that showed true tactical insight. If he had allowed himself to be diverted from his movement in order to deal with this unexpected enemy all Moreau's plan would have fallen to pieces. But Richepanse fully realized that everything depended on his falling on the flank of the Austrian main attack. He therefore took the risk of leaving a single brigade to delay Riesch's advance, and pushed on with the rest of his division and Decaen's.

At six o'clock Ney's division was in action at Hohenlinden. The first attack of the enemy came in on his right. Grouchy brought up his division to assist him in repulsing it. Several Austrian batteries had come into action along a wooded ridge to the north of the village, and the heads of infantry columns showed in the same direction. Moreau had ridden over to Ney's position, and "judging that the greater part of the Austrian column was still on the road and in the defile he ordered an attack on the troops already deployed". Ney led his infantry against the ridges held by the Austrians.

The attack was made with a rapid rush. There was all the enthusiasm of the old armies of the Republic, and officers and men were eager to wipe out the memory of their repulse of two days before. With fixed bayonets and beating drums the men rushed at the white-coated Austrians, singing the Marseillaise as they came on. Some of the battalions exchanged fire with the enemy at close quarters, but most trusted to their bayonets. As the enemy gave way several guns were dragged up the ridge and opened fire on the Austrians retiring down its reverse slope. The enemy made more than one attempt to reform and renew the fight, but Grouchy broke their left south of the road, and Moreau, noticing that their fighting line was not being reinforced, concluded that Richepanse's flank attack must be already coming upon their line of advance and holding back the rear of the column about Mattenpot. He therefore ordered Ney and Grouchy to press the enemy vigorously.

There was now a running fight through the woods. The two French divisions pressed steadily forward, driving the Austrians before them with cannon, and musketry and frequent bayonet charges. The enemy never made a serious stand, and as Ney hustled them back towards the road, regiments and batteries became crowded together and mixed up in an armed mob. The retreat had degenerated into a rout. And now as the fight surged eastwards towards the Mattenpot defile the roar of Richepanse's cannon was heard thundering through the woods. He had caught the Austrians moving in a long slender column of route through the hollow defile. They now fought only to extricate themselves from the dangerous position into which they had marched in full confidence of an easy victory. The main column had been beaten before the two others could come into action. Legrand and Bonet had only to meet and repel a half-hearted attack, for Kienmayer and Baillet-Latour had not been long in action north of the road when they received the Archduke's orders for a general retreat towards the Inn. Riesch was also ordered to retire on Wasserburg after he had pressed back Richepanse's detached brigade towards Ebersberg.

The only hard fighting had taken place about Hohenlinden and along the line of retreat of the main column. With its collapse the day had been lost for the Archduke. Ney was able to report next day to Moreau an enormous capture of prisoners and trophies during the last hours of the battle:—

> "The vigorous efforts of my division," he wrote, "assisted by the combined movements of those near it, placed in our hands more than 80 guns, with an immense quantity of ammunition wagons, many standards and about 10,000 prisoners, amongst whom are several generals and many officers of rank."

It was the greatest battle at which Ney had yet been present, and he had borne a splendid part in a decisive victory. Though the Austrians had set some 90,000 men in movement on the morning of Hohenlinden it is estimated that not more than 57,000 were actually engaged against 49,000 French. The Austrian loss was very heavy, 5460 killed and wounded, and 7200 prisoners, and 74 guns. The French loss was only 2500 killed and wounded.[1]

It was the victory of Hohenlinden that made Moreau a possible rival of Napoleon, and secured for him the enmity of the First Consul. But having won his great victory he failed to reap its full advantages. There was no vigorous pursuit of the enemy. It was not till the 9th—six days after the battle—that Lecourbe, with his corps acting as the vanguard of the army, crossed the Inn at Rosenheim. He advanced on Salzburg followed by Moreau with the divisions of the centre. At the same time the divisions of Grenier's corps—the left wing—crossed the Inn; Ney at Muhldorf, Bonet and Legrand at Wasserburg. The Austrians were retiring on Linz, Moreau's slowness having given them a good start. Richepanse overtook and had some fighting with their rear-guard on 16, 17, and 18 December. Ney's division saw no enemy. Joba's brigade was detached from it to blockade the small fortress of Braunau.

On 22 December Moreau had reached Steyer, half-way from the Inn to Vienna, when the Archduke Charles, who had taken command of the retreating Austrian Army, sent to his head-quarters a flag of truce with proposals for an armistice. This was concluded on Christmas Day and the negotiations were resumed between Paris and Vienna, which ended in the peace of Lunéville.

During the armistice the Army of the Rhine was dispersed in cantonments in Upper Austria and Bavaria. Ney occupied the town of Burghausen, which among other contributions paid daily twelve louis (240 francs) for the expenses of the general and his staff. On 30 January, 1801, Ney received from the Commander-in-Chief Moreau a letter containing four orders on the treasury, one for 10,000 francs, two for 6000 each, and a fourth for 3000. The first was for himself, in recognition of his services during the campaign; the two next were for his brigadiers, Generals Joba and Desperrières, and the last for his chief of the staff, Adjutant-General Ruffin.

[1] These are the figures given by Captain Otto Berndt of the Austrian staff in his work on military statistics, "Die Zahl im Kriege" (Vienna, 1897). Ney's report of 80 guns and about 10,000 prisoners taken, was a rough estimate formed when the firing had just ceased, and slightly exaggerating the results obtained.

On 16 March orders came for the return of the army to France. On the 22nd Ney transferred his head-quarters to Landshut, and on 1 April to Donauwörth. There he obtained leave of absence and handed over the command of the division to General Desperrières, who was to take it back to the Rhine.

Ney reached Strasburg on 4 April, and next day arrived at his country house near Nancy, La Petite Malgrange. He was to enjoy a well-earned rest there with those who were dearest to him. His father, old Pierre Ney, was awaiting his arrival, and with him was Ney's sister Marguerite with the husband she had married the year before. The house had become a home with such guests to keep him company and hear his stories of the years of warfare, through which he had passed since he left the cooperage at Saarlouis to put on the uniform of a private in the king's hussars.

CHAPTER VII

NEY MEETS BONAPARTE—MARRIAGE—MISSION TO SWITZERLAND (1801-1804)

NEY spent the greater part of the year 1801 at La Petite Malgrange. He was now 34 years of age, but he had done enough hard and successful work for a lifetime. In seven years of warfare he had won his way to the rank of general of division, and without one dishonourable act he had acquired a modest fortune. Unlike so many of his comrades he had never sought to enrich himself by methods that savoured rather of the brigand than the soldier. And he had throughout held aloof from political intrigue. The position he had won, the commands he had held, were due to hard fighting and good service in the field. While others were using every influence at their command to obtain promotion, Ney had more than once refused it. Honours he had modestly declined had been forced upon him. It was characteristic of the man that he had not yet seen Paris, or tried to penetrate into the charmed circle that surrounded the First Consul. He admired his genius but he was no suitor for his favour.

He had made many friends, but few of them were to be found in the immediate entourage of Bonaparte. The First Consul's personal lieutenants were mostly men of the Army of Italy. He regarded with suspicion the men of the Army of the Rhine, the lieutenants of Moreau. They were the generals who had made the reputation of his one possible rival, and they were supposed to be inspired with a loyalty to the Republic that might make them dangerous opponents of his personal policy. It is remarkable that so many of the best soldiers of the Rhine disappear from the military annals of France in the days after Hohenlinden. Some like Moreau himself were driven into exile when the time came for Bonaparte to break down all opposition to his personal rule. Others lived in retirement till in the closing years of the Empire they were called to take their part in the last struggles against invasion.

Some, however, were destined to play a great part in the wars of the Empire, and of these was Ney. Bonaparte knew the reputation the young general had justly acquired in the Army of the Rhine, and in May, 1801, he was invited to come to Paris and present himself to the Consuls. This was his first meeting with the future Emperor. But he asked for nothing, showed no disposition to attach himself to the great man's fortunes, and, after a brief stay in the capital, he returned to enjoy his long holiday at his country house. It lasted nearly to the end of the year. In the latter part of November he received a letter from the Minister of War informing him that he was appointed Inspector-General of Cavalry, and was to enter upon his new duties on the first day of the new year. It was suggested that he should come at once to Paris to make the necessary arrangements for taking up his appointment.

He went at once to the capital, but he did not much like the routine duties of the Inspectorship, and hearing that reinforcements of cavalry were to be sent at an early date to San Domingo, where for years the French Government had been trying to put down a negro insurrection, he wrote to the Minister of War on 4 December asking to be allowed to go out to the West Indies in command of the cavalry. His request was granted and on the 18th the First Consul signed a decree appointing General Ney to the command he had asked for.

The main expedition for San Domingo had just sailed from Brest under the command of the First Consul's brother-in-law, General Leclerc, who was accompanied by his wife Pauline Bonaparte. There had been an eager competition among the officers of the French Army for employment with it. For it was expected that there would be a brief campaign, an easy victory, and rich rewards for the victors in the confiscated lands of the island. The expedition was, however, doomed to failure, not so much by the efforts of the insurgents as through the effects of the climate, to which Leclerc himself fell a victim.

Thus, too, Ney's career might have closed, if he had gone to the West Indies. But he no sooner had received his appointment than he hesitated about accepting it. On 19 December—the very day after the decree was signed—he asked the Minister to suspend its execution till 2 January, as family affairs might require him to remain in France. And on the New Year's Day of 1802 he decided to take up the Inspectorship of Cavalry and relinquish his appointment to the West Indian command.

This change of plans appears to have been connected with a project of marriage for the young general in which Josephine, the wife of the First Consul, was interested. Amongst the friends of her daughter Hortense Beauharnais at Madame Campan's school at St. Germain, had been Mademoiselle Aglaé Louise Auguié. She was a niece of Madame Campan, the daughter of her sister Adélaïde Henriette, and Pierre César Auguié. Adélaïde Auguié had been one of the ladies of the suite of Queen Marie Antoinette, and her husband was a high official of the Finance Department under the old regime. When the mob invaded the palace of Versailles on 6 October, 1789, Adélaïde had saved the life of the Queen by facing their leaders in the gallery before her rooms, and keeping them back till she escaped into the King's apartments. During the Terror her husband M. Auguié was in prison, and narrowly escaped death. She herself, when she heard of the Queen's execution, had lost her reason and thrown herself from a window, and was killed by the fall.

Her widowed husband, after his release from prison, had saved something from the wreck of his fortunes, and had obtained a post in the Ministry of Finance under the Consulate. He had made a new home for himself and his daughters at the château of Grignon near Versailles. After her school-days with Madame Campan his daughter Aglaé was one of the circle of young girls who figured at Madame Bonaparte's receptions, like the maids of honour of an uncrowned queen, and her patroness formed the plan of marrying her to Michel Ney, and thus attaching the brilliant soldier of the Rhine to her husband's party.

When Ney first met his future wife at the New Year of 1802 she was just twenty—a tall, handsome brunette, with dark eyes, a pleasing expression, and a wit and intelligence that spoke well for the education she had received at St. Germain. For Ney it was a case of love at first sight. Thanks to Josephine's intervention he received an invitation from M. Auguié to visit the château of Grignon in February. But at first the course of true love did not run smooth. Mademoiselle Aglaé was disappointed in her admirer. She had been told of his exploits in the Army of the Rhine and of the many good qualities that had made him a general favourite among his comrades. She imagined him to be as handsome as he was brave and generous, and it was something of a shock to her, when he was presented to her, to find that he did not come up to the ideal of her day dreams.

The General had kept to old military fashions that seemed strange to the eyes of the lady used to the courtier-like modes of the Consulate. His round good-humoured face looked heavy and dull decorated as it was with a bunch of red whiskers on each cheek, and though the queue had gone out of fashion, it used to be worn in the hussar regiments, and Ney kept it still in memory of his first campaigns. All this gave him an awkward appearance, and this was not made the better by a certain shyness which still troubled him in a social circle. He was hopelessly deficient in "small talk" and the current forms of trifling compliment. Mademoiselle concluded that her hero was after all only a rather rough, old-fashioned, and stupid cavalry officer. Ney was disappointed in his turn by her studied coldness of manner.

But Josephine did not abandon her plan on account of a first check. She took care that Mademoiselle Aglaé should hear all manner of good things of Michel Ney, and the General's friends discreetly prevailed on him to bring his personal appearance more up to date before he ventured to see the lady again. The whiskers and the queue were sacrificed. Henceforth Ney was clean shaved in the fashion of the time. In the month of March, in an interval of one of his tours of inspection, he came again to Grignon, and this time he made some progress towards winning the lady's good will.

By the month of May matters had advanced so far that he thought he might venture on a formal proposal, and it was made in the proper French fashion to the father of the hoped-for bride, under the patronage of Josephine, who wrote for Ney, on 30 May from Malmaison, a letter addressed to M. Auguié asking him to bestow his daughter's hand on the General. This was sent to Ney with a covering letter in which Josephine wrote to him :—

> "I send you, General, the letter you have asked of me for Citizen Auguié. May I beg that you will read it. I have not said in it all the good things that I know and think about you. I want to let this worthy family have the satisfaction of discovering for themselves all your good qualities; but I repeat to you the assurance of the interest which Bonaparte and I myself take in this marriage, and of the satisfaction he feels in thinking that he will thus secure the happiness of two people for whom he has a special good will and esteem. I share with him both these feelings."

Such a communication as Josephine's letter to M. Auguié could have only one result. Within the week Madame Bonaparte received a letter from him telling her that he was only too pleased to accept the proposal made on behalf of General Ney. On 27 July the marriage contract was signed at Paris. In this document Michel Ney declares that he brings into the settlement his property of La Petite Malgrange near Nancy, valued at 80,000 francs, besides 12,000 francs in money and movable property. Mademoiselle Aglaé Auguié brings the fourth part of a property in San Domingo this portion of the estate being estimated at 5000 francs, a dowry of 60,000 francs, and a trousseau valued at 12,000. The date of the marriage was fixed for 5 August. Sending to his fiancée a little present of jewellery Ney made a proud apology for its small value. He could not offer her pearls and diamonds he said, because he had always held a soldier's sword should be used to obtain glory and not wealth.

Both the civil and religious ceremonies took place on that day at Grignon, the former at the *mairie* of the commune, the latter in the chapel of the château, which, after years of disuse, had been restored for the occasion. The famous artist Isabey, afterwards court painter to the Emperor, designed the decorations and organized the fête which followed. The aisles and roof of the chapel were hung with garlands of green foliage. Wax lights shone from chandeliers half hidden in masses of flowers, and a military band occupied the music gallery. The bridegroom wore the full parade uniform of a general and a jewelled Egyptian sabre the gift of Bonaparte. The bride was dressed simply in white with a wreath of roses on her bridal veil. Beside them at the altar stood a grey-haired peasant and his wife, servants of the farm attached to the château, who were celebrating their golden wedding. They wore the picturesque dress of the peasants of the district. Ney had provided that of the aged shepherd, Aglaé that of his wife. Their presence at the ceremony was suggested by Ney. He said that their fifty years of happy married life would be a good omen for his wedding and they would remind him of his own humble origin.

In the evening there was a rustic fête in the gardens of the château. The friends of the family and the farmers and peasants of the neighbourhood formed the audience before an open-air stage on which Aglaé's sisters and some of their friends performed a little play written for the occasion. Then the military band gave a concert, during which as the darkness came on, transparencies shone out among the trees bearing the names of the battles in which Ney had borne a distinguished part. Then a choir of peasant girls came forward and sang a song wishing long life and happiness to the newly wedded pair, and an aged peasant invited them to enter a rustic hut where he said they would find a wise old woman who would tell them something of their future. The gipsy predicted long years of happiness. Neither she nor anyone else could foresee the firing party in the Luxembourg garden only a few years away in the dim future. But she had no pretence to read such secrets, for the gipsy was only Aglaé's aunt and schoolmistress, old Madame Campan, and the "peasant" who introduced Ney and his bride to her was the artist Isabey, in the rustic disguise in which he presided at the fête.

Then there was a ball in the open air. In the first quadrille two of the couples were Aglaé and the old shepherd, and Ney with the aged peasant woman for his partner. There was a pause in the series of dances to witness a display of fireworks. Then the ball went on till near midnight the party broke up. It was a day long remembered at Grignon, and a happier wedding feast than the stately courtly ceremonials that were the usual forms of celebrating the marriages of Bonaparte's friends.

After a few days at Grignon the newly married pair set out for Ney's home at La Petite Malgrange. It was a happy marriage, and Aglaé's first great sorrow was the tragedy that made her a widow thirteen years later. Some six weeks were spent in the country house near Nancy. Ney had resigned the Inspectorship of the Cavalry and was looking forward to another long holiday. But on 29 September he received orders to proceed to Geneva, then a French city, where he would receive instructions for an important official mission to Switzerland. He left La Petite Malgrange on 1 October and arrived at Geneva on the 4th.

A crisis had arisen in Switzerland which threatened the French predominance. When the Republicans first invaded the cantons, and declared their intention of substituting for the historic Swiss Confederation, a new Helvetian Republic on the Jacobin model, the mountaineers had made an ill-organized and unsuccessful resistance. During the years that followed the inauguration of the new Republic with a centralized government at Berne, more than one effort at a counter-revolution had been made by the cantons that clung to their old ideals. The soul of the resistance from first to last was the brave Aloys Reding of Schwytz. He had served for some years in the Spanish Army and returned to Switzerland before the Revolution. In 1798 at the head of the men of the Forest Cantons he had defeated a French army on the historic field of Morgarten. Then the fortune of war turned against him and he had to bow to the new state of things, but he and his friends were still working for the restoration of the old federal constitution.

During the long war France had maintained large armies in Switzerland and on its borders. Now that the treaties of Lunéville and Amiens had given peace to Europe the French armies had been withdrawn within the new frontiers of the Republic. For some months a French Brigade remained in Switzerland to support the Berne Government, which had also at its disposal two demi-brigades of "Helvetian" infantry that had been organized and trained by French officers, but were now commanded by Switzers. In July, 1802, the First Consul considered that the Berne Government was now strong enough to maintain order with its own troops, and the last of the French garrison was withdrawn.

This had no sooner been done than the Swiss Confederates thought that it was a favourable moment for a new effort to overthrow the Berne Government. A league of the Forest Cantons was formed. A diet of delegates was summoned to meet at Schwytz under the presidency of Reding, and it was decided to levy an army which was to muster at Zurich under the command of General Bachmann. He had been an officer of the old Swiss Guard under Louis XVI. After the Revolution he had served with the rank of Major-General in the Sardinian Army, and he had then raised and commanded a Swiss Legion in the service of England. On its dissolution after the peace of Amiens he had returned to Switzerland with many of his comrades.

The Berne Government sent its two demi-brigades to capture Zurich. But Bachmann marched to meet them at the head of a small body of regularly organized troops and a great gathering of peasants, many of them armed only with scythes and pitchforks. He drove the Government troops back upon Berne and occupied the place on 18 September, 1802. The members of the Helvetian Government, escorted by their defeated troops and accompanied by the French Minister Verninac, took refuge at Lausanne, whence on 21 September they sent to the First Consul a request for intervention. This was the message that led to Ney's being suddenly sent to Geneva. The First Consul had announced on 30 September that he was about to take steps to restore order in Switzerland, and impose peace on "the contending factions, who," he said, "were ruining the country by their dissensions". In plain English he was going to put down the national party, in order to ensure that the Helvetian Republic should continue to be a useful dependency of France.

At Geneva Ney met the Chef-de-Brigade (Colonel) Rapp, one of Bonaparte's aides-de-camp who was on his way to confer with the French Minister and the refugee Government of Berne at Lausanne, and then proceed to communicate with the patriot Government at Schwytz. Ney's instructions informed him that he would find his definite orders in the hands of Seras, the commandant of Geneva, who would also give him full reports as to the state of affairs in Switzerland. He was directed to make all necessary preparations for a military occupation of the country, but to take no hostile step till the result of Rapp's mission was known.

He therefore remained at Geneva during the first weeks of October. On the 13th Rapp arrived there from Lausanne and reported that both of the opposing Governments, that of Lausanne and that of Schwytz, had been persuaded to accept the "mediation" of the First Consul. Rapp sent his report to Bonaparte the same day, and added to it an expression of his opinion that Verninac was not sufficiently energetic for his position and ought to be recalled.

Acting on this advice the First Consul on 18 October recalled Verninac and appointed General Ney, Minister Plenipotentiary to Switzerland as well as Commander-in-Chief of any French troops that might be sent into the country. He had already signed on 10 October a proclamation to the "inhabitants of Helvetia" in which he spoke of his "mediation" as the one hope of peace and prosperity for Switzerland; declared that he wished to act only as their friend, and invited them to disband all newly levied troops on both sides only maintaining such units as had been under arms for six months, to observe faithfully a truce between the rival parties, and send delegates to Paris to confer with himself on the permanent settlement of the affairs of Switzerland. He asked that the Senate—that is the Berne Government—should send three delegates and each Canton three more. The proclamation ended with a veiled menace of annexation in case his proposals were not accepted.

The patriots had evacuated Berne and disbanded most of their new levies. The Helvetian Senate and Executive were therefore able to return to their capital. Talleyrand, as the First Consul's Minister of Foreign Affairs, directed Ney to proceed to Berne, to do all he could to maintain the truce of parties, and endeavour to give effect to Bonaparte's mediation. He was advised to avoid as far as possible any communication in writing to the leaders on both sides, and to confine himself to verbal negotiations with them "as frequently a wrong use was made of written official communications". Talleyrand was obviously anxious to be able to disavow the envoy's arrangements if necessary. Ney was further advised to avoid anything that might hurt the feelings of the Switzers, and above all to take care not to pose as the commander of foreign troops concentrated on their frontiers. There was an allusion to rumours that the First Consul was anxious to be invited to become the President of the Helvetian Republic, as he had already accepted the Presidency of the Cisalpine Republic in North Italy. Ney was to reject any such proposal and declare that it was quite foreign to the First Consul's views. Talleyrand expressed his pleasure at being in correspondence with Ney, his high opinion of his good qualities, and his confidence that he would successfully discharge his important mission.

Ney received his appointment as plenipotentiary and Talleyrand's instructions on 21 October and next day left Geneva for Berne, without an escort and accompanied only by Rouyer, an attaché who had served with Verninac and one of his aides-de-camp, Captain Béchet (Baron de Léoncourt by right of descent, a title he resumed under the Empire).

That evening he reached Moudon, half-way between the Lakes of Geneva and Neuchâtel. There he met Commandant Lemarrois, who had been sent on to Berne for information and was on his way back to Geneva. Lemarrois told him that Rapp's report of the success of his mission had been too optimistic. The patriots of the Forest Cantons had not really disarmed, and accordingly Ney sent from Moudon a despatch to Talleyrand in which he said:—

> "The diet of Schwytz continues in session, under the presidency of Reding, and persists in its policy of maintaining a Government other than that which France protects. The Confederate troops, although sent back to their various cantons, remain under arms, and have orders to assemble wherever circumstances may require them. This perfidy will no doubt compel the First Consul to alter his resolution and to employ rigorous measures against the chiefs of the insurrection."

He reached Berne next day and thence he addressed a despatch to Bonaparte himself, in which, after describing the preparations for armed resistance made by Reding's party, he asked for authorization to march French troops into Switzerland:—

"I propose," he said, "to occupy the Helvetian territory with twelve battalions of infantry, six squadrons of cavalry, and twelve guns, drawn from the bodies of troops assembled at Chiavenna, Como, in the Valais, at Geneva, Pontarlier, and Huningen. [1] This operation will destroy for ever the hopes of the insurgents, and protect the election of the deputies, whom the eighteen cantons are to send to Paris in accordance with your proclamation."

Obviously Ney understood that his mission was to secure the predominance of the French party. He was not afraid of responsibility, and, without waiting for Bonaparte's reply and authorization, he proceeded to act. On the same day on which he sent his proposals to Paris he sent Béchet to Schwytz to inform Reding that he must at once dissolve the local Diet, and that his refusal would be treated as an act of rebellion. He also sent to General Seras at Geneva orders to proceed immediately to Huningen, take command of the division that had been concentrated there, and occupy Basel with an advanced guard. The division was made up of twelve infantry battalions, the 3rd Chasseurs-à-cheval, and a battery of artillery. He also ordered a movement of French detachments to occupy Berne, Thun, Freiburg, and Solothurn. On the 27th he directed Seras to march on Zurich and break up a gathering of Confederate troops reported in that direction. The same day he wrote to Talleyrand:—

"My aide-de-camp, whom I sent to Schwytz to notify to M. Reding the order to dissolve the Diet over which he presides, has not yet returned.

"According to the reports that have reached me the Confederate troops are guarding the right bank of the Reuss from Lucerne to its mouth. Those of the Grisons and of the districts of Schwytz and Altdorf are in front of Lucerne. A quantity of artillery and munitions of war have been collected at Zurich, Schwytz and Altdorf.

"Accordingly General Seras at the head of eight battalions, three squadrons of chasseurs, and a company (battery) of light artillery will march on the position of Olten, occupy the little fortress of Aarburg, and endeavour to seize Zurich either by a ruse or by any other method of persuasion."

"P.S.—It is 9 in the evening and I reopen my despatch to place in it the evasive reply just received from the Diet of Schwytz in answer to my

[1] The French frontier fortress near Basel.

formal demand for its dissolution. I can see no other course left to me but to set the French troops in movement as I have decided."

On the same day he had sent to the chief of the staff of the Army of Italy a request that two columns of troops should be sent over the Alpine passes to occupy Altdorf and Chur. Switzerland was thus to be invaded from north, west, and south simultaneously.

On the 28th Ney wrote to Seras that he was to spare no effort to secure the occupation of Zurich without an armed conflict. On the 31st he was able to report to Berthier, the Minister of War, that this had been successfully accomplished.

Seras had occupied Olten and crossed the Aar on 27 October his division marching in three columns. As he advanced towards the Reuss next day the Confederate troops guarding the line of the river had abandoned it in a panic, and retired in confusion on Zurich. Seras made a forced march that day, his columns covering thirty-five miles, and halting before Zurich. The old ramparts were still standing, but no attempt was made to defend them and at six a.m. on the 29th the French marched in by three of the gates, a military band playing at the head of each column as it passed along the streets to the open space in front of the town hall. Here Seras found a battalion drawn up and crowds of peasants armed mostly with flails, forks, and scythes. But there was no fighting. Some of the peasants, doubtless overawed by the French display of force, and anxious to make their peace with the General, even shouted, "*Vive le grand Bonaparte! Vive la France!*" Colonel Meyer, who commanded the Confederate regulars, contented himself with a formal protest against the French intervention in the affairs of his country. Seras disarmed the battalion and dismissed the peasants to their homes. Ninety guns on the fortifications were taken by the French as trophies, and a considerable quantity of munitions of war were found in the place.

A municipality favourable to the Berne Government was installed in office, and a number of French sympathizers, whom the Confederates had imprisoned, were released. General Bachmann was in the town. He presented himself to Seras, told him he had abandoned the quarrel as hopeless, and asked for a passport for Munich.

Ney made a flying visit to Zurich, and directed various movements of French detachments in order that the troops might show themselves in all the possible centres of insurrection. He countermanded the march of the two columns from Italy as no longer necessary, and was able to report that in various places cannon and military stores had been seized and the partisans of Reding peacefully disarmed. There was now no further danger of civil war.

But on 4 November, on a report that though the Diet of Schwytz had dissolved, the leaders of the movement were talking of another effort at resistance, he ordered the arrest of Reding and eleven other Confederate leaders and sent them to the fortress of Aarburg, directing that their imprisonment should be made as comfortable as possible consistently with their safe detention.

The Helvetian Senate was now again in session at Berne —a small council of twenty-seven officials and representatives of the Cantons. Ney took part in the debates, speaking sometimes in French, sometimes in his native German. He obtained a vote of 625,000 francs for the French Army of occupation. It was Bonaparte's plan to have his troops paid by the country where they were employed, whenever they were doing garrison duty beyond the frontiers of the Republic. Ney also arranged for a number of French military engineers to be employed in preparing a new map of Switzerland.

By the end of November the delegates from the senate and the cantons had been elected and set out for Paris to discuss with the First Consul and his ministers a new constitution for their country. The matter was settled by the middle of the following February, and the First Consul signed the decree setting forth the new arrangements and known as the "*Acte de Médiation*" (19 February, 1803). Ney was informed of the successful conclusion of the negotiations, of the fact that "the citizen D'Affry" had been chosen "First Landamann" or President of the Helvetian Republic, and of the First Consul's desire that he should be received with military honours by the French troops in garrison in any place in Switzerland through which he might pass on his way to Berne. The choice of D'Affry was likely to be popular with both parties. He was a man of moderate views, a soldier who had been a Colonel of the Swiss Guards under Louis XVI.

Ney received D'Affry at Berne on 1 March. He arrived in the evening and was welcomed with a salute of fifty guns. A squadron of chasseurs acted as his escort, and detachments of the French and Helvetian troops were paraded in his honour. He had expressed a wish that the seat of government should be transferred to Freiburg, the capital of his own canton, and Bonaparte had consented to this change. Ney left Berne with him, and the new Landamann was formally installed in his office at Freiburg on 10 March.

Ney had now to make arrangements for giving full effect to the Act of Mediation. It had been agreed that the Helvetian Republic was to keep no regular troops in its pay. The militia of the cantons would supply its defence with the assistance of a French auxiliary corps if necessary. The brigade that already formed its military establishment was therefore no longer required. It was settled these troops should be transferred to the French Army.

The brigade was made up of two line battalions and a battalion of light infantry, a squadron of chasseurs, and a company of artillery. All except the light infantry were at Berne under the command of the Swiss General Vonderwerdt. Ney went to Berne and ordered that the troops there should march to Auxonne in Burgundy, and that the light infantry battalion should go to Milan to be attached to the Army of Italy. The departure of the Swiss troops from Berne was accompanied by some unfortunate events. On 25 March Vonderwerdt reviewed the two line battalions, read them a letter from Ney, praising their conduct while in the service of the Helvetian Government, and announced to them their early departure for France. After the review they were taken out of the town for a route march. During this exercise there was some show of insubordination among the men. A baseless rumour had spread among them that they were to be shipped off from France to San Domingo, and they were showing their resentment at this prospect.

When they returned to their quarters there was some anxiety among the officers at this display of feeling, and at Ney's suggestion the guards on the barrack gates were doubled. All was quiet until about eleven o'clock, then the men were suddenly called out by a trumpeter of the chasseurs sounding the assembly. It was evidently a pre-arranged signal of mutiny. The men disregarded the orders of their officers, overpowered the guards, and broke out of barracks. A French officer with a patrol came up and tried to induce them to return to their allegiance, but some of the mutineers fired at his party, and a corporal of the 42nd French Infantry fell mortally wounded. The officer with difficulty prevented his men from firing back, and retreated with his patrol to give the alarm.

Ney turned out all the French troops in Berne. The mutineers were marching to the arsenal in order to seize the cannon there. The French barred their way, and drove them back towards their barracks. They then lost heart and obeyed the orders of their officers to return to their quarters. By 1 a.m. the mutiny was over, but Ney kept the French troops under arms till sunrise.

Five of the ringleaders had been arrested. Next morning a court martial was convened for their trial. One of them was condemned to death and shot in the presence of the regiments that had mutinied. The four others were sentenced to long terms of imprisonment. On the 27th the Helvetian Brigade marched off for the French frontier without any further trouble. The men had been assured that they had been misled as to their intended destination.

Madame Ney had left La Petite Malgrange for Paris during her husband's absence in Switzerland. She was now expecting the birth of a child and Ney was anxious to be with her. The affairs of the Helvetian Republic were so far settled that he felt he could ask for leave of absence. This was granted to him at the end of March, and he spent nearly three months at Paris.

There on 8 May, 1803, his eldest son was born. He was named Joseph Napoleon in honour of the First Consul and his elder brother who were his godparents at his baptism.

He lived to be an officer for some years in the Swedish Army, then a Peer of France under the Orleans monarchy, and the "General Ney, Prince de la Moskowa" of the opening years of the Second Empire.

Ney returned to Switzerland on 25 June, 1803. The Diet had been summoned to meet at Freiburg on 4 July. There was an imposing military display on the opening day of the session to do honour to the president and the members of the Diet. The assembly accepted the honour and closed its eyes to the meaning of the fact that it met surrounded by foreign bayonets. The Landamann D'Affry delivered an inaugural address in which he praised the First Consul as the protector of the peace, freedom, and prosperity of the country. Ney, as the representative of France, replied in a long set speech in the style of the period, when it was the fashion to hail Bonaparte as the greatest of men.

There was no need, he told the deputies, to assure them of the First Consul's goodwill towards Switzerland. The "great man" who governed France had given practical proof of it. He had put an end to discord and restored social order in their country, the character of whose people made them worthy of his special protection. Then Ney went on :—

> "The day of the 18th Brumaire, from which France dates the revival of her prosperity, is also the epoch at which the people of Switzerland began to have a ray of hope for a change that would produce a state of affairs more stable and more suited to their way of life. Their expectations have been justified, and if this did not happen at an earlier date it was because the deep wounds of the French Revolution could not be healed at once. Great changes in the state had become indispensable, and these fully occupied the precious moments that Bonaparte consecrated to the welfare of the peoples whose interests he had so gloriously defended. His successes have brought about the tranquillity you now enjoy, and which it depends on yourselves to perpetuate."

He spoke of the Act of Mediation as having been inspired by "the benevolence which is characteristic of this extraordinary genius". Then he argued that the welfare of Switzerland must depend on intimate friendship with France. There was proof of this in the advantages the country had derived from its cordial relations with the French monarchy "before the unhappy period of revolutionary disturbance". The same advantages were now offered to them by the First Consul. The enemies of European peace had sought to misrepresent the motives of his intervention in their affairs. But such insinuations could only gain credit among men "who were incapable of appreciating the greatness of the hero's views". He offered them the permanent protection of France. The deputies of the Diet would be asked to discuss a military convention and a treaty of defensive alliance with the French Republic, a treaty honourable and advantageous to Switzerland. Ney ended by declaring that it was a happiness to him to have taken part in securing a stable organization of their government and to act as the interpreter of the First Consul's benevolent views in their regard.

It was a strange speech for the soldier of Valmy and the Rhine, to whom the Revolution had opened the way to rank and a great career. But like so many others he had been disillusioned by the course of events. He was no politician, but he had come to see in the strong rule of Bonaparte the one hope of France. He spoke the language of the new time of reaction against the disorders that had been the outcome of the Revolution. It was a time when men's minds were ready to accept the personal rule of the brilliant soldier whose genius had dazzled and captivated them.

On 9 July Ney handed to D'Affry the draft convention and treaty of alliance to be submitted to the Diet. It was proposed that the cantons should maintain the local militia, which had always been the basis of the Swiss system of national defence. There was to be no regular army. In case of war a "stiffening" for the Swiss levy *en masse* would be supplied by a contingent of French regular troops. But for centuries Switzers had served in foreign armies, and it was proposed that the country should supply to the French Army four regiments of infantry each 4000 strong. Four companies of grenadiers selected from these regiments would have "the honour" of being attached to the Consular Guard.

During the debates on the proposed treaty and convention some of the deputies expressed a fear that the Swiss regiments would be sent to San Domingo or some other tropical country, and ask to have a clause inserted in the convention restricting their service to Europe. Ney explained that the First Consul intended that they should be employed in Europe as a rule, but he suggested that a formal restricting clause might be objectionable in certain cases. For instance, supposing the First Consul resolved to put an end to the piracies of the Barbary States, would the Swiss regiments like to have it established that while Frenchmen went to northern Africa on such a glorious enterprise they would have to stand aside? After some discussion he obtained the First Consul's consent to a clause by which it was agreed that the Swiss contingent should not be asked to serve either in Asia or in America. This satisfied the deputies as it excluded far distant, oversea expeditions.

The Convention and Treaty were signed in September by Ney as the plenipotentiary of France and by D'Affry as the first Landamann of the Helvetian Republic. Talleyrand informed Ney of the First Consul's satisfaction with the zeal and intelligence he had displayed in the negotiations.

During the long debates his wife and infant son, with her youngest sister and her father, M. Auguié, had come to stay with Ney at Freiburg. The ladies of the temporary capital of Switzerland organized a fête to welcome Madame Ney, and her stay at Freiburg was a very happy time.

The session of the Diet was closed at the end of September. Besides securing the signature of the Treaty of Alliance Ney had obtained the passing of a law for the construction of several new highways in Switzerland. Amongst these were a road from Basel to Constance along the left bank of the Rhine; a new road over the St. Gothard Pass to replace the narrow mountain track by which it had been traversed for centuries; the improvement of the path over the Gemmi Pass and the construction of roads linking it on one side with Thun, and on the other with the new road the First Consul was having constructed over the Simplon. Ney had some difficulty in persuading the deputies to agree to these projects. It was objected that they would divert trade and traffic from existing routes, and so impoverish certain of the cantons. He succeeded in overcoming these objections, urging throughout the general gain to the trade of the country as a whole, and keeping in the background the military importance of the routes dealt with—which was Bonaparte's real object in carrying through his plans.

His work in Switzerland was now completed. But France was again at war with England. The Peace of Amiens had proved to be only a truce and hostilities had recommenced. The First Consul was already assembling the "Army of England" the future "Grand Army" of the Empire on the shores of the channel. Ney was anxious to cease for a while being a diplomatist, and to become a soldier once more. On 10 September he had written to the First Consul praising the good services of M. Rouyer, the second secretary of the French Legation in Switzerland, and asking for his promotion to the post of first secretary. And he added:—

"He could even act as *chargé d'affaires* if you wish to employ me with the armies destined to act against England, and if, nevertheless, it should be your intention to keep for me—as I would desire—the position of Minister Plenipotentiary in Helvetia."

Rouyer received the promotion asked for. But on 17 December General Vial was appointed Plenipotentiary at Freiburg, and Ney was directed to hand over the legation to him and prepare to return to France for employment with the "Army of England". On the 27th he received a letter from the Minister of War ordering him to return at once to Paris, where he would receive his letters of service and instructions for the command of the camp of Montreuil near Boulogne.

Next day D'Affry handed to him an official letter conveying the thanks of himself and his colleagues for his services to the Helvetian Republic, expressing his personal feelings of friendship, and asking him to accept as a souvenir of his stay in Switzerland a gold snuff-box set with diamonds. Ney left Freiburg with his wife and child on 5 January, 1804, and reached Paris on the 9th. The great years of his military career were about to begin.

CHAPTER VIII

THE CAMP OF BOULOGNE—THE COMING OF THE EMPIRE
(1804-1805)

DURING his stay in Paris before joining the "Army of England" Ney met for the last time his old chief, Moreau, the victor of Hohenlinden. He was unemployed and took no part in public affairs. Napoleon regarded him as a dangerous man, for among those who formed the "old guard" of the Republican party and regarded the First Consul's absolutism as an undoing of the work of the Revolution, Moreau was spoken of as a possible leader in a last effort to avert a despotism. He was soon to be imprisoned and driven into exile by his all-powerful rival.

Moreau had a great liking for Ney and was disappointed at what he regarded as his defection from his former political creed. "So you go to the Tuileries now," he said to the young General when he met him,—as much as to say, "You are playing the courtier after all". The writer[1] of Ney's "Memoirs" puts into his mouth a defence of the First Consul's policy, and then goes on to tell how Moreau ridiculed Bonaparte's preparations for the invasion of England, and gave it as his opinion that to talk of ferrying an army across the channel in flotillas of small craft, despite the efforts of the British fleet, was a folly. Ney is made to reply with a long lecture on possible solutions of the problem and a final declaration of his

[1] This was the Marshal's second son, born in 1804, after the return of the Neys from Switzerland. He was christened Michel Aloys, the last name being that of the patriot, Reding. He was the Duke of Elchingen of the days of the Orleans monarchy and the Second Empire. He died of cholera at Gallipoli in 1854 when in command of a cavalry brigade sent to the East for the Crimean War. There were two younger children—Eugène Ney who entered the diplomatic service of Louis Philippe and died in 1847, and Napoleon Henri Edgar Ney born on the eve of the Russian campaign of 1812. He was the Prince Edgar Ney of the Second Empire, a senator and general of division and aide-de-camp to Napoleon III. He survived until 1882.

belief in the First Consul's genius. The alleged record of the dispute is not convincing. One cannot imagine Ney lecturing his old commander on the strategy of a cross channel expedition, or Moreau listening patiently to his somewhat long-winded theorizing. All we can safely say is, that, when the two old comrades met, they found that in the years since Hohenlinden they had drifted far apart. Moreau was still the old soldier of the Revolution. Ney had accepted accomplished facts and thrown in his fortunes with those of Bonaparte. He was to rise and fall with him.

The First Consul had assembled on the shores of the Channel the army destined for the invasion of England. It was never to venture on the enterprise that gave it its official name, but in the camps of Boulogne the men who had fought in Italy and on the Rhine were welded into the "Grand Army" that was to march victoriously across Europe. From first to last 172,000 men were collected together in the Boulogne camps, and an innovation of far-reaching importance in the methods of warfare was made when they were for the first time permanently organized in Army Corps—each a subordinate army, complete in all arms, and provided with its own transport and supply departments. The camps stretched out for miles along the coast on each side of Boulogne and reserves were assembled in the inland towns of the north. For the transport of the army across the Channel more than four thousand gunboats and flat-bottomed barges were constructed, and for their concentration in the harbours and creeks of the channel the ports were improved, estuaries of the rivers dredged and deepened, and batteries erected for the protection of the flotillas.

The 6th Army Corps of which Ney was given the command was on the extreme left of the line of coast camps. Its long rows of "baraques" or wooden huts had been erected about the village of Étaples and on both banks of the little River Canche, the estuary of which was crowded with the light craft of the transport flotilla and defended by powerful batteries on the land and lines of gunboats moored across the river mouth. The camp of the 6th Corps was known as the "Camp of Montreuil" from the little town of that name seven miles inland where Ney had his head-quarters.[1] There were three divisions of infantry and a brigade of cavalry, about 20,000 men in all. The 1st Division (General Dupont) was encamped on the right facing the sea behind the village of Camiers. The 2nd (General Loison) had a brigade on the right and another on the left of the town of Étaples; 3rd (General Partounneaux) was encamped 1500 metres in rear of it, near the River Canche, with a regiment detached on the left bank.

The Comte de Fezensac, who afterwards served on Ney's staff and rose to the rank of a general of division, was then serving in the ranks of one of Partounneaux's regiments. In his "Souvenirs Militaires" he gives an interesting account of the life of the Boulogne camps. Working parties of men and officers had constructed the *baraques* which gradually developed into a series of wood-built towns stretching for miles along the shore. To give more head room, without using too much timber to raise the height of the wooden walls, the floor had been sunk to a depth of about three feet below the general level of the ground. This made the huts very damp during the winter. The furniture was made up of rough wooden tables and benches, racks for arms and equipments, and hurdles supported on wooden uprights to serve as bedsteads. Once the huts were completed the men passed a great part of the day in comparative idleness. There were regimental parades and drills in the mornings. From time to time a company took its turn of service on board the flotilla. The men had very little to do except to learn to make themselves as comfortable as they could on board the boats and get used to life in such narrow and crowded conditions.

It has often been said that the camps by the shore of the Channel were "camps of exercise" where the Grand Army went through a prolonged course of training, divisions and army corps became accustomed to acting together, and the generals had frequent practice in handling great masses of men. But De Fezensac's evidence contradicts this. Parades of more than a single regiment appear to have been rare events.

[1] The commanders of the other five corps of the army were: 1st Corps, Bernadotte; 2nd Corps, Marmont; 3rd Corps, Davoût; 4th Corps, Soult; 5th Corps, Lannes; Cavalry Reserve, Murat.

There was some divisional route marches, but very few great field days or manœuvres. And we hear little of artillery or musketry practices. In such a camp in our own day one of the first works put in hand would have been the construction of rifle ranges. But in 1804 the recruit learned to load, fire, and clean his musket, and after his first course seldom fired a shot except in action. Then the firing was at such close quarters that it was considered he would do enough execution with his forty cartridges without having previously expended costly ammunition on mere target practice. In the Boulogne camps all that was required was that each man should fire *three* ball cartridges at a target at point-blank range.

Once enough huts had been erected to house the officers and men other rough buildings were run up to serve as canteens, theatres, concert halls, and gymnasium and fencing rooms. These helped the troops to pass away much of their idle time, and in the summer they amused themselves with laying out gardens and planting avenues of shrubs about their huts. Discipline seems to have been excellent and the health of the men after the first winter was good.

Madame Ney came to live at her husband's head-quarters, at first at Montreuil and afterwards at a small country house which he rented for her at Recque a few miles further inland. Both at Montreuil and at Recque there were numerous entertainments, at which the higher military society of the camps and visitors from Paris supplied the guests. Her old school friend Hortense Beauharnais, afterwards Queen of Holland, spent some weeks with Aglaé Ney and one of her sisters in the "château" at Recque. In connexion with this social side of the Boulogne camps we hear incidentally in De Léoncourt's memoirs of an unfortunate speculation of the Ney's. The aide-de-camp tells how the staff of the 6th Corps gave a fête in honour of Madame Ney, and had constructed a huge paper fire balloon to be sent up that evening, but abandoned this part of their programme when some one reminded them that it might be regarded by the General as an illusion to a project over which he had been victimized to the extent of 30,000 francs. An adventurer had come to Montreuil and persuaded Ney that he could construct a dirigible balloon for scouting purposes, and the General had been so pleased with the idea, that he had advanced the inventor the money he asked for with which the man had promptly disappeared.

There was from time to time a break in the monotony of camp life when English cruisers or gunboats approached the shore, and exchanged fire with the guardships of the flotilla or the batteries. And their were occasional scares—some of them ridiculous enough, including some wild outbreaks of the spy-mania. There would be reports of agents of "perfidious Albion" prowling about the camps, to learn what was well known to all Europe, and there were tales of projects for burning the huts over the men's heads. These alarms led to doubling of sentinels, extra guards, patrols moving round the outskirts of the wooden towns with orders to fire on anyone who approached after dark. The worst scare was caused by a report circulated in the middle of March, 1804, by General Vilatte, one of the brigadiers of Ney's corps. On 16 March Vilatte wrote from his post at the battery of St. Frieux to General Soult, at the head-quarters of the "Army of England" at St. Omers:—

"Mon Général,

"The English, unable to conquer us by open force, are having recourse to their last resource—*the plague*.

"Five bales of cotton have just been cast upon our coast; I hasten to inform you of it.

"From St. Frieux to the mouth of the Canche all the troops are at their posts; patrols are moving along the beach accompanied by custom-house officers.

"In sight of this battery and almost within cannon shot, are a frigate and two sloops of war of the enemy; also several small fishing boats, which I presume contain other bales of cotton.

"As no one is allowed to take out any boat or vessel I have just received orders to fire at everything that may appear in the waters within range of our batteries."

Vilatte was so full of the idea himself that he did not consider it necessary to explain to Soult that the cotton bales were supposed to be infected with pestilence—the plague with which the French soldiers had made a disastrous acquaintance in Egypt. The panic fairly took hold of the camps. The English were supposed to be capable of any abominable treachery.

It was the time of the conspiracy of Cadoudal and Pichegru. Assassins hired by the Bourbons and the British were supposed to be lurking everywhere in France. So Vilatte's suspicion of the "flotsam and jetsam" left by the receding tide in front of his battery found general credit. An order was issued which ran thus: "All are hereby forbidden to approach any boats or other objects that may be cast on shore." The alarm reached the capital and the First Consul wrote to Ney:—

"I am informed, Citizen General, that the English have thrown bales of cotton upon our coast, which has led to the supposition that those bales are poisoned. Give me all the particulars you can collect on this matter. It would be lamentable to think that every principle of humanity could be thus violated.

"BONAPARTE.

"MALMAISON, 30*th Ventose*, Year XII."
(21 *March*, 1804.)[1]

Bonaparte perhaps believed the story and would not have been sorry to add it to his indictment against "the English assassins". He was collecting all the evidence available as to the conspiracies against him, in order thoroughly to break up the opposition to the project of the Empire, by involving all the old-fashioned Republicans in the charges against the real plotters. Ney's investigations pricked the bubble of the "plague-infected" bales. The cause of all the alarm was found to be the stranding on the shore of some old hammocks lost from a ship in the channel.

The First Consul took advantage of the Royalist conspiracy to secure for himself the Imperial Crown. The first argument put forward in the Senate and the Corps Legislative in favour of the inauguration of the Empire was that, when once France had returned to a hereditary system of Government, and proclaimed that the death of one Emperor would be followed immediately by the accession of another, there would be no longer a motive for the enemies of France to seek to compass the assassination of her soldier-chief. During the period when the new imperial constitution was being debated the Army sent a

[1] This was the very day of the execution of the Duc d'Enghien.

number of addresses to the First Consul, calling upon him to assume the title of Emperor. In the Boulogne camps efforts were made at first to prevent the holding of large gatherings of the soldiers to discuss these addresses, and it was suggested that it would be sufficient for a delegate from the rank and file of each company to confer with the regimental officers. But the agitation was something of a diversion from the routine of camp life, and the assemblies of companies to select delegates were followed by meetings of regiments and brigades and even divisions, to the peril of military discipline.

Ney had received from many of his lieutenants—Divisional generals, brigadiers, and colonels—loyal addresses to the First Consul. He forwarded them to Paris adding to them an address from the 6th Corps as a whole, a long-winded rhetorical document. The Army was then invited to join in the plebiscite, which, by a majority of 3,572,329 votes against 2,569, called upon Napoleon to assume the Imperial Crown. On 18 May, 1804, the Empire was proclaimed, and in the Boulogne camps the event was announced amid the roar of hundreds of saluting cannon.

Having assumed a crown Napoleon proceeded to create a military aristocracy. On 21 February, 1793, the Convention had decreed the abolition of the rank of Marshal of France, which dated back to the time of Philip Augustus. At St. Cloud on 19 May Napoleon signed a decree reviving the dignity, and at the same time promoting to the Marshalate eighteen soldiers of the wars of the Revolution.

The name of Alexandre Berthier headed the list. He was his right-hand man as a soldier—his chief of the staff, on whom he relied for the execution of his orders. Next to Berthier came Murat, to whom he had given the hand of his sister Caroline. Then there came the names of Moncey, Jourdan, Masséna, Augereau, Bernadotte, Soult, Brune, Lannes, Mortier, Ney, Davoût, and Bessières. All these were men who had held high command in the field, and were still in the prime of life and fit to be the leaders of his armies in coming wars. Four names were added of men, who were more advanced in years, and whose promotion was a recognition of past services to France, and a link between the Empire and the earlier glories of the Republic. These were Kellerman, Lefèbvre, Perignon, and Sérurier.[1]

Ney's promotion to the Marshalate gave him with his new rank the annual income of 40,000 francs attached to it. To this was presently added 20,000 francs a year as the income attached to the decoration of Grand Cross of the Legion of Honour. These payments were in addition to the pay and allowances of any command that he might hold.

The regimental officers and the soldiers of the army were gratified by a liberal distribution of the decoration of the Legion of Honour. The enamelled crosses and red ribbons were given by the Emperor himself to the selected men of the Paris garrison at the great military review held on the Champ de Mars on 14 July. At the same time a supply of the same coveted decoration was sent to the commanders of the Boulogne camps. Ney received a parcel of 207 crosses of the Legion for the officers and men of the 6th Corps, which meant that about one man in every hundred would be decorated. But the officers and soldiers were disappointed at the idea that they were to be enrolled in the Legion of Honour by the Marshals, while their comrades of Paris had received the decoration from the hands of the Emperor himself. Ney therefore wrote to Napoleon on 25 July:—

> "It is my duty to acquaint your Majesty with the feelings of regret expressed by the general officers at not receiving this glorious decoration from your Majesty's own hands. They had flattered themselves that they would be as fortunate as those members of the Legion of Honour, who were present at the ceremony of 14 July at Paris. This desire, in which I participate, arises from our attachment to your Majesty, and you will give an additional value to your favours if you confer them in person."

Doubtless others addressed the same request to the Emperor. The result was the announcement that on 15 August Napoleon would visit the camps of Boulogne and preside at a great military display, at which the Legion of Honour would be distributed to more than 1500 generals, officers, and men of the "Army of England".

Marshal Soult, who was in general command of the camps,

[1] It may be interesting to complete the roll of Napoleon's Marshals and note that at later dates he promoted to this rank, Victor, Macdonald, Oudinot, Marmont, Suchet, Gouvion St. Cyr, Poniatowski, and Grouchy.

ordered that while leaving strong contingents to guard the coast and the batteries, 100,000 men should concentrate at Boulogne on the eve of the Emperor's fête. Two miles from the town on the Calais road a lofty platform was erected, on which the Emperor was to be enthroned facing the sea. Between him and the beach the selected troops of the six army corps were to be formed in a great semi-circle. On the water beyond some hundred ships of the flotilla were anchored. Boulogne was gay with flags, garlands of flowers, and triumphal arches. It was a cloudless day, with a breeze from the sea that tempered the midsummer heat. The Emperor rode through Boulogne escorted by the Cuirassiers of the Guard and surrounded by a brilliant staff, and as he reached the review ground he was greeted with the thunders of artillery from sea and shore, and the enthusiastic cheers of his 100,000 soldiers and of the tens of thousands of spectators that crowded the surrounding slopes. From his lofty throne he looked out on the vast array of glittering bayonets, and saw beyond the great semi-circle of ordered masses of men the forest of masts of the flotilla. And further still in the haze upon the distant sea the sunlight showed white flecks moving near the horizon. These were the only objects in view that could for a moment abate his pride in the spectacle, for he was told that they were the sails of British cruisers, watching Boulogne in the expectation that the sudden concentration of troops might be the prelude of an embarkation. The presence of these watchful enemies was a reminder to him that he had yet to solve the problem of obtaining the command of the channel even for a day.

On gilded pedestals to right and left of his throne two reversed helmets had been placed. They were said to have once been worn in battle by Duguesclin and Bayard. They now served as receptacles for the crosses, which the Emperor was to distribute, and were thus to be a link between the chivalrous traditions of old France and the new chivalry of the Legion of Honour. There was then a long procession of officers and men to the platform of the Emperor's throne. As each came forward to receive his decoration the Marshal, commanding the army corps to which he belonged, briefly recited his claim to the membership of the Legion. Napoleon as he pinned the ribbon on the men's uniforms had a word for each—a reminder of Egypt or Italy for those he had himself commanded, an allusion to campaigns and victories on the Rhine for those of the northern armies, which he had now fused into one great fighting force with his own veterans. During this part of the ceremony the bands played martial airs.

Then the newly invested Legionaries were grouped before the throne, and the Emperor rose and read the oath they were to take—a formula containing no mention of personal allegiance to himself, but so drawn up as seemingly to pledge them only to defend the results obtained by the Revolution, and naming not the Empire but the Republic that was still supposed to survive under Imperial forms:—

"You severally swear upon your honour to devote yourselves to the service of the Republic, to co-operate with all your power in maintaining the integrity of its territory and defending its government, its laws, and the rights of property recognized by these laws. You swear to oppose by every means, which justice, law, and reason allow, all attempts to re-establish feudalism with its titles and the privileges which they conferred. You swear, in short, to co-operate with all your might in the maintenance of liberty and equality. You swear to defend at the peril of your lives the honour of the French name, your country and the institutions and laws by which it is governed."

"*Nous le jurons!* We swear it!" shouted the Legionaries in chorus. The cry was re-echoed by the masses of troops beyond them, and then came shouts of "*Vive l'Empereur!*" with waving of swords and fluttering of hats held aloft on bayonets, while the cannon roared out again on sea and shore. During these salutes and acclamations a long line of gunboats under sail was seen making for Boulogne from the southward, hugging the coast, for the British cruisers were standing in towards the shore. For a while it seemed that the Emperor was to witness a naval engagement. The batteries of the port had been manned, but the only firing was the succession of salutes as the flotilla of forty-seven sail slipped into the port. It had twice narrowly escaped the enemy on its voyage from Havre.

The day ended with a banquet for the Emperor and his marshals, military sports for the men, who were supplied with extra rations and wine to drink Napoleon's health, and after dark a splendid display of fireworks. As the last great flight of rockets hissed up into the sky a *feu de joie* was fired by a line of 15,000 men, whose muskets were loaded with cartridges that shot out coloured stars.

Then the camps went back to the daily round of monotonous duty. On 1 October towards evening Lord Keith's squadron attacked the flotilla and tried to destroy it by sending a number of barges laden with explosives drifting in upon it with the tide. Little damage was done, but all through the night there was firing along the coast. After this for months to come the camps and flotillas were undisturbed. Ney arranged that during the winter the officers of each brigade should meet for military conferences, and he had prepared for them a series of elaborate essays on the manœuvres of all three arms. These must have cost him much time and labour. They were an attempt to simplify the somewhat complicated methods of command already in use, but the movements described were still of a kind that could only be carried out by highly drilled troops working with machine-like precision.

At the end of November Ney was summoned to Paris for the fêtes of the coronation. But on the great day he had no place in the ceremony itself. He was one of the crowd of distinguished spectators who looked on from the galleries erected in Nôtre Dame. On 9 January he was present at the fête offered to the Empress Josephine at the opera by the marshals. There was a concert followed by a ball. It was an expensive evening for him, for the marshals supplied the cost of the fête and the contribution of each of them was fixed at 10,000 francs.

He returned to his command at Montreuil in February and soon after this the camps were stirred with a new impulse to energetic activity. Villeneuve was about to make his dash from Toulon and through the Straits of Gibraltar and lure Nelson away to the Indies, and then he was to return swiftly across the Atlantic, and, if all went well, the French fleets were suddenly to combine in the Channel and secure the brief mastery of the narrow seas that was all Napoleon asked as the necessary condition for his invasion of England.

On 21 March Marshal Berthier sent Ney the detailed

instructions to be followed when the moment came for the embarkation, assigning to each unit of the 6th Corps the sections of the flotilla on which it was to make the voyage across the Channel. Then there was almost daily practice in embarking and disembarking. This was done first by regiments, then by whole brigades. Every man and officer learned to go to his place in the boats and dispose his arms and equipment in them. The horses were practised in walking up and down the gangways, and sometimes kept for a day and a night on board the horse boats. Then there were exercises in the embarking and disembarking of whole divisions. Finally it was announced that the whole army must be prepared to embark at the briefest notice. The Emperor and his personal staff had arrived at Boulogne. The word went round that the day had at last come for opening the "campaign of England".

Ney's corps was to embark in the estuary of the Canche. The transport flotillas were moored close to the shore along both banks. The order was issued to parade for embarkation. The troops formed up in parallel columns, the head of each column facing its own section of the boats. A gun was fired. Generals and other mounted officers dismounted, placed themselves on foot at the head of their men, and left their horses to be led by the grooms to the horse boats. The men unfixed bayonets. A second gun was fired, and the order passed along the lines "Prepare to embark". Then quickly came the report of a third gun, and the order "Forward, march". The men cheered enthusiastically as they marched to the boats. So well had they been trained by the preliminary practices that in ten and a half minutes the 25,000 men of Ney's corps were all on board of the flotilla. There was a brief pause and then came the report of a fourth gun. The men began cheering again, for they took it for the signal to the boats to unmoor and put to sea. But instead there came the disappointing order to disembark. It was only one more drill. In thirteen minutes all were out of the boats and reformed on the shore. After this successful experiment all the stores and most of the guns and horses were kept on board the transports.

In July it was known that Villeneuve had evaded Nelson

and was back in European waters. Napoleon sent him urgent messages bidding him join the Brest fleet and enter the Channel at any cost. He was already on his way when he was scared back to Cadiz by false information. Napoleon's great plan had failed.

At the same time there came news of danger on the Continent itself. England had formed a fresh coalition against the Empire. Austria had declared war against France. In August the marshals commanding the Army Corps of the Boulogne camps received sudden orders to make a rapid march to the Rhine. The "Army of England" had become the "Grand Army" and Napoleon's great career of victory was about to begin.

CHAPTER IX

THE CAMPAIGN OF ULM AND AUSTERLITZ (1805)

THE foundation of the Third Coalition against France had been laid as early as April, 1805, by the signing of a treaty of alliance between England and Russia. In August Austria, having completed her war preparations, joined the Coalition. Sweden had already entered the alliance. The Bourbons of Naples threw in their lot with it on the eve of hostilities. The allies had adopted an ambitious plan of operations. The Archduke Charles with 150,000 men was to cross the Adige and invade the territory of the former Cisalpine Republic, now Napoleon's "Kingdom of Italy". The Neapolitan Army reinforced by British troops from Malta and Russians from Corfu was to move northwards. There was to be a combined British, Russian, and Swedish expedition to recover the Kingdom of Hanover. From Vienna the Archduke Ferdinand was to march on the Rhine at the head of 60,000 Austrian and 90,000 Russian troops. A third Austrian army of 50,000 men in the Tyrol would be ready to co-operate either northward with the Archduke Ferdinand or southwards with the Archduke Charles. In all more than 400,000 were to take the field. It was estimated that the most that Napoleon could oppose to them would be 200,000.

But the allies were not ready to strike at once. Their main army was concentrating about Vienna. The Russians under Kutusoff were marching to join them, but they had many a hundred miles to go, and could not hope to cross the Inn for some weeks. Instead of waiting for them, the Austrians decided to send forward 60,000 men into South Germany, to enforce the neutrality of the Electors of Baden, Wurtemberg, and Bavaria, who were Napoleon's allies. The army that crossed the Inn and occupied Munich in August was commanded by General Mack, who had a quite undeserved reputation as a strategist and tactician. The Bavarians retired northwards, and Mack pushed on to the upper Danube, where acting on recognized traditions he took up his position along the line of the river Iller with his right at Ulm, his front facing the Black Forest, through the defiles of which he expected the French would advance as they had so often done in previous wars.

Napoleon was ready. He had the Grand Army in the camps by the Channel on a war footing and ready to march at brief notice. He recognized that the central theatre of war on the Danube was the place where the struggle would be decided. His plan was to strike swiftly there before the Russo-Austrian Army could concentrate, and to direct the first blow at Mack's advanced position. He could march against him with 150,000 men. Masséna in northern Italy had 50,000 more. He made no effort to reinforce him, told him to do what he could to delay the enemy on that side, and relied on deciding the conflict by his own advance on Vienna.

He did not mean merely to drive back Mack's army to the Inn. He meant to destroy it. He was about to carry out in the most decisive way a plan analogous to that which he had proposed to Moreau five years before. The Austrian army about Ulm was again the objective and in the coming campaign the knowledge of the ground about Ulm which Ney had acquired in the first stage of the campaign of Hohenlinden was to serve him to good purpose.

Ney's orders for the march of his corps to the Rhine were dated "9th Fructidor, Year XIII"—27 August, 1805.[1] They were sent to him by Berthier from Boulogne that morning. The cavalry and the 1st and 2nd Divisions moved off on the 31st, the 3rd Division on 1 September.

The following was the organization of the 6th Corps at the opening of the campaign of Ulm and Austerlitz:—

Corps Commander. Marshal Ney.

Chief of the Staff. General Dutaillis. Assistant chief. Colonel Jomini.

[1] It was on 26 August that Napoleon learned that Villeneuve had turned back to Cadiz.

MARSHAL NEY

FROM AN ENGRAVING BY W. READ

1st Division. General Dupont.
- 1st Brigade. General Rouyère. 9th Light Infantry (two battalions) and two guns.
- 2nd Brigade. General Marchand. 32nd and 96th of the Line (each two battalions) and six guns.

2nd Division. General Loison.
- 1st Brigade. General Roguet. 6th Light Infantry (three battalions), 19th of the Line (two battalions), and two guns.
- 2nd Brigade. General Vilatte. 69th of the Line (two battalions), and 76th (three battalions), and six guns.

3rd Division. General Malher.
- 1st Brigade. General Marcognet. 22nd Light Infantry (two battalions), 27th of the Line (two battalions), and two guns.
- 2nd Brigade. General Labassée. 50th and 59th of the Line (each two battalions), and six guns.

Cavalry. General Tilly.
- 1st and 3rd Hussars, 10th Chasseurs-à-cheval, and twelve guns.

The combatant strength of the corps was about 21,250 men. In a modern army the proportion of artillery for such numbers would be at least eighty guns. Ney had only thirty-six. And there must have been extra difficulty in the ammunition supply for they were of four different calibres and patterns including six field howitzers, six 4-pounders, eighteen 8-pounders, and six 12-pounders, and the guns of each type were not grouped together. The guns attached to the cavalry brigade were not horse artillery, but apparently the artillery reserve of the corps for they were not light pieces that could move rapidly with a mounted column, but howitzers, and 8- and 12-pounders.

Colonel Jomini, who had joined Ney at Montreuil, accompanied him on the campaign as his guest, without any defined duties. He was a Swiss officer of the Canton of Vaud, who had seen something of war on a small scale in the militia of his native country, and had studied its history and principles to such good effect that in 1804 he was preparing his "Traité des Grandes Opérations Militaires". Ney thought highly of it, brought it to the attention of Napoleon, obtained for Jomini a commission in the French Army, and attached him to his staff. Jomini served with Ney for some years, and in his subsequently published writings on Napoleon's campaigns he claims for himself the credit of having inspired some of the Marshal's most brilliant strokes of leadership and even asserts that more than once he saved his chief from disaster by inducing him to change his orders at the last moment. These claims of Jomini are at least open to some doubt, for the testimony of De Fezensac, De Léoncourt, and other officers, who served on Ney's staff all goes to prove that the Marshal when in command was very reticent, and equally self-reliant, never holding a council of war or even consulting his staff individually, but simply leaving it to them to transmit and execute his orders.

Ney having seen the last of his divisions march out of camp paid a flying visit to Paris and rejoined the 6th Corps at St. Dizier. It reached the Rhine at Seltz and Lauterbourg twenty-six days after its departure from Étaples. It was a march of 350 miles by way of Arras, Rheims, Châlons, Vitry, St. Dizier, Nancy, and Saverne. There was excellent discipline and order, and Ney gave leave to soldiers whose homes were within a moderate distance of the line of march to visit their families. All rejoined before the Rhine was reached. The troops lived on supplies requisitioned on the way, for which receipts were given. These were promptly turned into cash by the local authorities.

By the third week of August the six columns of the Grand Army were on the Rhine from Mayence to Strasburg.[1] Napoleon's plan of campaign was to send some of Murat's cavalry through the Black Forest to give Mack a confirmation of his idea that the French were advancing upon him from the westward, but to direct the march of the columns of his army in a great wheel round the northern end of the Forest hills, and then to the crossings of the Danube beyond Ulm with the view of cutting the Austrian Army off from its lines of supply and retreat and forcing it to surrender.

Ney had been informed that when he reached Seltz he would find a bridge ready for him, but though this had been ordered the work had not even been begun. He chose a place

[1] From left to right (north to south) they stood thus: 1st Corps (Bernadotte) Frankfurt-on-Main; 2nd (Marmont) Mayence; 3rd (Davoût) opposite Mannheim; 4th (Soult) Speyer; 6th (Ney) Seltz; 5th (Lannes), Imperial Guard (Bessières) and Cavalry Reserve (Murat) with Napoleon's head-quarters at Strasburg.

near Lauterbourg where roads on both banks led down to a ferry, and islands in the broad stream would facilitate the construction of his bridge, collected boats, barges and timber, and himself superintended the throwing of a floating roadway across the Rhine. The actual work was all done in fifteen hours. On 27 September the 6th Corps crossed the river. The men had fastened sprigs of oak leaves to their caps and coats "in anticipation of laurels," says De Fezensac. There was the utmost enthusiasm as for hour after hour the long column of foot, horse, and cannon poured across the floating bridges. On the right bank Ney was on horseback with his staff and the divisional generals, and was greeted with cries of "*Vive l'Empereur!*" as the men marched past him. The 1st Division occupied Carlsruhe the same day. Ney had the whole of his corps concentrated at Stuttgart on 30 September. There was a halt till 3 October, to enable the other corps to reach the points assigned to them on a long front extending from Stuttgart on the right to Wurtzburg on the left.

All were in position by the evening of 2 October, the heads of the columns facing to the east and south-east. On the 3rd there began the great wheeling march to the southward, the Army Corps gradually closing nearer each other, and their march being directed to the crossings of the Danube below Ulm. Ney's corps on the right formed the pivot of the wheeling movement and was nearest to the main mass of the enemy. Mack at Ulm was still in ignorance of the presence of the whole of the Grand Army to the north of him, and was expecting it to appear from the westward behind the cavalry screen thrown forward from the hills of the Black Forest.

The march to the Danube was a trying time for the men. The weather had become cold. There were frequent showers of chilling rain that later turned to sleet and snow. The supply arrangements of the 6th Corps had broken down, and the attempt to collect food and forage from the country gave but poor results and led to no little disorder and plundering, despite Ney's efforts to organize regular requisitions. Often the men and officers were half starved. But in wet, cold, and hunger they plodded on. On the 7th Murat on the left forced the crossing of the Danube at Donauwörth and began to advance on Ulm by the south bank, followed by the corps of Lannes and Soult and the Guard. Marmont and Davoût crossed next day further east at Neuburg, and began to sweep round to the south of the Austrian positions. Ney on the right was ordered to attack the bridges of Leipheim and Guntzburg.

He entrusted the operation to his 3rd Division under General Malher. The bad weather had made the approaches to the bridge at Leipheim impracticable. The ground had become a mere marsh. The attack was therefore directed against the bridges of Guntzburg. The town is on the south bank and there are several wooded islands in the river, across which the road and its bridges reach the place. The islands were occupied with little difficulty, and then it was found that the main span of the bridge between the last island and the south bank had been wrecked. Attempts to restore it under the fire of the enemy ended in failure and loss. An attack was then directed against another bridge further down the river. Here some of the roadway had been removed, but the bridge was still passable, and late on 9 October it was stormed by the 59th Infantry, whose Colonel was mortally wounded as he led it across. The French, as they formed on the shore, were attacked by infantry and cavalry, but beat them off, the fighting continuing till after dark. But De Fezensac, who was serving as a lieutenant with the 59th, says the Austrian attacks were very half-hearted, and gave him the impression that the enemy were only making a demonstration to cover their retreat from Guntzburg. On the morning of the 10th it was found that the place had been abandoned by the Austrians. It was occupied by Ney and the main bridge was repaired in a few hours.

It was only on 5 October that Mack had discovered the presence of the columns of the Grand Army moving from the north-westward towards the Danube. To use his own expression, he was like a man waking from a dream. He could easily have retired towards the Tyrol or the Lower Inn, but he could not form any fixed resolution, and day after day he changed his plans. First he concentrated most of his army between Ulm and Guntzburg. Then he pushed a corps under

General Auffenberg eastward on the south bank of the river as a prelude to a march in that direction. Auffenberg was beaten by Murat at Wertingen. Mack then jumped to the conclusion that the French were all across the river in this direction, and decided on crossing at Guntzburg and breaking out to the northward. But here on the 9th he found Ney attacking. He felt that wherever he turned the French barred his way, and ignorant of the fact that there was only a single corps in his front at this point he gave up his plan, and fought a rear-guard action at Guntzburg to cover his own retirement on Ulm. Fezensac had judged rightly that the Austrians were making only a half-hearted fight.

Napoleon expected that Mack would break out to the southward to reach the Tyrol, and was therefore directing the march of the left columns of the Grand Army on Memmingen. Murat followed by Lannes was moving directly on Ulm by the south bank. Ney was to watch Ulm and (greatly to his disgust) was told to take his orders from Murat. On the west and north the place was watched by a screen of cavalry detachments.

Neither Lannes nor Ney liked being thus placed under Murat's command. They felt that the young cavalry leader owed the position thus given to him chiefly to the fact that he was the Emperor's brother-in-law, and they had no confidence in his generalship, whatever might be his prowess at the head of a cavalry division on the actual field of battle. The very first order that Murat issued to Ney led to a dispute between them. On 10 October—the day after the victory of Guntzburg—Murat ordered Ney to bring over the whole of the 6th Corps to the south bank of the Danube, leaving only Bourcier's division of dismounted dragoons to watch the north front of Ulm. Ney rode over to Murat's head-quarters and, supported by Lannes, pointed out to him that part of the 6th Corps ought to be left on the north bank, for, if Mack broke out on that side, Bourcier was not strong enough to stop him, and the Austrians could make a rapid march to the eastward, sweeping up on the way the supply and ammunition trains of the Grand Army which were now toiling along the roads by which the various corps had reached the crossings of the river east of

Ulm. Murat yielded so far as to tell Ney he might leave Dupont's division on the north bank. Ney said this would not be enough, and, spreading out a map on the table, tried to make Murat realize the opportunity that was being given to Mack. Murat refused to continue the discussion, and turned away from the map. "I understand nothing of your plans," he said angrily. "It is my way to make mine in the presence of the enemy." And after this ill-tempered speech he reiterated his formal order to Ney to bring his cavalry and Loison and Malher's divisions across to join his own force, leaving only Dupont to assist in watching Ulm. He had the Emperor's orders he said to combine the 5th and 6th Corps with his cavalry force, and even in leaving Dupont on the north side he was departing from his instructions.

Murat was wrong and Ney was right, as events soon showed. The Emperor never meant that in order to command the two corps placed at his disposal he was necessarily to unite them on the same ground, and in a letter sent to Murat on the 12th he spoke of the advisability of his having a bridge thrown across the Danube between Guntzburg and Ulm to facilitate the combined action of the troops on both banks, and told him he must be ready to reinforce those on the north side if necessary.

But Mack had already moved. On the 11th he attacked Bourcier and Dupont along the north front of Ulm, from Haslach on the left to near Elchingen on the Danube on his right. Dupont had only some 6000 men against four or five times that number of Austrians, but he made such a splendid fight and such a determined show of opposition to the pursuit during his retreat on Albeck, that Mack thought he must have good support near at hand, and did not follow up his success. Next day the Austrians did nothing. Then at last Mack thought the way was open for a retirement north-eastwards to Bohemia, sent off an advanced guard 18,000 strong under General Werneck, prepared to follow with the main body, and posted Riesch's division at Elchingen on the Danube to protect the crossing there from a possible advance of the French against his flank. Riesch was to follow as the rear-guard as soon as the main column was well on its way.

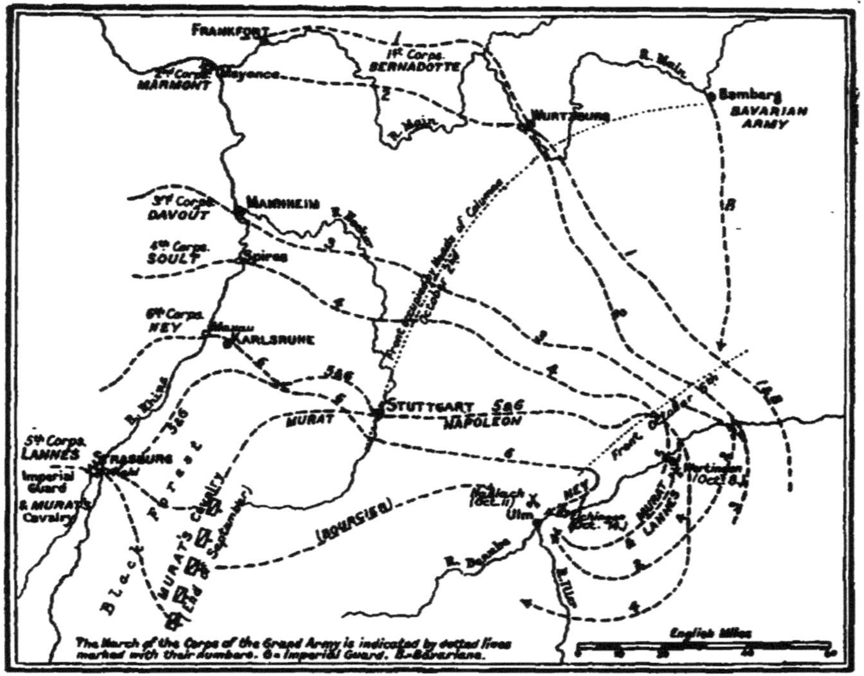

THE CAMPAIGN OF ULM. 1805.

When he heard of Dupont's defeat Napoleon realized that it left Mack free to march out of Ulm. He hastened to repair the mischief that Murat's blunder had caused, but if Mack had been more decided and energetic it would have been too late. Thanks to his slowness the Emperor was able again to shut him up in Ulm. Napoleon had hurried to the front, and reached Murat's head-quarters on the south bank near Ulm on 13 October. Ney heard in silence the unjust reproaches addressed to him by the Emperor for having left Dupont unsupported on the north bank. But the lecture ended with what was good news to him. Napoleon told him he must make up for his failure by next day attacking Elchingen and driving the Austrians back upon Ulm.

Riesch had occupied the crest of a plateau looking down on the Danube, with a dense wood on the right and on the left the village and the strongly built monastery of Elchingen. He had removed the roadway of the bridge across the river leaving only the piers standing. In the grey of the morning the pioneers of Loison's division rapidly repaired the bridge, covered by the fire of Ney's artillery, and a screen of skirmishers pushed out to the front. Then Loison and Mahler's divisions moved across to the attack. The Emperor had watched these preliminary operations from the south side. Murat rode beside him. Ney came to take Napoleon's last orders before putting himself at the head of the attack. Turning to Murat he said to him with a meaning that only Lannes could have explained, but Murat himself understood and did not care to discuss: "Come, Prince, come with me, and *make your plans in the presence of the enemy!*"

Riesch, left unsupported by Mack, made a hard fight before he was driven from the heights of Elchingen by Ney's impetuous attack. There were moments when it seemed that the day would end in a defeat for the French. More than once Ney led in person the troops he threw into the fight, and he was one of the first to enter the village of Elchingen. He wore the full parade uniform of a marshal with the star of the Legion glittering on his breast, but in the thickest of the fight he was untouched. Early in the afternoon the Austrians were in full retreat on Ulm and the French were in possession of the

Elchingen plateau. Lannes' corps was sent across the river to assist Ney in following up his success.

Napoleon recognized in the victory of Elchingen the decisive action of the Ulm campaign, the success that sealed the fate of Mack's army. When he inaugurated a new nobility of the sword and gave his Marshals the titles of Duke and Prince, these dignities were not territorial, but each new patent of nobility commemorated a battle won. To Ney was given the title of "Duke of Elchingen". It was the first victory of the Empire thus commemorated.[1]

Next day the 5th and 6th Corps united in a combined advance on Ulm, driving the Austrians inside its old bastioned wall, Lannes on the left, Ney on the right, where his divisions, meeting with a very poor show of resistance, stormed the heights of the Michelberg. Mack was now shut up in Ulm. Werneck's division, and a smaller force under the Archduke Ferdinand, had escaped after Haslach, and were retreating towards Bohemia, hotly pursued by Murat, who captured most of them. Another division had surrendered to Soult south of Ulm at Memmingen. Mack had only about half his army left, and these were now blockaded in Ulm, which had not been provisioned for a siege, and was cut off from all supplies.

Ney's capture of the Michelberg on the 15th had completed the investment of the place. The night after the battle was intensely cold. Next morning was a miserable time, with dark skies and driving showers of sleet. "The weather was so awful," says De Fezensac, "that no one remained at his post. Even the artillery was not guarded; every one tried to find shelter where he could, and at no other time, excepting during the campaign of Russia, did I suffer so much or see the army in such disorder." The men of Ney's corps were weary with two days of marching and fighting following on a long period of bivouacks in bad weather and constant shortness of food. But the defeated Austrians, though they had the shelter of the town, were worse off for supplies, and their leader had

[1] Four titles were taken from victories won before the inauguration of the Empire. Kellerman was made Duke of Valmy in honour of the first victory of the Republic. The three other dukedoms were memorials of Napoleon's Italian campaigns. Augereau was made Duke of Castiglione; Masséna, Duke of Rivoli; and Lannes, Duke of Montebello.

utterly lost heart. Early on the 16th Napoleon's aide-de-camp, Philippe de Ségur, was sent to summon Mack to surrender. He was told that a reply would be sent out later, and in the course of the morning an officer with a flag of truce arrived at the outposts of the 6th Corps. The envoy was the Austrian General Prince Lichtenstein. He was introduced to Ney, and told him that Mack was ready to surrender Ulm on condition that his army was allowed to march out with its arms and artillery, pass through the French lines, and join the Austrian Army on the Inn. Similar terms had been granted by Melas to Masséna after his gallant defence of Genoa in 1800. Lichtenstein declared that if this offer, which he considered reasonable, were refused, the Austrians would neither make nor receive any further overtures but would bury themselves under the ruins of Ulm rather than surrender as prisoners.

Ney listened to all the Prince had to say, and then told him that he was convinced that the position of Mack's army was hopeless; that it could not hold out for many days and that it must bow to the stern necessities of war. No such terms as were asked for could be even considered. Lichtenstein returned to Ulm with this answer and then Mack made a final attempt to bluff Ney and the Emperor into making some concession by sending out this letter under a flag of truce:—

"The garrison of Ulm, understanding with regret that the equitable terms it considered it had a right to demand of His Excellency Marshal Neu [*sic*] have not been accepted, is firmly resolved to run the chance of war."

Next day (17 October) Mack was again summoned to surrender, and informed that if he persisted in holding out Ulm would be stormed. He then entered into negotiations, sending Lichtenstein to Napoleon's head-quarters. The Prince told Berthier that Mack could not surrender when he knew the Russians under Kutusoff must be already marching to relieve him. Berthier replied by assuring him that not a Russian had yet passed the Inn, and relief at any near date was hopeless. But on the Emperor's behalf he made Lichtenstein what seemed a liberal offer. He was anxious, he said, to meet the honourable scruples of the Austrian General, and he proposed that hostilities should be suspended round Ulm for eight days, and if at the end of that time a relieving army had not made its appearance Mack was to surrender the army and the place on 25 October.

The proposal was accepted and a convention to this effect was signed. But on the 19th Napoleon learned that Werneck had surrendered to Murat, and that Kutusoff was approaching the Inn. He was anxious to be free to move eastward as soon as possible, and he represented to Mack that the prolongation of the conditional armistice was only subjecting the troops of both armies to useless suffering and exposure. He therefore offered that if the surrender were made at once he would undertake that Ney's corps should not move from Ulm till the 25th. Mack should have known that Napoleon would not be so anxious to accelerate the surrender already agreed upon, unless the gain of a few days was very important to him. But he weakly consented to the new arrangement. On the 20th the garrison marched out with the honours of war, and 25,000 Austrian infantry and 2000 cavalry laid down their arms, and Ney's corps took possession of Ulm. The results of the campaign so far were 60,000 prisoners (including 18 generals) and the capture of 80 standards, 200 guns, and 5000 horses.

The French losses in battle had been comparatively small, but the long marches, the lack of supplies, and the exposure to cold and wet had filled the hospitals with sick. The system of living on the invaded country broke down when division after division traversed the same towns and villages, and great armies were concentrated within a few square miles. During the whole campaign of Ulm officers and soldiers were hungry, regular distributions of rations and forage were unknown, and the attempts to collect supplies at haphazard led to indiscipline and plundering. To quote De Fezensac once more: "When during the bad weather the soldiers went to a village to look for food they were tempted to stay there. So the number of stragglers wandering about the country was considerable. The inhabitants were subjected to all kinds of annoyances, and officers who tried to restore order were menaced by the marauders. All these details," he adds, "are unknown to those who read the history of our campaigns. They see only a valiant army of devoted soldiers, as emulous of glory as their officers. They do not know at how great a price of suffering the most brilliant success is often purchased—how many examples of selfishness and cowardice are to be seen in an army beside those of generosity and courage."

The Grand Army now marched on Vienna. The Austro-Russian Army retired before it. The enemy's capital was occupied, and on 2 December, the anniversary of his coronation, Napoleon won the great victory of Austerlitz, and then dictated peace from the palace of the Austrian Emperor at Schönbrunn. Ney had no share in the glory of Austerlitz. The arrangement by which the 6th Corps was to remain behind at Ulm, while the rest of the army advanced across the Inn, had condemned him to play a minor part in the second stage of the campaign. His command had been reduced. Dupont's division had been detached, and one of Loison's brigades detailed for garrison duty. When he marched from Ulm on 26 October he had with him only his 3rd division (Mahler) the 2nd Brigade of the 2nd Division (Loison), and for cavalry about 150 men of the 3rd Hussars and the 10th Chasseurs-à-cheval. The battalions had been so reduced during the Ulm campaign that his total fighting strength was only about 9000 men.

His orders were to advance into the Tyrol. It was no easy task that was thus imposed upon him. The Austrian army in the Tyrol had numbered 50,000 men at the outbreak of the war, but more than half of these had been sent to reinforce the Austrian armies in Italy and on the Inn. The Archduke John, who commanded in the Tyrol, had at his disposal at the beginning of November, 1805, about 20,000 regulars, but besides these there was the levy *en masse* of the province, thousands of hardy mountaineers, many of them armed with rifles and excellent shots, and all bitterly hostile to an invader.

The bulk of the Austrian forces had been drawn off to the eastern passes of the Tyrol to meet the advance in that direction of Deroy's division of Bernadotte's corps. Ney was to march against Innsbruck. On the eve of the expedition he introduced into his corps a new organization that afterwards became general in the French Army. Each infantry battalion had already a picked company of its tallest men, known as the "Grenadiers". He formed a second special company of the smaller and more active men of each battalion, and these were known as the "Voltigeurs" (literally "the vaulters") or, to use the name of similar companies in the British Army of the time, the Light Infantry Company of the battalion. They were relieved of part of the load carried by the infantry privates, and were intended to climb the rocks and hills to lead or flank the attack in the coming mountain campaign.

On 4 November Ney was at the entrance of the pass of Schernitz, defended by two forts perched high on the spurs of the mountains, the Fort of Scharnitz and the Fort of Leutasch. The latter was taken by Loison's brigade, the former by Mahler's division. In both cases a detachment led by the Voltigeurs climbed by narrow paths, known only to the local chamois hunters, and up steep rock fronts where the men clung to bushes and even made holds by driving bayonets into the crevices of the mountain side. They had to drive off the Tyrolese peasants who rolled stones down on them and fired on them at long range. But the very daring of the unexpected advance helped the attack. The French at last reached positions above and in the rear of the forts, points which the Austrians believed to be inaccessible to regular infantry. The Fort of Leutasch surrendered, with its garrison of 300 men. That of Scharnitz was carried by assault, a combined attack being made up the slopes in front and from the heights in the rear. Sixteen guns were taken and 1800 prisoners.

The Austrians had relied on the Fort of Scharnitz for the defence of Innsbruck, and, pushing on rapidly after his victory, Ney occupied the capital of the Tyrol next day (5 November) without further fighting. In the local arsenal he took possession of several cannon, 16,000 muskets, and a large quantity of ammunition, and the 76th Regiment regained possession of a standard they had lost six years before in the campaign in Switzerland.

Ney remained halted at Innsbruck till the 10th. He then sent Loison's division to occupy the Brenner. On the 11th and 12th there was hard fighting with the Austrian regulars and militia at Staufach and Gries on the road up the pass.

French writers claim these actions as victories, because the Austrians evacuated the Brenner after the fighting. But the Austrians count them as successful rear-guard actions. Loison marched over the Brenner and penetrated as far as Botzen, where he met with an undoubted reverse. He had only sent two of his battalions on to Botzen, apparently in ignorance of the fact that a strong Austrian column under the Prince de Rohan, retiring from the north-western Tyrol into the Adige valley on its way to Italy, was approaching the same place. Rohan drove out the two battalions inflicting heavy loss on them, and then continued his retreat. The fight at Botzen took place on 25 November. It was the last serious engagement of the campaign. There were skirmishes with irregular parties of the mountaineers, but with the news of Austerlitz all operations on a larger scale came to an end.

The 6th Corps received orders to rejoin the Grand Army near Vienna, and after rallying his troops at Innsbruck on 4 December, Ney marched by Lauffen, Rastadt, Klagenfurth, and Judenburg to the cantonments assigned to him in Austria. This march occupied the next fortnight. Leaving his corps in cantonments about Judenburg, some twenty-two miles from Vienna Ney went on to Schönbrunn, where he was most cordially received by Napoleon. On 25 December the Peace of Pressburg was signed by which Austria abandoned the coalition, and amongst other advantages handed over Venice to Napoleon. Ney was then ordered to withdraw his corps first to Salzburg and then to cantonments on the north shore of the Lake of Constance, where during many months of the next year the officers and soldiers of the 6th Corps lived among their Bavarian allies.

Ney returned to Paris. He had missed Austerlitz, but he was content with the honours of Elchingen, and the decisive part he had played in the great triumph of Ulm, and the occupation of the Tyrol.

CHAPTER X

JENA, EYLAU, AND FRIEDLAND (1806-1807)

NAPOLEON had secured the neutrality of Prussia in 1805 by arranging for the occupation of Hanover by Prussian troops. But there was increasing friction between Berlin and Paris in the summer of 1806, and in the autumn the war party in the Prussian capital persuaded King Frederick William to break with Napoleon. Like the Austrians in 1805 the Prussians hoped for the help of Russia, and like them they challenged the trial of combat before their allies were ready to act.

Napoleon had the Grand Army with the exception of the Imperial Guard in cantonments, in South Germany. As soon as war was imminent Ney's corps was concentrated at Nuremberg. With the 4th Corps under Marshal Lannes it was to form the right of the Grand Army, in the coming advance into Prussian territory [1].

Ney's corps was organized into two divisions with a cavalry brigade. The regiments had been together since the days of the camp of Montreuil and the "Army of England," and the

[1] There were six corps of the Grand Army in Germany. The 2nd Corps under Marmont was in Dalmatia. The strength of the six corps stood thus at the beginning of the campaign:—

1st Corps.	Marshal	Bernadotte	20,000 men
3rd "	"	Davoût	27,000 "
4th "	"	Soult	32,000 "
5th "	"	Lannes	22,000 "
6th "	"	Ney	20,000 "
7th "	"	Augereau	17,000 "
Cavalry reserve.	Prince Murat, Grand Duke of Berg		28,000 "
		Total	166,000 men.

The Imperial Guard was hurried up from Paris, the men being conveyed as far as Mayence in relays of a hundred four-horsed wagons. When it had joined the field army, it amounted with its reserves in the theatre of war to about 190,000 men.

officers of higher rank were all old comrades. This permanent organization was a great source of strength to the armies of the Empire. Dutaillis assisted by Jomini directed Ney's staff as in the previous year, but Jomini was frequently absent on duty at the Emperor's head-quarters. The first division was commanded by General Marchand. Mahler, who had been one of Ney's divisional generals in 1805, was in nominal command of the 2nd Division at the outset of the campaign, but he was absent on sick leave, and one of the brigadiers, General Marcognet, temporarily commanded the division. The following was the formation of the brigades :—

1st Division.

1st Brigade. General Liger-Belair. 6th Light Infantry. 39th of the Line.

2nd Brigade. General Vilatte. 69th and 76th of the Line.

2nd Division.

1st Brigade. General Marcognet. 25th Light Infantry. 27th of the Line.

2nd Brigade. General Labassée. 50th and 59th of the Line.

Cavalry Brigade. General Colbert. 3rd Hussars. 10th Chasseurs.

As to the general course of operations in the Jena campaign, suffice it to say that the Prussian Army, reinforced, by a Saxon contingent, had been massed about Eisenach, Erfurt, and Weimar north of the wooded hills of the Thuringian Forest, and fronting towards the French cantonments in South Germany. King Frederick William was with the army, which was commanded for him by the Duke of Brunswick. The Prussians, despite Brunswick's failure in the First War of the Revolution in France, regarded him as a skilful general, a master of the art of war trained in the school of Frederick the Great. The whole army was still living on the reputation acquired in Frederick's days, and had a thorough contempt for the new methods of the "Corsican upstart," who was so soon to teach them a terrible lesson. A hundred and fifty thousand men had been mustered in the Prussian camps, and the generals were discussing the plan of operations, opinion in Brunswick's councils of war being in favour of a bold offensive movement against the French but not yet decided as to how to carry it into practical effect, when in the first days of October came the news that the French were already advancing. They were moving on a broad front covered by Murat's cavalry, and at first no man could say whether the attack would be made through the Thuringian Forest against Brunswick's centre, or against one of his flanking corps. Then it appeared that Napoleon's march was directed on Leipzig. Brunswick, for whom campaigns were worked out as geometrical diagrams, saw in this hostile march past his left flank a splendid opportunity for himself falling on the flank of the nearest French column, so in the second week of October he moved to his right, concentrating in two masses towards Jena and Auerstadt.

For the first time Napoleon was marching in the array that was henceforth his typical formation for a great army. At first sight it suggested the old linear order of centre and right and left wings, but the three units of the combination were great columns of Army Corps. Their composition was:—

Left.	Centre.	Right.
5th Corps	1st Corps	4th Corps
7th "	3rd "	6th "
	Guard "	

The corps followed each other at an interval of a day's march. The heads of the columns, at first spread out on a front of some sixty miles, rapidly drew nearer each other by following converging lines of march until from right to left the distance was not more than twenty. The seven corps could thus within twenty-four hours concentrate for battle either to the front or to a flank. It was the order of march which General Bonnal in his studies of Napoleon's campaigns calls the "*bataillon carré*"—the square battle order. Napoleon's object was not to manœuvre his opponent out of a position or force him to retreat, but to bring him to battle under conditions that would enable all the French fighting force to come into action at the striking point. In this Jena campaign he moved his great fighting square of Army Corps to the left of the Army of Brunswick, his line of march being directed on Leipzig, but Leipzig was not his objective, it was the Prussian Army. When Brunswick concentrated towards his left to strike at the French line of advance, the French left column turned to meet him, the two other columns faced left and came up to support it. There

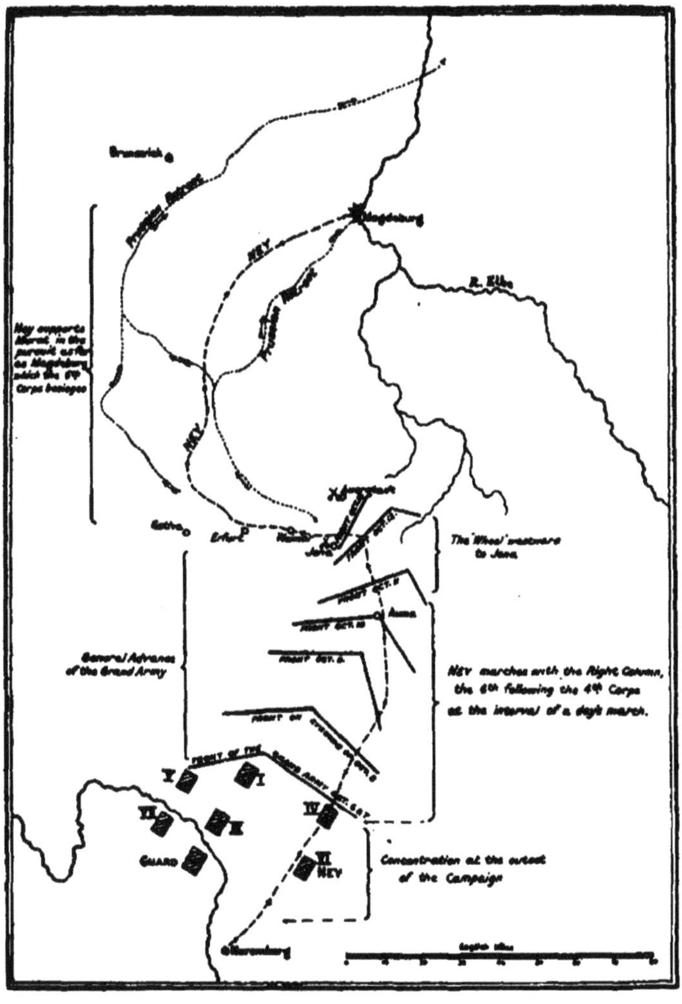

THE CAMPAIGN OF JENA

was no longer any question of the original right, centre, and left of the French advance. In the double battle of 14 October —Jena and Auerstadt—the 5th and 7th Corps were indeed on the left, but the 4th and 6th and the Guard were the centre, and the 1st and 3rd moved out to form the right attack at Auerstadt. By a blunder of Bernadotte's the 3rd Corps (Davoût) fought alone against superior numbers on the right, but at Jena the Emperor, though some of his troops arrived too late for effective action, met Brunswick with equal forces so far as numbers went, but with a marked superiority in fighting power. The Prussians had hoped to overwhelm the French left column. They had to fight the Grand Army, and, in that one day of battle and the fierce pursuit that followed, the Prussian Army was destroyed.

In the advance into Prussian territory Ney's corps formed the rear of the right column, following the 4th Corps (Soult). Nevertheless from the outset Ney marched in an order that made his command ready to act independently if need be. Colbert led the march with his mixed brigade of all arms, cavalry, the 25th Legère, and the picked infantry companies formed into provisional battalions, and the light artillery, a complete fighting unit. Then came the two infantry divisions commanded by Marchand and Marcognet.

Bayreuth was occupied on the 8th, and on the 10th the Saale was crossed at Hoff and the 6th Corps entered Saxony. Ney now found it no easy matter to obtain supplies for his men. It was the Napoleonic custom to live to a great extent on what could be collected from the country traversed, but as Soult's requisitions had already taken the cream of its resources, only the skimmed milk was left for Ney. So in those days of marching before the battle the men had often to tighten their belts and hope the trying time would soon be over. On the 11th the line of march diverged from that of Soult's for a while. Ney had been ordered to move on Auma, closing on the centre column, and that day Colbert's foraging parties rode through villages that had not been already cleared out by others, until in the afternoon they came on the track that had already been followed by the two corps of the centre and the Guard, and there they found that the whole country had been "eaten up". The village near Auma, where Colbert bivouacked that evening, was a mass of smoking ruins. There had been resistance to a requisitioning party and the place had been burned.

An incident of this day related by De Fezensac, who was then attached to Ney's staff, throws a strange light on his methods of command, and the whole machinery of the Imperial Army. As a soldier of the Republic Ney had lived on terms of familiar friendship with those who were associated with him in the work of command. As a Marshal of the Empire he kept aloof from them. According to one account his confidence had been betrayed by an officer, who served with him in the Boulogne camps, and henceforth he protected himself by trusting no one. According to another theory he felt that his rapid rise to rank made it prudent for him continually to assert his position in order to prevent others from presuming on their earlier association with him. However this may be, his staff officers were taught that they must not speak to him unless when he addressed them, or they had some communication to make to him in the routine of duty. Dutaillis and Jomini were the only officers of his military household with whom he spoke freely. On the line of march he rode alone. In camp or quarters he dined in solitary state.

But this lonely reticence was habitual to him in matters also that affected the practical working of his corps. The orders received from the Imperial head-quarters were usually not communicated to the staff generally. They only heard fragments of them when they were asked to carry an executive order to a divisional general or a brigadier. Thus they had only a vague idea of what was happening. And they consequently carried out their duties under considerable disadvantages. De Fezensac says that these unpractical methods were common in the Grand Army, and the source of serious losses in the difficult times that came before long.

On this October day at the town of Schletz Ney called up De Fezensac, handed him a despatch, and told him to convey it to Colbert. The aide-de-camp was asking where he should find him, when Ney dismissed him with a sharp—"No remarks. I don't like them." So he set off on a voyage of discovery. Evidently he had not been told that the column was moving on Auma, or he would have at once ridden off in that direction to find the advanced guard commander. He had first to inquire where Colbert was, and then to ask his way to the places named, for he had no map. "Officers of the Grand Army," he says, "did not carry such things." Map reading was apparently left to marshals. His first information proved misleading, and it was the accident of meeting one of Colbert's chasseurs that enabled the staff officer at last to find his bivouac and deliver his message.

Next day orders arrived from the Emperor to move to the left. The concentration for battle had begun. On the 13th Ney, eager for news, rode on in front of Colbert's advanced guard with a small escort and some of his staff. He met an officer from the Imperial head-quarters who handed him Berthier's final orders as Napoleon's chief of the staff:—

"BIVOUAC BEFORE JENA, 13 *October*.

"The enemy has concentrated his forces between Jena and Weimar. Bring up your Army Corps this evening to beyond Roda and as near to Jena as possible, so as to arrive there to-morrow morning. Try to come to Jena yourself this evening in order to be present at the reconnaissance of the enemy, which the Emperor will make during the night. I count on your zeal.

"ALEXANDRE BERTHIER,
"*Prince of Neufchâtel.*"

Ney had copies made of this letter and sent them to Generals Colbert, Marchand, and Marcognet, his cavalry and divisional commanders. Then, accompanied by the only two officers of his staff who were well mounted enough to keep up with him, he rode off in hot haste to Napoleon's head-quarters before Jena.

There had been some skirmishing already. When Ney reached Jena after dark the sky was reddened with a glare of a great fire. A number of the quaint wood-gabled houses of the town were ablaze, fired, it is said, by Prussian shells. Ney joined Napoleon who with Lannes and Berthier was on the Landgrafenberg, the ridge of hills beyond the town, examining a path that led to the crest and issuing orders that it should be widened and converted into a road, by which the artillery should reach the summit before daylight. From the hill-top, as the darkness deepened, the Prussian watch-fires marked out the enemy's positions, and there, map in hand, Napoleon explained to the marshals his plans for the coming battle.

Colbert broke up his bivouac between Roda and Jena at two in the morning, and marching through the darkness and a dense fog halted before daylight near the position occupied by the Imperial Guard. When the sun rose a thick mist hung for some hours over hill and valley. Officers sent by Colbert to report his arrival to Ney had some difficulty in finding the Marshal. It was not till near nine o'clock that he took command of Colbert's brigade, all that had arrived of the 6th Corps.

Long before this the battle had begun. Lannes had driven in the advanced troops of the enemy commanded by Prince Hohenlohe and cleared the nearer heights for the deployment of the army, which had mostly passed the night huddled together behind the Landgrafenberg ridge. There was a lull while the French formed, and Hohenlohe brought up his main body. During this time the mist cleared and the sun shone out brightly.

Then Ney, eager for the fight, and regardless of the strict letter of his orders from the Emperor, brought his small force into action on the left of Lannes. He had with him Colbert's two cavalry regiments, a battery of six guns, and the three battalions of Grenadiers, Light Infantry, and Voltigeurs—not 3000 men in all. He pushed so boldly forward towards the Prussian left centre in front of the village of Vierzehn-Heiligen, that for awhile he was unsupported, and had to meet single handed a furious counter-attack of the enemy. The Chasseurs, forming under cover of a clump of wood, had charged a line of Hohenlohe's guns, scattered the gunners and captured the teams and limbers of seven cannon, when they were charged in their turn and driven back by a mass of Prussian cuirassiers and dragoons. The 3rd Hussars saved them by dashing at the flank of the hostile cavalry, but then had themselves to retire under a heavy fire. The Prussians then rode at Ney's infantry, but formed in three squares they beat off

THE BATTLE OF JENA, 1806

FROM THE PAINTING BY MEISSONIER

several charges. Then Lannes came up on Ney's right, and the leading troops of Soult's corps began to arrive on his left, and the squares reformed in line and column to renew the attack.

In the hard fighting that followed Ney was always well to the front—"risking his life like a corporal of Voltigeurs," to use De Fezensac's expression. Two of his staff were wounded at his side. It was a bitter disappointment to him that only his vanguard was on the well-fought field, and it seemed as if he was trying by his own reckless energy to make the most of the small force at his disposal.

The infantry divisions, which had been marching all day towards the sound of the cannon, only reached the field as the sun was going down and the Prussian army was broken and in full retreat, hotly pressed by Murat's cavalry. Ney was marching after Murat to Weimar, where thousands of prisoners were taken. Murat established his head-quarters at the Grand Duke's palace. There was room enough there for Ney also, but he was jealous of the dignities that had been lavished on the Emperor's brother-in-law and had not forgotten the dispute of the year before. Instead of going to the palace he took possession of one of the local inns.

The town was the scene of disorders that the officers could not repress. Houses were being plundered on all sides by the victors. Ney's infantry divisions reached the suburbs after dark. The men were so exhausted with their long march that many of them threw themselves on the ground to sleep, and it was only after half an hour that the officers could rouse them to light fires and cook a meal.

The pursuit was continued next day. As Ney's infantry divisions had not been engaged in the battle they were reckoned as fresh troops, and sent to support Murat's cavalry in a forced march to Erfurt. Ney was anything but pleased at finding himself thus once more associated with Murat and under his orders, for as second on the list of Marshals and an Imperial Prince the younger soldier was his senior in rank. Outside Erfurt Murat captured a huge convoy and made 800 prisoners, then circling round the place he cut off the retreat of the corps of Marshal Mollendorf who was in the town, with the Prince of Orange-Nassau. The two generals refused Murat's summons to surrender and tried to make terms. He replied that it must be "surrender at discretion" or he would storm the place. But he knew that he could not do this with his cavalry alone. It was the arrival of Ney's infantry and artillery that determined the German generals to surrender. So Erfurt was taken with 14,000 prisoners (6000 of them wounded from the battle-field) and 100 guns. It was a new grievance for Ney that Murat claimed the success as his own. But he had to leave it to Ney to dispose of the place and the prisoners, for he was eager to push on with the pursuit of Hohenlohe's beaten army. Ney had the satisfaction of installing his chief of the staff Dutaillis as governor of Erfurt.[1]

Ney's corps as well as the 4th Corps (Soult) was at once sent to support Murat's pursuit of the Prussians to the northward, by way of Nordhausen and Halberstadt to the crossing of the Elbe at Magdeburg. Never was pursuit more vigorously pressed. And De Fezensac adds that "never too was pillage carried on to such an extent as along the route, and the disorder rose to the point of insubordination. At Nordhausen," he adds, "Colonel Jomini and myself thought we would have been killed by the soldiers whose excesses we were trying to repress. We had to draw our swords in order to make our way through the town."

Murat was before Magdeburg on the 20th. The Prussian Army had crossed the Elbe there and Murat summoned General Kleist, the commandant of the fortress, to surrender. Kleist refused, and as Murat had to continue the pursuit he left it to Ney to besiege Magdeburg. Ney established his head-quarters at Schönebeck, two leagues from the place, on 25 October, and commenced the investment. The infantry divisions closed in upon the fortress on the left bank of the Elbe. Colbert's brigade was established in front of it on the right bank, and a bridge of boats was thrown across the river to keep up communication between the besiegers.

[1] On occupying Erfurt Ney learned that Mollendorf, a veteran of the wars of Frederick the Great, was unable to leave his house as he was suffering from a wound received at Auerstadt. He went to visit him, and said as he entered his room: "The youngest of Marshals is come to pay homage to the senior of them all".

Ney then summoned the place. Kleist was a veteran of over 80 years, in such bad health that he could hardly mount his horse. The garrison was weak in numbers and encumbered with thousands of sick and wounded left in the fortress by the retreating army, and the civil population was terrified at the idea of a siege and anxious for a prompt surrender. Nevertheless the old commandant replied to Ney's summons that he could not surrender until the French had at least given him some proof that they had the means of compelling him to do so.

Ney had no heavy artillery and no means of undertaking a regular siege, but some mortars were sent to him from Erfurt and he threatened to bombard the city and actually shelled and set fire to the suburb of Krakau. This increased the alarm in the town, and Ney was able to send Kleist the news that the French had occupied Berlin, and the scattered corps of the field army were everywhere surrendering. Kleist then lost heart and decided that further resistance could serve no useful purpose. On 7 November a capitulation was signed. Magdeburg was to surrender next day. The garrison was to march out with the honours of war, the officers were to keep their swords and be set free on parole; the men were to be prisoners of war. Eighteen thousand men marched out and laid down their arms. Four thousand more sick and wounded were in the hospitals of the town.

Ney was then ordered to leave a garrison at Magdeburg and march with the rest of his corps to Berlin where it would be reviewed by the Emperor. The 59th Regiment was left to hold the captured fortress. The 6th Corps had then the satisfaction of marching into the capital of Prussia, parading before the Emperor, hearing his warm praise of its services during the campaign, and receiving an immediate reward in a distribution of promotions and decorations.

The corps was allowed a few days' rest at Berlin and then took the field again for a more trying campaign. The Russian Army was now moving, but only a mere handful of Prussians remained to co-operate with it, and King Frederick William had taken refuge at Königsberg. His flag still flew over Danzig and some of the minor fortresses of Silesia and the

Polish border. These were to be reduced, the Russians were to be met in the field, East Prussia conquered, perhaps Poland restored.

When the Grand Army advanced from the Oder to the Vistula in the beginning of November, Ney's corps was at first in the second line. It was ordered to march from Berlin to Posen. All the intervening country was clear of the enemy, and Ney and his staff travelled on in advance of their corps in post carriages, leaving the cavalry and the two infantry divisions to follow them by easy stages. The 59th Regiment was called up from Magdeburg to rejoin.

Ney arrived at Posen on 15 November. Davoût had already occupied the city where he had been received with enthusiasm by the people, who saw in the coming of the victorious French Army a possible prelude to the restoration of the Polish Kingdom, under a Prince of Napoleon's family.

The Emperor arrived at Posen on the 27th. Next day Warsaw was occupied without resistance, the Russians retiring to the suburb of Praga on the other side of the Vistula. Ney with the 6th Corps remained at Posen till the end of the month, and was then ordered to march on Thorn, which was still held by a Prussian garrison. He was to reduce the fortress in order to secure another crossing over the Vistula below Warsaw.

He set out from Posen on 1 December. General Lestocq with 15,000 Prussians (almost all that was left of the Prussian Field Army) was at Thorn. The place stands on the right bank of the Vistula, and was connected by a wooden bridge with the suburb of Podgurtz on the left bank. Lestocq had destroyed the bridge. The river had frozen over, but there had been a thaw, and the surface of the Vistula was now a mass of drift ice, so that Thorn was completely cut off from Podgurtz, which was occupied by a detachment of the 7th Corps (Augereau). The 1st Division of Ney's corps reached the left bank of the Vistula near Thorn on 4 December, and the line of the river was being reconnoitred with a view to bridging it above or below the place, when Colonel Savary of the 14th Infantry (7th Corps) who held Podgurtz was informed that Lestocq's Prussians were evacuating the town. Though it was no easy matter for boats to cross the river amid the drifting ice a number of Polish boatmen volunteered to ferry Savary's men across. He accepted their offer, embarked some of his companies, crossed the Vistula under a heavy fire of musketry, and after a sharp fight gained a footing on the right bank. The rest of the regiment then crossed, and General Marchand sent over reinforcements from Ney's 1st Division. Most of Lestocq's corps was already miles away to the eastward on its march to join the Russian Army. The rear-guard evacuated the town, and when Ney arrived at Podgurtz on the 5th he learned that it was in Marchand's possession. He crossed over next day, concentrated his corps at Thorn, and repaired the bridge over the Vistula. Lestocq had demolished so much of it that the work of reconstruction was not completed till 15 December.

Ney remained at Thorn till the 18th. By this time the long-expected Russian advance had begun, and an army under Benningsen was moving towards the line of the river Narev, a tributary of the Vistula which joins it a few miles north of Warsaw. The great mass of the Grand Army under the personal command of the Emperor was near Warsaw. Besides Ney's corps at Thorn, the 1st Corps under Bernadotte had been left to guard the lower course of the Vistula. Ney was now ordered to march eastward and hold the country to the extreme left of the Grand Army's main positions, while still further northward Bernadotte moved from the Vistula to observe Königsberg where King Frederick William had taken refuge.

Ney marched from Thorn on 18 December by way of Gollup and Strasburg to Soldau on the River Ukra. He soon found that Lestocq's Prussians were in his front, retiring as he advanced. On 26 December Marchand, with the 1st Division, overtook and roughly handled the Prussian rear-guard at Soldau. The enemy continued his retreat and was not followed any further. A continual thaw, with frequent showers of cold rain, had made the level country into a wide-spreading morass. Even on the so-called roads men sank to the knee and wheels to the axle. All further movement had become nearly impossible. It was difficult to collect supplies, and men and horses suffered terribly.

There had been fighting on the Narev between Benningsen and Napoleon, on 24, 25, and 26 December—a Christmas of miserable bloodshed in the midst of seas of mud, and deluges of sleet and rain. The enemy was repulsed at all points, losing 20,000 men in killed, wounded, and prisoners, and leaving eighty guns in the possession of the French, for the weather conditions and the state of the ground made it impossible to withdraw them. This series of engagements is known as the Battle of Pultusk. It was a success that it was impossible to follow up—the first of Napoleon's indecisive victories. Then came a period of enforced inaction for both armies.

At the end of the year Ney's corps was in cantonments in and about the towns of Mlawà and Niedenburg, the Marshal's head-quarters being at the burgomaster's house in the latter town. Bernadotte's corps on his left was about thirty miles away to the north-westward at Osterode. Soult's corps forming the left of the main body of the Grand Army was about twenty-five miles to the south near Golymin on the Narev. The weather was still wretchedly bad, and the chief problem was how to supply the troops.

Thus the New Year of 1807 opened under trying conditions. Sharp frost and snow would have been more tolerable, for a hard winter would have made the plains beyond the Vistula passable in all directions and bridged every river with thick ice. The comparatively mild weather, on the contrary, inflicted endless sufferings on man and beast.

Fatigue, exposure, sickness, and semi-starvation had thinned the ranks of the Grand Army to an extent far exceeding the losses in action in a brief hard-fought campaign. Although some 12,000 recruits had arrived from the depôts since Jena, Napoleon had not much more than 100,000 men available at the front at the end of January, 1807. Ney's corps had marched from Nuremberg four months earlier with a fighting strength of 20,000 men. It was reduced to 10,000 though it had lost very few in battle, only the advanced guard being engaged at Jena, and the corps having had no serious fighting since that day.

On 11 January the weather had improved a little, and Ney,

acting on his own initiative and without any orders from Napoleon, changed the positions of his Army Corps. The infantry divisions marched northwards to Wartemburg and Allenstein, and Colbert's advanced guard brigade was sent still further north to Bartenstein with orders to send patrols towards Königsberg. By this movement the 6th Corps was placed to the eastward of the 1st (Bernadotte), and Ney left open a wide gap of nearly sixty miles between Bernadotte's right and Soult's left.

His primary object seems to have been to reach new ground, where the available supplies from the villages had not yet been swept up by requisitions. But he also had heard rumours that Königsberg was ill supplied and might soon surrender, and he was anxious for the glory of occupying the old capital of Prussia, the last refuge of its King and court. Thiers in his history expresses the opinion that at this moment Ney might have taken Königsberg, but there was really not the remotest prospect of such a success, and Colbert's patrols never came within twenty miles of the place.[1] Ney was anxious about the view the Emperor would take of this new move, and on the 15th he sent off his aide-de-camp, De Fezensac, in a sledge from Bartenstein to report personally to the Emperor and give any explanations that were asked for.

De Fezensac had a trying and dangerous journey of 150 miles to the Imperial head-quarters at Warsaw, where he arrived on the 17th. To the aide-de-camp Napoleon said nothing. But next day he sent him back to Ney's head-quarters accompanied by Colonel Jomini, who had been for some time in Warsaw. Jomini was carrying a letter to Ney from Napoleon written in a tone of severe censure, and was also charged with a verbal message for the Marshal, and during the northward journey he told De Fezensac its purport. The Emperor had been seriously displeased at the news from Ney. "What is the meaning," he had asked, "of these movements that I never ordered, which fatigue the troops and may even endanger them? To obtain supplies? To extend the occupation of the country and enter Königsberg? But it is my business to

[1] A nearer approach was stopped by a local truce concluded for a few days with the commander of the Prussian outposts.

direct the movements of my army and to provide for its needs. And who authorized Marshal Ney to conclude an armistice—a right that belongs to the Emperor alone as commander-in-chief? Generals have been brought before a court of inquiry for an act like this." Napoleon was angry, and Jomini was to express his displeasure to Ney.

While Jomini and De Fezensac were travelling from Warsaw to rejoin Ney the Russians were again moving. A hard frost had made the country practicable for their columns, and they had planned a stroke that was full of peril for Napoleon, which was likely to fall first upon the advanced positions occupied by Ney's 10,000 men of the 6th Corps.

Benningsen, who so far had been facing the right and centre of the Grand Army in Poland, had left only small detachments in front of Napoleon and had marched northwards, uniting on the way with Buxhovden's corps of Russians and Lestocq's Prussian corps. His plan was to fall suddenly on the French left (Ney and Bernadotte) by marching into East Prussia, and having overwhelmed them he hoped to turn the whole French line, raise the siege of Danzig, and meet Napoleon with all the advantage of numbers and position on the allied side. Ney's movement towards Königsberg had if anything facilitated this plan of operations.

De Fezensac and Jomini reached Allenstein on 20 January, and found Ney had his head-quarters there with his 2nd Division. Jomini communicated to the Marshal the unwelcome message from the Emperor. Ney was deeply depressed and wrote to Berthier a letter of excuses and protestations of fidelity to the Emperor's last wish. The news he received that same day afforded a startling confirmation of the Emperor's remark that he had perhaps endangered his troops by this change of position made without orders, for Colbert was retiring from Bartenstein, having learned in the nick of time that the vanguard of a great Russian army was moving on Heilsberg and might cut off his detachment if he delayed his retreat. Ney's 1st Division was a few miles to the south of him at Hohenstein. He decided to withdraw Colbert's brigade and the 2nd Division to Hohenstein, and send Marchand with the 1st Division back to Gyllenburg, so as to bring his corps nearer to Bernadotte and withdraw it further from the line of Benningsen's advance.

On the 21st he sent off De Fezensac with written orders to Marchand. Once more a strange light is thrown on his methods of command (which were those of the Grand Army) by De Fezensac's narrative. Ney told him not a word of the Russian advance. He rode to Hohenstein in the darkness of a bitterly cold night, and on arriving there found that Marchand had left the place with his division, without informing the head-quarters. He was told the general was at a village seven or eight miles away. He arrived there, but found no sign of a French occupation, and for some time could get no news as the villagers spoke only Polish. At last he met a man who knew some German, and who told him there was a general at a château about six miles from the village. Here at last he found Marchand. He had been told at starting that he was to rejoin the Marshal at the village of Neidenburg. Having no map, but asking his way, he reached the village on the 22nd after a long ride amid ice and snow. Ney was not there, but by good luck he met at Neidenburg Colonel Jomini on his way back to Warsaw. The Colonel told him Ney was at Hohenstein that day, and also informed him of the Russian advance and the sudden change in the situation. This was the first that De Fezensac had heard of it. One wonders how with staff officers left in ignorance of important news, and blundering about the country without maps when they conveyed orders, and with generals moving their commands from village to village without reporting to head-quarters, the Grand Army worked so well as it did as a fighting organization.

Colbert had had a narrow escape on the 21st. He had to cut his way through the advanced Russian cavalry at Bischofstein to the east of Heilsberg. Next day he rejoined Ney at Hohenstein. The Marshal concentrated his corps in and around the place and remained there till the morning of the 27th. During the 26th the Cossacks were skirmishing with his outposts and surprised one of his pickets. On the 27th Ney evacuated Hohenstein and concentrated his corps at Gilgenburg on the 29th, making a leisurely retreat without any sign of pursuit. Even the Cossack raiders had disappeared.

Benningsen had allowed Ney to withdraw from his line of march, for he was hurrying forward to attack Bernadotte, and open the road to Danzig. On the 25th he attacked and drove in a division commanded by Bernadotte in person at Mohrungen, north of Osterode. The French claimed that the action had been only a successful rear-guard engagement, but the Russians had a trophy of victory in the capture of part of Bernadotte's convoy. Benningsen, having got so far, had to halt for some days to rest his troops, who were exhausted by their long march.

By this time Napoleon had heard of the Russian attack, and, leaving the 5th Corps to cover Warsaw, he was marching northwards with the rest of the Grand Army. The general direction of his march was towards Königsberg. He hoped to interpose between Benningsen's left rear and Russia, cut his line of retreat, and force him to fight under conditions in which defeat might mean another disaster like that of Ulm. To Bernadotte he sent orders to retire even as far as Thorn if necessary, in order to draw the enemy still further to the westward.

But as the Emperor advanced he received information that showed the Russians were suddenly retiring—falling back towards Königsberg, as if they had divined the secret of Napoleon's plan. The fact was Benningsen had read the Emperor's order to Bernadotte. Cipher was not used at this time in the Grand Army even for such important dispatches, and staff officers usually travelled without an escort and cheerfully took serious risks of capture. In this case the officer, who was carrying the order to Bernadotte, was taken by a roving party of Cossacks while asleep in his sledge, and had not time even to tear up the precious dispatch.

On 1 February Benningsen was concentrating on the line of the river Passarge. That day Ney reoccupied Hohenstein. The 7th, 4th, and 3rd Corps extended the line to the right. Murat's cavalry was out in front. Bernadotte's corps was closing up to the left, and the Imperial Guard coming up in the rear. With the reduced strength of the various corps Napoleon had about 65,000 men in hand. Benningsen with Lestocq's Prussians on his right could muster some 90,000, but the Emperor was eager to fight notwithstanding the disparity of numbers, and at first it seemed that Benningsen was anxious to avoid a pitched battle. He fell back from the Passarge during the next four days. On the 4th Ney on the left was in contact with a Russian rear-guard, and there was desultory fighting all day. He was well to the front throughout the action, and one of his staff was wounded beside him.

Lestocq, who had pushed towards the Vistula during Benningsen's halt at Mohrungen, was still on the left bank of the Passarge and separated from the Russians by a considerable distance. On 5 February Ney was sent to pursue him and try to cut him off. He crossed the Passarge at Deppen, moved up the left bank and overtook the Prussians at Waltersdorf. Lestocq left a strong rear-guard to make a stand against the French, while his main body crossed the river at the bridge of Wormditt. Ney reinforced with two regiments of dragoons made a furious attack on the rear-guard, and all but completely destroyed it, taking more than 2000 prisoners, several guns, and a large convoy of waggons.

On 6 February Ney crossed the Passarge and reached Wormditt, without any further fighting, Lestocq having gained some miles while his rear-guard was being destroyed the day before. During the night Ney received orders to march by Landsberg on Kreutzburg (fifteen miles south of Königsberg). Benningsen was still slowly retiring followed up by Napoleon. On the 6th Murat had driven his rear-guard out of the village of Hoff after a hard fight and had occupied Landsberg. On the 7th the French were in close contact with the retreating Russians all day, and there was more fighting. In the evening Napoleon occupied the town of Preuss Eylau. He expected that next day the enemy would continue his retreat towards Königsberg and there would be further rear-guard fighting.

On the evening of the 7th Ney had reached Landsberg on the left and to the rear of Napoleon's army, and with Lestocq's corps on his right front on the road to Kreutzburg. After dark he sent off De Fezensac to the imperial head-quarters at Eylau to inform the Emperor that he had reached Landsberg, and would next day march on Kreutzburg driving Lestocq before him. The aide-de-camp had a terrible ride over frozen tracks and amid darkness and driving snowstorms. Six times his horse fell, and it is a wonder he ever reached Eylau. He found the town crowded with troops, its outskirts strewn with dead and wounded, roads and streets encumbered with wagons and the townsfolk in a panic. He had some difficulty in discovering the house occupied by Berthier, and after handing over his dispatch to the Marshal he had a hasty supper with the staff and was told to remain in Eylau till next day. He slept on a bench with his horse still saddled tied to a cart close by.

When he rose in the morning he saw that the army was forming for battle. Benningsen had stopped his retreat. Against the white background of the snow-covered slopes north of Eylau the dark masses and lines of the Russian army stood out boldly, some 40,000 infantry, more than 20,000 cavalry, and 450 guns. Napoleon had actually on the ground only Murat's cavalry corps, the infantry corps of Augereau and Soult, 200 guns and some 40,000 men with whom to begin the battle. Officers rode off to hurry up the corps of Davoût and the Imperial Guard, and De Fezensac was ordered to ride back to Ney and tell him to give up the march on Kreutzburg, and move to his right so as to form the left of the French battle line.

The artillery had opened on both sides amid a heavy fall of snow when De Fezensac rode off. Before he left Eylau he felt that his horse was still dead beat from the effects of the night ride. He happened to have 500 francs in gold in his belt, and he spent the money on bribing a soldier to exchange a horse he was leading for his own tired steed. It was all important to reach Ney quickly, but still more important to reach him with certainty. The 6th Corps would be somewhere on the road between Landsberg and Kreutzburg, but Lestocq's Prussians were also in that direction, and to attempt a direct ride would be to risk capture. It was no use to ask for an escort, such things were unheard of in the Grand Army. He decided that "slow and sure" was the best plan, so he first rode back to Landsberg, and then followed the track of Ney's corps northward along the Kreutzburg road. Through the driving snow came the muffled roar of the cannonade at

Eylau, where for hours the Emperor barely held his own and was saved only by the furious charges of Murat's cavalry. As De Fezensac turned north from Landsberg the sound of the battle had died away in the distance into a dull muttering like a far-off thunder-storm, but as he rode towards Kreutzburg there was for a while another cannonade in his front. Ney was again in action with a Prussian rear-guard.

When De Fezensac at last rejoined his chief about 2 p.m. the local fight was over. Lestocq had received earlier tidings of the great battle, and had drawn off to join Benningsen. Ney began at once to march to the eastward, his columns tramping across country over ice and snow, guided by the ever-increasing sound of the cannonade.[1]

Napoleon had been reinforced and had repulsed the Russian attack and was in turn pressing the enemy when, towards the close of the short winter's day, Lestocq's 6000 Prussians came into action on Benningsen's right. As so often happens when both sides are nearly exhausted, the appearance of this reinforcement for awhile restored the fight on the Russian side. Napoleon had again an anxious time. But it did not last long. The red sun was going down on the western snow-fields and it showed the heads of columns appearing on the right rear of the Allies. Ney's corps was arriving, and Benningsen, alarmed at this appearance of new enemies, and suspecting some deadly manœuvre against his flank, drew back Lestocq's corps and broke off the battle as the sun set and the short twilight began to deepen into night.

Ney's corps had not fired a shot, but its arrival was the decisive incident of the day. Benningsen abandoned during the night the position he had held all day. He left 18,000 dead and wounded on the ground, more than a fourth of the force engaged, and the French had taken twenty-four guns and

[1] In his "Souvenirs Militaires" (p. 159) De Fezensac says: "According to M. Thiers, Napoleon sent during the evening of the 7th several officers to Marshals Davoût and Ney to bring them to the field of battle. This is an error so far as regards Marshal Ney. He received no information, and had no idea there was a battle in progress when I joined him at 2 o'clock on the 8th, in the direction of Kreutzburg." The misstatement of Thiers is one of many instances of the way in which the historian of the Consulate and the Empire represents Napoleon as having done what was ideally right under the circumstances, and throws the blame of failure on his lieutenants.

sixteen flags. But they too had lost heavily in the long hours of close and desperate fighting. Fifteen thousand men had been killed and wounded, and Benningsen carried off as trophies of the day five eagles and seven flags. Both sides claimed the victory.

Ney spent the night with his staff in a peasant's cottage in the village of Schmolditten, and had a scanty supper and a hard bed. He had no idea that the enemy were already retiring, and naturally expected the battle to be renewed next day, when his corps not having yet been engaged would be given a leading part in it. He told his staff to try to get to sleep at once as there would be hard work in the morning, and added somewhat theatrically, "If need be I shall dismount sword in hand, and I hope you will all follow me". "We assured him," says De Fezensac, "that we would all be happy and proud to conquer or die with him. Then he stretched himself on a plank and fell into a deep sleep."

At daybreak the enemy had everywhere disappeared. They had retired on Königsberg and behind the frozen Pregel. There was no attempt at pursuit, only some of Murat's patrols rode forward till they could see in the distance the spires of the old Prussian capital. Ney was ordered to occupy Eylau, and while his troops were marching across from Schmolditten the Marshal with his staff went over the battle-field. "It was horrible," writes De Fenzensac. "The field was literally covered with dead. Gros' celebrated picture only gives a very faint idea of what it was like. But he at least paints with a fearful fidelity to truth the effect of these torrents of blood shed upon the snow. The Marshal traversed the ground in silence, his features betraying his emotion, and at last turning away from this frightful spectacle he said: 'What a massacre, and all to no purpose!' We returned to Eylau, the wretched appearance of which did not alleviate the impression made upon us by the battle-field. For the houses were full of wounded, for whom no help was available. The streets were strewn with dead. The inhabitants had taken to flight. We ourselves had absolutely nothing to eat. The weather was awful, and those who have served in the field know how this increases one's fatigue and makes one more sensitive to privations." Nevertheless in the afternoon the 6th Corps was ordered to move out and take up a line of outposts facing Königsberg.

After Eylau there was a halt for a few days. The armies on both sides were not far from the breaking-down point. The indecisive battle, followed by a seeming collapse of the campaign, though it was described in Napoleon's official bulletin as a brilliant victory, produced a depressing effect on the feeling of the army and on public opinion in France. Napoleon himself was anxious and irritable, and men began to ask if he was still the invincible soldier of Marengo, Jena, and Austerlitz. He had talked of marching on Königsberg, but that was obviously impossible. The most he would be able to do for awhile would be to maintain himself beyond the Vistula. A week after Eylau he decided to retire to the line of the river Passarge, and establish his army there in the villages and in camps of wooden huts, to cover the siege of Danzig.

The retreat began on 16 February. Benningsen followed up the movement at a respectful distance, assuming the air of a victor and making a show of pursuing the French columns. Ney was furthest to the rear and in order to teach the Russians a lesson he was ordered, on the morning of 2 March, to turn upon them and drive them out of the town of Guttstadt. They did not make a very determined stand and Ney turned them out of the place, capturing some welcome supplies, and pursuing the Cossacks towards Heilsberg. There was a running fight till late in the afternoon, with slight loss to the victors. There was some skirmishing on the 4th and 5th, and then the Russians abandoned their half-hearted pursuit.

Napoleon installed his army in its winter quarters between the Passarge and the lower Vistula. He had his head-quarters in the centre at Osterode with the Imperial Guard camped around him. Ney's corps had done the work of a rear-guard during the retreat, and was now given the post of danger in advance of the main line and on the right bank of the Passarge, with head-quarters at Guttstadt the scene of his victory.

Then for four months there was almost absolute inaction. Reinforcements arrived from France. Stragglers rejoined their corps. Many of them had been playing the part of marauders, levying unauthorized requisitions, and preying on the wretched peasants in the villages away from the line of march of the corps they had deserted. During this period of rest and recuperation for the Grand Army, Ney lost his aide-de-camp, De Fezensac, who was taken prisoner by a party of Cossack raiders, while carrying a despatch to Marshal Soult.

The siege of Danzig was vigorously pressed and, on 25 May, the fortress surrendered and thus set free the 30,000 men who had been engaged in blockading and reducing it. By the end of May Ney's corps had been again raised to 20,000 men. The Grand Army had grown into a formidable force. Behind Ney's corps, which acted as an advanced guard for the cantonments between the Passarge and the Vistula, Napoleon had under his immediate command a field army of 150,000 men (Imperial Guard; 1st Corps, Victor; 3rd, Davoût; 4th, Soult; 8th, Mortier, lately before Danzig; Reserve Corps, Lannes; and Murat's Cavalry Reserve, of seven divisions). Besides these the 5th Corps, now under Masséna, 30,000 strong, was about Pultusk on the Narev, covering Warsaw. Between Masséna and the main mass of the Grand Army was the newly raised Polish corps of General Zajonczek, 10,000 strong. In the rear of the army Brune with 50,000 men was blockading Stralsund where Blücher with 20,000 Prussians was holding out since the pursuit after Jena. A corps of 10,000 men was besieging Graudenz and 15,000 more were with Prince Jerome in Silesia. Thus Napoleon had about 210,000 men at the front and 75,000 more in the second line. Benningsen had only between 80,000 and 90,000 Russians and Lestocq's Prussian corps now raised to 20,000 with which to face the main body of the Grand Army. He was expecting reinforcements, and had about 20,000 more men watching Masséna on the Narev.

The Russian Commander-in-Chief was quite aware of Napoleon's ever-increasing superiority in numbers, and wished to stand on the defensive, retiring when the French advanced, and adopting the tactics that the Russian Generals used so effectively five years later. But as the weeks went by and he made no move, there was a growing discontent with his inaction in Prussian and Russian official circles. At the beginning of June, against his better judgment, he yielded to the rising clamour against him, and suddenly moved forward to attack Ney.

Napoleon was just then preparing to advance with the object of driving the enemy across the Niemen, cutting off Königsberg from all hope of succour, and invading Russia itself, and the news of the enemy's onset came as a surprise to him. The first brunt of the attack fell on the 6th Corps in its advanced position beyond the Passarge. Attacked by the enemy on 5 June, Ney—a master of rear-guard tactics—fell back very slowly towards the river, showing a bold front and fighting continually, but only making a sufficiently long stand at each point to compel the Russians to deploy a considerable force against him. In the evening he concluded his report to the Emperor with the words: "I shall make the enemy lose another day to-morrow". On the 6th he defended the ground foot by foot till he reached the bridge of Deppen on the Passarge, and then he made a vigorous counter-attack which effectually covered the retirement of his corps across the river. Thanks to his skilful and determined leadership and the steadiness with which his men fought, the Russians had gained only ten miles of ground in two days. This delay had given the Emperor time to concentrate his army in order to assume the offensive, with the result that the Russian advance came to a dead stop on the eastern bank of the Passarge.

Ney had not been very fortunate since his victory of Elchingen, more than two years earlier. Delayed at Ulm he had missed Austerlitz; he had been able to bring only a weak advanced guard into action at Jena; he had incurred Napoleon's grave displeasure by his movement towards Königsberg in January, and he had arrived too late to fire a shot at Eylau, though his coming had had important results. But now he had rendered an exceptionally valuable service to the Emperor, and Napoleon fully appreciated it.

The Grand Army came pouring across the Passarge, Napoleon throwing forward his left to turn Benningsen's right and cut him off from Königsberg. The Russians retreated on Heilsberg and halted there in a strong position. While Napoleon was concentrating to fight a battle there, in which he counted on destroying the Russian Army, Murat, who was well to the front with his cavalry supported by Davoût's corps, attacked on 10 June without orders, drove the Russians from their position at the cost of heavy loss, and gained a victory that had no decisive result, to the disappointment of Napoleon, all whose plans were deranged by his brother-in-law's precipitate action.

Benningsen retreated along the right bank of the River Alle, the Grand Army marching on a roughly parallel line a few miles away on the other bank. On the 13th Ney's corps was at Eylau where the Emperor had his head-quarters. The scene had changed in the four months since the great battle. Instead of the dreary waste of snow and ice there was a sunlit landscape of green woods and fields, and shining lakes. Only the signs of the havoc wrought in the partly rebuilt villages, and the huge mounds that marked the graves of the dead, told of the terrible day of 8 February.

From Eylau Murat with Davoût and Soult's corps was detached towards Königsberg. The rest of the Grand Army moved forward towards the crossing of the Alle at Friedland. Lannes had pushed on in advance and sent one of his Hussar regiments into the town, which stands on the left bank of the Alle in a loop of the river, concave towards the west, the direction from which the French were coming. Lannes, hussars were hardly in the town when they were driven out by a strong force of Russian cavalry. Benningsen's army was crossing the bridges of Friedland to offer battle on the low range of hills west of the town with its flanks protected by the winding river.

As Napoleon marched to support Lannes at sunrise on the 14th he heard the sound of a cannonade in the direction of Friedland, and rejoiced at the prospect of bringing Benningsen to action. "It is a lucky day," he said. "It is the anniversary of Marengo." As the various corps came up they formed for battle, but the attack was not pressed till late in the afternoon, when Napoleon had in line the corps of Mortier, Lannes, Victor, and Ney, the Imperial Guard and several divisions of cavalry. Ney was posted on the extreme right with his two divisions partly hidden at first in the woods of Sortlack. Napoleon had decided to entrust to him the movement that was destined to make the Russian defeat a disaster for Benningsen.

Opposite the Sortlack woods the Russian left was posted

with its flank resting on the Alle on the crest of a long slope, behind which lay the town of Friedland with its three bridges on the river. There was one more bridge behind the Russian centre and a ford in the rear of their right. Napoleon's plan was to make a feint against the enemy's right in order to draw the Russian reserves to that side, then send Ney to attack on the left where Bagration's corps was posted, interpose between it and the river, and seize the town of Friedland cutting the Russians off from three out of the four bridges. As Ney broke in on the Russian left there would be a general advance, and the Imperial Guard would be sent against the left centre of the enemy. Napoleon hoped thus to press the Russians back upon the Alle and secure many guns and thousands of prisoners while they tried to struggle across the ford and the one bridge left open to them.

From Ney's position in the woods the ground sank to a wide valley, and then rose again to the heights in front of Friedland. A strong body of the enemy's cavalry was posted on Bagration's left. Ney was anxious to have them broken up before he advanced across the hollow, and suggested to the officer commanding a brigade of the cavalry of the Guard, which was posted near him, that he should charge the Russian horsemen. The cavalry officer replied that he could not do so without orders from the Emperor. But Ney forced his hand. He had a squadron of hussars with him acting as his escort, and he ordered them to charge the Russian cavalry brigade. It seemed a mad order, but without "asking why" the squadron commander rode at the Russians. Down on the hussars came the enemy's cavalry in full charge driving the handful of light horsemen before them. The cavalry of the Guard could not look on without attempting to save their comrades. They charged in their turn and rode over the enemy while they were still disordered with their success.

Ney now advanced from the woods, his 1st Division leading, and the columns formed in echelon of brigades, and covered by lines of skirmishers. Up the slope went the French attack, the Marshal riding well to the front with one of Marchand's regiments. A heavy fire of artillery met him in front, and the leading brigade came under a cross fire from batteries posted on the other bank of the Alle. General Senamont, the artillery commander, sent some guns to check this flank fire, but the sorely tried 1st Brigade wavered and began to fall back. For a moment it seemed that the whole attack was on the point of collapsing. But Ney rode in among the men of the retiring brigade, and threatening some with his drawn sword, appealing to all with his voice which rang out clearly amid the din, he rallied them and brought them on once more to the attack. A mass of cavalry moved out to charge his left, but the danger had been marked by La Tour Maubourg who, with a brigade of dragoons, was covering the advance. He charged and drove back the Russians, and then Dupont's division of Victor's corps came into action on the left of Ney's 2nd Division. Thus supported the 6th Corps crowned the height, and led by Ney in person pushed in between Bagration's flank and the river, driving the opposing Russians down the slope towards Friedland, hurling many of them into the Alle, and fighting its way into the streets. "That man is a lion," exclaimed Napoleon when he heard of Ney's exploit.

As the Russian left gave way, the French attacked all along the front, and the Imperial Guard came marching into the Russian centre. Ney was fighting his way through Friedland with the wooden houses of the place ablaze, as Benningsen's centre and right retired down the heights, and unable to enter the town made for the one free bridge and the ford below it. With such scanty means of retreat and a victorious enemy pressing on their rear the Russians lost heavily. Ten thousand had fallen on the field, many were drowned in the Alle and some thousands of prisoners and eighty guns were the prize of the victors, who themselves lost nearly 12,000 men.

"The battle of Friedland is worthy of being numbered with those of Marengo, Austerlitz, and Jena," wrote Napoleon in his bulletin announcing the victory. On the day of the battle Königsberg surrendered to Davoût. In the evening Murat arrived with several divisions of cavalry, and early next day he was in hot pursuit of the Russians, who were retreating to the Niemen, the frontier stream of their Empire. Napoleon could now follow them up with overwhelming numbers. On the 19th he entered Tilsit on its left bank just as Benningsen

had completed the transfer of his army to the other shore. Here Napoleon was met by an envoy from the Czar Alexander asking for an armistice and offering to open peace negotiations. Three days later the Emperor and the Czar met in a tent erected on a raft moored midway between the banks of the Niemen, and the Treaty of Tilsit was signed by which Napoleon and Alexander became allies.

As soon as peace was arranged Ney handed his corps over to Marchand and hurried back to Paris with a well-earned leave of absence. He had been two years away from France and had taken a distinguished part in three campaigns. The Emperor had acknowledged his services by granting him an annual revenue of 28,000 francs payable by the exchequer of the Grand Duchy of Warsaw; and when a few months later (on 23 September, 1807) further largesses were bestowed on the marshals, Ney's share was 300,000 francs in cash, and 300,000 more in bonds of the National Debt of France. He was becoming a wealthy man. War in the great days of the Empire was a profitable business.

CHAPTER XI

SERVICE IN THE SPANISH PENINSULA (1807-1811)

AFTER the campaign of Friedland Ney was able to enjoy a few months of home life. He bought the country house and the small estate of Coudreaux near Châteaudun, and divided his time between this quiet retreat and his house in Paris. He could afford to spend money, though, compared to some of his brother marshals, he had still only a modest fortune. He had always held aloof from the disguised brigandage, which so many of them practised, and he was too honest for the wholesale peculation that went to the private accounts of others among those adventurous soldiers of the Revolution and the Empire.

Ney had been more than a year in France when the Emperor's intervention in the Spanish Peninsula again called him into the field. Spain had long been the subservient alley of Napoleon, and he had begun to work out a scheme for making the country a vassal state of his Empire. Under the mask of an armed alliance for the partition of Portugal a French army had occupied the northern provinces, and then advanced to Madrid. The dissensions in the royal family were skilfully used to secure the abdication of the King and of Prince Ferdinand his successor, and Napoleon's brother Joseph was accepted as King of Spain by a subservient assembly of Spanish Notables at Bayonne. But even before he was installed at Madrid the Spaniards had risen against the foreign ruler imposed upon them by the Emperor. There was it is true a French party in Spain, but it was a feeble minority. King Joseph could rely only on the French army of occupation. And a great success helped to spread the rising all over Spain, when, on 22 July, 1808, General Dupont with 17,000 men was forced to surrender at Baylen.

A few weeks later came the British intervention in Portugal

and Junot had to sign the Convention of Cintra, by which the French evacuated that country which then became a base of operations for the British against the French power in Spain. With insurrection all around him Joseph was compelled to abandon Madrid, and his rule was limited to the country north of the Ebro. Even there it extended no further than the French outpost lines and garrisons.

In the early autumn Napoleon went to Erfurt in Germany to have an interview with the Czar Alexander. Austria was becoming restless, and there was prospect of another war on the Danube next year. It was all important to crush the resistance of Spain, and drive out the British auxiliary corps operating from Portugal before facing this new danger. Hitherto the troops that had fought in Spain were chiefly young conscripts. While at Erfurt Napoleon determined to send to the Peninsula from their cantonments in Germany some of the veteran corps of the Grand Army under his best marshals. "I have sent the Spaniards lambs whom they have devoured," he said; "I shall send them wolves who will devour them in their turn."

The 6th Corps was one of those thus transferred to Spain. Marshal Ney rejoined it and took command, while it was marching across France. Its journey from the Rhine to the Pyrenees was a triumphal progress. Every city, town, and village, through which the veteran regiments passed, hailed in them the victors of the campaigns of Jena and Austerlitz, Eylau and Friedland, the conquerors of Europe on their way to an easy success in Spain. Officers and men were everywhere fêted, and the march was a long holiday.

As his veterans passed the Pyrenees, Napoleon himself hurried to the front, and on 5 November established his headquarters at Vittoria, where King Joseph with his Franco-Spanish court had taken refuge. Encouraged by the successes they had already won, three insurgent armies had advanced against the French in the north of Spain. They had rashly divided their forces. On the left Blake with 45,000 men was marching on Bilbao; on the right Palafox with 18,000 was moving on Pampeluna; between them Castaños with 30,000 men was on the Ebro near Logrono. A British army of 25,000 men under Sir John Moore was advancing from Portugal. Moore had been assured that he would be joined by a much larger force under the Spanish General, Romaña. His British troops were to act as a "stiffening" for the patriot levies, and with them to interpose between the French and Madrid.

Napoleon, with some 70,000 men in a central position, meant first to destroy the Spanish armies in the north, and then make a dash for Madrid before Moore could reach it. He marched on Burgos, and occupied the place after routing a large gathering of insurgents. Marshal Victor's corps defeated and dispersed Blake's army at Espinosa on 10 and 11 November. Castaños in the centre had meanwhile joined hands with Palafox on the right, but their united forces were routed by Marshal Lannes at Tudela on 22 November.

The Emperor had pushed forward Ney and the 6th Corps from Burgos to Aranda on the road to Madrid before launching the attack against Castaños and Palafox. He further directed Ney to move to his left towards Agreda, so as to watch the passes of the Sierra Moncayo through which the Spaniards were likely to retire, as Lannes and Moncey drove them south. He thus hoped to catch the enemy between hammer and anvil. Ney had only between 14,000 and 15,000 men with him at Aranda. He marched as far as Soria, but when he arrived there he realized that campaigning against a regular army, while the civil population stood practically neutral, was a different business from carrying on war in a country where every man's hand was against him. It was with the utmost difficulty that he could collect supplies for his men. No information either from the Emperor or his colleagues reached him. He found himself isolated among enemies and there were persistent reports that Castaños, at the head of 60,000 men (some said 80,000), had beaten Lannes and Moncey. The aggressive attitude of the Spanish population and the absence of any official communication seemed to give colour to these rumours. For the first time in his life Ney hesitated to advance, though his orders told him to do so. He feared that in the hill country in his front a disaster such as had befallen Dupont at Baylen might be waiting for him.

Had he blindly obeyed his orders and marched at once to Agreda he probably would have cut off the retreat of Castaños. But when, after a three days' halt at Soria, he at last moved, it was too late. He crossed the Sierra, occupied Agreda, and then finding no Spanish army within striking distance marched by the south bank of the Ebro by way of Tarragona to Alagon, where he arrived on 28 November, and found Marshal Moncey's corps preparing to besiege Saragossa.

The Emperor was very disappointed at the news that Ney had failed to carry out his orders. He wrote to him blaming him for the halt at Soria, though, at the same time, he admitted that he had had some cause for prudent hesitation. But when he heard of the march to Alagon he told him that he ought not to have gone there. He had nothing to do with the coming siege, and must keep his troops separate from those of Marshal Moncey and devote himself to hunting down Castaños.

Immediately after the French victories in the north the Emperor had made a dash for Madrid, forcing the pass of the Somo Sierra, and reoccupying the Spanish capital on 4 December. Thence he at once sent an order to Ney to bring the 6th Corps to Madrid. It was to form part of the army that was to be employed against Moore and the British expedition.

Ney marched from Alagon up the valley of the River Jalon and down that of the Henares, thus avoiding any high mountain passes, and reaching Madrid by way of Catalayud, Medinaceli, Siguenza, and Guadalajara. He arrived in the capital on 14 December. A few days later the 6th Corps was reviewed by the Emperor. He had by this time forgotten his discontent with Ney's leadership in the north, in his general satisfaction at the apparent collapse of the Spanish resistance. He was prodigal of his praise of the men, and told Ney and his officers that he was about to send them to new victories, this time over the English, the traditional enemies of France.

Moore's little army, now reduced to about 20,000 effective men, was slowly making its way across the snowy plateaus of Leon, scattering in more than one sharp action the French cavalry that harrassed its advance, but finding no sign of the co-operation promised by the Spanish patriots. Day by day came news that in the north the French Generals had driven the Spanish armies before them like flocks of sheep. Still Moore hoped to reach Madrid in time to co-operate in the defence of the mountain defiles that are the approach to the capital from the northward. But then came the tidings that the boasted defences of the Somo Sierra pass had been rushed by a few squadrons of Polish lancers, and the Emperor was in Madrid. But even then there were rumours of a new rising of the people, a rally of the Spanish armies, and Moore pushed on as far as Sahagun, where in the grey dawn of 23 December, Paget, afterwards the famous Marquis of Anglesea, with the 10th and 15th Hussars, dashed into the town, surprised the French cavalry who held it, and drove them out in twenty minutes, taking more than 150 prisoners. But from some of these prisoners and from the despatches found on a captured officer Moore learned that several French columns were converging upon his line of march, and the Emperor himself was advancing against him from Madrid with 50,000 men. To persevere in his enterprise unaided against such odds would have been to court destruction. He began his retreat to Corunna.

The Emperor had crossed the passes of the Guadarama in deep snow, through which the troops moved only at the cost of considerable suffering and danger. Ney's corps started from Madrid on 20 December and in its turn struggled through the ice and snow of the mountain passes, then advanced north westward across the wintry uplands of Old Castille and Leon by Tordesillas and Rio Seco to Astorga. Soon there were signs that the column was moving on the track of the enemy. Abandoned wagons, starving stragglers who were glad to surrender for the sake of food and protection from the Spanish irregulars, the new-made graves on the scene of a skirmish, all told their tale. But Ney's corps was in the second line. Soult was a day's march in advance and in contact with the British rear-guard. So the infantry of the 6th Corps saw no fighting. Ney sent on his cavalry to assist Soult. The gallant young Colbert still commanded it. He was shot dead by a skirmisher of the 95th in a rear-guard fight at Calcabellos on

3 January, 1809. His loss was a great blow to Ney, with whom he had served in three campaigns.[1]

Ney reached Astorga on 2 January. He found Napoleon there. The Emperor had suddenly changed his plans. Disquieting reports had reached him from Paris, and he had decided to return there at once leaving it to Soult to "drive the English into the sea". He considered that Soult did not need the 6th Corps to help him in dealing with what was left of Moore's sorely tried force now reduced to about 15,000 effective men. He therefore ordered Ney to march to Lugo and make that place the centre for operations against the insurgent bands still in arms in the province of Galicia.

Lugo was occupied without difficulty and small flying columns were sent to clear the neighbouring country of the guerillas. Napoleon had returned to Paris. Moore had fought the battle of Corunna against Soult on 16 January (1809) to cover the re-embarkation of his army, dying in the moment of victory. After occupying Corunna, Soult had compelled Ferrol to surrender, and then marched his corps into the north of Portugal leaving Ney to complete the subjugation of Galicia and reorganize the province.

The 6th Corps had to provide garrisons for the chief towns, and detachments to patrol the main roads and deal with the few bands of patriots (or as the French called them insurgents) who still kept the field. He left these active duties to his subordinates and established his head-quarters at Corunna, visiting the other important centres in turn. Communications either with the Government at Paris, or with King Joseph at Madrid, were difficult and uncertain. British warships were cruising off the port of Corunna, the Province of Asturias was held by a patriot force, and the roads to Madrid were beset by bands of guerillas. Ney thus became, by the force of circumstances, for some months an almost independent viceroy of Galicia.

[1] Only two days before, when Colbert's cavalry joined the advanced guard, Napoleon had reviewed the regiments and said to their young commander: "General, you have proved in Egypt, Italy, and Germany that you are one of my bravest soldiers. You shall soon receive the reward due to your brilliant successes." "Make haste, Sire," replied Colbert, "for though I am not yet thirty, I feel that I am already growing old."

Martial law was in force but he was a moderate and kindly ruler and was not unpopular with the people. He organized a regular collection of taxes, out of which by careful management he was able to supply and pay his army and provide for the civil administration of the district. He even found means to assist some of the Spanish victims of the war. One of his acts of generosity was of a very exceptional character. In Corunna and Ferrol he found some of the wives and families of officers of the regular Spanish Army, whose husbands were then actually in arms against King Joseph. Separated from them and having no claim on the new government the women were in the direst poverty. Ney arranged that they should be allowed from the revenues of the province half the pay of their husbands' rank. By this act of humanity he was actually helping to pay the enemy's officers.

There was a current belief among the French that the Spanish convents were full of unwilling recluses pining for freedom. In every city and town he visited in Galicia, Ney went to the local convents, and after assembling the nuns and novices told them they were at liberty to put off their conventual dress and return to their old homes. Ney's aide-de-camp, Béchet, Baron de Léoncourt, tells how during one of these military visitations a young novice threw herself on her knees before the Marshal, and with tears in her eyes made a long petition to him in Spanish, of which language neither Ney nor his staff understood a word. The impression of the officers was that she was pleading for freedom. The interpreter was asked to explain. Then it was found that instead of asking to leave her convent the young nun was imploring the Marshal to use his influence to obtain permission for her to take at once the vows that would bind her to the conventual life. She was under the age at which, by the law, women were allowed to take these vows, but permission to anticipate the date could be granted by the joint consent of the ecclesiastical and civil authorities, and the novice told how she had thought that it was revealed to her in prayer that before long a powerful personage would come to the convent, and secure her the desired dispensation from the law's delays. She believed that this hoped-for intervention had come, when the French

Viceroy of Galícia appeared at the convent. Ney and his officers found that all their sympathy had been wasted. De Léoncourt says that in all the convents visited, Ney only found one nun anxious to lay aside the veil. It is very likely that she was a novice, free to go in any case. Later on she married one of the French officers. The final result of Ney's visitation of these Spanish convents was to prove that the story of cloisters crowded with unwilling inmates was a baseless legend.

The marshals operating in or holding the various provinces of Spain were under a divided authority. They were nominally under the command of King Joseph and his "major-general," or chief of the staff, Marshal Jourdan. But they were also receiving instructions in the name of the Emperor from the Minister of War at Paris, Clarke, Duke de Feltre. These commands were often in disaccord with those that came from Madrid. But in any case the marshals showed but scant respect for the orders that emanated from the Madrid Government. Joseph they regarded as a *pékin*, an ignorant civilian who had no right to dictate to soldiers, and they had something like contempt for Jourdan's military capacities. Ney curtly rejected a plan of campaign sent him by the latter. "This order," he wrote to Jourdan, "is drawn up by some one who knows nothing of our business. The Emperor has given me an army to conquer with and not to capitulate. You may tell the King that I have not come here to play the part of Dupont." The state of mind manifested in such an utterance, the contempt for the puppet King and his major-general, the possibility of playing off the Madrid and the Paris War Offices against each other, the semi-independence resulting from the difficulty of communications, all helped to produce a tendency to insubordination towards authority, and when one of the marshals was placed under another's orders there was friction and lack of hearty co-operation. This helps to explain, though it does not justify, Ney's action in the crisis that, later on, brought to an abrupt end his command in the Peninsula.

Without troubling himself about the views of the Madrid Government he worked out a plan of campaign of his own in the early summer of 1809, as soon as the pacification of Galicia made him feel equal to an enterprise beyond its borders. The

Spanish General Romaña held the neighbouring coast province of Asturias, with his head-quarters at Oviedo. Ney, at the end of April, organized a column of the 6th Corps, with which he was to enter Asturias and march on Oviedo from the westward, while General Kellerman, who commanded in the Province of Leon, advanced against it from the southward. The Asturias is a narrow tract of mountain land, and Ney, having to move by rugged hill-tracks, took with him only what baggage and supplies could be carried on pack mules, and reduced his artillery to a single mule battery of four light guns.

The march through the mountains was a trying operation. There were times when the column from Galicia had to move for a while in single file. A more enterprising commander than Romaña would have offered serious resistance, but he contented himself with retiring on Oviedo. Ney had hoped to bring him to action, but the difficulty of obtaining information prevented this. Everywhere the inhabitants had fled from their homes on the approach of the French. Those who were captured refused to answer questions, or gave misleading replies. Ney afterwards found that one night the column had bivouacked within five miles of Romaña, without having any idea that he was anywhere in the neighbourhood. By the middle of May Ney had been joined by Kellerman before Oviedo, and Romaña had evacuated the place by embarking his troops on English transports. Then Ney had to hurry back to Galicia for there was bad news from Portugal. On 12 May the British under Wellesley had forced the passage of the Douro. This was the first step in a series of operations that ended in Soult having to retreat across the northern frontier of Portugal, bringing with him only some 6000 men out of the 25,000 he commanded a month before and having lost and abandoned all his baggage and artillery.

Ney received him at Lugo on 30 May. Wellesley had turned to the preparations for his march into central Spain which ended at Talavera, so Galicia was allowed still to remain a French province. Ney helped Soult to refit the remnant of his army, turned over some of the guns of the 6th Corps to him, and from its well-stored magazines gave his brother marshal clothing, ammunition, and food for his men. It was agreed that Soult should lead them into northern Leon and give them a rest there. But first there was a project of surprising Vigo, the only place in Galicia where the Spaniards had kept their flag flying, thanks to the co-operation of a British squadron. The enterprise came to nothing. De Léoncourt says it was Soult's fault. Ney's column was on the spot on the day agreed, but Soult was late at the rendezvous.

He marched off to Toro in Leon; and now Ney found his own position in Galicia becoming difficult. The French had been driven out of Portugal, Wellesley was threatening Madrid, Ney at Lugo with all the ports of his province blockaded by the British navy, and the prospect of British, Portuguese, and Spanish forces appearing on his landward frontier, and the district showing signs of a coming rising, decided that he must follow Soult into the Province of Leon and abandon Galicia for the time being. At Corunna there were in the hospitals a number of sick and wounded officers and men of the French Army. He feared to trust their fate to the inhabitants, and he had no means of removing them. He communicated under a flag of truce with the blockading squadron, and arranged that simultaneously with his evacuation of Corunna, a landing party of British sailors and marines should take over the guard of the hospitals. Then he concentrated the 6th Corps at Lugo and marched into Leon, skirmishing on the way with guerilla bands that gathered like flocks of vultures to hang upon his line of march.

After Talavera (27 and 28 July) Wellesley, though he had been victorious and had won his title of Lord Wellington, had been obliged to withdraw into Portugal. Ney was directed to move down to Salamanca with the 6th Corps, establish his head-quarters there, and maintain order in the surrounding district. He was at Salamanca for some months, during which his corps received considerable reinforcements. At the end of October he obtained leave to return for a while to Paris. He left Marchand, his senior divisional-general, in command of the corps, with his chief of the staff, the Swiss strategist Jomini, to assist him.

Ney had not been many days with his wife at their house in Paris, when news arrived that Marchand had been unlucky in some operations he undertook against an insurgent force on the Portuguese borders of the province. The Emperor was very angry, and ordered the Marshal to return post-haste to his command at Salamanca. Ney arrived there in very bad humour. He had a quarrel with Jomini whom he blamed for the mischance that had so abruptly cut short his leave of absence. The Switzer resigned his place as chief of the staff, and the Baron de Léoncourt was given the vacant post.

The winter and the spring of 1810 passed quietly enough at Salamanca. "We had a very agreeable time," says De Léoncourt, "and at our head-quarters there was high play." Whist, at a gold Napoleon for each point, seems to have been the favourite game. Wellington was entrenching himself in the famous lines of Torres Vedras, and the Emperor had planned an invasion of Portugal and a march on Lisbon for the coming summer. The first step in the campaign was to be the siege of Ciudad Rodrigo, the fortress that barred the road across the frontier into Portugal.

Ney was hoping for the command. But in May Masséna arrived as Commander-in-Chief of the "Army of Portugal" to organize and direct the march against Wellington. Ney with the 6th and Junot with the 8th Corps were to serve under him. In the first days of June, detachments of the 6th Corps were sent forward to besiege Ciudad Rodrigo: the Commander-in-Chief was with Junot's corps at Valladolid.

Then came Ney's first open quarrel with Masséna. De Léoncourt only briefly alludes to it, but Madame Junot, who was with her husband at Masséna's head-quarters, tells the story in detail in her memoirs. The first parallel had been opened before the fortress on the night between 15 and 16 June, and then, under the direction of his chief engineer officer, Major Conche, the approaches were rapidly pushed forward and batteries were being erected and armed for the bombardment of the town. All was going well and Ney, who had returned to Salamanca, was expecting an early reduction of the place, when one morning there arrived from Valladolid a young engineer officer of Junot's staff, Lieutenant-Colonel Valazé. He produced a letter from Masséna directing Ney to put him in command of the siege works before Ciudad Rodrigo. Ney was indignant at what he regarded as a plan for giving to a protégé of Junot the credit of taking the fortress, after his own officer had done the hardest part of the work. He told Valazé that he had plenty of good officers of his own, and the Prince of Essling (Masséna), "prince though he was," had no right to interfere with his staff. He sent the young colonel back to Valladolid with this message: "I don't want the Duke d'Abrantès" (Junot) said Ney, "to trouble me with his protégés. If they are good, let him keep them for himself."

Valazé told his story, and Masséna was furious, and talked of removing Ney from his command, and sending him back to France. Junot generously intervened to dissuade him. "You will see," said Masséna as he gave a reluctant consent, "You will see that this proud fellow will upset all our plans with his stubborn self-will and foolish vanity."

Valazé was sent back to Ney, only to return to Valladolid, a couple of days later, bearing a letter from the Marshal which was an open act of insubordination. Here is the strange document, evidently written while he was under the sway of one of his characteristic outbursts of temper:—

"MONSIEUR LE MARÉCHAL,

"I am a Duke and a Marshal of the Empire like you; as for your title of Prince of Essling, it is of no importance outside the Tuileries. You tell me that you are Commander-in-Chief of the Army of Portugal. I know it only too well. So when you tell Michel Ney to lead his troops against the enemy you will see how he will obey you.

"But when it pleases you to disarrange the staff of the army, appointed by the Prince of Neufchâtel (Berthier), you must understand that I will no more listen to your orders than I fear your threats. See here, just ask the Duke d'Abrantès (Junot) what he and I did a few weeks ago when we received from that other (who is major-general to the King and who did such pretty things there where we are going)[1] orders differing from those that came to us from Paris and were therefore the orders of the Emperor. Do you know what we did? We obeyed the orders from Paris, and we did right for they praised us for it, and praised us warmly. I had letters from Madrid in which I was called—I believe—a rebel. As that is about as absurd as calling me a poltroon, I took no notice of it, and General Junot would certainly have acted in the same way.

"Adieu, Monsieur le Maréchal. I esteem you, and you know it. You esteem me, and I know it. But why the devil sow discord between us over a mere caprice? For after all, how on earth are you to know that

[1] Marshal Jourdan.

your little man can throw a bomb better than my old veteran, who is, I assure you, a reliable fellow. They say your man dances prettily: all the better for him; but this does not prove that he can make those mad Spaniards dance, and that is what we want.

"I remain, Monsieur le Maréchal, etc.,

"NEY"

One can imagine the rage of Masséna when Valazé came back with this letter. That Ney should have written it, and still more that he should have been able to retain his command after such an outburst against his chief, throws a flood of light on the indiscipline of the French armies in Spain.

"You see it is impossible to do anything with that man," said Masséna to Junot. The latter tried to calm him, but he broke out in a fury: "Am I then only a sham Commander-in-Chief. I mean that this young man shall conduct the siege, and by the devil in hell Monsieur Ney shall bend the knee before my will, or my name is not Masséna."

He hurried off to Salamanca with Valazé. Ney had gone to the lines before Ciudad Rodrigo. Masséna followed him there, and gave Ney the choice of returning to France or accepting Valazé. Ney hesitated to take a course that might have removed him once for all from the Emperor's service, and gave an unwilling submission.

On 9 July the rampart was breached and all was ready for the assault when the Governor surrendered. He came to meet Ney on foot in civilian dress and leaning on the arms of two officers. He explained that he had had a fall and could hardly walk, and that this was why he was not in uniform and ready to give up his sword. Ney replied with graceful courtesy, "Monsieur le Gouverneur, you have made too good use of it, for us to think of taking it from you".

Masséna then concentrated his army and crossed the Portuguese frontier with 65,000 men. The 6th Corps was employed in the siege of Almeida, but as the Commander-in-Chief was present, Ney left the direction of the attack to him, and took as little personal part as possible in the operations. The advance was then continued by way of Coimbra on Lisbon. On 25 September Wellington's army of 40,000 British and Portuguese barred the way over the Sierra d'Alcoba at the ridge of Busaco on the Coimbra road. The attack was arranged for next day. De Léoncourt relates an incident, which occurred on the eve of the battle, and which shows how deeply Ney's resentment against Masséna still rankled in his mind. The Marshal was dictating to his chief of the staff the orders for the coming fight. De Léoncourt interrupted him to ask if there was not an omission, pointing out that the troops that would come first into contact with the British had no support, and would be exposed to serious risk of defeat. "Write on," replied Ney, "these are not *my* orders." Next day following the letter of Masséna's orders he attacked on the ridge on the British left centre after Reynier's attack further up the ridge had been repulsed. The massive columns of the 6th Corps were driven back in their turn, and Busaco was a French defeat.

From the scene of his victory, Wellington, carrying out his pre-arranged plan, fell back within the fortified lines that protected Lisbon. Masséna's army, forced to maintain itself in a hostile and wasted country before the entrenchments that defied attack, dwindled rapidly week after week. In the middle of November he fell back from immediate contact with the British positions, but still persisted in the determination to remain within striking distance. By the end of February, 1811, he had no more than 30,000 effective men left, and when Wellington issued from his lines to attack him he began a retreat towards the frontier. Ney, with what was left of the 6th Corps, protected the retirement.

The movement began on 3 March by the road to Coimbra. On the 9th Ney fought his first rear-guard action at Piombal and was somewhat roughly handled by the pursuing British. On the 12th there was another fight at the village of Redinha. Then came the news that Coimbra was in the hands of the allied troops and Masséna had to change his line of retreat, following the south side of the Mondego valley, and reaching Miranda by a difficult march over wretched tracks through hilly country. At Miranda, after another action in which his troops were driven from position after position, Ney determined that it was impossible to continue the retreat, unless a large part of the huge wagon train that encumbered the army was sacrficed. He gave orders that most of it should be burned. He set fire first to the wagon that carried his own property, but he also condemned to the flames a number of carriages belonging to the Commander-in-Chief. This enabled extra horses to be attached to the teams of the remaining waggons, and thus facilitated the subsequent movements. In the fighting next day he had a narrow escape from disaster. One of his brigades broke its ranks in a temporary panic at the crossing of the bridge of Foz-d'Arienna. Two guns were lost, numbers of men were hustled into the river below the bridge, and amongst them the standard-bearer of the 39th Infantry was thus drowned, and the eagle he carried was lost. It was only the steadiness of the rear-guard brigade that saved the situation.

On the 23rd the army was at last concentrated at Colerico near the frontier. Masséna was anxious to make an effort to remain on Portuguese ground. Ney regarded this as a useless proceeding that could only lead to further disaster. The event proved that he was right in his judgment,[1] but this does not excuse the action he took. Masséna ordered a movement to the town of Guarda. Ney, who had from the first been on the point of a quarrel with him, refused to obey, and declared that he would lead the 6th Corps by Almeida into Spain. Masséna's patience was now exhausted. He issued an order transferring the command of the 6th Corps to General Loison, and directed Ney to proceed to Madrid and there await the Emperor's decision on his conduct.

But Napoleon had by this time come to regard dissensions and indiscipline among his marshals as something like an inevitable evil. He could not afford permanently to dispense with the services of a leader like Ney, but neither could he disregard his conduct towards Masséna, and to give him another independent command in Spain would have been to put a slight upon the Commander-in-Chief, whom he often spoke of as the best of his marshals. He sent Ney a letter of strong censure and told him to go home to Coudreaux. Perhaps the Marshal was not greatly disappointed at leaving a country where there was now small hope of gathering further laurels, and at being allowed to spend a few months in peace with his wife and children.

[1] On 3 April Masséna was badly defeated by Wellington at Sabugal.

CHAPTER XII

THE MARCH ON MOSCOW (1812)

IF Ney's career as a general had closed with his retirement from the army in Spain, he would not have held more than a secondary place among Napoleon's marshals, and his name would be little known beyond the comparatively narrow circle of students of military history. The real greatness of the man was yet to be revealed. So far though he had had a successful career, others of his contemporaries had risen to a higher eminence. They had won for themselves a fuller share of their master's glory, attached themselves more closely to his fortunes, rendered him greater services and reaped a richer reward.

To some extent what was best in Ney's character had retarded his advancement. He was no fortune hunter. He had none of the spirit of intrigue that led others to push their way to the front at the expense of their comrades, and he was quite free from brigand touch that made so many of the soldiers of the Empire enrich themselves with almost open peculation and plunder. From the days when, as a Republican officer, he had more than once refused a well-earned promotion he had done his duty as a soldier without troubling himself much about tangible rewards.

And he had not always been lucky. In the famous years after Boulogne, when the Grand Army was marching about Central Europe making swift conquests and tumbling down thrones, he had missed some of the greatest battles. In Spain he had failed at the outset to carry out the Emperor's orders. He had been given no high command, and as a subordinate he had drifted into a dispute with his Commander-in-Chief, which had temporarily severed him from the armies in the field. But his great opportunity was to come. The terrible campaign in Russia revealed him as "the bravest of the brave," and the tragedy of the final downfall of the Empire involved him in a fate that has given him an enduring and a pathetic place in the world's history.

Napoleon knew his solid qualities as a leader of men, and when in the early months of 1812 he was preparing to break with his ally of Tilsit, and stake his fortunes on an invasion of Russia by the united armies of the Empire and its vassals, he summoned Ney from his retirement. His old corps, like the first "Grand Army," had long since been broken up. It had been frittered away in the endless campaigns of Spain and Portugal. Ney was given the command of the 3rd Corps of the new Grand Army—an army of many nations and languages, of which not more than a third was French, and which included as many conscripts as veterans in its ranks.

The 3rd Corps was a larger body of troops than the old 6th Corps. It was formed of two French divisions, from Metz and to which later a third division of King Jerome's Würtemberg troops was added. There were two brigades of light cavalry. The total strength of the corps was 35,000 infantry and 2400 cavalry.[1]

The officers were mostly strangers to their commander. General Gouré acted as his chief of the staff. An old friend rejoined him when the Würtemberg division was added to the corps. It was commanded by General Marchand, who had been one of his divisional commanders in the 6th Corps and before that had served with him in the Army of the Rhine.

The concentration of the Grand Army along the right bank of the Vistula began in the month of February and was not completed until May, 1812. From Metz the 3rd Corps marched across the whole of Germany to the cantonments assigned to it in West Prussia between Thorn and Strasburg. We are now so used to the idea of armies being rapidly concentrated by railway that we forget these enormous marches

[1] The organization of the corps (before the Würtembergers joined it) was:—

1st Division. General Ledru des Essarts. 24th Light Infantry and 46th and 72nd of the Line.
2nd Division. General Razout. 4th, 18th, and 93rd of the Line.
Two cavalry brigades. Generals Beurmann and Valmabele.
Artillery Commander. General Fouchet.

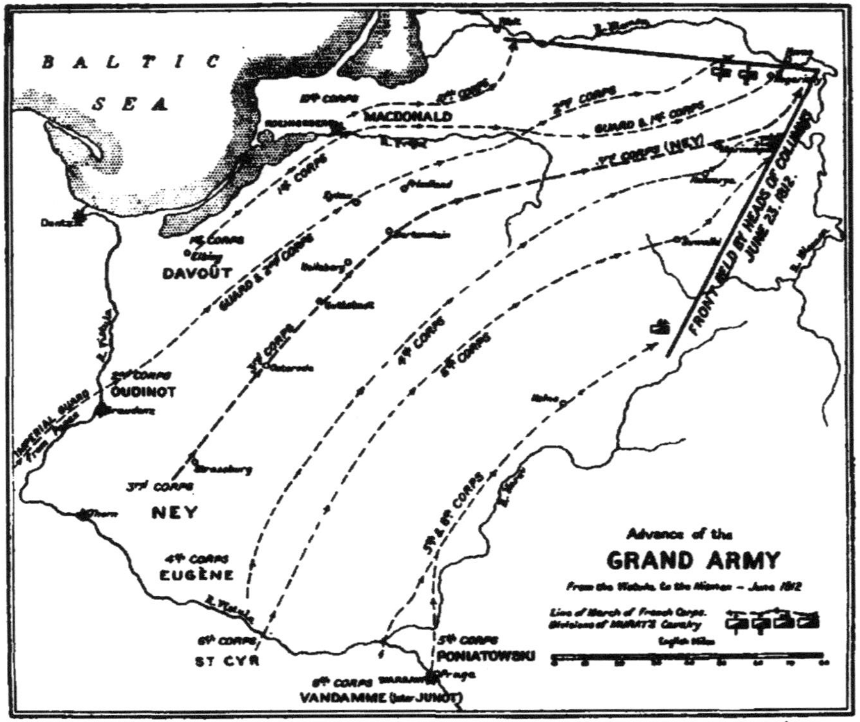

BALTIC SEA
MACDONALD
DAVOUT
OUDINOT
NEY
EUGÈNE
ST CYR
PONIATOWSKI
VANDAMME (later JUNOT)
1st CORPS (NEY)
GUARD & 1st CORPS
2nd CORPS
3rd CORPS
4th CORPS
6th CORPS
5th CORPS
8th CORPS
5th & 8th CORPS
GUARD & 2nd CORPS
FRONT HELD BY HEADS OF COLUMNS JUNE 23, 1812.
Advance of the
GRAND ARMY
From the Vistula to the Niemen – June 1812
Line of March of French Corps.
Divisions of MURAT'S Cavalry
English Miles

of the Napoleonic wars, when the French infantry tramped for weeks at a time across half a continent.

By the end of May the Grand Army was arrayed on a front of several hundred miles along the Vistula, its left near the Baltic at Elbing and Königsberg, its extreme right resting on the Carpathians in Austrian Poland.[1] The Emperor was at Dresden holding his "Congress of Kings". It was not till 5 June that orders were given for the first stage of the general advance, and next day the columns of the Grand Army began their converging march towards the Niemen. By 23 June the front of the army formed a great wedge with its point threateningly directed towards Russia. That point was just inside the bend of the Niemen near Kovno. Here Napoleon had close at hand the Imperial Guard, the 1st, 2nd, and 3rd Corps and two divisions of Murat's cavalry. Macdonald about Tilsit on the left watched the lower course of the Niemen. Away to the right on the other front that looked directly eastward were Eugène with the centre and Jérôme with the corps of the right wing.

Ney's corps had been marching for a fortnight, passing on the way over ground that had become familiar to him in the campaigns of Eylau and Friedland. He had seen again Deppen and Guttstadt where he had fought successful engagements, and Bartenstein and Heilsberg, and had passed just

[1] The general arrangement may be thus shown in tabular form:—

Extreme left (north). 10th Corps. Prussians (Macdonald), Königsberg.

Extreme right (south). The Austrian Army about Lemberg under Prince Schwartzenberg.

Main army of operations under Napoleon.

Left Wing	1st Corps (Davoût) from Hamburg 2nd " (Oudinot) from Holland 3rd " (Ney) from Metz Cavalry Reserve. (Murat)	The Emperor.
Centre	4th Corps (Eugène) Italians 6th " (St. Cyr) Bavarians	The Viceroy Eugène.
Right Wing	5th Corps (Poniatowski) Poles 7th " (Reynier) Saxons 8th " (Vandamme) Westphalians 4th Cavalry Division. La Tour Maubourg	King Jérôme of Westphalia.

Imperial Guard at Posen, to join the Emperor in Russia.

Reserve Corps { 9th at Berlin / 11th at Mayence } in process of formation.

south of the field of Friedland. At last he camped by the shore of the frontier river amid the dark pine woods. His corps was not to be the first to cross, so he had to wait till the passage was free, and he received his orders to follow.

The crossing of the Niemen began on the night between 23 and 24 June, four bridges being thrown across the river near Kovno. A few Cossacks had watched the covering party row across the river while the bridges were being built, but on the French approaching them they disappeared into the woods. The incident was typical of the experiences of the invaders during the first days of the advance. The few enemies who showed themselves rode away to the eastward, and evaded every attempt to close with them. Wilna was abandoned, the Russians setting fire to the great magazines of supplies accumulated there. Napoleon occupied the place on 29 June.

During this first stage of the advance, Ney, with the 3rd Corps, had followed a line of march some miles to the north of that taken by the main body under the Emperor. On the 28th, when it was thought the enemy might make a stand at Wilna, Ney had closed in nearer to Napoleon's line of advance, diverging again to the north-eastward next day. Oudinot with the 2nd Corps marched on his left.

After the occupation of Wilna, there was a pause on the advance, enforced by a sudden change in the weather and some days of abnormal cold and torrential rain. The loss in horses was heavy. An equally sudden change to dry warm weather was the signal for resuming the march. And again for Ney and his corps there were some days of uneventful plodding eastward along the monotonous plain between the dreary belts of fir and pine woods. There was no sight of an enemy. Murat's cavalry well out in front were in contact with the swarms of Cossack irregular horsemen that protected Barclay's retreat.

At the entrenchments that guarded the crossing of the Dwina at Drissa the Russian General halted, and there were rumours of a coming battle. Ney hurried up to support Murat in the attack on the works, only to learn that the enemy had abandoned them without firing a shot, and was retiring up the right bank of the river towards Witebsk. There Barclay hoped to be joined by the Russian army of the South under his colleague Bagration.

On 16 July Ney turned from the direct road to Drissa to march along the left bank of the Dwina, following Murat and closing with him on the main central mass of the Grand Army, which the Emperor was concentrating for a hoped-for battle near Witebsk. On the 25th Murat and the advanced guard came upon the Russians in position west of that place, and the two days' fighting known as the Battle of Ostrovno followed. Ney had joined hands with the Emperor on the 22nd and, during Murat's advanced guard battle, was moving up to take part in the anticipated general engagement. But on the morning of the 28th, which was expected to be a day of battle, it was found that the enemy had disappeared. They had slipped away quietly in the night, on Barclay's learning that Bagration had been headed off by Davoût and could not yet join him. Witebsk was found deserted, and the Emperor established his head-quarters there.

All touch with the enemy had been lost. Had Barclay retreated eastward towards Smolensk or north-eastward along the Dwina? Murat was sent out to feel for the Russian rear-guard in the latter direction, while Ney marched out along the road leading to Smolensk. His cavalry came upon the Cossacks, and he found abundant evidence that a large army had traversed the ground over which he was moving. But he soon received orders from the Emperor to halt.

For once, even to a keen soldier like Ney, such orders were welcome. The sun was blazing with tropical heat. The ground was burned up and the men marched in clouds of stifling dust. Water was scarce. The horses were breaking down. It was the collapse of thousands of cavalry and artillery horses that forced the Emperor to call a halt at Witebsk. But though there had been hardly any fighting, the men had also suffered in the prolonged march into a half-desert country, from which all supplies had been swept by the retreating enemy. Regiments that had not yet fired a shot were already reduced by invaliding to two-thirds of the strength with which they had crossed the Niemen.

Napoleon announced that the campaign of 1812 was over. The army would be put into cantonments and standing camps, Lithuania and Poland would be reorganized during the autumn and winter and in the spring of 1813 there would be an advance to Smolensk. Thence two roads radiated, one to St. Petersburg, the other to Moscow. Both capitals would be attacked, if need be, in the great campaign of 1813. Till then the Grand Army would hold the country it had already occupied.

The positions assigned to Ney were in the centre of the line of cantonments east of Witebsk, along the course of the little River Moczna, where the Smolensk road crosses it at the village of Lozna. North of him to his left lay the 4th Corps; south of him to his right the 1st and then the 8th. Behind him the Imperial Guard held Witebsk. In his front, towards Smolensk, Murat had formed a strong outpost line.

But these positions had not been occupied for many days when the Emperor again changed his plans. On 8 August Barclay, urged by those who had from the first been ill-pleased with his persistent retirement, had suddenly assumed the offensive and driven in Sebastiani's advanced cavalry at Inkowo. Murat had hurried up to restore the fight, but the Russians claimed a victory, and Napoleon felt that even a doubtful success for the enemy might be a danger to him. He thought Barclay's stroke at Inkowo was the prelude to a general advance of the enemy, and he had heard that Barclay had been joined by Bagration. He conceived the plan of a concentration against the Russian left to drive the united armies away to the north of the Smolensk-Moscow road.

The French flank march from the cantonments about Witebsk south-eastward to the south bank of the Dnieper began on 10 August. For some days the Russians did not suspect it for they still had a screen of French outposts in their front which held its own so firmly against a partial attack, that they believed the Grand Army must be behind it. The Dnieper was crossed on the 13th, and Napoleon had thus a new line of supply in his rear passing through Minsk. The line of march was now eastward on Smolensk.

Ney's corps was well to the front supporting Murat's

cavalry. On the 15th there was the first fighting. Krasnoi, a town of wooden houses at the crossing of a little stream running into the Dnieper, was found to be held by a Russian regiment. Ney's infantry quickly drove them out. It was his first victory in the campaign, and the name of Krasnoi was a few months later to be associated with the most famous of his exploits.

East of the captured town, as the advance continued, Ney and Murat came upon some 6000 Russians in line of battle. It was the rear-guard of General Neverovskoi's corps which Bagration had left upon the Dnieper. It was late in the day, but before Murat's fiery charges and the onset of Ney's infantry the Russians broke, leaving a 1000 prisoners and eight guns in the hands of the victors. Neverovskoi fell back upon Smolensk.

Contemporary French accounts speak of the city of Smolensk as a fortress. It was a walled town, with a low rampart flanked only by a few towers and a ruinous citadel of the middle-age type. It stood on the slope of a hill rising from the margin of the Dnieper, with a suburb on the other side connected with it by a bridge. A few guns were mounted on the old walls, but in places buildings and plantations gave cover for an attack up to the edge of the narrow ditch.

The place looked so ill fitted for defence that Ney, pushing forward at the heels of the retreating Russians, thought that Smolensk could be carried by a *coup-de-main*, when he came in sight of it on the morning of the 17th. He opened fire with his artillery and sent his infantry forward to rush the low ramparts of the citadel. They were driven back with serious loss, and the Marshal himself was slightly wounded by a bullet which grazed his neck.

He drew off from the attack. The firing died away to an occasional spatter of musketry between the Russians on wall and rampart and Ney's advanced posts. He rode up to the crest of a wooded sandy hill looking down on the Dnieper, in order to reconnoitre the town. But the wide outlook afforded to him showed him an unexpected sight. Beyond Smolensk, from the undulating country north of the Dnieper, great clouds of dust were rising. They stretched far towards the western horizon, and through them came here and there the flash of sunlight on weapons, or a glimpse of dark masses in movement.

It was the army of Barclay and Bagration returning from the direction of Witebsk. The Russian Generals had learned from Neverovskoi that great masses of French troops were marching by the south bank of the Dnieper, and had made a forced march to bar Napoleon's advance on Smolensk.

Ney galloped off to find the Emperor, and brought him back to the hill-top, guiding him through thickets and hollows of the ground to avoid drawing the fire of the town. He pointed to the moving dust clouds far away beyond the river. Napoleon saw in the approach of the enemy promise of the long-desired battle. "*Enfin, je les tiens!*" he exclaimed. "At last I have them!"

Poniatowski's Poles were coming up eager to attack Smolensk. The Emperor held them back. He hoped to draw the Russians into attacking him, and formed the Grand Army in battle array along the low hills facing the town with a level stretch of open ground in front, across which he hoped soon to see the enemy advancing. Ney was in the first line with the 4th Corps under Davoût and the 1st, now commanded by Lobau, on his right. The Imperial Guard was in reserve. Murat was setting his squadrons in array, Junot and the Westphalians were called up to strengthen the battle line.

Meanwhile the Russians were showing themselves in ever increasing numbers along the right bank of the Dnieper, but not even the Cossacks came across the bridges of Smolensk. The Emperor sent swarms of skirmishers down to the river's edge to try to provoke the enemy to an attack, but the Russians contented themselves with keeping up a desultory fire across the stream. This mere show of fighting went on till near sunset.

The Emperor confidently predicted that there would be a battle next day. Barclay, he supposed, was only waiting to have all his available force in line. If he did not attack the French he would await them on the Dnieper, and make a stand to save Smolensk. Napoleon had pitched his tent almost in the outpost line opposite the town. There he discussed the situation with the marshals. Davoût shared his opinion, but Murat and Ney predicted that Barclay would not risk a battle. If he had meant to fight, they argued, he would have attacked already.

At sunrise there was no sign of a Russian advance but it was thought that they were still holding the heights on the right bank. Smolensk was strongly occupied, and parties of Cossacks were moving about on the left bank beyond the extreme right of the French line. Napoleon clung to the hope of a battle. A detachment of Murat's cavalry was sent to drive off the Cossacks, and sent back the report that they could see great columns of the enemy retiring eastward along the other bank of the river. Barclay had in fact sent off Bagration's army the day before, and was following with his own, leaving only a strong rear-guard to hold Smolensk.

Although the place would in any case be soon evacuated, Napoleon, in his irritated disappointment, gave orders to storm the town and seize the bridges. The Russians attacked by superior numbers made a magnificent defence. Davoût and Lobau fought their way into the suburbs. Ney once more tried to rush the citadel, and once more the soldiers of the 3rd Corps were hurled back from its ruinous ramparts. Towards evening the assault was abandoned. The twelve-pounder batteries of the Guard were brought up to breach the walls, and Lobau placed some howitzers in one of the captured suburbs, and after dark threw some shells into the town. This bombardment had hardly begun when fires broke out here and there among the houses. The French thought it was the result of their shells, but the Russians themselves were burning the place, determined to leave only its ruins to the invader.

By midnight Smolensk was blazing like a huge furnace. No one could be seen on the walls and parties sent forward to the gates were neither challenged nor fired upon. Before sunrise the French pushed into the burning streets and found that the place was abandoned. The Russian rear-guard had retreated in the night. Part of the town was saved, but most of it was a mass of smoking ruins. Napoleon dated a bulletin of victory from Smolensk, but it was at best a doubtful and a costly success. Ney's dash at the citadel on the first day had cost between 300 and 400 casualties. The unnecessary attack ordered by the Emperor had sacrificed more than 5000 men.

Now that he was once more in contact with the Russian army, the Emperor was eager to overtake and bring them to action, and at any risk to occupy Moscow. Murat's cavalry were already moving out on the Moscow road. Ney was sent to support him. On the 19th—the day after the occupation of Smolensk—he came upon a strong Russian force in position on the plateau of Valutina.[1] Ney thought he was in presence of a rear-guard that would probably retire after a mere show of resistance. But it was a corps of Barclay's army posted on the ridge to cover the movement of heavy convoys moving across in the rear of the height to reach the main Moscow road beyond it. Ney's attack was met with a determined and prolonged resistance, and it was not till late in the day, after he had been reinforced with Gudin's division of Davoût's corps, that he stormed the plateau. There was hard fighting with the bayonet, and the victors lost some 3000 men. The Russians retired under cover of the darkness without losing a gun or a single prisoner. Napoleon rode out to the battlefield next morning and made a liberal distribution of crosses of the Legion of Honour among the soldiers.

Ney's losses at Smolensk and Valutina had been so heavy, that the 3rd Corps was now withdrawn from the advanced guard and replaced by that of Davoût. Thus till the beginning of September Ney had no more fighting. He marched with the central column of the general advance. The country through which the invaders were now moving was well cultivated, and there were numerous villages, and some fine country houses. But every house and cottage was deserted, and the retiring Russians swept up or destroyed most of the available supplies. Town after town was given to the flames, the Russian rear-guard on more than one occasion fighting for a while in order to hold back Murat and Davoût just long enough to allow the conflagration to take a complete hold of the doomed streets and houses.

[1] Walutinagora, of the Russian and Austrian maps, a few miles north-east of Smolensk.

Pine Woods
Marshy Ground
Borodino
EUGENE
MILORADOVITCH
PLATOFF (Cossacks)
GUARD
BAGRATION
JUNOT
MURAT
DAVOUT
Schwardino
Semenovskoi
Military Bridges
BATTLE OF
BORODINO
Cavalry
Infantry
French
Russian

The town of Gzatz, which the Emperor occupied on 31 August, was partly rescued from the flames, thanks to the speedy victory of the French advanced guard. During the last few days the men and horses of the Grand Army had suffered terribly. The heat was intense, the march was amid clouds of stifling dust that hung like a fog round the columns, and water was scarce. Some of the corps could obtain only a scanty supply from the muddy pools in the beds of dried-up streams. Then the advance was stopped by a sudden change in the weather. There were three days of heavy rain that turned the country into a swamp. Ney was amongst those who urged on the Emperor the advisability of deferring the further advance on Moscow till the next spring.

But on 4 September the weather changed again. There was bright sunshine and the intense heat rapidly dried the ground. Next day Murat, who had been meeting with more and more determined resistance from the Cossacks, sent back a report that the Russian army was halted in an entrenched position about the village of Borodino, its right flank resting on the River Moskowa. The long-desired battle was at last to be fought. The growing murmurs of the Russian Army against the policy of continual retreat and ruthless destruction of town and village as the invader approached them, had led to Barclay resigning his command to General Kutusoff. The new Commander-in-Chief was the General who had been beaten at Austerlitz, and he was now nearly seventy years of age. But his one great defeat had not diminished his popularity with the Russian soldiers, among whom he had served for more than half a century. He was regarded as a fighting general, and his appointment had been hailed with acclamations. He justified the confidence reposed in him. For Russia he is still the heroic figure of 1812. Tolstoi writes of him as "the genius of Russia and of the war".

He had chosen for the great battle that was to decide the fate of Moscow a position seventy miles west of the city, near the junction of the Moskowa and its affluent, the little River Kologha. He had with him 121,000 men and 640 guns. But 15,000 of the men were raw militia who had just joined him. He had entrenched a line of over six miles running along the crest of a rise in the general level of the steppe. The right towards the Moskowa was protected by the Kologha, the marshy banks of which made it a formidable obstacle. Near the bridge over the Kologha, at the village of Borodino, the line left the river and ran along the hills to the dense pine woods of the Utitza Forest. This part of the front was defended by several redoubts, the largest of them near the river. An advanced redoubt had been constructed in the plain south of the village of Schwardino. It was too far to the front to be effectively supported by the main battle line, and it was stormed by Davoût's infantry when the French advanced guard came up on 5 September.

The next day was spent by both armies in preparations for the battle. Napoleon had actually with him 120,000 men and 587 guns. The troops bivouacked in battle array, and officers and men were told to put on their best uniforms. Ney's corps was posted in the centre, between Schwardino and the south bank of the Kologha. A mile to his front a straggling belt of pine woods was held by the Russian outposts; behind them, beyond the swampy hollow of a stream, the ground rose to the great redoubt bristling with cannon, to the left of which were arrayed the dark masses of Bagration's corps.

With most modern armies the tactical necessity of concealment has taken all the glitter and colour from the battlefield. Men march into the fight in dull khaki or bluish grey. But when the sun rose on 7 September, 1812, the French Army looked as if it was prepared, not for a murderous life and death struggle, but for a spectacular review. It was an army of many nations and there was a strange variety of brilliant uniforms. The sky was a cloudless blue, and the sun rose behind the Russian position and shone in the faces of the attack. "It is the sun of Austerlitz," exclaimed Napoleon.

There was a rolling of drums, and then the colonels read at the head of their regiments the Emperor's proclamation telling the men that the coming victory would give them possession of Moscow, abundant supplies, comfortable winter quarters, and the prospect of an early return to their homes, where each as long as he lived would be proud to say: "I was in that great battle before the walls of Moscow". A signal gun fired from the captured redoubt was to have been the signal for the general advance, then the heights on the Russian left were to be stormed and their line rolled up by a succession of attacks towards the centre and right.

The signal was delayed. Ney, ever eager for battle, had sent an officer to Napoleon asking for permission to attack the Russians in the woods in his front. There was the same impatience everywhere. The men had been under arms for two hours, and the long wait was becoming a strain on their nerves. Suddenly from the left beyond the Kologha came the sound of heavy firing. Without waiting for orders Eugène was attacking Borodino. He drove the Russians out of the village, seized the bridge, and pushed on towards the main position about Gorki. While Eugène was still clearing Borodino, Ney had ordered his batteries to open, and sent swarms of skirmishers forward into the pines. On his right Davoût moved to the attack and Poniatowski's Poles were tramping forward through the Utitza woods. The battle had become a frontal attack all along the line, a struggle to be decided by sheer fighting with but little manœuvring. And for perhaps the first time in his life the Emperor did little or nothing to control or direct the fight. More than one of those who were with him testifies that he was ill. He was almost a spectator of the conflict. He never rode forward from the Schwardino redoubt, and during most of the day he was nearly a mile from the firing line, and depended largely on the reports brought by staff officers for his knowledge of the progress of the battle.

It raged from early morning till darkness set in, and Ney was hotly engaged throughout all the fifteen hours of hard fighting. First he drove in the advanced line of the Russians in the plain, and then, concentrating towards his right, co-operated with Davoût and Murat in the attack on Bagration's corps holding the heights about the village of Semenovskoi, which was set on fire early on the morning and blazed like a furnace in the midst of the battle. The line of redoubts in front of the village was taken and retaken. It was not till noon that Ney was firmly established on the plateau. By that time the Russian left had been pushed back, and Kutusoff's line of battle was a salient with the Great Redoubt for its apex.

Round this the fight raged during the afternoon. Ney and the other generals sent more than one message to the Emperor begging him to bring the Guard into action. But hour after hour he kept these fine regiments idle spectators of the distant battle, which their intervention would have at once decided. He hesitated to risk his last reserve. The most he would agree to was that some of the batteries of the Guard should be sent forward to the heights.

Ney was beside Murat in front of the Great Redoubt when General Belliard, Murat's chief of the staff, rejoined him, and told him that he had tried in vain to persuade Napoleon to send even a portion of the Guard into action. Belliard said he had found the Emperor depressed, unlike himself, giving his orders in a languid hesitating way. Ney completely lost control of himself. "What is the Emperor doing in the rear of the army?" he exclaimed. "If he will not conduct the war himself, if he is no longer a general, if he wants to play the Emperor everywhere, let him go back to the Tuileries, and leave us to command for him!" Murat was calmer and remarked that Napoleon was ill and they must do the best they could for him.

Attack after attack of the infantry was hurled back from the Grand Redoubt. Davoût had been unhorsed and stunned early in the day. Murat was commanding his infantry as well as the cavalry. The French line along the captured heights had to hold its own against repeated counter-attacks of the Russians. On the right Barclay had not lost a foot of ground. Ney was fighting in the centre, near the Great Redoubt, exposing himself freely in the thickest of the battle. But it was Murat's cavalry that decided the struggle at this point, a mass of cuirassiers charging through the enemy and pouring victoriously into the open rear of the Redoubt.

The day was drawing to a close, but still the Russians held on obstinately to the ground between the villages of Gorki and Tzarevo. The batteries of the Guard came galloping up from Schwardino and opened fire. The battle became an artillery duel which died away as the sun went down. Some thought it would be renewed at daybreak, and the Emperor congratulated himself that he had still the Imperial Guard intact. But

when the sun rose it was seen that the enemy had retreated during the hours of darkness.

The battle had been terribly costly for both armies and both claimed it as a victory. The Russians had taken away with them some thousands of French prisoners, and thirteen captured guns as trophies of the stubborn fight. They had lost no less than 37,500 men killed and wounded, 31 per cent of the force engaged. Twenty-two of their generals were among the casualties of the day. Bagration had been killed in the fight before Semenovskoi. Thirty Russian guns and 5000 prisoners had been left on the field.

The French—or rather the Imperial Army, for only half of it was French—had lost 24,500 killed and wounded and 7500 prisoners and missing. Thirty-one generals were killed or wounded. The peasants of the district had fled. The troops were exhausted, so very few of the dead were buried, and thousands of the wounded were left for days uncared for and died. Seven weeks after the battle, when the Russians, following up the French retreat, took possession again of the battle-field, they found it strewn with some 50,000 corpses and more than 30,000 dead horses, in all stages of decay, and for weeks burial parties were at work hiding these horrors out of sight.

The Russians call the battle Borodino, and its name is always commemorated in that of a battleship of their navy. They claim that Kutusoff's splendid resistance wrecked the French Army and prepared the way for the disasters that so soon overtook it. Napoleon in his bulletin of victory called it the Battle of the Moskowa, perhaps wishing to recall the fact that it was fought to open the way to Moscow. He singled out Ney among all the marshals as the leader who had most largely contributed to the victory, and he rewarded him with a new title in his military peerage. Henceforth Michel Ney besides being Duc d'Elchingen, was also Prince de la Moskowa.

CHAPTER XIII

THE REAR-GUARD OF THE GRAND ARMY (1812)

FROM the death-strewn field the Grand Army marched on to Moscow, with its ranks sadly thinned, and with the consciousness that the Russian Army, even if it had been defeated, had not been destroyed, and was still to be reckoned with. Murat had started off in pursuit of the enemy early on 8 September, but when in the afternoon he came on the rear-guard under Milarodovitch at Mojaisk, there was no sign that the Russians were in the least demoralized by their losses. They met his attacks with a stubborn resistance, and when night fell they still held the town. Napoleon rode up with Davoût's corps, and as the darkness came on he saw the camp fires of 60,000 men glimmering along the slopes to the eastward, a warning that, far as he had advanced, he was not yet a conqueror.

Once more the sunrise showed that the Russians had disappeared. Only the irregular swarms of Cossacks scouring the country in the French front told of the presence of an enemy. Then day after day the Russians steadily retired before the advance of the invaders. It was expected that there would be another fight before Moscow was reached, but there were only insignificant skirmishes. Kutusoff retired through the city which was abandoned by nearly all its inhabitants, and on 14 September Murat rode into Moscow with the cavalry of the French vanguard.

Ney had been joined by an old comrade on the 12th, when De Fezensac, who had formerly served on his staff, and had been attached to the Emperor's head-quarters at the outset of the campaign, took up the command of the 4th Infantry, vacant since its Colonel, Massy, had been killed at Borodino. The regiment had crossed the Niemen 2500 strong. When De Fezensac took command, it mustered only 800 bayonets. In the whole of the 3rd Corps Ney had now not more than 8000 men. The 3rd Division (the Würtembergers under Marchand) had lost so seriously that there were only 1000 men in its ranks.

To the disappointment of the officers and men Ney's corps did not enter Moscow. It was ordered to camp on the hills to the westward, whence there was a splendid view of the great city with the pinnacles and towers of the Kremlin, and the gilded and painted domes of hundreds of churches. On the night of the 14th the bivouacs of the 3rd Corps were roused by the news that there was a great fire in the city. The men watched it for hours and saw it die out before morning. On the next night there was another alarm. This time the fire blazed all through the night, breaking out in new places as the wind changed, and in the morning a dense pall of smoke hung over the city. Moscow had been set on fire by the Russians, and burned for six days and nights. News was brought from the city that the troops who held it were being allowed to plunder it from end to end, on the plea that what they took was doomed to destruction by the Russians themselves, and there were wild rumours of the enormous store of wealth to be found in the houses of the nobility and the shops and warehouses of the business quarters. At the same time Ney received orders to prevent any of his men from leaving camp and going into the city. But there was such excitement among the soldiers, that the Marshal and his officers decided that a strict enforcement of these orders might result in widespread insubordination, and they therefore connived at parties of men from each regiment going into Moscow to secure a share of the loot for themselves and their comrades. It is quite clear that the discipline of the army was already breaking down. De Fezensac is not alone in his statements that the heavy losses incurred, the hardships of the long advance through a wasted country, and the disappointing conviction that the war was only beginning, had told on officers and men alike. After the first hopes excited by the sight of Moscow there was a general depression. Hitherto the capture of an enemy's capital had meant the speedy termination of a campaign. But the sight of Moscow blazing from end to end told that in this case the enemy meant to continue his resistance after destroying the prize the Emperor had won at the cost of so many dangers and so much loss and suffering for his army. He had promised his men comfortable winter quarters, and abundant supplies once Moscow was occupied. The city was a smoking ruin, and the men were heaping up useless plunder in the camps, where they had to live from hand to mouth, and where the horses were dying for want of forage.

For some days all touch with Kutusoff's Army had been lost. Then it was reported to be on the Vladimir road north-east of the city. Napoleon tried to communicate with the Czar through the Russian head-quarters, and spoke confidently of dictating a peace, or, alternatively, marching on St. Petersburg; but at a conference at the Kremlin, at which Ney was present, the Marshals told him that any further extended operations were out of the question, and some of them even ventured to suggest that it would not be easy to hold on to Moscow much longer.

In the last week of September Ney was ordered to transfer his corps to the north-east side of Moscow, and take up a position on the Vladimir road. The 3th Corps had now been rejoined by numbers of stragglers left behind in the advance and slightly wounded men dismissed from the hospitals, and its strength had been brought up to 10,000 men, just two-fifths of the force that Ney had led across the frontier river. The march through Moscow gave most of the officers and men their first close view of the burned city. It was a wilderness of blackened ruins, amidst which, here and there, rose a church or a mansion that had escaped the flames. Some of the wretched inhabitants who had stayed in the place were wandering among the wreckage, searching for the dead bodies of animals or digging for roots in the gardens in order to find some food. Among them were several disbanded Russian soldiers. Ney made prisoners of some fifty of them and handed them over to an officer of the French garrison, who remarked that it would have saved a lot of trouble if they had been shot.

The 3rd Corps for some days occupied a number of villages on the Jaroslav and Vladimir roads. Then it was ascertained that there was no large force of the enemy in this direction.

Kutusoff had marched round to the south side of Moscow and established himself in a position across the Kaluga road. There he threatened the French line of retreat and cut the invaders off from the unwasted southern provinces. Ney's corps was withdrawn to the Vladimir suburb of Moscow. It was a region of villas and gardens and had escaped the conflagration. Here many of the officers and men could find roofs to shelter them, but supplies were woefully scanty. "It was with difficulty," says De Fezensac, "that we could procure black bread and beer. Meat began to be very scarce. We had to send strong detachments to hunt for cattle in the woods where the peasants had taken refuge, and these parties often came back in the evening bringing nothing with them. Such was the alleged plenty procured for us by the pillaging of the city. We had liqueurs, sugar and jam, but we were short of bread and meat. We could wrap ourselves in furs, but we were soon without coats and shoes. There were diamonds and jewels and various objects of luxury, and we were nearly dying of hunger."

In the first part of October there were cloudy days with showers of cold rain. Then there were nights of hard frost and occasional snow. It was the first menace of the Russian winter. But still there were rumours of peace, and men looked forward hopefully to a speedy end to their present hardships. The Emperor was holding a series of reviews on the great parade ground of the Kremlin, and on 17 October Ney was informed that the 3rd Corps would be inspected there next day.

On the morning of the 18th he once more marched through the ruined city at the head of his 10,000 men. They had spent the day before preparing for the review. The parade uniforms had been carefully preserved and muskets and bayonets had been polished up, so that at first sight the thinned ranks of the regiments presented a brave show when they were marshalled at the Kremlin. But the men's boots were broken and roughly patched, and their thin haggard faces told of how much they had had to endure. At the sight of the Emperor there was an outburst of the old enthusiasm. He passed along the lines to the cry of "*Vive l'Empereur!*" He distributed some crosses of the Legion, spoke familiarly to officers and men, and congratulated Ney on the appearance of his corps. But he must have been unfavourably impressed by its diminished numbers. Regiments had shrunk to weak battalions. Companies were represented by squads. In almost every case there were two captains and several lieutenants to each company. So many men had disappeared from the ranks, that two or three companies had had to be combined into a new unit with this superfluity of officers. Then there were companies of dismounted cavalry troopers acting as infantry, and it was with difficulty that sufficient horses had been found for the gun teams.

While the review was in progress a staff officer of Murat's cavalry corps rode on to the parade ground and handed a dispatch to the Emperor. Those who were near him saw by his change of countenance that it conveyed serious news. It told Napoleon that at dawn that morning Murat had been attacked by overwhelming numbers at Winkowo, south of Moscow. His outposts had been surprised and driven in by the grey light of the winter dawn; for a while his retreat had been cut off; he had cleared the way by desperate hand to hand fighting, but he had left several guns in the hands of the Russians and a large number of prisoners. It was a disaster that might be the prelude of worse things.

The parade was dismissed, and Ney marched back to the Vladimir suburb, a shower of snow whitening the roads as the men tramped through the ruined city. He had hardly reached the suburb when a staff officer arrived with orders. Moscow was to be abandoned, Ney was to be ready to march at daybreak next morning. He would receive detailed instructions later.

The day was spent collecting and piling on the transport wagons all the supplies that remained. The soldiers insisted on adding to the loads some of the plunder they had secured, and further burdened themselves with all kinds of portable property, soon to be thrown away by the roadside. In fact sooner or later all the loot of Moscow was destined to fall into the hands of the pursuing Cossacks. Shortly after midnight the marching column was formed and moved off by the light of a burning monastery, for the French were vengefully eager to destroy all that they were forced to abandon. Daylight showed Ney's soldiers that the 3rd Corps was a unit in a great multitude moving southwards from Moscow along the "new road" to Kaluga and on the open ground on both sides of it. More than a hundred thousand men were on the march encumbered with thousands of wagons and hundreds of carriages of all kinds, from the equipages of French residents in Moscow who were now fugitives with their countrymen, down to hand-barrows laden with loot from the city. "The march looked more like that of a caravan than an army," said one of the spectators. The guns had been horsed with difficulty, and their number was out of all proportion to the available gunners and ammunition, but Napoleon had refused to leave any of them behind. They would be trophies for the enemy, he said. This was nevertheless to be their fate before long.

Two roads from Moscow lead to Kaluga. The army was moving by the eastern or "new" road, that on which Kutusoff's army was posted, and on which he had surprised and defeated Murat. But this first movement was a feint. Napoleon's plan was to transfer his army by cross roads and tracks to the western or "old" road, and marching along the latter, pass round the enemy's flank and reach Kaluga without a battle. Ney's corps was posted on the new road at Tschirkovo, two days' march from Moscow, to cover this movement. He expected to be attacked by the Russians, but there were only skirmishes between his outposts and the Cossacks. The fact was that Kutusoff had discovered the French flank march to the old road, and was moving more rapidly on a parallel line of march to cut off the Emperor from Kaluga.

After a three days' halt, Ney received orders to follow the main body. The march of the 3rd Corps by the cross roads, unpaved wagon tracks, proved to be a trying operation. It began in the night of the 23rd under a heavy downpour of chilling rain, that converted the track, already badly cut up by hoof and wheel, into a prolonged swamp, through which horses and men toiled wearily.

At daybreak the Cossacks began a series of harrassing attacks on flank and rear. It was not till the 26th that the 3rd Corps rejoined the head-quarters of the Grand Army at

Borovsk. There Ney heard what had been happening during the last few days. The Emperor had found his way barred by Kutusoff at Malo-Jaroslavetz. There had been hard fighting with heavy loss and indecisive results. For a while Napoleon had thought of forcing his way through at all costs, but he had realized that even a victory would leave the Grand Army too crippled to continue its march southward, and he had reluctantly decided to fall back on the northern route by which he had advanced, and to retreat by way of Smolensk and Witebsk through a devastated tract of country. He hoped to draw supplies for the Army from magazines at Smolensk, and to have further supplies brought up from Germany to other points on the route, in time to provide for the wants of his troops as they reached Witebsk, Wilna and Kovno.

In the first stage of the retreat Davoût with the 1st Corps formed the rear-guard, but even so Ney's corps was continually worried by attacks of the Cossack irregulars. They swarmed on the flanks of the long columns of the Grand Army. Once a strong body of these wild spearmen broke through the French line of march close to the spot where Napoleon himself was riding with his staff, and would have captured or killed the Emperor if they had not been eager to plunder a convoy of wagons laden with the loot of Moscow.

Ney's men were already enduring the first trials and sufferings of the retreat, though its worst horrors were still to come. The country was utterly desolate. The men had to live on the scanty supplies they carried with them, and on rations provided by killing the horses that showed signs of breaking down. During each day's march wagons and guns had to be abandoned for want of teams to drag them further. The artillery caissons thus left on the track were set on fire and blew up with loud explosions. Every man that straggled from the ranks was mercilessly speared by the Cossacks. The French were exasperated by the miseries they endured. Every village was fired as they passed through it, and one day Ney's corps found the track strewn with disarmed Russian soldiers lying dead with their skulls smashed with musket butts. A division that was marching in front of the 3rd Corps was escorting a column of prisoners, and had killed in this way all who were too exhausted to keep their places in the ranks.

On 29 October Ney marched past the ruins of Mojaisk and traversed the battle-field of Borodino. The dead bodies of men and horses in all stages of decay still cumbered the ground. The day of horrors ended with a bivouac near the monastery of Koletkoi on the western edge of the battle-field. It had been used as a hospital after the battle, and was now a huge tomb of unburied dead. Those who visited it found only corpses and skeletons lying on rotten straw. In another abandoned hospital, the only remaining building of the ruined town of Gyat, a search party headed by Colonel de Fezensac found and rescued a few survivors of the 3rd Corps. They had been lying there for weeks in the midst of filth and misery without doctors, nurses or medicine, almost without food. The unburied dead were heaped up in the courtyard.

On 1 November the 3rd Corps reached Viasma. One of the suburbs had escaped the conflagration that destroyed the town, and here Ney and some of his officers and men spent a night under a roof, after sleeping for a fortnight in the open. In this stage of the retreat Eugène with the 4th Corps (Italians) followed Ney and then came Davoût with the 1st Corps acting as the rear-guard. Kutusoff had not been content merely to follow the retirement. While pressing the rear-guard with a mass of Cossacks and regular cavalry under Platoff, he had detached a strong force under the most enterprising of his lieutenants, Milarodovitch—the "Murat of Russia"— to fall upon the flank of the Grand Army. Miloradovitch marched rapidly through the yet unwasted region south of the line of retreat, and struck at the flank of the 4th Corps east of Viasma, and on 2 November had cut off Eugène and Davoût from Ney's position there. Ney had to remain halted in order to hold Viasma while his two colleagues fought their way through the Russians to rejoin him. He was himself attacked and on 3 November was for five hours in close action with the enemy. By evening he had beaten them off, and was again in touch with Eugène and Davoût, who, after repulsing the repeated onsets of Platoff's Cossacks, had forced their way through the Russian lines at the cost of heavy losses, and after abandoning many guns and long convoys of wagons. The 1st Corps was so reduced in numbers and so exhausted that Ney was ordered to relieve Davoût, and take his place with the 3rd Corps as the rear-guard of the retreating army.

On the 4th Viasma was abandoned, and the remaining houses set on fire. Ney's corps held the border of a pine wood along the banks of the Viasma river and easily repulsed some irresolute attacks of the enemy, while the 4th and 1st Corps passed through its lines to continue the retreat. Ney and his officers were startled at the sight of the disorganization of these two corps. They streamed along the forest roads in disorderly masses, encumbered with crowds of men who had thrown away their arms and lost their regiments. One unit only, the Italian Royal Guard, still moved with some show of order and discipline. Hundreds of the fugitives lay down and slept in the woods, though the officers urged them to push on. When in its turn the 3rd Corps moved off on the morning of the 5th, the masses of stragglers, for whom there was no food to spare, came crowding upon the rear-guard. Then there was a horrible scene as the soldiers drove them back first with blows of musket butts then by firing on them. But to allow them to encumber the rear-guard would have been destruction for all. They were mercilessly repulsed, and before long the lances of the pursuing Cossacks put an end to their misery.

Across a wide plain and through another belt of wood the 3rd Corps retired during the next day, harassed by the Cossacks in the daylight, and fired upon by artillery at random during the night. On the 6th it became suddenly colder and during the night snow fell heavily hour after hour. A gale of wind made it almost impossible to light the bivouac fires, and the men were chilled to the bone. In the morning the whole aspect of the country had changed. It was an unbroken expanse of snow. The streams were rapidly freezing. The sky was a mass of dark-grey clouds.

The army was now approaching Smolensk and the vanguard was crossing the Dnieper. To give time for the slow movement of the long columns and the heavy convoys across the river, Ney was ordered to make a stand at Dorogbuz. He had in vain written to the Emperor urging that the retreat should be accelerated by abandoning useless guns and a large part of the convoys. Napoleon was reluctant to leave any trophies to the enemy, and did not realize the full extent of the danger impending over the Grand Army.

The defence of Dorogbuz collapsed in a few hours. The enemy rushed the town, an attempt to recapture it ended in failure, and Ney realized that he could not ask any more of his wearied and half-starved soldiers. He was in a bad temper as he gave the orders to abandon the position and continue the retreat, and under the strong feeling of the moment he unjustly blamed his officers. Beating off continual attacks of the Russians, and abandoning crowds of wounded and exhausted men on the way, the thinned ranks of the 3rd Corps plodded slowly back to the crossing of the Dnieper at Solovievo.

The weather was fearful. A high wind drove the snow in dense whirling showers that often blotted out the view beyond a few yards. Deep drifts, in which the men sunk to the knee or the waist, encumbered the track. Where the snow lay less deeply the way was marked with the white mounds that covered the dead left behind by the corps that had already passed by. The track was strewn with abandoned arms and equipments, and here and there lay dying and starving men whom it was impossible to succour. The long nights in the frozen bivouacs always ended with scores of men being left on the ground, dead or so exhausted with starvation, cold, and frostbite that they could not move. There was no transport for the sick and wounded. Day after day the horses were breaking down, and numbers of wagons had to be abandoned to the Cossacks.

On 10 November the Dnieper was reached. The other corps had already crossed. Ney fought a rear-guard action on the right bank on the 11th to cover the crossing of his own corps, but he had to leave most of his guns and wagons behind him. Two days' march now lay between him and Smolensk where the men were promised that they would find rest, shelter, and abundance of food and warm clothing. But hundreds who had passed the Dnieper broke down before they reached the city. On the night of the 13th Ney's corps bivouacked in the pine woods about two miles to the east of it. Of the 10,000 who had marched out of Moscow only some 3000 were left. The Würtemberg division had ceased to exist. The few officers and men who survived from it had been attached to the other divisions. The cavalry was represented by a few mounted officers and troopers, not even one squadron could be mustered. Most of the artillery had been left on the road. Ney had only twelve badly horsed guns and hardly any ammunition for them.

On the 14th the remnant of the 3rd Corps marched into Smolensk. The city was half in ruins. Of the buildings that were left most had been converted into hospitals, where 7000 sick and wounded were huddled together in utter misery. The doors and woodwork of the houses had been pulled down and burned for firewood. Worst of all Ney's exhausted soldiers could obtain hardly anything in the way of food or clothes. The corps that had already reached Smolensk had fairly pillaged the magazines. There had been no orderly distribution but only waste and confusion. Some regiments had secured a temporary abundance, others next to nothing. Ney's men, whose devoted courage had protected the retreat of their comrades, fared the worst of all. They were glad to get a little flour and a number of broken-down horses to be slaughtered for the camp kettles. Even the promise of rest and shelter for a while, which had buoyed them up during the last days of their terrible march, ended in disappointment. The Grand Army was already moving off, for there was news of fresh hosts of the enemy coming up from the south to be beforehand with the retreating invaders at the crossing of the Beresina.

Ney received a reinforcement of a few hundred men, the remnant of the 129th French regiment of the Line, and an Illyrian regiment. He also obtained a much-needed supply of ammunition. His corps was still to act as the rear-guard. On the 14th it took up a position in the suburbs to keep the Russians at bay during the evacuation of Smolensk. In the night the cold was so intense that it was with difficulty that the sentries could be kept at their posts. At daybreak the enemy appeared, but the men of the 3rd Corps fought with a steady courage and beat off every attack. Ney was pleased with the day's work and spoke to the officers of his satisfaction with the men. The victory thus won seemed to augur well for the future. He did not realize that the Russians had not seriously pressed the attack and were in no great force. Kutusoff had pushed westward with 80,000 men and gained the flank of Napoleon's line of retreat. He was not anxious about the mere recapture of Smolensk. His hope was that he would be able to strike at the long straggling column, separate corps from corps, and destroy or capture the Grand Army piecemeal. He nearly succeeded.

On the 17th Ney marched from Smolensk, abandoning perforce to the enemy the crowded hospitals and a large number of guns and ammunition wagons and quantities of military stores that he could neither move nor destroy. Various detachments of troops that had remained to the last brought his fighting force up to a little over 5000 men. He reduced his artillery to six guns. Of his cavalry all that was left was formed into a weak troup to do escort and messenger duties. His march was encumbered by a miserable crowd of some 7000 disorganized fugitives. During the first day he had only to deal with the irregular attacks of the Cossacks. He bivouacked for the night at Koritnya and at sunrise on 18 November resumed his march, hoping to reach Krasnoi that afternoon and there find Davoût's corps awaiting him.

All the morning the Cossacks hung on his flank and rear and cut off numbers of the fugitives, but were always driven back from the ordered ranks of the marching column by a few volleys. Presently the sound of cannon was heard in the distance, and then numbers of Cossacks showed themselves in front of the 2nd Division which was leading. No special attention was paid to this fact, as the Cossacks often cut in upon the line of march. Then Ney's vanguard, approaching Krasnoi, came upon General Ricard's division belonging to the 1st Corps, a few hundred men with six guns. Ricard reported that he had been in action with a greatly superior force of the enemy and had been cut off from his corps commander Davoût. Krasnoi was held by the Russians. Except for the hovering bands of Cossacks there was no enemy in sight, but the view did not extend far. The weather had become warmer, or rather less cold. The snow showed signs of a coming thaw, and a damp fog drifted over the plain.

Uniting Ricard's small force to his own, Ney formed up his corps for battle and advanced through the fog till suddenly forty guns opened upon him at a short range, and he had a glimpse of ordered masses of the enemy waiting in battle array. He fell back and halted, expecting to be attacked. He had hardly done so when a Russian officer with a flag of truce rode into his lines.

The Russian was brought to Ney, and told him he was sent by General Milarodovitch to demand the surrender of the 3rd Corps. "A Marshal of France cannot surrender. You may go back to those who sent you," was Ney's indignant reply. But the Russian asked to be allowed to explain what was the actual situation. Kutusoff and Milarodovitch, he said, had so high an opinion of Ney's courage and military talents, that they would never think of proposing to him anything that was dishonourable or unworthy of him. But a capitulation was inevitable. To refuse meant the useless sacrifice of brave men's lives. Kutusoff had attacked the Emperor and his Imperial Guard near Krasnoi. Napoleon had continued his retreat after being for a while separated from Eugène and Davoût. These had in turn been attacked. They had rejoined the Emperor at the cost of leaving in the hands of the Russians most of their guns, their convoys, and thousands of prisoners. The Grand Army had moved on leaving Ney isolated, and he had in front of him at that moment 80,000 men. There was no need of giving an immediate answer. There could be a brief truce during which Ney might send some of his officers to verify the statements made to him.

An officer sent with a flag of truce is a picked man. The Russian in his brilliant cavalry uniform, with a fur pélisse wrapped round him and mounted on a sleek charger presented a striking contrast to the Marshal and his officers, a group of haggard-looking men in ragged uniforms, huddled together amid the fog and the snow, with the weary battalions halted close by, and crowds of disorganized fugitives waiting anxiously to know their fate. The Russians must have felt sure that the surrender would be soon settled. But suddenly away to the front a red flash tore through the fog and there came the ringing report of a Russian gun and the whistle of a shot in the air. On some false alarm, probably the result of a band of disorganized fugitives wandering towards the hostile line, a battery had opened fire. "You are a prisoner, Sir," said Ney to the astonished envoy; "Your people have fired on us while you are in my lines and that forfeits the protection of your white flag." The officer protested, but had to give up his sword, and for three weeks shared the hard fortunes of the 3rd Corps.

Ney had taken the desperate resolution of trying to break through the enemy in the fog, and hoped that the failure of the envoy to return would help him, by leaving the Russian commander in doubt to the last moment as to what was coming. The fight did not last half-an-hour. General Razout with the 2nd Division, formed in columns of regiments, led the attack. But it was driven back by a hail of grapeshot discharged from a long row of guns at close quarters. The Russians then attacked in turn. The infantry came on in great masses with the bayonet. A storm of cavalry charged out of the fog, and fell on both flanks of the French. Only by desperate exertions Ney, with the 1st Division and Ricard's men, checked the onset for a moment, covered Razout's retirement, and extricated his little force from the disastrous engagement. Numbers of beaten men never rallied. They mingled in the confused crowds of disbanded fugitives that fled aimlessly through the fog, and the Cossacks only drew off from the pursuit of them as the darkness came on.

The losses had been terrible. Six guns were saved. De Fezensac's regiment, the 4th, had gone into action over 400 strong. Only 200 were left. The Illyrian regiment and the 18th had suffered still more heavily. The 18th had lost its eagle. General Lenchantin had been taken prisoner. Razout was wounded.

A man of less iron will than Ney might well have despaired, and tried to make terms with the victors. He had reformed his little army in column of march, and, to the surprise of all, was leading it back towards Smolensk. All the wounded, who could still keep on their feet, marched in the ranks. From time to time a few of the fugitives rejoined him. It was near the end of the day and in the gloom of the coming darkness the Cossack spearmen pressed upon the rear. The position seemed utterly hopeless. "But," writes De Fezensac, "the presence of Marshal Ney was enough to reassure us. Without knowing what he intended or what he could do, we knew that he would do something. His confidence in himself was equal to his courage. The greater the danger the more prompt was his resolution, and once he had decided what course to take he never doubted of success. Thus, even at a moment like this, his face showed no sign of indecision or anxiety. Every one turned his eyes to him, but no one ventured to question him. At last seeing one of his staff near him, the Marshal said in a low voice: 'It is not well with us.' 'What are you going to do?' replied the officer. 'Get to the other side of the Dnieper.' 'Where is the way to it?' 'We shall find out.' 'But what if it is not frozen over?' 'It will be.'"

This was the first revelation of Ney's plan for avoiding surrender. Somewhere to the north of the track he was following, and not many miles away, ran the Dnieper. He would reach it after dark, cross on the ice and thus evade pursuit and rejoin the Grand Army by a march on the north side of the river. He hoped to overtake Napoleon at Orsza, where a reserve magazine of supplies had been formed.

He had a wretchedly imperfect map, which could only give him vague and general indications. But presently he led the column away from the road across the snowy fields to the left. In a hollow he dismounted, cleared some snow away, and found as he expected the ice on a stream. He broke the ice and found out in which direction the water was running. "The stream must flow into the Dnieper," he said. "It will guide us to the river bank." At sunset he halted at a large village. The peasants had fled leaving their small stores of food in the houses. Fires were lighted, more fires than were actually needed, in order to impress the pursuing Cossacks with a false idea of his numbers. The men bivouacked and had supper. The many wounded were sheltered in the houses where the surgeons dressed their wounds. An outpost line was formed, and after the exchange of a few shots the Cossacks drew off to a respectful distance. They were quite satisfied that they had marked down the column for destruction next morning.

But at eight o'clock, leaving a few men to keep the fires alight and follow later, Ney silently reformed his column and marched to the Dnieper bank, guided by one of the villagers, whom some of Ney's Polish soldiers had captured and who promised to show him a bend of the river where the ice was firm enough to cross. At nine o'clock he stood on the river bank. The ice had partly thawed, but there was a hard frost, and he decided not to attempt the crossing at once but to wait till after midnight. The three hours would make the ice firmer, and give time for more of the stragglers to come in. His perfect self-possession was shown by the fact that, as soon as he had reconnoitred the river and given his orders, he wrapped himself in his cloak and lying down on the snow slept soundly till midnight.

Then the Marshal rose and began to direct the crossing. The ice was treacherous, and it was found that the only safe way to cross was by sending over the men in single file at several points. Fires lighted on both banks showed the way. When most of the infantry and some thousands of the disbanded fugitives had crossed, an attempt was made to send some horses and wagons over the ice. A few horses crossed safely, but several broke through and were lost. A wagon laden with wounded men crashed through the ice and disappeared, and a few of the wounded were seen struggling in the chilly water or clinging to fragments of floating ice. Some of them were rescued. In one case Ney himself was the rescuer. Crawling on hands and knees along the ice, he reached the edge of the huge gap that had opened in it and dragged out of it a man who was clinging to the broken edge. It proved to be a staff officer, Captain De Briqueville, who had the good fortune to survive the horrors of the retreat and return to France.

After this accident it was decided that all the guns and wagons must be abandoned on the south bank. The ranks were formed and the march began, at first for a few miles northward in order to gain some distance from the river, then once more to the westward. For some hours of the long night the men bivouacked in a belt of pines and made fires to warm themselves. Ney hoped that he had shaken off all pursuit, and that there were no Russians north of the river. He expected that two long marches would bring him to Orsza.

But early next day there was a disappointing discovery. Before dawn some Cossacks were surprised asleep in a farm. Then after the column had been moving across open snow-covered fields and through belts of wood, at last it came upon a highway, and there the snow was trampled with horse hoofs and there were the tracks of sledge runners. A large body of mounted troops had evidently passed that way within a few hours, for the tracks were quite fresh.

Platoff, the hetman of the Cossacks, had crossed the Dnieper the day before at the head of some thousands of his men, irregulars such as had been harrassing the French retreat day after day, and with them several squadrons of drilled regulars accompanied by a number of light field guns mounted on sledges. It was not expected that any French troops would be found on the north bank, and the column was sent there to make a rapid march, in order to fall upon the right flank of the Grand Army. It was not long before Cossack patrols came upon Ney's little column toiling through the half-melted snow, with the miserable crowd of disbanded men straggling after it. Some of the Cossacks galloped off to carry the news to their hetman, the rest, rapidly reinforced by other bands of wild spearmen, rode in among the fugitives, killed numbers of them, and drove the rest back to the protection of the column.

Platoff was between Ney and his objective Orsza, and further from the river than the French. He turned back to attack them. At first Ney had hoped that he would have to deal only with the worrying tactics of the irregulars. They never charged home, and were easily driven off by musketry fire when they came within close range, but no one who straggled from the formed ranks of the French escaped their spears. The situation became more serious when Platoff's main body came in sight and his light artillery opened fire. It needed all Ney's courage and energy to face this new danger.

He now commanded only a small force of infantry, encumbered by a mob of disbanded men, and having with them not a gun or a wagon, so that they had only the small supply of cartridges and food that the men carried. They were opposed by a numerically superior force of mounted men with artillery. If they marched with closed up ranks the Cossack leader could choose his own distance and keep them under artillery fire. If they opened out the cavalry would be upon them. But for two days and the intervening night Ney faced this terrible danger, marching slowly for most of the time, snatching a brief rest when for a while the enemy's attacks slackened, and losing men continually. In the course of the 19th all the disbanded men had disappeared. Some had been made prisoners, a few were wandering about the country or hiding in the woods, but most had been mercilessly massacred by the Cossacks. There was hope only for those who could keep their places in the marching ranks. For those who fell wounded by the enemy's fire, or out of sheer exhaustion, there was no chance. They mostly accepted their fate with stoical indifference. A sergeant of the 4th Infantry dropped with his thigh shattered by a shot. "Here's another man done for," he said coolly to his comrades, "Take my knapsack. You will find it useful." But there were moments when it seemed as if the nerve of the sorely tried men was breaking down. More than once it was all that Ney and his officers could do to steady the ranks, as with a wild "Hurrah!" the storm of Cossack lancers came surging round them.

Ney marched in two columns, one under his personal command, the other under General Henin. When in close action with the Russians one would show a bold front and beat off the charges, while the other moved on and gained ground. If both had to make a stand they could cross their fire. During the 19th he gradually drew nearer to the course of the river and in the afternoon found some respite from the enemy's attacks, when he gained the shelter of the pine woods along the Dnieper. Here he rested for a while in the night, but marched again before dawn. He left the woods, and the ground became difficult as the track was intersected by the numerous ravines formed by streams running down to the river. At each of these obstacles some of the weary men broke down and were left behind. The attacks of the enemy had begun again at daybreak. Platoff marched on a parallel track to Ney's rapidly dwindling force, now cannonading it with his sledge-mounted artillery, now launching his Cossack cavalry in charge after charge. Ney was the life and soul of the dogged resistance that was everywhere offered to these onsets. Moving on foot among the men, now here, now there, he encouraged them by telling them that the worst was over; that next day they would be resting in safety at Orsza; that he had sent on an officer to tell the Emperor they were coming, and that soon a helping hand would be held out to them.

Ney's messenger had started before dawn. Badly mounted on a starved horse, ignorant of the country, and forced frequently to hide from roving Cossacks, it was only by a series of happy chances that he reached Orsza after dark. The Emperor had that day marched off with the Imperial Guard, now reduced from 35,000 to 6000 men. Eugène and Davoût were still there. All hope of seeing Ney again had been abandoned, and the two Marshals could hardly believe their ears when the tired officer was brought to them, and told them he had parted from Ney that morning, and that a remnant of the 3rd Corps was fighting its way to Orsza.

A force of all three arms under the command of Eugène was at once sent out. After marching for some miles and finding no sign of the column, he halted in the darkness and fired salvoes of artillery at regular intervals, as a signal to Ney in case he should be within hearing. Presently a reply was heard—distant volleys of musketry, for Ney had no guns with which to answer. Eugène moved on for awhile, and then fired some more signal guns to guide his colleague. At last the little column appeared, less than 900 men—not a few of them wounded—all that was left of the 6000 who had marched out of Smolensk. Ney was at their head. Eugène ran to meet him, and the two leaders fell into each other's arms.

Ney was excited and angry. Davoût, he said, should have held on at Krasnoi until the 3rd Corps could reach the place, or if he could not do that he should have sent him timely warning, instead of allowing him to march into a trap. He continued speaking in this strain during the night march back to Orsza. There he met Davoût. The Marshal tried to explain his retirement from Krasnoi and his failure to warn him. Ney gave him an angry look and replied: "As for me, Monsieur le Maréchal, I do not reproach you. God sees us and will judge us."

When the Emperor heard of Ney's exploit he exclaimed, "He is the bravest of the brave," and then he spoke of the way in which Ney had extricated the remnant of the 3rd Corps from imminent destruction as a good augury for the whole army. "I shall yet save my eagles!" he said.

Eighteen days of marching and fighting, culminating in the disaster at Krasnoi, had reduced Ney's corps to the strength of a battalion. Only one of his generals and two of his colonels were still capable of further service. He had lost all his artillery, cavalry and transport. He had looked forward to receiving reinforcements at Orsza, reorganizing his corps, and giving the weary men a rest.

But once more, as at Smolensk, a bitter disappointment awaited him. The supplies collected at Orsza had already been for the most part distributed to the Imperial Guard and the other corps. He could only obtain very little for his men. And they could not even have the much-needed rest for there was a halt of only a few hours.

For the Emperor had hurriedly marched off with the Guard and ordered the other corps to follow him immediately. He had heard serious news. Two Russian armies were converging upon his line of retreat a few marches to the westward. Tchitchagoff, an admiral serving for a while as a general, after leaving 30,000 men to oppose Schwartzenberg's Austrians, had marched up from the southward with 40,000 more, and captured Minsk, where a vast amount of supplies had been stored for the Grand Army. Wittgenstein, with 35,000 men, was coming down from the northward and forcing back the corps left with Victor to protect that flank. Napoleon had intended to retreat by way of Minsk. He was now directing his march on the crossing of the Beresina river near Borisov. There was no considerable depot of stores nearer than Wilna, and there was a terrible risk that among the half-frozen swamps of the Beresina he would find his way barred by Tchitchagoff and Wittgenstein, while Kutusoff with the main Russian army fell upon his rear.

Orsza was evacuated on 20 November. Davoût's corps now formed the rear-guard, and Ney's handful of men had only to endure the hardships and dangers that were the common lot of all the French Army. During the next few days a broad highway led through the wooded country that was once part of the great forest of Minsk. The partial thaw during the day made the marching difficult. During the nights there was intense cold, and in a week the handful of men that now represented the 3rd Corps had lost 200 more officers and soldiers through hunger, exposure, and sickness. Some of the regiments had entirely disappeared. Others were represented by one or two weak companies and a squad of officers, who no longer had men to command, and had armed themselves with muskets to fight as privates. As the army approached the Beresina, it was joined by the corps of Victor and Oudinot—reduced in numbers but still in good fighting form, with some well horsed batteries and well mounted regiments of cavalry. The two Marshals and their soldiers were startled at the sight of the ragged, war-worn remnant of the conquerors of Borodino and Moscow, and the miserable crowd of fugitives, men, women, and children, that accompanied their march. With the reinforcements supplied by these two corps Napoleon had some 50,000 men at his command, but the mob of disbanded soldiers and civilian camp-followers and refugees was almost as numerous—some estimates placing their numbers as high as 40,000.

The situation had become, if anything, more perilous during the march from Orsza. Tchitchagoff, moving up the western bank of the Beresina, had beaten Dombrowski's Poles and seized the bridge at Borisov. Wittgenstein was closing in from the northward on the other bank. Happily for the French Kutusoff, with his army suffering almost as much as the invaders from the terrible weather, was pursuing them very slowly. They had gained a little on him—but for this the position would have been hopeless. Even so Napoleon considered the outlook so menacing that he burned his private papers and the reports of his ministers, and ordered the eagles of his regiments to be destroyed. He showed, however, an unwise persistence in endeavouring to save scores of now useless guns from becoming the trophies of the enemy. Wagons were abandoned, officers and cavalry troopers dismounted to provide horses with which to drag every gun that yet remained over the snowy roads.

The awful story of the crossing of the Beresina has so often been set forth with all its grim details of suffering and death, that there is no need to do more than tell of Ney's part in the operation. He had so few men with him that at first he was a mere passive spectator, anxious only to find the opportunity of moving his 600 officers and soldiers across the river. The first bridge was not ready till late on the 26th. It was only on the following day that Tchitchagoff discovered that he had been misled as to the crossing place and began to march back to bar it. Wittgenstein was now attacking the French rear-guard under Marshal Victor on the east bank and Kutusoff, Milarodovitch and Platoff were hurrying up to his assistance. Ney crossed the river during the night of the 26th, with his 600 men. For the next two days they were bivouacked on the right bank. The cold had suddenly become more severe, and during this enforced halt, though the 3rd Corps was not in action, it had heavy losses. Men who had held out against suffering and exposure while they were actively engaged from day to day, broke down on this wretched bivouac in the midst of a battle, in which they were spectators.

The crossing of the river was painfully slow. This was partly the result of the Emperor's order that as many guns and wagons as possible should be taken across, partly the outcome of the general confusion and the increasing collapse of discipline. On the 28th the Russians were fiercely attacking on both sides of the Beresina. The Emperor was with his last reserve, the remnant of the Imperial Guard, near the bridge-heads on the western bank. On the other side rows on rows of guns and wagons and a huge multitude of fugitives were protected by Victor's stubborn defence against the attack of Wittgenstein's army. On the west bank Oudinot's corps (2nd) was holding back Tchitchagoff. About midday Oudinot was badly wounded. Most of his generals had already been hit, and there was imminent danger of the defence collapsing. It was then that the Emperor called upon Ney to save the situation. He was only too eager to act. He took command of the 2nd Corps and his vigorous measures restored the fight. He surprised the Russians by organizing a counter attack. Doumerc's Cuirassiers were sent to charge their artillery and came back with five captured guns and 2000 prisoners. After this the Admiral gave up the attempt to force the French lines, and contented himself with a distant cannonade. He showed indeed such slackness that he was accused of conniving at the escape of the enemy. A Russian caricature showed Kutusoff and Wittgenstein tying Napoleon up in a sack, and Tchitchagoff cutting a hole in it through which he slips out. The wits of the time also suggested that as the wind was blowing from the north the Admiral could not understand how he was to bring up his army dead against it.

The Emperor was effusive in his praise of Ney. He told him he had once more saved the army. The sight of the captured guns and prisoners raised the courage of all. The fate of the unfortunate Russians was terrible. Dragged with the retreating army that was itself half-starved they mostly died of cold and hunger. It was said that there were even cases of cannibalism among them.

Victor withdrew across the river early on the 29th, leaving thousands of disbanded fugitives on the east bank. The artillery bridge had broken down under the fire of Wittgenstein's guns. The other bridge was burned by the engineers as soon as the last of Victor's corps had crossed. Many lost their lives in a desperate effort to force their way across the flaming bridge. Many more were drowned in the attempt to pass on the rotten ice. Still more were massacred by the Cossacks on the left bank. In the spring the Russians collected and burned in great heaps nearly 30,000 corpses.

Only Tchitchagoff's strange lack of enterprise saved the Grand Army from destruction on the morrow of its disastrous passage of the Beresina. The line of march for many a mile lay across the half-frozen marshes of the west bank. There was one narrow roadway, often carried for hundreds of yards at a time along wooden bridges. They had been prepared for destruction by the Cossacks, who had heaped up piles of dry brushwood at the entrance to bridge after bridge. But the order had not been given to fire them. They were seized by the French vanguard, and as Ney and Victor, with the rear-guard, passed over them they burned them to check the enemy's pursuit. But once the marshes were passed the harrassing attacks of the Cossacks began again, and the rear-guard was in action day after day. Tchitchagoff was following on the track of the Grand Army. To right and left of him Wittgenstein and Kutusoff were marching on parallel lines.

The miseries of the retreat had hardened Ney into something like insensibility to the losses and sufferings that were the experience of each recurring day. Captain De Noailles of the general staff had been killed in the battle of 28 November on the Beresina. He was a friend of De Fezensac, and the young colonel spoke to Ney of his loss. The Marshal's comment was: "Well, it is better that we should be regretting him, than that he should be regretting us". A soldier fell wounded beside him, and begged to be carried off and saved from the pursuing Cossacks: "What do you want me to do? You are one more victim of the war," said Ney coldly, and passed on. The worst horror of the retreat and pursuit was that it made men heartless. There were exceptions. Some endured endless toil and suffering to aid a comrade, and the soldiers in the ranks especially showed a devoted care for their officers in all the remnants of regiments in which discipline still survived.

On 30 November, after the passage of the long defile formed by the causeways and bridges of the Beresina marshes, the Russians had begun a series of furious attacks on the rear and flanks of the rear-guard formed by Ney's men and a portion of Victor's corps. They were repulsed only at the cost of heavy loss, Ney more than once fighting in the ranks, musket in hand, as if he were a sergeant instead of a marshal of the Empire. The cold increased day by day, and the losses from exposure in the miserable bivouacs each night were heavier than those incurred during the fighting by day. Men and officers lost heart, abandoned their regiments, and joined the mob of stragglers. But the rigour of the winter told upon the Russians themselves. The pursuit slackened. The attacks on the rear-guard became half-hearted demonstrations. It was well that there came this partial relief, for, on 4 December, Ney had with him only some sixty men, belonging to various regiments. He told Victor that he could no longer assist him, but must leave the rear-guard and try to collect the remnants of his corps. Victor replied that he was himself about to withdraw from the extreme rear of the column, that his men were worn out and needed some rest. There was an angry altercation when Ney told him to go, but to leave him as much of the 9th Corps as was still fit to make a stand, and he would answer for the safety of the army. Victor replied that he would not give him one of his men. The dispute was ended by the arrival in the nick of time of an order from the Emperor bidding Ney join him at once at Smorgoni, and confiding the command of the rear-guard to Victor.

Napoleon was about to leave the Grand Army and return to Paris. He had rightly recognized that he could do more to save the tottering Empire by resuming the direction of affairs in his capital, than by journeying slowly back to the Niemen amid the wreck of the Grand Army. It needed no prescience to see that the coming year would bring with it a desperate struggle against Europe called to arms by the tidings of the catastrophe on the snowy plains of Russia. He would bring new armies into existence to replace the veteran legions, whose unburied dead strewed the line of the disastrous retreat. He did not desert the Grand Army. He had shared its perils so long as his presence was of the least help to his officers and soldiers. It was now becoming an embarrassment to them.

In his farewell interview with the marshals at Smorgoni he spoke hopefully of the future. He was leaving his brother-in-law, Murat, in command. Ney would hurry on to Wilna and organize the defence. Loison's division was coming up from that side to reinforce the army, and Wrede with the 6th Corps was rejoining from the north. The pursuit would be stopped at Wilna, and in the spring he would have fresh armies concentrated on the Vistula to meet the enemy if he tried to invade Germany.

Napoleon left Smorgoni on 5 December. If he seriously

believed that the Russian advance would stop short of the Niemen, or that Wilna could be held against the enemy he was doomed to a speedy disappointment. Under the rigours of the intense cold and constant exposure the reinforcements brought by Loison and Wrede melted away, and the regiments seemed to catch the contagion of disorder that had already wrecked the other corps of the Grand Army. Ney had got together a few hundred officers and men of the 3rd Corps. These he placed under the command of General Ledru and they marched with the Imperial Guard, "under its protection" to use the expression of De Fezensac. They were too worn down and exhausted to be any longer fit for combatant duties. The rear-guard, which Ney formed to cover the retirement of the army through Wilna, was made up of a few thousand men of Loison's division and Wrede's Bavarians. During these first days of December, while the *débris* of the Grand Army was straggling along the road from the Beresina to Wilna, the sufferings of the unfortunate soldiers had reached a climax. Half of Loison's division had disappeared in two frozen and almost fireless bivouacs. The pursuing Russians had become weary of slaughter, and were too short of supplies themselves to be able to take any prisoners. One of their officers told how the road was strewn with dead and dying; how the French bivouacs were marked by smouldering fires, round which a crowd of miserable men lay or sat huddled together, some already dead, others too exhausted to move another step; and how starving fugitives were wandering all over the country.

Wilna had escaped the horrors of war so far. There were well-stored magazines of supplies, the shops were open, and the local traders had been doing good business during the campaign, and now sold various comforts to the officers and soldiers at extravagant prices. The hospitals and many of the public buildings were crowded with sick and wounded men, and from the hospitals fever had spread among the people. When the beaten army poured into the streets many thousands, who were already ill and broken down, gave up the attempt to go further. In two days the number of the invalids rose to 20,000. The general disorganization was such that Murat despaired of holding the place, and at once decided on continuing the retreat to the Niemen. Ney was directed to defend the eastern suburbs during the evacuation of the town.

The vanguard of the army had entered Wilna on 8 December. Ney held the suburbs during the 9th and next day retired through the town, with some 2000 men of the rear-guard. The Russians immediately occupied the place, securing 20,000 prisoners, mostly invalided, and with them an immense quantity of abandoned guns and wagons, including the Emperor's baggage. Most of the supplies in the magazines also fell into their hands. The utter disorganization of the Grand Army had resulted in very little being distributed to the men.

If it had been possible to halt even for a few days at Wilna the army might have been reorganized there, the men given rest and food and warm clothing, and then there would have been an orderly retreat to the Niemen and thousands of lives would have been saved. But as it was, the march from Wilna to the frontier town of Kovno was the most disastrous stage of the whole retreat. The Grand Army had become a helpless mob. Even the discipline of the Imperial Guard had broken down. If any of the fugitives at last repassed the Niemen it was due to the dauntless courage, iron will, and unbroken energy of Ney. To the last he managed to keep some remnant of a rear-guard together, and with an ever-dwindling handful of men stood between his comrades and destruction. Ségur's description of his method of covering the retreat tells us what was the order for each day: "At five in the afternoon he took up a position to check the Russians and allowed his men to have a meal and rest. He started off again at ten o'clock. During the whole of the night he drove the crowds of stragglers before him with shouting of orders, entreaties, even blows. At daybreak, about seven o'clock, he halted, took up a position, and rested under arms and with watchful outposts until ten o'clock. Then the enemy would again come in sight and he would have to fight until evening, gradually retiring over more or less ground. At first the length of the march had been decided by the orders for the day, but later it depended on circumstances, for the rear-guard, at first 2000 strong, was reduced to 1000, then to 500, and at last to only 60 men. But nevertheless Berthier, whether of set purpose or through mere routine, had made no change in the form of his orders. He went on issuing them as if they were addressed to a corps of 35,000 men. He detailed with complete imperturbability in his instructions to Ney all the positions that were to be taken up and held till next day by divisions and regiments that no longer existed. And each night when, on receiving a pressing message from Ney, he had to wake up the King of Naples (Murat) and make him continue his journey, Berthier expressed the same astonishment. It was thus that Ney protected the retreat to a point a few versts beyond Evé. There as usual the Marshal had stopped the Russians and given his men some rest during the first hours of the night. About ten o'clock he and Wrede who was with him discovered that they were all alone. Their soldiers had left them abandoning their arms, which were to be seen glittering in rows beside the deserted bivouac fires."

Luckily for Ney and Wrede the intense cold of the night kept the Cossacks, who were close at hand, in stupid drowsiness around their watchfires. So the French Marshal and the Bavarian General, after a long tramp through the night, safely rejoined the straggling column that was making its way to Kovno. Attempts to rally even a handful of men proved useless. At dawn some prowling Cossack spearmen were sighted. If they had attacked, the French were at their mercy, but they kept a respectful distance, and peering through the haze that hung upon the snowy ground they failed to discover that there was no formed rear-guard between them and their prey.

That day Ney reached Kovno. The frontier town was a scene of hopeless disorder. The troops had been plundering the magazines and the shops, wasting and destroying as much as they took. They had found some large stores of rum and brandy, and had been drinking freely. In their enfeebled, half-starved condition even a small quantity of spirits was enough to intoxicate them, and some 2000 men were lying dead drunk in the streets. Many of them never rose from the ground again, the bitter cold ending what the drink had begun. Others, not so far gone, sat about fires lighted in the streets and open spaces, and refused to obey orders or to join the column of fugitives that was streaming across the bridge on the Niemen.

The disorder at this point was such that more than once there was a complete block in which men were crushed and trampled. Not a few, who had survived all the horrors of the retreat, met their deaths thus as they tried to cross the frontier stream. It was frozen hard, and thousands could have passed freely on the ice, but there was so much confusion and panic that officers and men huddled like sheep through the narrow defile of the bridge.

Ney set to work at once to organize another rear-guard, with which to protect the evacuation of the place. He brought two guns up to an earthwork on the Wilna road, and got together some weak companies of Wrede's Bavarians to support them. Then, leaving the artillery officer in command, he went into one of the houses and lay down to snatch an hour or two of sleep. He was roused by the sound of firing, and hurrying towards the earthwork he met the Bavarians and the gunners bolting into the town in a complete panic. A Russian battery had suddenly opened fire. The first shot had dismounted one of the guns. The gunners had spiked and abandoned the other. The artillery officer had tried to stop them, and failing this had blown his brains out. The sight of Cossack lancers advancing, with the head of an infantry column behind them, had been enough to send the Bavarians running out of the work. Their nerve was already badly shaken by the fire of the enemy's cannon, and the collapse of their own artillery. There was nothing to prevent the Cossacks charging into the streets of Kovno.

Threatening the fugitives with his drawn sword, appealing to them in their own language, his mother-tongue, the Marshal rallied a few score of men and led them back to the abandoned work. Setting the example himself by taking up a musket and cartridge box and shooting down the nearest Cossack, he got the Bavarians to open an effective fire on the attack. The Cossacks, who had expected to dash unopposed into the town turned and rode away. The low rampart gave some protection against the enemy's artillery, and the Russians contented themselves with firing on the earthwork with musket and cannon. If they had come on with the bayonet there was nothing to stop them for Ney's force was soon reduced to only thirty men. With these he made a show of defence till nightfall. At dawn next day he retired across the river.[1] Kovno had been by this time evacuated by all the troops that could still march and were obeying their officers. Some thousands of stragglers and of broken down or drunken men were made prisoners by the Russians.

Less than 300 officers and men, the remnant of the 35,000 that had crossed the Niemen under Ney's command a few months before, were all that represented the 3rd Corps at Kovno. They had taken no part in the defence. Under General Marchand they had been among the last to cross the Niemen during the night between 13 and 14 December. Next morning they marched by the Gumbinnen road, the one organized body of troops in an irregular column of fugitives. Less than 200 men and officers were under arms, commanded by General Marchand, assisted by General Ledru, and Colonel de Fezensac. They had with them about a hundred sick and wounded, whom they were transporting on sledges, and a few more sledges conveyed a small reserve of ammunition and

[1] There is a more sensational version of Ney's defence of the Kovno breastwork which appears to me to be a legend. De Fezensac who was in Kovno and met Ney next day, and who proudly relates the exploits of his illustrious chief, does not give any of the sensational details to be found in more than one popular French history of the campaign and in some English books. According to these stories Ney was abandoned by all the Bavarians, and remained alone to defend the work, collecting the muskets they had thrown away and firing them over the parapet. For a while he was himself the "rear-guard of the Grand Army". I take to be equally baseless General Dumas' romantic and dramatic story of Ney's meeting with him at Gumbinnen, for the simple reason that after crossing the Niemen Ney found the road to Gumbinnen held by the Cossacks, and had to reach Königsberg by way of Tilsit. Here is one version of the story, reproduced as a sample of the romantic embroidery of popular history:—

"In Gumbinnen, Mathieu Dumas was sitting down to breakfast, when a man in a brown coat entered, his beard long, his face blackened and looking as though it had been burnt, his eyes red and glaring. 'At length I am here!' he exclaimed. 'Don't you know me?' 'No,' said the General, 'Who are you?' 'I am the rear-guard of the Grand Army. I have fired the last musket shot on the bridge of Kovno. I have thrown the last of our arms into the Niemen, and come hither through the woods. I am Marshal Ney.'"

To what has been already said of the improbability of this story, it may be added that there was no firing at the bridge of Kovno, and no arms could have been thrown into the Niemen, for it was frozen so hard that the Cossacks rode across it on the ice.

supplies. Now that they were across the Niemen they thought all danger was over, for there was a fixed belief in the Grand Army that the pursuit would not be pushed across the frontier river. But the danger was not over. They had not gone far on the road when, as the column began to ascend the long slope of a flat-topped ridge crowned with pine woods, the fugitives in front came running back in a disorderly crowd calling out that the Cossacks were in front, barring the way. At first this was thought to be a mere scare, but suddenly there was the report of a gun from the pine woods at the top of the hill and a cannon ball crashed into the crowd. Shot after shot followed. It was evident that the hill-top was held, not by some roving band of Cossack irregulars, but by a body of troops with artillery. The fact was that a flying column of Russians had crossed the Niemen above Kovno on the ice, and occupied the Gumbinnen road.

Marchand halted his men. The position seemed desperate. To attack the heights would have meant destruction. To retire would be to invite a charge of superior numbers, and even if they beat it off and escaped to Kovno, they risked being massacred by Kutusoff's Cossacks, who would soon be masters of the town, if they were not there already. The men lay down to get some cover from the enemy's artillery fire. The two Generals and De Fezensac realized that, under the shock of this great disappointment, there was no fight left in the men. They were in despair. Even some of the officers lost heart. Two of those who survived in the little handful of men that represented the 4th Infantry told their Colonel they were going back to Kovno to surrender and ask for quarter. They had fought bravely and suffered uncomplainingly during the long retreat, but now they had broken down, and turned back to Kovno followed by some of the men. They were never heard of again.

The Russian balls were making more victims in the thinned ranks of the 3rd Corps. Men lay dead by the roadside. Others badly wounded were carried to the sledges. The destruction of the corps was now only a question of time. But the officers expected that presently the Russians would come on to attack at close quarters with overwhelming numbers. Then they could hope at most to sell their lives dearly in a last desperate fight.

It was at this moment of despair that Ney appeared. He had found a horse in Kovno and rode up accompanied by a few of the Bavarians. "He showed," says De Fezensac, "not the least excitement or anxiety in the midst of this desperate situation." Here, as after the defeat of Krasnoi, his calm confidence restored every one's courage. Now, as on that occasion, "they felt he would do something". And he made up his mind at once, took command, and issued his orders. He led his men not back to Kovno, but to their right, into scattered belts of wood through which he gained the road along the west bank of the Niemen in the direction of Tilsit. Only a handful of Cossacks pursued and they were easily driven off. The Russian officer who held the ridge on the Gumbinnen road had no idea that the handful of men was commanded by a Marshal of France, and that a vigorous attack would have given him Ney and two generals as prisoners. His instructions were simply to hold the road in order to prevent the escape of any more of the French from Kovno before its occupation, and he kept to the letter of his orders.

Five miles below Kovno Ney left the Tilsit road and marched through the woods to the westward. Some of the soldiers, who went on towards Tilsit, were killed or captured by the Cossacks, who were now swarming across the frozen Niemen at various points. The night of the 14th was passed by Ney and the 3rd Corps in a village in the woods. He had now with him only about 200 officers and men, half of them wounded, sick or broken down and conveyed on the sledges. An officer of the 4th Infantry died that night, another next day. But the miseries of the retreat were now over. The Cossacks no longer pursued the detachment. They were too busy following up the main body on the Gumbinnen road. The way to Königsberg lay through a country which had not been wasted by war, which abounded in supplies, and in which the country folk were not yet hostile. On the 15th Ney handed over the command to Marchand, and hurried on to Königsberg in a well-horsed sledge. The debris of his corps rejoined him there on the 20th—200 men, half of them invalids, out of the original force of 35,000.

Ney had not received even the slightest wound during the continual fighting of the retreat, and though he looked worn and haggard when he reached Königsberg, he was in perfect health. He had evidently an exceptional physique. It was men of this stamp that survived the horrors of the Russian campaign. The weaker had all been swept away.

His service with the rear-guard of the Grand Army was undoubtedly the most brilliant episode in his military career. Never was there a more conspicuous illustration of the fact that in war the man counts for more than the men. It was to Ney's iron will, calm courage, ready resource and initiative, and his influence as a leader that Napoleon owed it that even the debris of his army reached the Niemen, and that he himself escaped from captivity or death. It was the dauntless chief of the rear-guard who averted an anticipation of Sedan on the plains of western Russia.

CHAPTER XIV

THE CAMPAIGNS OF DRESDEN AND LEIPZIG (1813)

AFTER a short stay at Königsberg and then at Berlin, during which he was engaged in work connected with the reorganization of the Grand Army, Ney was recalled for awhile to France.

He found the whole country plunged in mourning. For the first time, after long years of victory, there had come tidings of disaster that could neither be concealed nor minimized. It was "the beginning of the end". But the great majority of the French people were still loyal to Napoleon—still believed that his genius could reverse even the most terrible of defeats. They responded, if not with enthusiasm, at least with patriotic generosity, to his call upon them to make new sacrifices to uphold the honour of the French arms. Eighty thousand men of the National Guard were formed into marching battalions and incorporated in the regular army. Fifty thousand men were withdrawn from Spain. Fifty thousand of the contingent liable to the conscription of 1813 had already been called up in September, 1812. They were sent into Germany from the depots. On 11 January, 1813, the Senate accepted a decree calling out 100,000 men who had escaped the conscription in the years 1809 to 1812, and summoning to the colours 150,000 young men who in the ordinary course would not have been liable to the military law till 1814. These mere boys learned their drill while marching though France and across the Rhine. Two thousand officers, who had come back from Russia without any men to command; retired officers called back to the army; officers from Spain, and a numerous promotion of non-commissioned officers to higher rank, supplied the cadres for organizing this huge mass of men—470,000 recruits—who had to be trained and made ready to take the field in the spring beside the 50,000 old soldiers withdrawn from Spain and the remnants of the army that had marched into Russia.

Ney was again to command the 3rd Corps. Its reorganization had begun in East Prussia, then when Prussia joined the Russian alliance, and the French held only the fortresses in the north, the Corps was withdrawn to South Germany. The handful of men who had reached Königsberg became the nucleus for the reinforcements, and new drafts of recruits hurried up from France, and by the end of the winter had grown to a corps of 37,800 infantry and 1300 cavalry. But though Ney had now nearly 40,000 men under his orders, they were not to be compared to the veteran divisions and regiments of the old army that had been destroyed in Russia. Ten thousand of those war-worn soldiers would have been better fighting material than Ney's whole corps, mostly made up of new levies. The wonder is, not that these young soldiers did not win back victory to Napoleon's eagles, but that they fought so well and averted for so long a time the final catastrophe.

Austria had withdrawn from the French alliance, but at first stood neutral. The Emperor Francis was loth to declare war against his son-in-law, but his army was kept on a war footing and massed in Bohemia, ready, if need be, to intervene in the struggle. Saxony and the states of South Germany were at first on the side of Napoleon. The rulers of these minor territories owed too much to him, and had too long been accustomed to act as his satellites, so that they stood by him, although their people were already wavering under the impulse of the patriotic movement that had swept over the north. Eugène had been forced to abandon all the country up to the Elbe, and had retired from Berlin on Magdeburg. Dresden and Leipzig had been occupied by the Allies.

But Napoleon was able to assemble his new army in the same South German territories that had been the starting point of more than one of his greatest campaigns. His garrisons held fortresses not only along the middle Elbe, but also on the Oder and the Vistula, in the heart of the enemy's country. His plan of campaign was to make a dash at Leipzig, drive the enemy from Saxony, then turn northwards to march on Berlin and win his way from the Oder to the Vistula, relieving the blockaded fortresses, calling Poland again to arms, and dictating peace on Russian ground, so as to wipe out the baleful memories of 1812. He would have to face the armies of Russia, Prussia, and North Germany, and a Swedish contingent under one of his own Marshals, Bernadotte, now Prince Royal of Sweden, and the enemy of France.

The Emperor established his head-quarters at Erfurt on 25 April. He had with him the Guard, no raw levies these but the surviving veterans of many a hard campaign. They mustered about 15,000 bayonets. Marmont with the 6th Corps (30,000 men) was marching from Gotha. Bertrand with the 40,000 men of the 4th Corps was coming up from Saalfeld. Out in front, nearest to the enemy, lay Ney's corps. It was in cantonments and camps on the old battle-field of Auerstadt. Two divisions had been added to it, bringing up its total strength to about 50,000 men. Ney was to lead the vanguard of the new Grand Army. His divisional commanders were Ricard, Brenier, Girard, Souham, and his old comrade Marchand. General Beurmann led his handful of cavalry.

The advance on Leipzig began across the famous plains of Lutzen, the scene of the last battle of Gustavus Adolphus. The Viceroy Eugène was marching down from Magdeburg with 65,000 men (5th Corps, Lauriston; 7th, Reynier; and 11th, Macdonald), to combine with the main body under Napoleon before Leipzig. All that was known of the Russian and Prussian armies was that they held Leipzig, and had their main masses somewhere behind the line of the river Elster on the eastern border of the Lutzen plains. The Elster was an effective screen for them. The river, divided into many branches and backwaters, flows through a tangle of swamps and islands covered with dense willow woods and osier beds.

Ney marched through Naumburg on 29 April, and next day his young soldiers had their baptism of fire at Weissenfels on the Lutzen road. They had to face a trying ordeal for such raw troops, for they were charged again and again by masses of Russian cavalry. But the squares stood firm and the conscripts felt at the end of the day that they were real soldiers. A similar attack at the crossing of the river Rippach next morning was defeated in the same way, and the hostile cavalry drew off to the eastward, forming a screen in the direction of the Elster, that completely hid any indication of the Allied movements on that side.

Lutzen was occupied that May day, and the Emperor established his head-quarters in the town. Ney had opened the campaign with two victories. The young soldiers were behaving excellently. Eugène had joined with his three corps. The army was now concentrated within easy striking distance of Leipzig. The Emperor determined to seize it on 2 May. But his spies reported that Wittgenstein's Russians and the Prussians under Yorck were moving to cross the Elster at Zwenkau and Pegau, and that the Czar and the King of Prussia were with them. Napoleon had no accurate information as to the Allied strength, but he still ventured to move on Leipzig. Eugène's three corps and the Imperial Guard were to carry this out. Ney was to occupy the villages immediately to the south and south-east of Lutzen, and thus cover the movement by holding the Allies if they attacked from the crossings of the Elster. He might count on being reinforced by the corps of Marmont and Bertrand which were to reach Lutzen early in the day.

Ney sent Beurmann's squadrons to scout towards the Elster, and placed his five divisions in the villages, Souham's men holding the most advanced of them, Gross Görschen, on the road from Pegau to Lutzen. The village gives its name to the battle that followed in German histories of the campaign. French writers call it the Battle of Lutzen. Then at ten o'clock Ney joined Napoleon's staff and rode with him towards Leipzig. As the Emperor passed the long columns of troops that were tramping towards the city he was enthusiastically cheered by the men.

Cannon were booming at the head of the column and when Napoleon and Ney reached the scene of the engagement they found that an easy victory was being won. Maison's division of Lauriston's corps was fighting its way across the succession of bridges and causeways that led over the Elster and its swamps into Leipzig. The enemy, Kleist's Prussians, were giving way so rapidly that it was evident that no determined effort was being made to hold the place. By eleven o'clock Maison's men were in the suburbs. The Emperor rode forward and watched Lauriston's corps pouring across the bridges to complete the victory. The artillery had ceased firing, for its work was done.

Then suddenly from the south-westward, the direction of Lutzen, ten miles away, came the dull rumble of a heavy cannonade. The feeble resistance offered at Leipzig, the sound of battle from Lutzen, told Napoleon at once that the Allies must have left a mere detachment to hold the former place, and thrown the mass of their forces against the latter. He said quietly to Ney, "It looks as if while we have attacked their flank here, they have been turning us. But there is no harm done. They will find us everywhere prepared to meet them." Then he told him to ride back, resume command of his corps, and hold Gross Görschen and the neighbouring villages at all costs, and he promised to support him with the Guard and the rest of the army, all but Lauriston's corps, which would be left to complete the occupation of Leipzig.

Staff officers dashed away with orders to the corps commanders. Ney set spurs to his horse and galloped off by the road that leads to Kaya, the centre of his position, between Lutzen and Gross Görschen. Louder and louder came the roar of the battle with each mile of his eager ride. He was hurrying to add one more brilliant exploit to his long record of soldierly service to France.

As he clattered over the bridge on the Flossgraben brook and up the slope into Kaya, he was at once in the thick of the fight, and could see that it had been going badly for the Emperor. Gross and Klein Görschen and Rahna were in the hands of the enemy. On the lower ground around the captured villages—ground intersected with willow-bordered streams that formed stretches of swamp with shining pools of water—columns of Prussian infantry were moving forward to the cry of "*Vaterland! Vaterland!*" Four hundred guns were thundering against the long swell of the plain on which Kaya and Starsiedel stand, the two villages that now formed the strongholds of the French line. To the right front some thousands of Russian cavalry, Cossacks, dragoons, and cuirassiers, were moving over the more open ground. Souham had been driven out of Gross Görschen by an overwhelming attack. A stand had been made in Klein Görschen and Rahna. Marmont had arrived on the French right with two of his divisions—Bonet's infantry and Campan's marines. These had for awhile restored the fight. There had been fierce bayonet encounters, furious charges of the Russian cavalry, and just as Ney reached Kaya the French had been driven in, the two villages were lost and Blücher was leading an attack on the last position of the defence, the Kaya-Starsiedel ridge.

But then was seen the magic influence that one man can sometimes exert on the fortunes of a battle-field. Ney's very appearance, calm, alert, confident, in the midst of the lost battle, inspired all who saw him with new courage. Grasping at a glance the possibilities of the situation he issued a few swift orders. He sent his trusted comrade Marchand to lead his division against the right flank of the attack. Riding forward sword in hand he himself led Ricard and Brenier's divisions to meet Blücher's advance with a vigorous counter attack, instead of awaiting it on the crest. Souham and Girard, who had already suffered heavily, were to follow in the second line.

Bayonets were crossed on the slope below Kaya. After a severe struggle the Prussians were hurled back. Ney riding in the thick of the fight seemed once more to have a charmed life. Following up the retiring enemy he fought his way towards Gross Görschen. The villages of Klein Görschen and Rahna were retaken. The guns came rushing down from the Kaya ridge to support the victorious advance. Blücher clung to Gross Görschen, but it was the most he could do. Macdonald was coming up on his right joining hands with Marchand. And now Napoleon rode on to the field, the man whose presence was held to be worth a reinforcement of 10,000 men.

Ney had done his work. He had snatched victory from the jaws of defeat, and held the enemy till Napoleon and the first reinforcements could arrive. But the battle was not yet over. The Czar and the Prussian King had still in hand large forces not yet engaged. Blücher's reserves included the infantry and cavalry of the Prussian Guard, and several line brigades.

He sent a brigade to check Macdonald's advance; ordered the Guard cavalry to support the Russian attack on Marmont on the French right, and himself led forward a strong column of attack headed by the grenadiers of the Guard. Ney's hard tried troops, exhausted by the strenuous fighting in which they had been so closely engaged, gave way before the charge. Klein Görschen and Rahna were retaken. Blücher was wounded, but refused to quit the field. The Prussians pushed up the slope to Kaya, stormed that village, breaking deep into the French centre. If at this moment Wittgenstein had sent the Russian infantry to support Blücher it would have gone hard with the French. But the Russians showed a strange slackness, and contented themselves with pressing the attack on Marmont.

At this critical moment Bertrand's corps began to arrive to support Marmont on the right, and on the left Macdonald pressed forward towards the line of the Flossgraben stream, bringing a long line of guns into close action against the enemy's flank. Behind Kaya Ney's four divisions had fallen back in a confused mass. Ricard's men alone showed some steadiness and closed up their thinned ranks. The rest were breaking away into a hurried retreat that would soon be a rout. But the Imperial Guard was approaching. If even a brief stand could be made in the centre the battle might yet be won. Napoleon rode in among Ney's conscripts. "Young men," he said to them, "I counted on you to save the Empire. Are you going to desert me?" Ney and his officers helped to rally the broken divisions, and once more the Marshal led them against the enemy. The Prussian Guard, unsupported and temporarily disordered by their very success, were driven out of Kaya, and Ney's men again advanced on the villages below the slope.

But now Wittgenstein flung into the fight his infantry and the Russian Guard, with Yorck's Prussian corps. These masses of fresh troops were directed against the French centre. If only Ney's divisions had opposed them the result must have been a disaster for Napoleon. But he was ready for the crisis. Drouot galloped into the fight eighty fresh guns, the artillery of the Imperial Guard, and down the slope between

Starsiedel and Kaya came the columns of bearskin-capped infantry, more than twenty fresh battalions of the veteran Guardsmen, whose advance had been the presage of decisive victory on so many famous fields. The Russian Guard met them bayonet to bayonet, but were forced back after a stubborn fight. The French Guardsmen now swept all before them. Ney led the remnant of his four divisions beside them in the triumphant march that carried the eagles through Rahna and Klein Görschen into Gross Görschen.

The sun was going down and the Allied commanders were breaking off the fight. Covered by their masses of splendid cavalry, they drew off without leaving any trophies of the victory to the French. Not a gun or a standard was lost, and very few prisoners. His weakness in cavalry made it impossible for Napoleon to reap the full results of a hard-won success. The Allies withdrew across the Elster, and then continued their retreat eastward through the Kingdom of Saxony. Napoleon followed them up. They abandoned Dresden to him without risking a stand in its defence, and, on 8 May, he had the satisfaction of occupying it, and bringing his ally the King of Saxony back to his capital.

He had marched on Dresden with the Guard and the 4th, 6th, 11th, and 12th Corps. After his success at Lutzen he had felt strong enough to detach Ney with a cavalry division and three corps to Torgau on the Elbe. Ney's presence there was a threat against Berlin, and yet he was near enough to be quickly recalled for combined operations with the Grand Army.

That of all the marshals Ney should have been chosen for this semi-independent command shows the high esteem in which the Emperor held him. The French Army of the North at Torgau was made up of Ney's own corps, the 3rd, with the 5th Corps under Lauriston, and the 7th under Reynier. Between him and Berlin there was only a weak Prussian corps under Bülow. But great as would have been the impression caused by the occupation of the Prussian capital, Napoleon knew that his real objective was not this or that city, however important, but the main Allied army, which had at last halted and taken up a position on the hills behind the upper course of the River Spree near the town of Bautzen, some thirty-six miles east of Dresden.

He formed a plan for the attack of the Bautzen position, with the object of not merely driving the Allies from it, but of destroying them. A frontal attack by the Grand Army from Dresden was to be combined with the sudden appearance of Ney and the northern army on their right flank. He was not simply to drive that flank in and roll up the hostile line, but he was to gain the right rear of the position and cut the Allied line of retreat. Napoleon's plan of attack was, in its main lines, much the same as that of Moltke at Sadowa more than fifty years later. He wanted not a victory but a decisive victory, another Marengo, Austerlitz, or Wagram, after which he could dictate peace.

The Allied position was occupied by 97,000 men with 627 guns. The left rested on the high wooded hills of the Austro-Saxon frontier. The front ran for about ten miles along the heights east of the River Spree. The right was thrown back along the spurs of the high ground, in the hollows of which at this point were a number of small lakes, that formed a series of obstacles diminishing the actual front to be held against a turning attack. The Allies occupied the town of Bautzen and the line of the Spree only with advanced detachments, which after delaying the development of the French attack would fall back on the main position. General Kleist with 5500 Prussians was on the river north of Bautzen. The town and the river banks south of it were held by Milarodovitch with 15,000 Russians. When he retired from the river, he was to defend the heights on the left. The centre was occupied by the Russians under the Grand Duke Constantine and the Prussian corps of Yorck. To their right was Blücher for whom Kleist's corps was to act as a reserve in the second stage of the battle. The Russian corps of Barclay de Tolly was on the extreme right. At various points the heights had been entrenched.

On 17 May the Allies, well served by their numerous cavalry, were aware that Ney was coming down from the north-west with obvious designs on their right flank. He had moved out from Torgau to Luckau as if about to make a dash for Berlin, and then changed the direction of his march towards Bautzen. He had with him the 3rd and 5th Corps—his own and Lauriston's. Reynier had been left at Luckau to watch Bülow's Prussians.

A Russian column under Barclay and a Prussian force under Yorck were sent out to meet the threatened danger. On the 19th Barclay was in action with Ney's advanced guard, and later in the day Yorck had a fight with Lauriston. But the Allies could only afford to attempt a delaying action against the forces opposed to them. They fell back to the Bautzen position and on 20 May in the forenoon Napoleon, who had left Dresden only the day before, was in front of it with the main body of the Grand Army.

He had received considerable reinforcements since Lutzen, and had a very marked superiority in numbers. Including the detached force under Ney he was marching against the Allies with 164,000 men and 530 guns. The fighting began about noon with an attack on the advanced corps of Milarodovitch and Kleist holding the river line.[1] The crossings of the Spree were forced, Bautzen was occupied, and the Russians and Prussians driven back to the heights with serious loss. Ney, with the flanking force, took only a small part in this first day's battle. About half-past seven in the evening, with the vanguard of the 3rd Corps, he drove Barclay's advanced troops out of the village of Klix. Darkness ended the fighting. Napoleon had the Imperial Guard and his head-quarters at Bautzen. Macdonald and Oudinot (11th and 12th Corps) were partly over the river on his right, Marmont and Soult (6th and 4th Corps) on his left—all in touch with the enemy and ready to attack his entrenched positions next day. Ney with part of the 3rd Corps had crossed the river at Klix. Lauriston with the 5th was close behind him, and had orders to cross the Spree below Klix next morning and come into action to the left of the 3rd Corps.

[1] The engagement of 20 May, 1813, is sometimes called the "Battle of Bautzen," and next day's fighting on the heights the "Battle of Wurschen". The fighting of the two days really amounted to the first and second stages of a great battle, which it is most convenient to describe as the "Battle of Bautzen".

Napoleon's plan for what he intended to be the decisive battle of the 21st was to send forward his right (Oudinot and Macdonald) at sunrise to make a fierce attack on the left of the Allies, in order to induce them to move their reserves to that side. The Guard was to be held in reserve, and in the centre Marmont and Soult were at first to confine themselves to a cannonade and mere demonstrations against the heights. The decisive movement was to be made by Ney. Barclay had wheeled back the Allied right so that it faced nearly north to meet the flank movement. Ney was to attack Barclay in front sending Lauriston to drive in and turn his extreme right. The two corps were to converge on the village of Preistitz. Napoleon told Ney he was to occupy this place by 11 a.m. The flanking force would then be in rear of the Allied right and the point of direction for Ney's further advance was to be the tower of the village church of Hochkirch, appropriately named, for it stands high on the hills in the rear of the ground held by the Allies, on the road from Bautzen to Lobau, and the tower is visible for many miles. As Ney thus moved across the enemy's rear cutting his lines of retreat, Soult, Marmont, and the Guard under Napoleon, would be driving the Allies from the central heights. The enemy would be caught between hammer and anvil. Napoleon counted on capturing tens of thousands of prisoners and hundreds of guns, and ending the war at one blow.

The battle began well for the Grand Army. The attack on the Allied left made steady progress, and Milarodovitch, who commanded there, had soon to ask for support from the centre. From Bautzen northwards the French artillery was pouring a storm of fire into the positions held by the Grand Duke Constantine and Blücher, and swarms of skirmishers, pushed well up the hills, seemed to prelude an immediate attack in force all along the line. Ney had moved in the early twilight, hurried his two corps across the river, and attacked Barclay in front and flank. By eight o'clock he had 60,000 men in line. Barclay could only oppose to them 13,500 Russians. He sent repeated messages to the Czar asking for support, but Alexander for some time took no notice of these appeals for he was seriously alarmed at the rapid progress of

Oudinot's fierce attack on the left. Here the French were coming on steadily, storming village after village, and crowning the conquered ridges with their artillery. The Czar for a while regarded this as the real point of danger, and Barclay, left to his own resources, fell back on Preistitz and Baruth about 9 a.m.

Ney now rode forward, and sent two divisions, led by Souham, to attack Preistitz. He moved another division nearer the Spree, against the village of Pliesskowitz, in order to link his advance directly with the left of Soult's corps. It is very likely that if Ney had had under his command the war-worn veterans he had led at Friedland and Borodino he would not have minded much having a gap between his advance and the nearest corps of the main attack, and would have concentrated all his efforts on the turning movement. But with his young and inexperienced troops he saw a risk in plunging boldly into the Allied positions and leaving his own right for a while "in air" and exposed.

Preistitz was cleared of the enemy after a hard fight, and between ten and eleven Napoleon heard plainly the cannon thunder of Ney's victorious advance, and saw the smoke and flashing of his guns on the heights well into the Allied right. The Emperor therefore ordered Marmont to advance against the enemy's centre.

Marmont was somewhat slow about coming into action, and the danger to Barclay and the whole position on that side was so obviously pressing that the Allies began to send what reserves they could spare against Ney. As Souham's division issued from the south end of Preistitz, it was attacked by there battalions of the Prussian Guard supported by a mass of Russian and Prussian cavalry. The French were driven back into the village. Kleist's corps then came up with the remaining battalions of the Guards, and Preistitz was attacked by the Prussians and recaptured after a sharp fight and heavy losses.

Marmont was now beginning to make the pressure of his attack felt on the centre. So Kleist, holding on to Preistitz himself, sent away the Prussian Guards to reinforce Blücher. Ney for a while did not attempt any further advance. Lauriston's corps was working round to the east of Baruth, and Ney was waiting for this flank movement to tell upon the Allies before he tried to retake Preistitz.

By two o'clock the attack was general along the French front. On the extreme left Lauriston was pressing Barclay hard at Baruth. Ney brought three of his divisions into action again against Kleist about Preistitz. Within an hour he captured the village for the second time, and Kleist's Prussians were falling back on Belgern. Ney had now one of the great opportunities of his life. He had only to keep strictly to his orders, take the high church tower among the wooded hills as his guiding mark, and push straight forward on the heels of Kleist. He would first have separated Barclay from the Allies, and then cut their central line of retreat through Wurschen. But strange to say he allowed his corps to drift away from its proper line of direction, and swing to its right against Blücher in the enemy's right centre, only a mere detachment following up Kleist's retreat.

Blücher, already closely engaged with Soult's corps, saw at once the danger of his position when Ney's victorious troops appeared upon his flank. He rapidly withdrew his corps behind the deep hollow of the Blossaer Wasser, and formed on a new front, facing nearly north, with his left at Purscwitz, a large village that had been elaborately fortified. Kleist rallied behind Blücher's right, and Barclay's Russians, falling back from Baruth and extricating themselves from Lauriston's turning movement, prolonged the line to the right through the villages of Rackel and Kortnitz. Behind the line thus formed the Allies began their retreat from the heights. It was a defeat, but Ney's error had saved the beaten army from the disaster Napoleon had prepared for it. How well the retreat of the Russo-Prussian Army was conducted, and how little the French were able to interfere with it, is shown by the fact that out of more than 600 guns only nine were left in the hands of the victors. Very few prisoners were taken. The Allies lost 10,850 killed and wounded. The French storming fortified villages and entrenched heights lost nearly 25,000.

There was practically no pursuit. The Allied right retreated through Wurschen to Weissenberg, the left through Hochkirch to Lobau. The two columns then evacuated

Saxony and united about Gorlitz in Silesia. Once more Napoleon had to regret that he no longer commanded an army of seasoned veterans. The young men who filled the ranks of his regiments were exhausted by their efforts and incapable of further exertions without some days of repose. But on the other hand the Allies were disheartened by their failure. They had expected an easy victory over the improvised army of the Emperor, and they had been badly beaten at Lutzen and then at Bautzen and expelled from Saxony. In three weeks Napoleon had victoriously won back the old prestige of his arms, and while he was overrunning Saxony, Davoût had recaptured Hamburg. No wonder there was depression in the Allied councils, and they welcomed the friendly mediation of Austria proposing an armistice and peace negotiations. Napoleon, temporarily unable to follow up his success, and anxious to secure the fruits of victory, accepted the proposed suspension of arms. The armistice was signed on 4 June.

From Ney's failure to carry out Napoleon's plan at Bautzen dates the beginning of the final stage of the Emperor's downfall. Had the Allied army been destroyed on 21 May he could have dictated peace on his own terms. The armistice held his hands, but with his army in its exhausted condition and a formidable enemy still in the field he could not reject the good offices of the Emperor Francis, without running the risk of seeing the Austrian army at once arrayed against him. He might even now have saved his crown and his dynasty if he had made the best of a difficult situation and concluded a peace though at the cost of great sacrifices. But he felt he was still a conqueror, and when the Allies and Austria proposed as a basis of the peace that he should resign most of his conquests and withdraw from his overlordship of Germany he resolved to tempt once more the fortune of war. The terms finally formulated for Napoleon's acceptance at the Congress of Prague included the yielding up of Poland to Russia and Illyria to Austria, the evacuation of Spain, Holland, Belgium, and a great part of Italy by the French, and the organization of a free Confederation of the Rhine. Napoleon hesitated for awhile. Then he prepared again for war. 10 August, the last day of the armistice, passed without his even sending a reply to the Allies. Next day Austria, which had kept a large army ready mobilized in Bohemia, declared war against him.

Napoleon began the autumn campaign in the face of terribly unequal odds. During the armistice the forces on both sides had been considerably increased. The Allies had now some 700,000 men in the field, of whom about half a million would soon be available in the main theatre of war. In the first days of August, 50,000 Russians under Barclay and 50,000 Prussians under Kleist had been marched from Silesia through Austrian territory to reinforce the army under Schwartzenberg in Bohemia. As he had already concentrated 130,000 of his own troops this brought his fighting force up to 230,000 men. These would march from the southward against Napoleon.

The Army of Silesia under Blücher, with its head-quarters at Breslau had left, after thus reinforcing Schwartzenberg and the Austrians, a total of 110,000 men (60,000 Prussians and 50,000 Russians). These would march against the Emperor from the eastward. Northward lay another allied army about Berlin, 20,000 Swedes under Bernadotte and 70,000 Prussians and Germans under Bülow and Tauentzien. Finally a Russian reserve army of 60,000 men under Benningsen would soon be ready to march to the scene of operations in Saxony.

To these half-million men Napoleon would be able to oppose a little more than 300,000 men after providing for garrisons and line of communication troops. Dresden was to be the centre of his defensive operations. He hoped to be able to strike from this central point now at one, now at another of the allied armies. Under his immediate command he had the Imperial Guard, eight army corps and three corps of cavalry, in all about 250,000 men. At the close of the armistice these were divided into three groups. In and near Dresden were the 14th Corps (St. Cyr) and the 1st (Vandamme). Further east at Bautzen, Gorlitz, and Zittau were the Guard, and the 2nd Corps (Victor) and the 8th (Poniatowski). Facing Blücher's army in Silesia stood Ney at Liegnitz, with the 3rd Corps. On his right, and under his orders, was the 5th (Lauriston). The 11th (Macdonald) was still further to the right about Löwenberg. In his rear in support was the 6th Corps (Marmont).

A smaller army under Oudinot lay about Luckau, watching the Allied Army of the North and threatening a march on Berlin. It was about 60,000 strong and was made up of 4th Corps (Bertrand), the 7th (Reynier), and the 12th (Oudinot).

Ney's position during the campaign was remarkable. For most of the time he was not in command of his own corps, but withdrawn from it and employed now here, now there, in special duty with other troops of the Grand Army. Napoleon had learned to rely upon him as the man to cope with an emergency. His mistake at Bautzen was not allowed to count against him, but he did not escape the ill fortune that was now linking with defeat so many names that hitherto had been held to mean unfailing success.

The Allies opened the campaign with a forward move of Blücher and the Army of Silesia, a feint meant to draw Napoleon with the central mass of the Grand Army eastward, and give Schwartzenberg the opportunity for issuing from the passes of the frontier range with the Army of Bohemia, overwhelming the French left, and occupying Dresden. The brunt of Blücher's attack fell upon Macdonald's corps. Napoleon marched to the help of the Marshal and Blücher was defeated at Löwenberg on 21 August. But Schwartzenberg was hopelessly slow in taking advantage of the opportunity made for him by his Prussian colleague. On the 22nd Napoleon heard that the Austrians were on the move, and he at once began a forced march on Dresden with Marmont's corps, leaving Macdonald only to watch Blücher, sending everything else towards the point of danger, and calling Ney temporarily away from his own corps to hurry up the divisions of the Young Guard that had been moved towards Gabel.

Schwartzenberg, advancing slowly with the Army of Bohemia, was before Dresden on the morning of the 26th. He held a front of seven miles, but one of his corps was late in arriving, and with an excess of caution he wasted the whole morning waiting for it. St. Cyr held the southern suburbs which had been strengthened with redoubts, trenches, and barricades, but he was so weak in numbers that there is no doubt that a determined attack by the Allies early on the 26th would have given them Dresden.

Napoleon arrived in the city with the first reinforcements shortly before noon. It was not till after one o'clock that Schwartzenberg at last attacked. By that time the French were marching into the city in a steady stream. But few of the newly arrived troops had reached the southern front, and at first the attack seemed likely to succeed. St. Cyr was being driven in by the pressure of numbers. The first check to the attack, the first warning to the Allies that they had more than St. Cyr's corps to deal with, was the appearance in the French centre of line upon line of bear-skin caps, as two strong columns of the Guard came into action. They were led by Ney in person. They had not merely come up to strengthen the defence. They made a fierce counter-attack with the bayonet, and drove back Kleist's Prussians with heavy loss. After this the attack made not another foot of progress. The fighting went on till nightfall, the French being continually reinforced and everywhere holding their ground. Towards evening heavy rain began, and during the night it came down in a deluge on the hostile armies which had bivouacked on the ground on which they had fought, waiting to renew the battle in the morning.

Napoleon was still outnumbered two to one by the Allies. On the morning of the second day he would be able to put only 96,000 men in line against an army of 200,000. Nevertheless he had decided to abandon the defensive and venture upon an attack on both flanks of the enemy. Mortier, with two divisions of the Guard, was sent to the right to turn the enemy's flank on that side. But this movement, like Oudinot's attack at Bautzen, was chiefly intended to divert Schwartzenberg's attention from the real point of danger. Murat, after long hesitations had joined the Grand Army and with every available squadron massed in a great column had marched before dawn to gain the right flank of the Allies, pushing in between them and the Elbe. Victor's infantry corps supported him, attacking in front while Murat charged through the driving rain upon the Allied flank and rear. The infantry formed in squares to meet the charge, but as the horsemen dashed forward only a few straggling shots were fired at them. The rain had soaked the paper-covered cartridges and the priming of the muskets, and most of the ammunition was useless. Under these circumstances square after square was broken. The horse artillery, acting with the cavalry, opened at point blank range upon the masses drawn up in solid squares to resist the charges. By two o'clock Murat had routed the Allied right taking some 12,000 prisoners. Mortier had broken their left. Ney in the centre had attacked with the Guard supported by his own corps. Schwartzenberg lost heart and retired covered by his cavalry.

The French had about 10,000 men killed and wounded. The losses of the Allies were much heavier. Fifteen thousand were killed and wounded, 23,000 prisoners. Two generals were among the latter. Napoleon's trophies of the day were fifteen captured standards and twenty-six guns. Had he been able to follow up his success and reap its full results the victory of Dresden might have saved his throne. But on the morrow of the battle he was prostrated by an attack of illness, and none could supply his place. The great scheme of operations he had devised for destroying the beaten enemy during the retreat into Bohemia miscarried for want of his directing genius. Vandamme, with the 1st Corps launched against the flank of the retiring Allies, was left unsupported, cut off from the Grand Army, and completely defeated at Kulm on the 29th. Of his 40,000 men, only one half extricated themselves from the disastrous fight. All the artillery was lost, and Vandamme himself was wounded and taken prisoner.

Even before he heard of Vandamme's failure, Napoleon had bad news from Oudinot. He had advanced on Berlin with the French Army of the North about 60,000 strong (4th, 7th, and 12th Corps and 3rd Division of Cavalry). But on 23 August he had been beaten by Bernadotte at Gross Beeren, with a loss of thirteen guns and many prisoners. His defeat was partly due to the misconduct of the Saxon troops who formed a large element in the 7th Corps and whose hearts were not in the struggle. Oudinot retreated to Wittemberg on the Elbe.

Then came news that on the very day of the first fighting before Dresden Blücher had beaten Macdonald on the Katzbach.

The Emperor used the breathing time allowed him while the Army of Bohemia was recovering from its defeat to turn upon Blücher and the Army of Silesia. On 4 September he encountered and defeated the Prussians at Hochkirch on the old battle-field of Bautzen, and following up his success won another victory next day at Makersdorf.

While he was thus driving back the Army of Silesia he had found work for Ney elsewhere. He was anxious to avenge the defeat of Gross Beeren (which he felt all the more because it was Bernadotte who commanded the victorious enemy), and he attached great importance to the moral effect that would be produced by an occupation of Berlin. On 1 September he gave Ney the command of the northern army at Wittemberg with orders to march against Bernadotte, who had now nearly 100,000 men at his disposal. Ney, usually so sanguine and self-confident, did not disguise his dislike for the mission entrusted to him and his doubts of success. He reached Wittemberg on the 4th, and began his march on Berlin next day. He had no reason to complain of the zealous co-operation given to him by Bertrand, who commanded the 4th Corps. But the other two commanders were a source of trouble and anxiety to him from the first. Reynier (7th Corps) was notoriously self-willed almost to the point of open insubordination. Oudinot (12th Corps) was in continual bad humour at having been deprived of the chief command and placed under the orders of his brother marshal. At times it seemed almost as if he would rather see a failure than a success, if only to show that Ney could do no better than himself.

On the 5th the advanced parties of the enemy were driven from the villages of Zalma and Seyda. Three corps were now concentrating to bar Ney's advance. Tauentzien and Bülow's Prussians were on his right front, Bernadotte's Swedes away to the left. He decided to attack the Prussians early on the 6th before they were joined by the Swedes. The result was the battle of Dennewitz. Ney's plans for the attack were executed in a way that brought his three corps into action in succession instead of simultaneously, and thus exposed him to be beaten in detail. Bertrand with the 4th Corps obeyed his instructions, and was the first to engage the enemy. Reynier with the 7th left the line of march appointed for him with fatal results. Oudinot had been directed to follow Reynier's corps. He waited a long time for the 7th Corps to appear, and when time went by and there was no sign of Reynier, who had taken another road, he at last marched off hours too late, and even when he arrived in sight of the battle-field did not come into action till he received a pressing message from Ney. By this time the Marshal was barely holding his own against the united forces of Tauentzien and Bülow. Oudinot's arrival restored the fight for awhile, but then the appearance of Bernadotte's army on the left of Ney's line forced him to retreat in order to avoid an utter disaster. Reynier's Saxons had already given way and their retirement was very like a rout. The French and Italian regiments of the army did better. The pursuit was hotly pressed and the three corps, retiring by different lines, only concentrated on the 8th at the fortress of Torgau after heavy losses. Large numbers had surrendered as soon as the fortune of the day turned against France, the only consolation was that most of these were not Frenchmen. Ney had brought 58,000 men into action, 20,000 at a time against a solid mass of 54,000 Germans. He had lost 10,000 killed and wounded, 13,000 prisoners, eighty-three guns and 400 wagons. The German loss was about 7000 men.

The defeat was all the more serious because Ney had failed. Hitherto his name had been a talisman of victory. Not unjustly he attributed the disaster to the indiscipline of his subordinates. On the 10th he wrote to Berthier:—

> "The *morale* of the generals and of the officers as a whole is strangely shaken. To command under such conditions is only to be half a commander and I would rather be a grenadier. I beg that you will obtain from the Emperor either that I shall be sole Commander-in-Chief, with generals of division under me as my subalterns, or that His Majesty will be so good as to take me away from this hell. I think I need not speak of my devotion to him. I am ready to shed the last drop of my blood, but I want it to be shed for some useful end. In the actual state of things the presence of the Emperor is the only chance of pulling things together."

And a little later he wrote again:—

> "I cannot but go on repeating that it is absolutely impossible to make General Reynier obey. He never executes the orders he receives. I request that either this general or I myself shall be sent elsewhere."

Despite this strong protest no alteration was made in the commands. Napoleon had become used to friction between his marshals and generals and left them to settle their differences as best they could. But Ney had other causes of anxiety besides the troubles caused by his corps commanders. The spirit of officers and men was breaking down. The officers had found that they could not expect from their young troops the endurance and the efforts, which with the men of the Grand Army of other days had been a matter of course. In the earlier battles of the campaign the young soldiers, many of them only half-trained, had shown that they could fight well, but the exertions of the day of battle are the least trying part of a soldier's experiences. The young men could not march like the veterans of earlier campaigns. They broke down under exposure to bad weather and the trial of living on supplies that were often too scanty to allow full rations to be distributed. After the defeat of Dennewitz there was a general depression, which, as so often happens, was accompanied by an increase of sickness. Men began to shirk duty. They straggled on the line of march despite stern orders from Napoleon that stragglers were to be treated as deserters. They wandered from their camps in search of food. There were even cases of soldiers deliberately mutilating themselves of two or three fingers by firing a musket against them in order to report themselves as accidentally disabled and so obtain dismissal from service. Replying to a letter of the Emperor's proposing another march on Berlin, Ney, for the first time in his life, replied that he could not depend on his men. "In case of such a movement," he wrote, "a battle must be looked for, and if my army is to take part in it other corps must support it, for if we mean to force the line of the Elster[1] we must expect another check, such is the depression of spirit (*abattement*) of my troops." It must have pained a soldier like Ney very deeply to have to make such a confession.

When, therefore, after striking now at Schwartzenberg now at Blücher as the two main armies of the Allies menaced him

[1] Not the Elster near Leipzig, but another river of the same name, the Schwarze Elster (Black Elster), a tributary of the Elbe which runs parallel to it east of Torgau and joins it below the fortress.

in turn, Napoleon was at last forced to abandon Dresden in order to meet a converging movement of the enemy on Leipzig that threatened to cut him off from his communications with France, Ney fell back before the advance of Bernadotte without attempting a stand. Blücher and the army of Silesia had made a flank march to join hands with Bernadotte and move with him against the north and east of Leipzig, where Napoleon was now concentrating the Grand Army. Schwartzenberg was advancing against it from the southwards. These movements occupied the first two weeks of October.

During the retirement Ney had been joined by his old corps, the 3rd, and had resumed command of it, while exercising a general direction over those that were acting in concert with it. As he drew near Leipzig and the detached corps were once more units in the great concentration, he became again for a couple of days a mere corps commander, the French Army of the North having no longer a separate existence.

Then came the three days of battle round Leipzig—the greatest battle of the nineteenth century. The Grand Army mustered 170,000 men with 700 guns. The Allies brought into action 301,500 men (including 56,000 cavalry) with 1384 guns. The Germans call it the "Völkerschlacht"—the "Battle of the Nations," not without reason, for besides the French there were in the Grand Army the soldiers of many nations whom the great Emperor had made his tributaries, and the Allied armies were those of Russia, Austria, Prussia, and Sweden.[1]

On 16 October, the first day of the battle, Ney and the 3rd Corps had no opportunity of taking any useful part in the action. It was not his fault. In the morning he was posted on the north-east side of the circle of positions held by the Grand Army around the city. From the southward Schwartzenberg with the Army of Bohemia was attacking along a front of six miles. North-westward Blücher was in action with Marmont

[1] The English Army was also represented in the great battle, not only by the officers attached to the Allied head-quarters, but also by a fighting detachment, a "Rocket Troop" of the Royal Artillery, commanded by Captain Bogue. It was with Bernadotte's army. Bogue was killed in the fight. Lieutenant Strangways then took command, the same officer who as General Strangways was mortally wounded at Inkerman in 1854.

about Mockern. Bernadotte was approaching slowly from the north-east. Early in the day Napoleon became anxious about his positions south of the city, and Ney was ordered to transfer his corps to that side and act as a reserve for the defence there. The 3rd Corps accordingly made a march of about eight miles, passing through the eastern suburbs of Leipzig, and then moving out by the Lieberwolkwitz road to Probsteyda, where beside the windmill, on the highest ground south of the city, the Emperor was watching the battle, with the Imperial Guard waiting in ordered lines on the slopes to the left of the village. Here there was a brief halt while Ney conferred with the Emperor. Then he moved his corps forward to near the village of Dosen.

There was now good prospect of the 3rd Corps being actively engaged, but there came from Marmont pressing messages asking for help. The southern line of battle was making a good stand. The danger on the north was more imminent, and Ney was ordered to retrace his steps and support Marmont. Once more he marched through the narrow streets of Leipzig. Issuing from the northern suburbs he took up a position in the rear of Marmont's line, but his corps was never seriously engaged. He had been marching instead of fighting during the day, and had for him the novel experience of being a spectator of a great battle.

The firing ceased about six o'clock as darkness came on. The French had maintained their positions on the whole, but at the cost of heavy losses. It is true that the losses of the Allies had also been serious, but they could better afford them. Bernadotte had not yet come into action. The Russian corps of Benningsen and Colleredo's Austrians had not yet joined Schwarzenberg. The Allies could spare many thousands of men. Time and numbers were on their side.

Sunday the 17th was a dull, sunless day, with frequent storms of wind and rain. Beyond a few shots exchanged here and there between the outposts of the hostile armies there was no fighting. The Allies were waiting for their reinforcements. Bernadotte's vanguard (Wintzigerode's Russian division) showed itself beyond the Partha. In the evening Colleredo and Benningsen joined Schwartzenberg. The counter attacks of the French the day before had made the Austrian generalissimo anxious about his position, and before these reinforcements joined him he had withdrawn Gyulai's corps from the left bank of the Elster by the bridge at Pegau. This was a piece of good luck for Napoleon, for it cleared his line of retreat. It was a piece of characteristic over-caution on Schwartzenberg's part, and needlessly sacrificed a great advantage.

Napoleon spent an anxious day. He was strangely irresolute, and there were times when he spoke of beginning a retreat at once. On the south side he drew in his lines nearer to Leipzig. During the night he slept little. At 3 a.m. on the morning of the 18th he sent for his carriage and drove amid rain and darkness through Leipzig to Ney's head-quarters on the north side. He roused the Marshal and spent an hour in conference with him. Map in hand he pointed out the positions of the Allies and the general arrangement of the defence, and after an exchange of views with Ney, put him in command of all the troops on the north side of Leipzig.

Before dawn the weather had cleared up and the sun rose brightly on the morning of Monday the 18th. Leaving Marmont to hold his own against Blücher, just outside the northern suburbs of Leipzig, with his left protected by the Elster swamps, Ney prolonged the line with the 3rd and 7th Corps, his own and Reynier's along a rising ground east of the village of Schönfeld. The Partha ran parallel to his front about two miles away in the plain, and then swept round his left flank by the village of Mockou. Masses of the enemy, the Allied Army of the North reinforced by other corps, were crossing the Partha in his front and working round by Mockou to threaten his flank.

An artillery duel opened the battle. Ney's guns, though heavily outnumbered, made a good fight, and he sent forward lines of skirmishers to delay the hostile advance across the Partha. But it was not till near noon that the Allied attack began to develop its full force. Then Langeron's corps stormed Mockou driving out Ney's left and seizing the bridge on the Partha. By this crossing, and the fords close by, they came pouring over the river. Ney drew back his left to Schönfeld, where he was in touch with Marmont's right.

On his own right towards Sellerhausen Reynier was attacked by Bubna's corps, supported by Wintzigerode's regular cavalry and some thousands of Platoff's Cossacks. Here the English Rocket Troop came into action, and although the rockets did little damage, the flying trails of smoke and the loud explosions were trying to the nerves of Reynier's young troops, who were facing a novel weapon that seemed something as terrible as it was strange. Unfortunately, too, for Reynier, he had in his command the Saxon troops whose half-hearted slackness had been so largely responsible for the defeat of Dennewitz. About two o'clock first one, then another, regiment of these deserted its post, marching over to the Allies with bands playing a patriotic German air and muskets sloped on their shoulders. Then the Saxon cavalry galloped across to the attack with sheathed swords. Three batteries of artillery ceased firing, limbered up, and trotted away with the deserters. A cuirassier regiment charged after them to try to capture the guns, but the Saxon artillerymen promptly unlimbered and stopped the charge with a blast of grapeshot fired at close quarters, then limbered up again and continued their march. Thus in half an hour Reynier was abandoned by the whole Saxon contingent, eleven battalions, three squadrons, and three batteries. The Allies did not bring their new comrades into action but at once sent them into bivouac a league away on the banks of the Partha.

The remnant of Reynier's corps had now to fall back by Sellerhausen, supported by some reinforcements hurriedly despatched by Napoleon from the south front. Meanwhile Ney was fighting hard with Langeron and Bülow about Schönfeld and Paunsdorf. He had two horses killed under him. Late in the afternoon Bülow took Paunsdorf, and Langeron stormed Schönfeld. Ney rode back towards Leipzig amid the wreck of his corps, hardly able to remain in the saddle, for in the defence of Schönfeld he had been badly wounded by a ball in the shoulder. Marmont had been driven into the suburbs. The whole defence of the northern line had collapsed.

On the south the French had barely held their own against Schwartzenberg's attack, and it was evident that the struggle could not be prolonged for another day. The Emperor rode over to see for himself the situation on the north side, but he had already given orders for the retreat to begin. Days before it had been proposed to throw additional bridges over the branches of the Elster, but Napoleon had neglected this precaution, and the whole army with its guns, wagons, and commissariat cattle had to march in a single column through the narrow winding streets of old Leipzig, and then along miles of causeways and bridges, the roadway being never more than thirty feet wide. Twenty-four hours would hardly have been enough for the uninterrupted march of the Grand Army through this defile.

The retirement began during the night and was continued for some hours during the 19th, rear-guards holding the suburbs of Leipzig. The first bridge on the Elster had been mined, and on a detachment of the enemy seizing a neighbouring island and threatening the bridge the engineer in charge prematurely blew it up. Thousands had not yet crossed. With their line of retreat thus cut they became the prisoners of the Allies. Marshal Macdonald escaped by swimming the Elster, but the gallant Poniatowski was drowned in the attempt.

The losses during the three days' battle had been terrible. The Allies had 48,000 killed and wounded, including 21 generals and 1800 officers. The Grand Army had lost 45,000 killed and wounded, and 15,000 prisoners. Thirty-six generals had been killed, wounded, or taken prisoners, and the Allies captured on the battle-field or secured in Leipzig 28 standards and eagles, 325 guns, and 900 wagons.

Ney was invalided, recovering from his wound, during the retreat of the Grand Army to the Rhine. Only the slackness of Schwartzenberg's pursuit enabled Napoleon to save the remnant of his army. All his German Allies had now abandoned him. The Bavarians under Wrede (Ney's old comrade of the Russian retreat) even tried to bar his way, but were badly beaten at Hanau, so that the disastrous campaign closed for Napoleon with a parting gleam of victory.

CHAPTER XV

THE CAMPAIGN OF FRANCE AND THE ABDICATION (1814)

NEY was disabled by his wound during the retreat across the Rhine, but he made a good recovery, and before the end of the year was able again to take the field. There had been for a moment a hope that peace would be concluded under conditions that would leave to Napoleon his crown and to France the Rhine frontier. But the informal negotiations came to nothing. Wellington had crossed the Pyrenees; Bülow was in the Netherlands with a Prussian Army; the Austrians were overrunning Switzerland. Two great armies of invasion were preparing to pass the Rhine. The outlook could not be more menacing. A year ago by extraordinary exertions the Emperor had replaced with new levies the old army that had disappeared among the snows of Russia. Only a remnant of the new Grand Army remained to him. By decree after decree he called to arms three-quarters of a million of men. But now at last France failed to respond to his call. Not one-third of the men he summoned to the colours ever appeared. Not more than half of these took the field before the final catastrophe.

There were for a while hopes that the Allies would avoid a winter campaign, and that there would be some breathing time in which to prepare for the defence of France. But on 21 December Schwartzenberg's army, more than 200,000 strong, was crossing the upper Rhine near the Swiss frontier. On the New Year's Day of 1814, Blücher crossed the middle Rhine with 80,000 more. Bülow had 60,000 in Holland and would soon enter the north of France. Marshal Macdonald had about 15,000 men in Cologne and Coblentz. Another 15,000 was with General Morand at Mayence, and Marmont had about 20,000 at Durkheim. Marshal Victor had collected 20,000 men behind the Vosges. Ney had 5000 or 6000 at Nancy, and Mortier about the same number at Langres.

Unable from lack of numbers to risk a serious engagement with the invaders, the French commanders in the east of France retired before the advance of the enemy, leaving garrisons in the fortresses and walled towns. Marmont retreated through Metz. Victor joined Ney at Nancy, and the three Marshals united their forces at Châlons. Reinforcements were sent from Paris, regiments of the Imperial Guard and drafts from the depôts, and on 25 January the Emperor himself arrived at Châlons. He gave to Ney, a Marshal of France who had commanded Army Corps numbering forty or fifty thousand men in earlier campaigns, the command of a division of the Imperial Guard. Two years before it would have ranked as a weak brigade, or it might have been organized simply as a regiment, for it mustered only 2500 officers and men. That such a command should have been assigned to a Marshal was a startling evidence of the way in which the great Emperor's military power was dwindling to comparative insignificance.

Ney's weak division belonged to the latest formations of the "Young Guard". Many of his men were little more than recruits. Many of his officers had been lately promoted from the ranks, or called back from half-pay, or were fresh from the military schools. He had to act as a brigadier on the march and in battle, and in the bivouacs and on the outpost line give every possible moment he could spare to teaching his men their duties. Now he was doing the work of a general, now of an adjutant, or a sergeant-instructor. The splendid physique that had sustained him through the dangers and fatigues of the retreat from Moscow without an hour of illness, without even an hour of over-fatigue or exhaustion, enabled him to work day and night with only snatches of sleep.

Ney's division was included in the little army of about 40,000 men with which Napoleon marched up the valley of the Marne by Vitry, and on 29 January startled Blücher by falling upon the Prussian rear at Brienne and winning the first victory of the campaign. The Prussian abandoned his advance on Paris, drew back to unite with Schwartzenberg, and on 1 February the Allies opposed 130,000 men to Napoleon's

40,000 at La Rothière. The French were beaten, leaving fifty guns and 2000 prisoners in the hands of the enemy. But they made good their retreat towards Paris; there was no pursuit, and the Emperor was able to halt at Troyes to rest and reorganize his army.

But at this crisis of the campaign the Allies adopted a plan which delayed the catastrophe, and offered Napoleon new opportunities of victory. La Rothière had made the invaders over confident. They thought that the Emperor's army was not only defeated, but utterly demoralized. The more easily to supply their large forces from the country they divided into two columns. Blücher was to move northwards towards Châlons, and then advance on Paris by the valley of the Marne. Schwartzenberg was to follow that of the Seine; he marched with a cautious deliberatión that permitted Napoleon for the moment to neglect his operations, and aim another blow at Blücher's column. On 10 February he fell upon the Russian corps of General Olsuvieff at Champaubert, and completely defeated him, taking fifteen guns and 2000 prisoners, among them Olsuvieff himself and two other generals. He had thus cut through the centre of the long column in which Blücher's army was trailing towards Paris, and by a series of rapid manœuvres he used his central position to engage and defeat his enemy in detail. Sacken and Yorck turning back with the leading corps were met and beaten at Montmirail on the 12th. Then Napoleon turned upon Blücher and defeated and nearly captured him on the 14th at Vauchamps. Abandoning the pursuit of the Prussians he then marched to check the slow advance of the main Allied army under Schwartzenberg, the cavalry of which was already approaching Fontainebleau.

The reports of Blücher's failures had for the moment paralysed Schwartzenberg's advance. For three days he kept his forces halted where they stood "in order to await the development of the Emperor Napoleon's movements," to quote the words of his order to the army. He had not long to wait, for Napoleon was hurrying by forced marches to reunite with Victor and Oudinot and fall on the Austro-Russian flank. On the 17th with 50,000 men he swept Pahlen's corps out of Mormant, and next day won a victory at Montereau over the

Prince of Würtemberg's corps. To avoid being beaten in detail like Blücher, Schwartzenberg began a retreat, drawing his corps together as he marched. All the ground the Allies had gained in the three weeks of campaigning was abandoned. Schwartzenberg fell back across the Aube. The plan of the Allies was now that he should hold his positions on the river against Napoleon, while Blücher made another dash for Paris. For this purpose he was to be reinforced by the Prussian corps of Bülow and the Russians under Wintzigerode who were marching down to Laon from the Netherlands. A further Russian reinforcement was advancing from Lorraine. But Blücher believed that even without this help he was strong enough to sweep away the small force under Marmont that guarded the direct road to Paris. Napoleon had early information of the movement and decided to repeat the manœuvre which had given him victory a fortnight before. Leaving Oudinot at Bar-sur-Aube to keep a mere screen of troops in front of Schwartzenberg, he marched from Troyes on the 27th to attack Blücher. He had about 35,000 men with him. Ney's command had been raised to 5000 men, organized on the small scale then characteristic of Napoleon's army, in two weak divisions and a brigade. The two divisions, each of the strength of a regiment of former times, were the infantry of the Young Guard under Generals Meunier and Curial. The brigade mustering little more than a thousand bayonets was made up of veteran soldiers withdrawn from Spain, and commanded by General Pierre Boyer.

Blücher was driving back Marmont when he heard of Napoleon's northward march. He had a very exaggerated idea of the forces at the Emperor's disposal,[1] and dreaded

[1] The remembrance of how the Emperor had before this improvised grer armies, and how he showed himself in force now here, now there, had given the Allies this idea, and Napoleon did his best to foster it. After his first victories in February, he had written to the Government in Paris: "You must really have lost your heads to say that we were one against three, when as for myself I am giving out everywhere that I have 300,000 men, and when the enemy believes it, and we must go on repeating it everlastingly. This is how with a stroke of the pen you destroy all the good result of my victory. You ought to understand that there is here no question of vain boastfulness, and that one of the first principles of war is to exaggerate one's strength. But how am I to get this into the heads of a lot of poets who think only of flattering me and flattering the

being attacked by him before he could join hands with Wintzigerode and Bülow. He drew back to evade Napoleon's blow and to facilitate their junction with him. His line of march was north-eastward towards Laon, where he hoped to concentrate his army. Soissons, held by a French garrison, lay in his way, but Bülow got possession of it, thanks to the feeble defence made by a weak commandant.

Napoleon had hoped to attack Blücher before Soissons. He was indignant at the news of its premature surrender. But still unaware that Blücher had been so largely reinforced he decided to attack him at Laon, drive him away to the northward and then march back to deal with Schwartzenberg. Leaving Soissons on his left he marched to the crossing of the Aisne at Berry-au-Bac.

In the first stages of the campaign Ney with his handful of men had done his full share of the work without fortune giving him the opportunity of performing any exceptional service. Now with somewhat larger numbers at his command his chance came, when the Emperor sent forward his little corps of Guardsmen and veterans of Spain to act as the vanguard of the advance on Laon. At their head Ney took a leading part in the desperate fighting of 5 and 6 March when the Allied rear-guards were driven from the plateau of Craonne and the way to Laon was thus opened.

Blücher had six army corps, 100,000 men—Russians and Prussians, in and around the city, partly holding its approaches, the open ground eastward by Athies, the passages over the marshes of the Ardon brook—partly on the long ridge-like plateau crowned by the city with its towered cathedral and ruined walls—but mostly in reserve behind the screen of the isolated height. Napoleon had no idea his enemy was so strong. He

self-esteem of the nation." And again before this dash at Blücher he wrote to his brother Joseph (24 Feb.): "Only a few days ago the Allies thought I had not an army. Now their imagination stops at nothing. Three or four hundred thousand are not enough for them. They say the French army is stronger than ever. It is necessary that the reports inspired by their fears should be re-echoed by the Paris newspapers. Newspapers are not history, any more than bulletins are history." It is likely that Napoleon had the same purpose in organising his army in "Army Corps" 4000 or 5000 strong and "divisions" of 1500 or 2000 men. The allies hearing of divisions and corps commanded by Generals and Marshals would multiply these numbers freely.

sent Marmont to attack by Athies. He himself advanced from the south by the Soissons road. To Ney he confided the task of surprising and capturing the bridges and causeways across the Ardon marshes, near the villages of Étouvelles and Chivy, held by 6000 Russians under Woronzoff.

The weather had become suddenly colder. On the evening of the 8th snow began to fall. There was a sharp frost, and fog hung over the marshy course of the Ardon. Breaking off from his bivouacs at midnight Ney led his corps to the Soissons road, and then marched swiftly and silently on Étouvelles through fog and snow. There was no danger of missing his way with the broad high road to guide him. The Russian sentinels were suddenly swept away by a rush of bayonets, that burst through the veil of darkness and whirling snow. Led by Ney in person the French poured into Étouvelles. The Russians were bayoneted, knocked down, and captured as they rose from their sleep. A mob of panic-stricken fugitives, mostly unarmed, fled along the causeway and over the Ardon bridge with the French bayonets at their backs. The defenders of Chivy were overwhelmed by the mingled rush of routed friends and exultantly victorious foes. Beyond the second village Ney halted, rallied his men, disordered by the rush through the darkness, and collected and sent back his prisoners.

Before daybreak Victor's corps had passed the causeway in his rear, moved out to the right of Chivy, and formed up to attack Ardon village. Ney was at the same time to rush the suburb of Semilly. The French advanced just before daybreak. The snow had ceased falling and lay thick on the ground, and over it a dense marsh fog was drifting. In the half-light of dawn and hidden in the fog Ney dashed into Semilly, and stormed the suburb from end to end. At the same time one of Victor's divisions cleared the Russians out of Ardon. Ney then pushed up the steep slope towards the ruined ramparts of Laon. As he reached the higher ground he was above the fog, and Blücher watching the attack from the ramparts was surprised to see by how small a force he was being attacked. Bülow's men drove the French down into Semilly and Ardon, but at first made no attempt to recover the lost suburbs. Blücher and his staff were in a state of anxious perplexity as to the situation. The fog hid all the lower ground from them. They knew only that what was comparatively a mere handful of men had been flung against the southern suburbs, and they had a report from the cavalry on the west side of the city that there was a considerable French force in that direction (Marmont's corps beyond Athies). Blücher concluded that the attack on Semilly and Ardon must be a diversion, intended to distract his attention from the real danger-point. Then he thought that Napoleon would hardly risk an advance against him along such two lines so wide apart as the Soissons and Rheims roads. There must surely be between these two wings of the attack a strong central force. He remained on the defensive, and even when the fog lifted did little more than attempt the recapture of the suburb. Meanwhile Marmont had taken Athies, but did not follow up his success. He did not believe in ultimate victory, and he hesitated to push forward with the masses of Ziethen's cavalry threatening his flank.

Night ended the battle. Marmont's young soldiers were dangerously careless about outpost duties. In the darkness four columns of hostile infantry broke through their ill-guarded line, and as the troops in bivouac behind them rushed to their arms, and before they could form, Ziethen's cavalry burst in amongst them in a thundering charge. Marmont's men broke and fled. When he rallied the remnant of his corps about Festieux on the Rheims road at daybreak he found he had lost some 6000 killed, wounded, and prisoners, all his baggage and ammunition train and nearly all his guns.

Napoleon only heard of the disaster next morning when he was preparing to renew the attack on the south front of Laon. By this time Yorck and Kleist's corps, abandoning the pursuit of Marmont, were moving to fall upon the Emperor's flank and rear. Bülow and Wintzigerode were to hold him in front. The other two corps were to turn his left. But Blücher had suddenly fallen ill, and Gneisenau, who took over the command, still so over-estimated Napoleon's strength that he feared to divide his forces, abandoned the plan of attack that might have given decisive results, recalled Yorck and

Kleist, and gave orders for an almost passive defence of the Laon position. The most he would attempt would be to drive the French advanced troops from the ground they held in the suburbs of the city.

Napoleon after hearing of Marmont's defeat had also given up the plan of a vigorous offensive. But he still clung to the idea that Blücher would not maintain his position, and he kept in touch with the enemy intending to push home his attack on the first sign of a retirement having begun. The brunt of the fighting on 10 March fell on Ney's corps. During the morning hre epulsed repeated attacks of Wintzigerode's Russians. But he was himself in turn repulsed when, on the Emperor's order, he attacked through Semilly. Napoleon thought he saw Bülow's Prussians withdrawing from the heights above the suburb, and under this mistaken impression gave the order. It cost Ney's corps serious losses, and the only result was that the vigour of the onset made the enemy keep more strictly to the defensive during the afternoon.

By evening Napoleon had discovered that he was in the presence of fourfold odds, and that he had taken a completely mistaken view of the situation. To remain longer before Laon would be to incur further useless losses and to risk disaster. Orders were given for a retreat across the Aisne during the night. Ney was to remain in position till morning to conceal the movement from the Allies, and then act as the rear-guard. He had lost heavily during the two days' fighting and accepted with reluctance the task assigned to his weary and sorely tried battalions. He wrote to Berthier that it was a difficult business to cover the retreat with "a handful of men" in presence of a great army, and that it would have been better if the Old Guard had been left in his place.

At Soissons—after the failure before Laon—the Emperor reorganized his army. Ney's corps had suffered so severely that the remnant of his Guardsmen were turned over to the Old Guard under Mortier, and for Ney a new command was formed—the veterans of Spain, the Polish "Regiment of the Vistula" and a new battalion of the 122nd of the line, mostly conscripts. He had in all about 2500 men. Ney was in reserve in Napoleon's splendid dash at Rheims, when the city was captured, the Russian corps of St. Priest beaten, and the operations of the Allies for a while paralysed by their fear of Napoleon's energetic counter attack.

The Emperor now formed the daring plan of marching against the flank of Schwartzenberg's advance, then turning eastwards driving off the detachments blockading the fortresses, reinforcing his army with the garrisons thus relieved, and with thousands of National Guards and insurgent peasants who were reported to be in arms in the eastern departments. He would thus paralyse the allied march on Paris by cutting their lines of communication, and force them to turn back to meet him, when he would be at the head of an army flushed with local successes and reinforced by tens of thousands of old soldiers and new recruits.

While he was elaborating this plan he had sent Ney to raid the depôt of supplies established by Blücher at Châlons. It was weakly guarded and Ney seized the place after a mere skirmish on 15 March. He was received by the people with enthusiastic rejoicings. From the captured magazines of the Allies he was able to send a convoy with abundant supplies to Rheims. The raid on Châlons was like some of his early exploits as a soldier of the Republic, and he evidently had a longing to be allowed to make his column a nucleus for the partisan warfare that had begun in the east of France. Napoleon had suggested through Berthier that Ney should issue from Châlons a proclamation to the people of Lorraine and Alsace, encouraging them to rise against the invaders and promising the speedy coming of the Emperor to their aid. But Ney wrote to Berthier:—

"Before sending me this order your Highness might have pointed out to His Majesty that a proclamation of such importance and from which such great results are expected ought to come from the Emperor himself. In fact, however high may be the position I hold in the army, what can be expected from any appeal made by me to populations that have been so long accustomed to respond only to the voice of their sovereign? If I had under my command a corps strong enough in numbers for the Emperor to consider it advisable to allow me to act independently, the distance between me and His Majesty might perhaps compel me to employ such a means of announcing my early arrival to the inhabitants, whom I might be able to rid of the enemy's presence. But except in this case, it seems to me that it belongs to the Emperor only to forewarn of his intentions the provinces which he means to succour."

The letter was an indirect suggestion that he should be reinforced and given a free hand to organize the rising in Alsace-Lorraine. Napoleon reinforced him with a division of fresh troops drawn from the garrison of Mezières—2900 infantry under General Janssens and a few hundred cavalry. This brought his command up to a little over 5000 men. But the Emperor could not spare Ney for detached operations. When he began his march from Rheims towards the Aube he ordered Ney's corps to move as the left column of the general advance. Leaving Châlons on 18 March Ney was across the Aube at Arcis on the 20th, with his corps and Sebastiani's cavalry. The Emperor was a few miles away to his right. Napoleon had hoped to surprise his enemies scattered over a wide tract of country before they could concentrate. But Schwartzenberg, after a brief period of confused alarm and hesitation, during which he issued orders and counter orders and nearly gave away the game, had begun to concentrate with remarkable rapidity, his general movement being eastwards in order to secure his communications at the same time as he drew his forces together. From Macdonald's reports Napoleon learned that the enemy were falling back from Troyes, but he did not credit the sluggish Austrian generalissimo with enough enterprise to use his superior forces to attack him. The hard-fought battle at Arcis-sur-Aube on 20 and 21 March thus came as a surprise to both the French and the Allies.

Schwartzenberg, who had with him the Czar and the Prussian King, had only the vaguest knowledge of the numbers and position of the French columns when he marched on Arcis-sur-Aube on the morning of the 20th. Ney had halted on the south bank of the river east of the town. Sebastiani had driven back some of the enemy's cavalry and was marching through Arcis, after sending a young officer forward to examine the undulating country immediately to the southward. The officer did not go far enough, and reported that there was nothing in front but small parties of the allied cavalry. Sebastiani did not rely entirely on this report and rode out with a mounted detachment to drive in the hostile cavalry and see what was behind them. He had not to go far to make a startling discovery. As he cleared the first ridge he saw great masses of infantry, cavalry, and artillery moving steadily towards the Aube, and realized that he would hardly have time to ride back and give the alarm before a considerable part of Schwartzenberg's army would be ready to attack the few thousand men who held the south bank of the Aube at Arcis.

Ney's troops had formed in two lines, Janssens' brigade (the Mezières regiments) in front of the village of Torcy, about 2000 yards east of Arcis; Rousseau's brigade (the 122nd, the Vistula regiment, and the veterans of Spain) in the second line between Arcis and Torcy. The town was held by Sebastiani. His cavalry (about 2600 sabres) were in front of it, and the engineers were repairing the bridge over the Aube. A little after 1 p.m. Napoleon rode across it with his staff, and inspected Ney's position.

About two o'clock he was in the village of Torcy, discussing the situation with the Marshal, when Sebastiani was seen spurring fast for Arcis followed by his escort, and over the crest of the long slope to the southward came a great wave of mounted men, and then there was a thunder of guns as the horse artillery of the Allies unlimbered and opened fire. Sebastiani had put himself at the head of his division and rode up the slope to meet the hostile advance with a charge. A line of guns sent a storm of shells into his front. Kaisaroff's Cossacks supported by a brigade of Austrian hussars dashed at his flank. The French cavalry gave way, and, mingled with the victorious Allies, came streaming back into Arcis. At the same time sixty guns opened upon Ney, and his old comrade of Russia, General Wrede, with an Austro-Bavarian division advanced to attack Torcy.

Telling Ney to hold out to the last, Napoleon rode hard towards Arcis. As he approached it he was involved in a rush of broken cavalry, mingled with the pursuing Cossacks. He saved himself by taking refuge behind the bayonets of the Vistula regiment. The Poles, posted nearest to Arcis, had formed a square, and their steady fire drove back the Cossack. spearmen. As soon as the ground was clear of them the

Emperor left the square and galloped into the town. The streets were full of fugitive cavaliers, but Napoleon reached the bridge before them, and there, facing them sword in hand, checked their flight and rallied them. Sebastiani led them again to meet the enemy, and for the moment Arcis was saved.

Ney was meanwhile fighting hard against more than twofold odds. Wrede had carried Torcy village with the first rush, driving out Janssens' brigade. Ney brought up Rousseau's regiments, and lending them himself sword in hand, recaptured the village at the bayonet's point. There was then a momentary lull in the fight, and during this respite Friant arrived with the Old Guard and the long column of bear-skinned veterans began to cross the bridge. Napoleon sent the first three battalions to reinforce Ney on the left, and led the remainder to the position before Arcis, himself pointing out the places to be occupied by battalions and batteries. The arrival of the reserve batteries, soon after Friant came into line, further strengthened Napoleon's hands and the fight in front of Arcis became for some time an artillery duel. But on the left at Torcy Ney had to meet repeated attacks of Wrede's corps, which was steadily reinforced until the enemy had nearly 20,000 men in action against Ney's force of not more than 7000. Twice the Allies gained a footing in the south end of the village, twice they were driven out. The Bavarian General, Hebermann, was killed at the head of his brigade. Ney's brigadier, General Janssens, was severely wounded and General Lefol took his place. Torcy burst into flames under the concentrated bombardment of the Allied batteries, but in and around the burning village Ney's men stubbornly held their own. The battle did not end till after dark. In the twilight there was a fierce cavalry melée in front of Arcis, and at Torcy Schwartzenberg made a last effort to break down Ney's resistance. Two batteries of heavy guns opened on the village at short range, and Wrede reinforced with 4000 grenadiers of the Russian Guard and two regiments of cuirassiers made a last onset upon the handful of Frenchmen and Poles that had so long defied all his efforts. There was a hard fight by the light of the burning houses, and it was after eight o'clock when

Wrede abandoned the hope of forcing the position and drew off to the long ridge from which he had advanced six hours before. Fighting against more than threefold odds, with the river in his rear and destruction the penalty of defeat, Ney had not yielded an inch of ground. He had lost more than a thousand men. Impressed by this stubborn resistance Schwartzenberg drew his army together and fell back behind the crest of the high ground looking down upon the Aube from which he had attacked Ney and Napoleon. At daybreak on the 21st the French could see only some cavalry vedettes posted along the ridge.

Napoleon had gained touch with Macdonald and Oudinot and had received considerable reinforcements. He, too, misjudged the situation. The Austrians thought they had engaged the vanguard of a great army about to debouch from Arcis. Napoleon considered that the battle had been the counter-attack of a mere flank guard covering the retreat of the Allies, and that he had now no large force in his immediate front. He ordered Ney and Sebastiani to move up to the crest of the slope, the cavalry general having now at his command 9000 sabres and several batteries of horse artillery. The enemy's vedettes rode off as the French advanced, but as they reached the crest of the hill Ney and Sebastiani found themselves face to face with the whole of Schwartzenberg's army, 100,000 men and 370 guns drawn up in battle array. The artillery opened fire on both sides, and there was some skirmishing between the mounted troops, but the Allied commanders maintained otherwise a passive attitude, waiting for the French attack and believing that, on the slopes behind the troops they could see, there were hidden large masses of Napoleon's army. The Emperor now knew that he had made a mistake, and issued prompt orders for a retreat across the Aube. It was only when the retirement had been in progress for some hours that Schwartzenberg realized what was happening and gave, too late, the order to advance. The French held Arcis till nightfall against a series of desperate attacks. Then the rearguard crossed the Aube and the bridges were destroyed to check any attempt at pursuit.

The Emperor now resumed his project of a march into

Eastern France, and the retirement from Arcis was directed to the crossings of the Marne near Vitry. The town was held by a garrison of 5000 Russians and Prussians. Ney had bivouacked on the night of the 21st at Sommepuis, between the Aube and the Marne. He moved before dawn on the 22nd, and as the sun rose he was marching through the ford of Frignicourt on the Marne above Vitry, having with him his infantry and artillery and the cavalry of Milhaud and Defrance. In retreats he commanded the rear-guard; now that the retreat had become an advance he was in the van. Wheeling to the left he appeared before Vitry, and, having formed his corps for an assault, he summoned Colonel Schurchow, the commandant, to surrender, offering to allow him to retire with arms and baggage, and telling him that he was completely isolated from Schwartzenberg's army, which was in full retreat towards Switzerland. Schurchow in reply asked to be allowed to send an officer to verify Schwartzenberg's alleged position, saying that, if the Austro-Russian Army had already withdrawn beyond the line of the Marne, he would be willing to enter into negotiations for surrender in order to avoid useless bloodshed. Ney could not agree to this, and opened fire with his artillery in the hope of intimidating the Colonel. Napoleon was by this time crossing the Marne with his army by the ford of Frignicourt and two bridges constructed near it. He could not afford to waste any of his force in besieging Vitry, and he therefore called off Ney and ordered him to move with the rest of the army towards St. Dizier.

The Emperor's forces were concentrated in and around that town on the 23rd. He had pushed out cavalry reconnaissances in all directions, and sent peasants and disguised gendarmes to collect information, but the reports received were vague and contradictory. Weighing the various probabilities, he at last concluded that Schwartzenberg was marching towards Vitry, following up his own eastward move, and he suddenly changed his plan. He would cross the Marne again at St. Dizier, double back towards Troyes, and place himself once more between the Allies and Paris. The movement began at dawn on 24 March. The Emperor with the vanguard reached Doulevent, his cavalry sweeping the country to the south and west. Ney, with Sebastiani and the cavalry of the guard, bivouacked nearer St. Dizier, between that place and Vassy, having gone only a few miles.

Next day the Emperor once more changed his plans. He was puzzled at the contradictory reports he received. Troyes had been abandoned by the Allies. They were also preparing to leave Langres. But Schwartzenberg had not arrived at Vitry. There was no news of his huge army. Ney reported a mass of cavalry moving from the north-west on St. Dizier. Was this an isolated corps or the vanguard of an army? The probability was that it was part of a force detached to cover the flank of some movement of the Austro-Russians. In the early morning the Emperor had ordered all corps commanders to remain where they were for some hours, till he could clear up the situation and decide what was to be done. In the afternoon he issued sudden orders for a march back to the neighbourhood of St. Dizier. He was going to turn upon and crush the detached force of the enemy reported to be now crossing the river in that direction. "The intention of the Emperor," wrote Berthier to Ney, "is to attack the enemy to-morrow morning and drive him back into the Marne. The enemy's forces are dispersed. Everything points to our having a good day to-morrow."

Ney's corps was present but was not closely engaged at the action of the 26th, the Emperor's last victory in the campaign. The French infantry, pressing into St. Dizier with drums beating, met with the merest show of resistance. The advance was continued across the bridge while the cavalry crossed by the fords. Only about 500 of the enemy were killed and wounded, but the cavalry, pressing the retreat along the Vitry road, took eighteen guns and some 2000 prisoners. And then came the surprise of the day. The prisoners were all Russians of Wintzigerode's corps—against whom Napoleon had been fighting at Laon a fortnight ago. Schwartzenberg's army had disappeared, and here was one of Blücher's corps on the upper Marne. It was a "fog of war," through which for a while the Emperor could see nothing. He discussed the position with Ney and other generals.

Prisoners were questioned. Reports from various sources

anxiously compared. At last the truth was discovered. Blücher had marched southwards by Rheims to Châlons to bring his line of operations nearer to Schwartzenberg, detaching Wintzigerode by Vitry to watch the Emperor's movements. Schwartzenberg, after some hesitation, had cancelled the orders for a retreat eastward and decided to stake everything on an immediate combined advance on Paris. He was to march by the valley of the Seine, Blücher by the lower Marne. They had nothing between them and the capital, but Marmont and Mortier's corps cut off from Napoleon by their own converging movement.

The insurrection was spreading in Eastern France, and Napoleon's best chance of prolonging the struggle was to carry out his original projects. But once more he changed his mind, and at the news of the enemy's march on Paris he resolved to reach the capital before them. On the 27th the army would begin a forced march by Troyes, Sens, and Fontainebleau. Marmont and Mortier would delay the enemy, and Napoleon hoped to enter Paris by its southern barriers before the Russians, Austrians, and Prussians could attack and force the new entrenchments of the capital on its eastern and northern fronts.

Ney's corps reached Troyes in the afternoon of 30 March. The army was strung out over many miles of road. Macdonald was behind Ney, and the Guard, which was the foremost corps, was already approaching Fontainebleau. There were stragglers left behind in every town and village. But this dispersed march was safe enough, for all the Allied army was concentrated that morning far away on the other side of the Seine for the attack on Paris.

Napoleon had driven on with a few officers far in front of the vanguard. After dark, near the inn of the Cour de France, a few miles from Paris on the Fountainebleau road, he came upon Marmont and Mortier's troops retiring from the capital to the Loire, and learned that that morning there had been a battle round Montmartre and before the eastern barriers, the French line had been driven in, and a capitulation had been signed, according to which the regular troops of the garrison were to withdraw behind the Loire. The Allies were in Paris, and the Empress and Napoleon's brothers were on their way to Blois.

After an indignant outburst at the failure to hold the capital till he could come to its succour, the Emperor turned back to Fontainebleau and ordered the army to concentrate there. He would attack Paris, he said, call its people to arms, and destroy the invaders in its streets.

Marmont and Mortier's corps and the garrison of Fontainebleau were in position on a line covering Fontainebleau on 31 March, but it was four days before the whole of Napoleon's army had arrived. By the evening of 3 April he had concentrated nearly 60,000 men. Ney's corps was by this time reduced to the strength of a regiment. It mustered only 2270 officers and men.

A Provisional Government had been formed at Paris, and the first steps were being taken for the recall of the Bourbons. The Allied generals had occupied the approaches to the capital from Fontainebleau and were prepared to concentrate some 150,000 men if the Emperor advanced. The proclamations of the Provisional Government and the Allied Sovereigns, and newspapers printed in Paris that called for Napoleon's abdication as a necessary condition of peace, were passed through the French outpost lines and secretly circulated among the troops.

The most that the friends of the Emperor hoped for was that he would be allowed to abdicate in favour of his son, with the Empress as regent during the minority of "Napoleon II." The first overtures made at Paris in this sense were met with a demand for his unconditional abdication. He had heard this news when on 4 April he reviewed the Guard before the Palace of Fontainebleau, and told them that he would soon lead them to the reconquest of the capital. The answer was an enthusiastic outburst of cheering—cries of "*Vive l'Empereur! À Paris! À Paris!*"

On the terrace not far from the Emperor stood Ney, in the midst of a group of marshals, generals, and officers of rank. During the inspection of the troops they had exchanged their impressions of the situation. One after another expressed the view that the game was lost for good and all, and that a march on Paris would be hopeless. All that could be done had been attempted. It was a marvel that, after the disastrous campaign of Leipsig, the Emperor had been able to resist the invaders for three months. The time was come to make peace, and if Napoleon was an obstacle to it, he must be persuaded to withdraw. The enthusiasm of the soldiers was for the dispirited and disillusioned generals only a warning that there might be difficulties with the army, still so susceptible to the magical influence of its great leader. Ney, who had saved the remnant of the Grand Army amid the Russian snows, led his raw battalions of young troops on field after field in Germany, and taken such a prominent part in the obstinate struggle on the soil of France itself, was now foremost in declaring that all was over. "It is only an abdication that can get us out of this," he said.

It was agreed that a deputation of the marshals should wait upon Napoleon after the review. It needed some courage to beard the lion. The Emperor was in a desperate position, and might take a desperate course. He was quite capable of arresting the marshals and sending them before a court martial, for he felt he could count on the soldiers still, whatever the leaders might say. Ney, always ready to take risks, offered himself as spokesman of the deputation. Two of the elder marshals joined him, Lefèbvre, Duke of Dantzig, and Moncey, a veteran of the armies of Spain, now 60 years of age, who had commanded the National Guard of Paris on the day of the Allied attack, and who was to show next year on the occasion of Ney's trial that his moral courage was as great as the soldierly resolution he had so often displayed in the field.

Napoleon had gone back to the palace, and was with Berthier, Bassano, Caulaincourt, and Bertrand in his study, when the three marshals asked for an immediate audience and entered the room almost before a reply could be given. There was an awkward pause. Then Ney asked the Emperor if there were any news from Paris. Napoleon, though he had just heard from Caulaincourt of a hostile vote of the Senate, answered that he had no news of any kind. Then Ney said that he himself had bad news from the capital. The Senate had declared for the abdication of the Emperor. Napoleon showed no surprise, but quietly pointed out that this was beyond the powers of the Senate, and a matter for a vote of the whole nation. "As for the Allies," he said, "I am going to crush them before Paris." Ney protested that further military operations were now hopeless, and at this point Lefèbvre supported him. "It is a pity," said Ney, "that peace was not made sooner. Now there is nothing for it but abdication." Napoleon still remained calm. He began to argue about the military possibilities of the situation. He counted up the forces at his command about Fontainebleau, and those he could summon from other parts of France. The Allies, he said, could not maintain themselves with a large army at Paris. He would cut them off from their communications, and the first success he won would be the signal for a widespread rising against the invaders. The marshals listened in stony silence. Berthier and the others said not a word in support of the Emperor's plea to be allowed one more throw of the deadly dice of war. They were of Ney's opinion.

While Napoleon was thus arguing to deaf ears, Macdonald and Oudinot entered and reported the arrival of their army corps. The Emperor hoped that they would support him, and spoke of the projected march on Paris. But they sided with Ney. "I declare to you," said Macdonald, "that we do not mean to expose Paris to the fate of Moscow. We have taken our decision, and are resolved to make an end of all this." Once more Napoleon argued that the struggle could be resumed with good hope of victory, and finally declared that, notwithstanding the contrary opinion of the marshals, he would attack Paris. Ney interrupted him. "But the army will not march on Paris," he said. For the first time Napoleon raised his voice, and looking the Marshal in the face said to him: "The army will obey *me!*" "Sire," replied Ney sternly, "the army will obey its generals."

It was a declaration of war. The two men stood face to face. The others looked on silently, expecting an outburst of anger from Napoleon. But after a pause he resumed his calmer tone, and asked the Marshals to withdraw and leave him alone with Caulaincourt. The very name indicated a coming surrender. Caulaincourt was his Minister of Foreign Affairs and had been his envoy at the Châtillon conference, and his intermediary in the negotiations with the Provisional Government since the fall of Paris. In the trial of strength Ney had carried his point. As soon as he was alone with Caulaincourt the Emperor dictated and signed a conditional act of abdication in favour of his son, and told Caulaincourt to communicate it to the Allies.

If the throne was to be saved for the boy Napoleon, it would be well to show the Allied Sovereigns that this was the will of the army. He told Caulaincourt to take Ney and Macdonald with him and to invite Marmont also. Caulaincourt drove off with the two first-named marshals to Marmont's head-quarters at Essonnes. It was four in the afternoon when they arrived there. Marmont hesitated and seemed embarrassed when he was asked to accompany them to Paris. Then he made a surprising confession. He informed them that, in concert with his divisional generals, he had been in correspondence with Schwartzenberg and the Czar, and had actually agreed to march his corps of 11,000 men over to the Allied lines within the next twenty-four hours. He had believed the cause of Napoleon to be lost, and was anxious, he said, to avoid civil war. But this new proposal changed the situation. He would go with them, see Schwartzenberg, and withdraw his engagement with the Allies. He handed the command of his corps over to his senior divisional general, Souham, telling him to make no movement till his return, and meanwhile to inform the troops of the conditional abdication of the Emperor.

It was six o'clock when Caulaincourt and the marshals left Essonnes. They stopped at Schwartzenberg's head-quarters near Chevilly to leave Marmont there. He was to follow them to Paris. It was after midnight when they drove up to Talleyrand's palatial residence in the Rue St. Florentin, where the Czar was staying. Three hours before Talleyrand, now the centre of the Provisional Government, and the prime mover in the restoration of the Bourbons, had received from a trusted agent at Fontainebleau the news that the Emperor's envoys were coming. He had seen Alexander, and urged him to stand firm, but he had told some of his colleagues that he was not sure of the Czar who was prone to act on impulse and was very impressionable.

THE ABDICATION OF NAPOLEON AT THE PALACE OF FONTAINEBLEAU

It was between midnight and 1 a.m. on 5 April, when Caulaincourt and the two marshals were presented to the Czar. They read the conditional act of abdication and then pleaded with the Czar to use his influence to obtain its acceptance. Ney was highly esteemed by Alexander, and he now made every effort to win the Russian Emperor over. The Marshal was sincerely anxious to secure the adoption of Napoleon's proposal, and he joined his colleagues in urging that France did not want the Bourbons, that the Allies had announced that they would leave the country free to direct its own destinies, that what all wanted was peace, and that this would be secured far better by the withdrawal of Napoleon and the regency of Marie Louise, than by imposing the Bourbons on a divided people at the risk of civil war. The Czar seemed to be moved by these arguments. He spoke of the rising in the east of France, and said he was anxious to have a settlement that would put an end to such dangers. At last he told the envoys he would see them again at nine in the morning. Meanwhile he would communicate their proposals to his allies and would support them.

It was between two and three in the morning when the interview ended. Ney went to his own house in Paris, taking with him Marmont who had joined him at the Rue St. Florentin, and told him that in view of the changed situation Schwartzenberg had released him from his engagements. Ney snatched a few hours' sleep, and had an early breakfast with his wife and Marmont. Only then he learned that the latter had hardly gone to rest, when he was called up by his aide-de-camp, Colonel Fabvier, who had ridden in to Paris to tell him that his 11,000 men, led by Souham, had marched into the Allied lines before Versailles after midnight. It appeared that the Emperor had summoned all the corps commanders and divisional generals to meet him at the Palace of Fontainbleau at ten in the evening of the 4th. His object was to obtain a joint declaration of their support for the dynasty. But Souham and his colleagues suspected that the Emperor had discovered their negotiation with the Allies, and fearing the result they marched their men into the enemy's lines in the darkness, the soldiers having no idea where they were going, until they halted in the midst of masses of the Allied cavalry and were ordered to break up and bivouac among them. "I would give my right arm to have prevented this happening," said Marmont to Ney. "Your arm!" replied Ney indignantly, "Your head would not be enough!" He foresaw that the defection of several generals, and a whole corps, the most numerous in the Army of Fontainebleau, would convince the Allies that Napoleon was no longer worth negotiating with.

At nine o'clock Ney, Macdonald, and Caulaincourt again met the Czar. The King of Prussia was with him. It was a brief interview. Alexander told them that, after consulting his Allies, it had been decided that the conditional abdication could not be accepted. Napoleon must abdicate absolutely. He would be allowed to retain the title of Emperor, and be given the island of Elba. The Bourbons would again reign in France. The Czar and the King refused to listen to any argument, and the envoys withdrew.

They did not at once start for Fontainebleau. Ney had an interview with Talleyrand, in which he told him he would recognize the Provisional Government and any other to which it transferred its powers, and promised to report to him that evening the result of his coming interview with Napoleon.

It was after nine in the evening when the three envoys reached Fontainebleau. They told the Emperor the result of their mission. Napoleon was not at first disposed to surrender. "War," he said, "can now offer us nothing worse than such a peace would bring." Then he told them he was determined to fight on. He had still 50,000 men. He could summon many thousands more to his standard. He had already issued orders for a retreat to the Loire. He explained his new plan of campaign. Ney and his colleagues replied that further resistance was hopeless. They would have no part in a civil war. He must accept the inevitable. At last he seemed to yield and told them to come to him in the morning, and they would settle the form of the act of abdication. At half-past eleven Ney, immediately after leaving the Emperor, wrote to Talleyrand that all was over.

Napoleon had, nevertheless, sent off the orders for a march to the Loire to begin at sunrise on the 6th. But none of the troops moved. The rumour of the coming abdication paralysed the army, and early in the day Ney joined Caulaincourt and Macdonald in formally warning Berthier that he was henceforth to transmit no orders from the Emperor to the troops. In the forenoon Napoleon summoned all the marshals to the palace. He made a last effort to persuade them to follow him to the Loire, and make one more fight for the eagles. Ney was among those who replied for the rest that they could not prolong a useless struggle. They were tired of the war, which no longer offered any chance of victory.

"You want rest. Well you shall have it," said Napoleon. Then he sat down and wrote :—

> "The Allied Powers having proclaimed that the Emperor Napoleon is the sole obstacle to the peace of Europe, the Emperor Napoleon, faithful to his oaths, declares that for himself and his heirs he renounces the thrones of France and Italy, because there is no personal sacrifice, even that of life, which he is not ready to make for the interests of France."

He signed the paper and handed it to Caulaincourt. Then he bade the marshals a formal farewell. Ney left the palace, handed over the command of the remnant of his corps to General Lefol, and hurried back to Paris. He was going to make his peace with the new rulers of France. He had served the Empire faithfully through its first years of victorious conquest and through these later days of disaster. And one may say that it was only when a further adherence to Napoleon's cause seemed to point the way to a miserable and useless civil war and the further humiliation of France, that he took the lead in insisting on peace, even at the cost of his master's abdication. Like so many of his colleagues he was tired of endless war and hoped that years of lasting peace were now beginning for France and for Europe. He looked forward to a life at home with his wife and children, and the enjoyment of the honours he had won. He had not the remotest idea that he would soon leave his home again for a new campaign under the chief to whom he had said "farewell for ever," and that the coming year would see the tragic end of his own life.

CHAPTER XVI

THE RESTORATION—NAPOLEON'S RETURN—NEY DECLARES FOR HIM (1814-15)

WHEN Louis XVIII landed at Calais on 26 April, 1814, after twenty-four years of exile, he proclaimed that he wished to bury the troubles of the past in oblivion, and unite all Frenchmen under the restored royalty of France in the common task of bringing back peace and prosperity to the country. Had he returned alone there might have been some prospect of his fulfilling this programme. But he brought back with him a host of other exiles, who were mostly inspired with the hope of restoring in France a condition of affairs that was as utterly beyond recall as the feudalism of 800 years ago. It was to the reactionary exaggerations of these men that the first failures of the Royalist Restoration were due; and it was thanks to them that within a twelvemonth Napoleon was able to make another bid for power.

Louis XVIII had accepted and ratified the new nobility created by the Empire. Ney was among those whose personal action had contributed largely to compelling the Emperor to abandon the struggle with the Allies, and he had thus indirectly helped to secure the Bourbon Restoration. Louis expressed a generous admiration for his prowess as a soldier, and for his services to France during his long military career. Ney's rank of Marshal of the Empire was confirmed with a slight variation of form. He now bore the older title of "Marshal of France and Lieutenant-General of the King". His purely military titles of nobility, the "Dukedom of Elchingen," the "Princedom of the Moskowa," neither of them having the least territorial significance, and both of them reminders of battles against the King's Allies, were nevertheless recognized and perpetuated, and Ney's name was further borne on the list of the "Peers of France," who were to form the upper house of the legislature under the new constitution.

But the old aristocracy of France, the men of the emigration who had refused for so many weary years to accept the new state of things, were in no mood to welcome to their ranks the new nobility of the Revolutionary Empire. Princes and Dukes and Marquesses, who traced their titles back to the Crusades or to half-legendary Frankish and Carlovingian days regarded the military peerage of Napoleon's creation as a set of upstarts with a further taint of brigandage. There were whispered jests in the royal circle of the Tuileries at a duchess who had once been a washerwoman; a prince who was the son of a cooper or an innkeeper. The Duchess d'Angoulême, daughter of Louis XVI, and sole survivor of the royal prisoners of the Temple, affected to be unable to remember the new titles of the marshals and their wives. "You are Madame Junot—is it not so?" she said to the Duchess d'Abrantès in the royal circle, and she greeted the Princesse de la Moskowa as "Madame Ney". Yet there was a link with the memories of the Temple that might have made the daughter of Marie Antoinette hesitate to put a slight upon the wife of Marshal Ney, in the fact that her mother, Madame Auguié, had been so devoted to the hapless queen, that, when she heard of her royal mistress's execution, her reason had given way and she had taken her own life.

Honoured though he was by the restored King, Ney felt deeply the half-veiled insults put upon him by the returned *émigrés*, and the treatment of his wife by Royalist Princesses and Duchesses made him furious. "It is well for you," he said one day to Lavalette, "that you have kept away from the court. You have thus escaped having to put up with insult and injustice." Then breaking out into a sudden burst of angry indignation he went on:—"Those people know nothing. They don't understand what the name of Ney means. Shall I have to teach them?"

In the winter of 1814-15 he kept away from Paris and lived quietly with his wife and children at his country house at Coudreaux. There echoes reached him of the growing discontent excited by the new government, and it seems that more than once efforts were made by those who were conspiring against it to ascertain whether he would be likely to favour an attempt to constitute a regency in the name of Napoleon II, or to assist in an Orleanist *coup d'état* that would place Louis Philippe on the throne. But Ney turned a deaf ear to every hint at a new revolution. He had never been a politician, and he was now convinced that the one hope of France was the maintenance of peace abroad and civil order at home. He more than once declared that no advantage could outweigh the risk of reopening a new period of foreign wars.

In the beginning of March, Ney was at his country house, where he had been living since the previous October. On 6 March he received a letter from the Minister of War, Marshal Soult, dated the day before, directing him to come to Paris at once and thence proceed to Besançon to take command of the troops of the 6th Military Division in the departments bordering on the Jura. The officer who brought the letter from Soult had been handed it as he left a ball-room the night before. He could tell Ney nothing of the nature of the crisis which had led to the issue of this urgent order. He dined with the Marshal and at once started on his return to Paris. Ney followed during the night. His uniforms were all at his house in the Rue de Bourbon, and he wished to see the Minister before setting off for Besançon.

He had hardly arrived (in the afternoon of 7 March) when his notary, M. Batardy, called upon him. "This is very extraordinary news," said Batardy. "What news?" asked Ney. "What! you don't know what has happened!" exclaimed the other. "No." "Don't you know that Bonaparte has landed near Cannes? That Monsieur, the King's brother, has started for Lyons this morning?" "No, the officer who brought me the Minister of War's letter told me nothing." Then Batardy informed him of the official news just published in the "Moniteur." The notary declared afterwards that Ney seemed startled and afflicted at the news. "What a misfortune," he exclaimed. "What a terrible business it is! What is to be done? Who is there to oppose that man?"

After having arranged some business matters with the notary, Ney put on his uniform and called upon the Duc de

Berry, and begged him to assure the King of his devotion to the royal cause. Then he went to the War Office to see Marshal Soult and obtain his letters of service and instructions. "Bonaparte has landed," said Soult. "So I have just heard. It is a piece of madness. What do you want me to do?" was Ney's reply. Soult told him he would find detailed orders in the hands of General de Bourmont at Besançon. Ney then expressed a desire to see the King at the Tuileries. "Don't go there," said Soult, "His Majesty is unwell and will not receive anyone." Ney insisted. "You will not prevent me from seeing his Majesty," he said, and he went on to the Tuileries.

It was late in the evening when he reached the palace, and he had some difficulty in obtaining an audience. Ney had been on terms of friendship with the King since he had first met him after the return from exile, and Louis had a pleasant manner and the royal gift of inspiring personal devotion. After kissing his hand the Marshal conversed for some time with him, and Louis made an appeal to him to do all that was possible to prevent the opening up of a new period of strife and bloodshed for France. Ney became very excited, declared that the King could count upon his acting most energetically against the invader, and ended by exclaiming, "Sire, I hope I shall soon be in a position to bring him back in an iron cage".

It was with this wild speech on his lips that he took his departure. As the Marshal turned away Louis said in a low voice to those near him, "I did not ask all that of him!"[1]

Ney reached Besançon on 10 March. He was to act as second in command to the Duc de Berry, but the Prince had

[1] At his trial in the following December Ney at first tried to explain away the evidence of the Duc de Duras and the Prince de Poix, who both deposed to his having promised to bring back Napoleon in an iron cage. Ney protested that what he had said was that, "for venturing on so mad an enterprise Napoleon deserved to be shut up in an iron cage," but he denied that he had himself proposed to act on this idea. The two witnesses repeated their statement, and then Ney practically admitted that it was true. His words were: "I thought I had said that Bonaparte deserved to be shut up in an iron cage, and not that I meant to put him in one. But nevertheless it may be that, in the state of agitation in which I was, this latter expression escaped from me. I have no reason to challenge the assertions of M. le Duc de Duras."

not yet arrived, had not even left Paris. Then he was disappointed at finding that he had hardly any troops to command. General de Bourmont had been so far in charge of Besançon, and he had sent off to the Comte d'Artois at Lyons all the garrison except some five hundred depôt troops, about whose fidelity to the white cockade there was serious doubt. The officers told Ney that if the men were kept in barracks nothing would happen, but if they were brought out and came in contact with the people they would probably cry, "*Vive l'Empereur!*"

Ney wrote to the Comte d'Artois at Lyons suggesting that he would be more useful there than at Besançon and asking to be employed with the vanguard of the Royal Army. The letter never reached the Prince, for that very day he had abandoned Lyons, into which Napoleon marched next morning amid scenes of the wildest enthusiasm. A few hours after despatching his letter Ney heard of the imminent evacuation of Lyons by the Royalists. A post-chaise rattled into Besançon bringing to Ney's head-quarters a great noble of the court, the Duc de Maillé, "*premier gentilhomme de Monsieur le Frère du Roi,*" or chief of the Comte d'Artois' household. De Maillé had expected to find the Duc de Berry at Besançon, and was surprised when Ney told him that his Royal Highness was still at Paris. De Maillé's news was bad enough. Grenoble had thrown open its gates to the "Corsican adventurer" who was now in full march on Lyons, and the capital of the south, once a stronghold of royalism, was so fiercely Bonapartist that D'Artois had decided to fall back from Lyons towards Paris. De Maillé had brought Ney no orders, but suggested that he should march to join D'Artois. The Marshal told him he could do better work by collecting all the troops in the eastern departments at Lons-le-Saulnier, and thence acting against the flank of Napoleon's advance or falling on his rear. He counted on getting together some 6000 men in a few days, and he estimated that Napoleon had as yet not much more than 10,000. He spoke very bitterly of his old chief. "I shall settle accounts with Bonaparte," he said. "We are going to attack the wild beast." The same evening he sent off orders for the concentration at Lons-le-Saulnier. He had two zealous lieutenants to assist him in his projected campaign—Bourmont, an old Vendean, and General Lecourbe, the veteran soldier of the Revolution, and his former comrade in the campaigns of Switzerland and the Rhine. Lecourbe had been dismissed from the army by Napoleon on the eve of the proclamation of the Empire. He was suspected as a friend of Moreau, and while Ney was winning his way to the Marshalate and a Princedom, Lecourbe had been living in obscurity on a little farm in the Jura. Louis XVIII had called him back to the army and restored him to his rank of general. Hatred for Napoleon made the ex-Jacobin soldier as zealous a Royalist as any of the *émigré* officers.

Next day (Saturday, 11 March) Ney left Besançon in the afternoon and drove to Lons-le-Saulnier. While changing horses at Poligny he had a talk with the sub-prefect of the department. He was very excited and repeated to the official his promise to the King that he would "bring Bonaparte back to Paris in an iron cage". "It would be better to bring him back dead in a tumbril," said the Royalist. "No, no," replied the Marshal, "you don't know Paris. The Parisians must see him." Then he added, "It is a good thing that the man of the island of Elba has attempted this rash enterprise, for it will be the last act of his tragedy, the *dénouement* of the Napoleon epic." He was in a strange humour, living in a turmoil of excitement.

He arrived at Lons soon after midnight. At the Hôtel de la Pomme d'Or, where he put up, he found a Monsieur Boulouze, a business man, who had left Lyons on the Saturday morning, and who told him that he had seen Napoleon ride into the city amid the frantic cheering of the garrison and the people, had seen him review the troops on the Place Bellecour, and heard him say to them: "My friends, we shall go to Paris with our hands in our pockets. It is all arranged for us to get there." Boulouze had secured one of Napoleon's proclamations, which had been scattered broadcast in Lyons. He handed it to Ney.[1]

[1] Napoleon had printed in Elba before embarking proclamations to the people and the Army of France. He declared that his defeats had been the result of treason. He had abdicated for the sake of the country, hoping that it would have a better fortune under the monarchy, but the Bourbons, forced upon France by the foreigner, "had learned nothing and forgotten nothing". They wanted to

The Marshal glanced at it and put it in his pocket. "Bonaparte says he has the support of Austria, and that the Empress Marie Louise and his son will come from Vienna," said Boulouze. "Nonsense," replied Ney, "that is only some of his usual boasting." "Ah! Monsieur le Maréchal," said Boulouze, "you have already been the saviour of France in forcing Napoleon to abdicate. You will save us a second time." Ney felt strangely flattered by this compliment from a commercial traveller, and told it next day to his staff with an air of complete self-satisfaction.

Boulouze went off to bed, but Ney sat by the inn fire waiting for the prefect of the Jura, to whom he had sent news of his arrival. When the prefect arrived he brought with him the Marquis de Saurans, an aide-de-camp of D'Artois. They found Ney reading the Emperor's proclamation. He showed it to them and said: "That is how the King ought to write. That is how one should talk to soldiers. That is how to stir them." He was evidently greatly moved by Napoleon's appeal to the army. He rose and walking up and down the room with the paper in his hand read aloud: "The eagle with the national colours will fly from steeple to steeple to the towers of Notre Dame". The two Royalists stared at him and at each other. Turning to De Saurans Ney asked him for news of D'Artois, and then went on to rail against the Royal Prince. The Comte d'Artois, he said, had blundered badly at Lyons. Then he burst out into an angry tirade in which fierce criticism of the policy of the Restoration was mingled with puerile complaints about his own personal grievances. "This Comte d'Artois," he said, "is too fine a gentleman ever to think of inviting a Marshal of France to a seat in his carriage, and is now leaving me without troops and without orders." Then he said the King had blundered as badly, in disbanding the Old Guard and

impose the feudal system again upon France. They regarded the old soldiers of the Revolution and the Empire as rebels. Soon the patriots would bear all the burdens, and the *émigrés* would have all the honours and privileges. "Frenchmen," he wrote, "you require the government of your own choice, which alone can be legitimate. I have crossed the sea to resume my rights which are also yours. Soldiers, rally to the colours of your old chief. His rights are also yours, and those of the people. Victory will march with us at the charging step, and the eagle with the national colours will fly from steeple to steeple to the towers of Notre Dame."

throwing himself into the arms of the *émigrés*. He had allowed the Princesse de la Moskowa to be insulted at his court. The Duchesse d'Angoulême's treatment of "Madame Ney" was evidently a very sore point with him. But then just as the two Royalists were expecting a declaration for Napoleon, Ney told them they need not fear that he would let Bonaparte escape. "That madman," he said, "will never forgive me his abdication. He would be quite capable of cutting my head off. I can count on my men. The first soldier that moves to join him will have my sword through his body—up to the hilt. But the soldier always marches where the cannon clears the way, and my aide-de-camp Vavasseur knows how to work the guns beautifully."

It was a pitiful scene. Ney had tired himself with his own wild talk and bade his guests good-night, leaving them puzzled and anxious. Next morning he was himself again, and during the Sunday and Monday he was busy hurrying up troops, collecting ammunition, sending out gendarmes in disguise and royalist volunteers to obtain information. On the Monday evening he arrested an officer who cried out "*Vive l'Empereur!*" at one of the cafés. De Bourmont was depressed by news he had received during the day, and told Ney the Emperor had 14,000 men, to whom they could oppose only 6000 at most, and some of these of doubtful loyalty. "We shall be short of numbers," replied Ney, "but we shall give him a good dressing down. I shall take a musket and fire the first shot myself, and then every one will march as he is told."

That Monday evening there was bad news. Regimental officers came to Ney with stories of growing excitement among their men, as rumours spread that everywhere the people and the troops were resuming the tricolour. Then Capelle, the prefect of Bourg, arrived thence in hurried flight, and reported that the 76th Infantry stationed there, instead of obeying the order to join Ney, had displayed the old colours and marched off to reinforce Napoleon. Capelle said it would be dangerous to march against Bonaparte. Better try to rejoin Masséna in the south, or make a forced march to Chambéry, where it was rumoured a Swiss army was coming to help the King. Ney flared up at the talk of a Swiss intervention. "If the foreigners set foot in France," he exclaimed, "it will be time for every Frenchman to declare for Bonaparte."

The Hotel of the Golden Apple was full of guests that evening. The prefect of Bourg was not the only arrival. Two civilians, who came in late, sent the Marshal a message that they had news that might interest him, and would like to convey it to him in private. Eager for information, Ney received them in his room. There they revealed themselves as old comrades—disguised officers of the Imperial Guard—sent off from Lyons to convey to him a letter from Bertrand, the Emperor's chief of the staff, an official order bearing the same signature, and a brief note from the Emperor himself.[1] Ney read the papers. Bertrand's letter told him that he must not mistake Napoleon's enterprise for a piece of child's play. It was a carefully organized movement, and everywhere the people and the troops were declaring against the Bourbons. So far not a drop of blood had been shed, and if Ney attempted a resistance doomed to failure he would be responsible for a hopeless civil war and useless bloodshed. Bertrand urged him to rejoin the old flag and act on the enclosed order to march with his troops to co-operate with the Emperor.

Napoleon's letter ran thus:—

> "MON COUSIN,—My major-general sends you your marching orders. I have no doubt that on receiving the news of my arrival at Lyons, you have already made your troops resume the tricolour flag. Execute Bertrand's orders, and come and rejoin me at Châlons. I shall receive you as I did on the morrow of the battle of the Moskowa.
>
> "NAPOLEON"

Ney questioned the officers. They told him of the Emperor's triumphal progress through the south of France. They added statements which were not true, but which were based on current rumours. The King, they said, had already fled from Paris. The Allies were quarrelling among themselves at Vienna. The Emperor's return to France was part of an international arrangement, still secret, but soon to be public property. The English squadron had been withdrawn on

[1] The officers were personally known to Ney. At his trial he persistently refused to name them, and the Government never discovered who they were.

purpose to enable Napoleon to leave Elba. Austria was his ally. Marie Louise and the King of Rome would soon leave Vienna for the Tuileries. Finally they handed Ney a proposed proclamation to his troops drawn up for him by Napoleon and with the Marshal's title already affixed at the end of it as a signature.

Ney hesitated. If he had still been as determined to act against Napoleon, as he undoubtedly was when he left Paris, he would have arrested the disguised officers. Instead of this he told them that they might remain in safety at the Golden Apple, but he had no answer to give them. He passed a sleepless night. He was in a desperate position. He was pledged again and again to make an effort to save the monarchy. His duty as a soldier was to obey the orders he had received at Paris. But could he trust his men? They were already on the verge of revolt, and if they obeyed him would he not be lighting up the flame of a brief and hopeless civil war? For it seemed that the movement for the restoration of the Empire had already gone so far that nothing could check it. He might, indeed, have acted as others of the marshals did. He could have declared that he considered resistance to Napoleon was now hopeless, and that wishing to avoid civil strife among Frenchmen he resigned his command and would watch the course of events as an onlooker. But this way of escape appears not to have entered his mind. He was far too agitated for a calm consideration of the position. He saw no other course open to him but a march against Napoleon, or a march against the Government. "I was in the midst of the storm," he said afterwards, "and I lost my head."

Next morning he sent for his two lieutenants, Lecourbe and De Bourmont, to discuss the situation with them. But he did most of the talking, and from the first it was plain that he had decided for Napoleon. Without revealing the source of his information he told the two generals what he had heard the night before of Napoleon's success, the alleged international plot, the certainty of all France resuming the tricolour. He added statements intended to make Bourmont and Lecourbe believe that he spoke from personal knowledge, and for once in his life he wove a kind of romance, posing as if he had been admitted to the inner circle of movements, of which he certainly had only a vague outside knowledge. "It is all a prearranged affair," he said. "Three months ago we were all agreed about it, as you would know if you had been at Paris. As the King had not kept his promises, it was decided to dethrone him. There was some talk about the Duke of Orleans, but the Bonapartists carried the day. A commissioner was sent to the island of Elba to lay down conditions to the Emperor. The Minister of War (Soult) himself is in the plot. At this very moment the King will have left Paris; or if not he will be carried off, but no harm will be done to him. All will pass off very quietly." It would be easy to analyse this story line by line and show that Ney was indulging in fiction. He had not been in Paris for months before he passed through the capital in the first week of March. He certainly knew nothing of the inner track of the abortive Orleanist and Bonapartist plots of 1814-15, and there had been no envoy of the conspirators sent to Elba. Ney had not played a treacherous part when he told the King that he would bring Bonaparte back a prisoner; he was not "acting a comedy" on the day of his farewell audience; and he had been desperately in earnest on the Royal side till the night before he wove this strange romance for De Bourmont and Lecourbe.

At his trial he attempted to show that they made no opposition to his suggestions, but according to their own accounts they both protested against his proposed defection. Bourmont reminded him that he had pledged his honour as a marshal and peer of France to lead his troops against Bonaparte. Lecourbe broke out into rough angry speech. "How can you ask me to serve that fellow?" he exclaimed, using a coarse expression. "He has done me nothing but ill: the King nothing but kindness. Then I am in the King's service, and look here, Monsieur le Maréchal, as for me I have some sense of honour."

Ney might have insisted on the impossibility of marching against Napoleon with troops that were only too eager to join him, and the futility of bloodshed when successful resistance was hopeless. Instead he tried to *justify* his action by complaining of personal grievances. "And I too have a sense of honour," he said. "That's why I don't mean to be further humiliated. I do not mean ever again to see my wife coming home to me with tears in her eyes at the humiliations to which she has been subjected. The King does not want us—that's plain enough. It is only with a soldier like Bonaparte that the army can ever be properly respected. Look at this—this is what I shall read to the troops," and he showed the officers the proclamation drawn up for him by Napoleon, not the original brought by the two officers of the Guard from Lyons, but a copy he had made in his own handwriting that morning.

Bourmont and Lecourbe protested for awhile, but finally took the strange course of submitting to be tacit witnesses of Ney's action, and even to give it the sanction of their presence.[1] Bourmont actually issued the orders for a parade of the troops on the Place d'Armes in the outskirts of the town, and then with Lecourbe called for Ney at the Golden Apple and rode with him to the parade ground.

The troops assembled at Lons-le-Saulnier were the 60th and 77th of the line, each two battalions strong, and six squadrons of cavalry (the 5th Dragoons and 8th Chasseurs-à-cheval). The artillery had not arrived, and this was why Ney had not yet marched. The 3000 men were formed in a hollow square facing inwards. Outside their ranks anxious crowds of the citizens were looking on. The soldiers seemed depressed, but there were signs of ill-controlled excitement here and there in the ranks, and a general unsteadiness that made some of the onlookers expect an outbreak of mutiny or revolt. Ney, De Bourmont, Lecourbe, and their staffs dismounted and entered the square on foot. Ney held a paper in his hand. There was a roll of the drums, then the Marshal drew his sword and in his loud clear voice began to read the proclamation:—

> "Officers, non-commissioned officers, and soldiers, the cause of the Bourbons is lost for ever——"

For some moments he could read no more. A thundering shout of "*Vive l'Empereur!*" burst from the soldiers, and was echoed by the crowd. Muskets, swords, caps, were waved in

[1] The two versions of the conference can perhaps be reconciled by supposing that Ney in his evidence had in mind this second stage of the conversation.

the air. Then as Ney's voice rang out again there was silence while he read on:—

"The lawful dynasty adopted by the French nation is again to be seated on the throne. It is to the Emperor Napoleon that it belongs to rule over our beautiful country. Soldiers, I have often led you to victory. Now I am about to lead you to the immortal phalanx which the Emperor is leading to Paris."

There was another burst of cheering. The ranks were broken. Officers and men threw themselves into each other's arms. Ney himself went through the ranks "looking like a madman," embracing officers, soldiers, sergeants, drummers, revelling in the cheers that greeted him. Here and there some of the Royalist officers looked on in silent indignation. One of them, Colonel Dubalen of the 60th, rode up to Ney, forcing his horse through the confused crowd that was shaking hands with him and embracing him. Bending from his saddle, Dubalen said calmly: "Monsieur le Maréchal, my oath to the King will not allow me to change sides. I give you my resignation." "I won't accept it," replied Ney, "but you are free to go. Get away quickly, and above all take care not to be roughly handled by your men." Already the Colonel was in danger, for even in the midst of the din many had heard his words. He set spurs to his horse and dashed for the main street of the town. Several dragoons rode wildly after him. One of them overtook him, but out flashed Dubalen's sword and down went the dragoon with a nasty wound in the head. The others thought it was enough to help their comrade to hospital and return to the scene of rejoicing on the Place d'Armes. Dubalen rode through the town and got away safely, and earned a general's commission when the Bourbons returned again.

On the parade ground the ranks reformed. The men returned to barracks and exchanged the white cockade for the tricolour. Then they were free for the day, and till late in the evening all the cafés and wine shops were crowded with men drinking success to the Emperor. Ney gave a dinner to the generals and colonels and the staff at the Golden Apple, but he seemed tired and anxious, the only dull man at the table. During the evening he received a dispatch from Bertrand changing his orders, and telling him to march his column to Dijon.

Next morning (Wednesday, 15 March) he left Lons-le-Saulnier with his troops en route for Dijon by way of Dôle. Several officers of rank refused to go farther with him, and De Bourmont slipped away during the march. When Ney reached Dijon on the 17th, he was informed that the Emperor had just occupied Auxerre, and wished to see him. Leaving his troops at Dijon he hurried to Auxerre, where he arrived on the evening of the same day.

He told Bertrand that he did not wish to go to the Emperor till next day, as he wanted to write a justification of his conduct during the night. "What do I want with his justifications," said Napoleon, when he was given Ney's message. "Tell him I shall embrace him to-morrow morning." On the 18th Ney saw the Emperor again for the first time since the forced abdication. He had worked for several hours during the night drawing up a strange document, which he handed to Napoleon when he was presented to him. It began with the words, "If you continue to govern tyrannically I shall be your prisoner rather than your partisan," and after several long-winded paragraphs, ended by warning the Emperor that he must now study the welfare of the French people and endeavour to repair the evils his ambition had brought upon them.

Napoleon glanced through the document, then turning aside tore it up and said in a low voice to those nearest him, "This fine fellow Ney is going mad". Then without making any further reference to the essay on statemanship he turned again to Ney, and began to question him as to his troops, the state of feeling among the people in the south-eastern departments, and the experiences of his march to Dijon. Ney was embarrassed and gave brief replies. The somewhat trying interview ended by Napoleon telling him to return to Dijon, and march his troops to Paris, where the Emperor promised him that he would be at the Tuileries before him. Ney rejoined his column at Dijon on the 19th, and the march to Paris began. Once more as at the dinner at the Golden Apple the Marshal was the only gloomy man in the party.

CHAPTER XVII

THE HUNDRED DAYS—QUATRE BRAS AND WATERLOO (1815)

"AFTER that wretched proclamation I wished only for death, and many times I had the idea of blowing my brains out." These words spoken by Ney during his trial were perhaps an exaggeration, but there is evidence enough that after the scene at Lons-le-Saulnier he was no longer the same man. He felt that he was not fully trusted even by Napoleon, who had been made aware of the language he had used regarding him, and the threats he had uttered in the first days of March, and who had not forgotten his conduct of the year before. He had reached Paris with his troops on 23 March, three days after the Emperor's triumphant return to the Tuileries. That very day he received from Napoleon's Minister of War, Marshal Davoût, an order to leave the Capital at once, for a tour of inspection in the departments of the North and East. He was to report on the condition of the fortresses, and on the state of public feeling, and suggest what changes should be made in the local, military, and civil administrations.

He was travelling about for three weeks. Perhaps to give a guarantee of his zeal for restored imperialism he had the bad taste to speak of the Royal family more than once at gatherings of officers and civilians in terms of unmeasured abuse. One phrase of his, that was repeated in Paris, was that the King and Princes, the whole family, were "a rotten lot". His friends felt that he was destroying his own reputation by these tirades, first against his old chief, and now against the King who had loaded him with honours and whom he had so lately sworn to serve. His enemies said openly that the man who was capable of the quick-change performance of Lons-le-Saulnier was not to be trusted. The Emperor received an anonymous letter, in which he was advised that if Ney was employed in the field, it would be well to surround him with a staff of thoroughly reliable officers.

He returned to Paris in the middle of April, and had an audience with Napoleon. During the conversation he suddenly referred to the story of his having told Louis XVIII that he would bring him to Paris in an iron cage. "It is quite true," he said, "but the fact is that I had already made up my mind, and I thought I could not say anything better calculated to conceal my real plans." Napoleon made no reply, but looked at Ney with a stony stare. To put it plainly, he knew the Marshal was lying.

All hope of peace had vanished. The Allies had pronounced sentence of outlawry against Napoleon, and a new coalition was arming against France. The Emperor was making unheard of efforts to form a great army. Commands were being assigned to old soldiers of the Empire, who were still faithful to their chief. There were new promotions to the rank of General of Division, and Grouchy had been given a marshal's bâton. But there was no command for the hero of the Moskowa and the retreat from Russia. The Emperor did not trust him. He went back to his château of Coudreaux, and for six weeks he lived there with Aglaé and her children, learning only from the newspapers and a few letters from friends what was happening at Paris.

In the last week of May he received a dispatch from the War Office. He opened it, hoping to find in it an appointment to a command. It was a mere invitation to the ceremonial display of the Champ de Mai, the great gathering at which the Emperor was to take the oath of fealty to the new constitution and distribute the eagles to the regiments assembled in Paris.

For the last time his wife accompanied him to the court, to share his honours, and find in them some compensation for the slights that had so lately been put upon her by Royalist duchesses. On 1 June, a day of brilliant summer sunshine, 45,000 soldiers formed in glittering lines around the altar erected in the Champ de Mars, and 200,000 spectators looked on at the last great ceremony of the Empire. Napoleon drove to the parade ground in a carriage drawn by eight horses, with four Marshals riding beside it—Ney, Soult, Jourdan, and Grouchy.

But Ney was a mere unit in the great display. To have left him out of it would have confirmed the current rumours that he was in disgrace and in danger of arrest. Though he had found no active employment for him, Napoleon could not afford to omit so famous a figure from the ceremonial display at a time when so many of the marshals had abandoned him. This, too, was the reason why next day Ney was informed that he had been named a member of the Chamber of Peers, the new Senate of the reorganized Empire. So far he had not had an audience with Napoleon, though he had ridden beside his carriage door as one of his state escort. But on the 6th he met him again. Ney had gone to the Palace of the Elysée to ask for the formal authorization to draw a sum of 37,000 francs from the treasury—arrears of his pay as Marshal and Grand Cross of the Legion of Honour and expenses of his tour of inspection. After seeing Davoût he met the Emperor. Napoleon gave him an ill-humoured greeting. "Here you are!" he exclaimed, "I was thinking you must have emigrated." "Perhaps I ought to have done so before this," replied Ney, and the Emperor passed by without another word. The Marshal was bitterly disappointed and discouraged. It seemed that notwithstanding his new dignity of Peer of the Empire, his career had closed, and closed in something like disgrace.

The army was concentrating on the northern frontier for the Emperor's great stroke against Wellington and Blücher. It seemed that Ney had been forgotten. On Sunday, 11 June—the day on which Napoleon was to leave Paris for the front—he went to the Tuileries again, in the hope of hearing that his services were required, but there was no news for him. But at the last moment the Emperor relented, and gave his old comrade a chance of volunteering his assistance in the coming campaign. Just before leaving Paris the Emperor wrote a note to Davoût in which he said: "Send for Marshal Ney and tell him that if he wishes to be present at the first battles, he ought to be at Avesnes on the 14th. My head-quarters will be there."

Davoût sent the message to Ney later in the day, and he

made hurried preparations to start early on the Monday. He had no horses, no staff and there was no time to wait for either. An old comrade not yet employed with the field armies, Colonel Heymès, who had served on his staff in more than one campaign, offered to go as his aide-de-camp. Early on Monday the Marshal bade Aglaé farewell and left Paris in a hired carriage for the north, with Heymès as his travelling companion. Hé was again cheerful. He might perhaps still have a command. In any case he would once more face hostile fire, and might die a soldier's death on some Belgian battlefield.

He reached Avesnes on the afternoon of Tuesday, 13 June. The Emperor's head-quarters were in the little town, which was then a frontier fortress surrounded by old bastioned works. The regiments and batteries of the Imperial Guard were marching to their bivouacs around the place. The other five corps of the army were closing into the space between Beaumont, Marchiennes, and Philippeville—a few miles to the eastward—whence on the Thursday morning they were to make the dash across the Belgian frontier.

Ney dined with the Emperor that evening, and had a more cordial welcome than he expected, but still there was no offer of a command. He was, it seemed, to be a spectator of the opening operations of the campaign. Next day the head-quarters moved to Beaumont. Ney had not yet been able to find horses for himself and Colonel Heymès, and to reach Beaumont he hired a trap belonging to a small farmer. At Beaumont he found Marshal Mortier laid up in bed with an attack of sciatica that made it impossible for him to ride. It was a piece of luck for Ney, who was able to buy two of the Marshal's horses. He secured a servant, bought various minor objects of equipment, found out what were the marching orders for next day, and decided to accompany the central column (3rd and 6th Corps and Imperial Guard) which was to move directly on the crossing of the Sambre at Charleroi.

To be thus a mere onlooker with no recognized position, no work to do, was a new and somewhat humiliating experience for the veteran soldier. It was in a mood of brooding discontent and disappointment that on Thursday morning he rode with Heymès from Beaumont along the Charleroi road, finding it no easy matter to get forward on the flank of the mile-long columns of men and horses, guns and wagons that crowded the tree-bordered highway. It was a bright summer day, and the heat was soon intense and the men marched amid a fog of white dust. Here and there the Marshal was greeted by younger comrades, who had the good luck to hold active commands. Now and again the soldiers cheered him. They seemed glad to see him, and he smiled as he acknowledged their salutes. Once he heard a soldier say to his comrades: "Things are moving. There goes *le rougeaud!*"—his old nickname when he was a private in the 4th Hussars—a word equivalent to "red head" or "carrots" in the language of Tommy Atkins.

As Ney gradually worked his way forward, the sound of cannon came from the front, at first in dull thuds and mutterings and then more distinctly. Early in the afternoon he crossed the bridge of Charleroi amid moving masses of soldiery and saw the signs of the fighting in and around the town, from which the Prussians had been driven in the forenoon. He heard that so far all had gone well, the left and centre columns driving in the Prussian detachments wherever they opposed the advance. Between two and three o'clock he at last found the Emperor, between Charleroi and Gilly, seated at a table outside a wayside inn on the slope above the Sambre, with his map and papers before him, and a group of staff officers around him, while the troops, tramping up the road in an endless column, cheered him as they passed.

Here a pleasant surprise awaited Ney. He dismounted, gave the bridle of his horse to Heymès, and went to greet the Emperor. "Good day, Ney," said the Emperor, "I am very glad to see you. You will go and take command of the 1st and 2nd Army Corps. I am giving you also the light cavalry of my Guard, but don't use it yet. To-morrow you will be joined by Kellerman's Cuirassier's. Go and drive the enemy back along the Brussels road and take up a position at Quatre Bras."[1]

[1] One of the many points of controversy in the story of the campaign is the question whether Ney was ordered to occupy Quatre Bras on the afternoon of

The left column of which the command was thus assigned to Ney was made up of the following units:—

1st Corps. General Drouet d'Erlon. Four divisions of infantry (Quiot, Donzelot, Marcognet, and Durutte); a division of cavalry (Jacquiminot, 7th Hussars, 3rd Chasseurs, and 3rd and 4th Lancers) and six batteries of artillery.

2nd Corps. General Count Reille. Four divisions of infantry (Bachelu, Prince Jérôme Bonaparte, Girard, and Foy); a cavalry division (Piré, 1st and 6th Chasseurs, and 5th and 6th Lancers) and six batteries of artillery.

Its strength was:—

1st Corps.	20,731	men and	36	guns
2nd „	25,179	„	36	„
Total	45,910	„	72	„

To these Napoleon had added the two regiments of light cavalry of the Imperial Guard under Lefèbvre Desnouettes, about 800 sabres. Kellerman's heavy cavalry, eight regiments, and a horse battery of six guns were to join next day. Instead of being a spectator of the great conflict, Ney thus found himself at the head of an army, with the important task of keeping Wellington at bay on the Brussels road, while the Emperor dealt with Blücher and the Prussians. Ney had the easier share of the work, for the Prussians had begun to concentrate the day before, while the mixed force of British, Dutch, Belgian, and German troops under Wellington's command was still widely dispersed, and was only beginning its concentration that evening.

It was with a light heart that Ney galloped with Colonel Heymès to join his command, after ascertaining that Lefèbvre-Desnouettes was ready to follow him immediately. The left column had marched at 3 a.m. that day, Piré's lancers

15 June. Heymès in his narrative (written in defence of Ney) gives Napoleon's words as above quoted, with the exception of the last phrase as to Quatre Bras. Napoleon himself and Gourgaud say that this order was given. Grouchy declares that he heard Napoleon blame Ney for not seizing Quatre Bras on the 15th. Finally, the Bulletin drawn up the same evening at Charleroi (while Napoleon still believed the order had been executed), and published in the "Moniteur" of 18 June, says: "The Emperor has given command of the left to the Prince of the Moskowa, who this evening has his head-quarters at Quatre Chemins (Quatre Bras)".

leading, followed by the 2nd Corps, with the 1st behind it. At 9 a.m. Reille was before Marchienne on the Sambre, west of Charleroi. The Prussians were driven out and the long column was hours crossing the narrow bridge. Piré scouting along the Quatre Bras road reported that the enemy had halted at Gosselies. Reille, taking with him Bachelu and Prince Jérôme's divisions and some guns, moved forward to drive them out, and arrived before the village about three o'clock, while Ney was with the Emperor at the inn on the Charleroi road. To prepare his attack Reille brought his guns into action against Gosselies, which was held by the 29th Prussian Infantry. It was towards the cannon thunder that Ney rode.

He arrived just as Reille was forming up his infantry in columns of attack. The Marshal took over the command. He was under fire again. Before the advance of 10,000 bayonets, one division marching on the front of the village, the other threatening to turn it, the Prussians gave way, after a brief show of resistance.

And now came the first indication that Ney was no longer the clear-sighted, enterprising leader of Friedland and Borodino, Krasnoi and the Beresina. As the French infantry, after their easy victory, followed the retiring 29th Regiment out of the north end of Gosselies, the enemy halted and several fresh battalions came up to support them. The Prussian General, Steinmetz, was moving past the village in pursuance of the concentration orders received that morning. He drove the French back into Gosselies, and held some houses north of it with a rear-guard, till his column was well on its way to the eastward. It was the moment when Ney, by vigorously following up his success and attacking Steinmetz with all the force he had at hand, might have disposed of some thousands of Prussian infantry who fought next day against the Emperor at Ligny.

With the capture of Gosselies and Steinmetz's retreat the road to Quatre Bras was clear, and there was no serious obstacle to prevent Ney occupying the group of houses at these important cross-roads before evening. But instead of moving onward in force and bringing up every man and gun to the front, Ney not only showed a strange lack of energy, but also disregarded the plain order of the Emperor. He sent three of Reille's divisions into bivouac about Gosselies; ordered Piré to move out to the village of Mellet with his lancers and Bachelu's infantry division, to guard against a possible return of Steinmetz from that side; and himself rode along the Brussels road with Lefèbvre Desnouettes and the cavalry of the Guard.

About half-past five, as he approached Frasnes, artillery opened on him from the village. It was held by an outpost of Wellington's army, a battalion of Nassau infantry, and a horse battery under Major Normann. The French cavalry halted. A galloper was sent off to Mellet to bring up some of Bachelu's infantry, and while waiting for them, General Colbert, with a detachment of the lancers of the Guard, was sent round the right of Frasnes. Colbert rode into Quatre Bras, which he found unoccupied, but feeling himself isolated, and hearing that a strong column was coming from the direction of Brussels, he fell back upon the main body before Frasnes. By this time one of Bachelu's brigades had joined Ney and sent forward a firing line of skirmishers against the village. Normann evacuated it and drew back to the south border of the wood of Bossu, near Quatre Bras, where he took up a position commanding the road. As he did so Quatre Bras itself was occupied by a brigade of four Nassau battalions under Prince Bernard of Saxe Weimar. The Prince had heard that the French were across the Sambre, and without waiting for orders had marched to hold the cross-roads. It was a point of the greatest importance, for there the Brussels-Charleroi Road crossed the great highway from Nivelle to Namur. On this latter road a few miles eastward the Prussians were concentrating, and the possession of the Quatre Bras position would enable Wellington to face the French with his left in touch with Blücher.

Ney, with the cavalry of the Guard and one battalion, found himself about seven o'clock in front of Quatre Bras, now held by Saxe Weimar with 4500 bayonets and six guns. Colonel Heymès, in his defence of Ney, says quite correctly that there was not one chance in ten of storming the position. But if Ney had not managed things so badly he might have had with him before Quatre Bras two or more of Reille's divisions and several batteries. With such a force he could have swept Saxe Weimar out of Quatre Bras, and the advance of the left column would have turned all Blücher's positions to the eastward. As it was, after an aimless skirmish between the cavalry and Saxe Weimar's outposts, Ney withdrew his force to Frasnes, and himself rode back to Gosselies. Reille and Prince Jérôme spent part of the evening with him, but he sent no report to the Emperor till late that night, and Napoleon believed till next day that he had reached Quatre Bras. On the other hand, Ney received no information or orders from Soult, the chief of the Emperor's staff. There was a general slackness about staff work on the French side during this campaign of Waterloo. Information was neglected, orders sent after long delays, and there was a hopeless waste of time and opportunity that went far to wreck the Emperor's plans.

On Friday the 16th this general slackness and slowness was at its worst. Blücher had nearly concentrated his army in the Emperor's front about Ligny. By 10 a.m. Wellington had reached Quarte Bras from Brussels. He found there the Dutch General Perponcher's division, including Bylandt's Dutch and Belgian battalions, and Saxe Weimar's Nassauers. He sent back orders to hurry up the British troops who were moving out from Brussels, and then rode over to Blücher's position to concert measures with him, returning later to Quatre Bras. All the morning, beyond an occasional exchange of shots between nervous sentinels on the outpost lines, there was absolute quiet in front of the position. Ney was wasting long hours of the summer morning. He had not even concentrated his two corps. Three of Reille's divisions were in bivouac all the morning about Gosselies. D'Erlon's corps was still farther back, between Gosselies and Marchienne. A few years before Ney would have been in the saddle by 4 a.m., and even if he waited for further orders before attacking Quatre Bras, he would have moved up all his forces to the fighting front, ready to strike as soon as the word was given. But as Napoleon said, the Marshal was no longer the same man.

At half-past six Ney received a letter from Soult, written about 5 a.m. It contained no orders, but informed him that Kellerman, with eight regiments of heavy cavalry, was to join him at Gosselies, asked if D'Erlon's corps had closed up to that point, and indicated that he would soon have orders to advance. Ney sent Soult the information asked for and shortly after rode forward to Frasnes, telling Reille to act on any orders that might in his absence arrive from the Emperor's head-quarters and communicate them to D'Erlon. It is strange that still no preparations were made for the coming movement. Ney remained at Frasnes inactive for hours. He did not even push a reconnaissance forward to ascertain the force in his front. He persisted in believing that it was only a rear-guard that could be driven in as soon as the advance began in earnest.

At eleven o'clock, when Count Flahault arrived from Charleroi with the order for him "to take up a position at Quatre Bras or beyond it," Ney dictated to one of his staff instructions, which implied that he did not expect any serious fighting. They were a simple marching order, not a plan of attack. Piré's cavalry were to scout towards Genappe. Reille was to move one division to the heights near Genappe, with another in support of it north of Quatre Bras, where his two remaining divisions were to be posted. D'Erlon was to bring three of his divisions up to Frasnes and send the other with his cavalry to cover the flank at Marbais. The cavalry of the Guard was to remain at Frasnes. Kellerman was to bring one brigade of his force there and post the remainder (three brigades) to the left rear at Liberchies. No one reading this order would suppose that Quatre Bras was strongly held by the enemy. Ney was under an illusion on the subject, which he had taken no steps to correct. He said that there was nothing to stop the advance but "the handful of Germans that had been cut up yesterday".

But even when the orders had been issued there was a delay of some hours before anything could be done. Ney was paying dearly for having wasted the long summer morning. Reille, anxious at having received a report of hostile columns moving to the eastward, did not march from Gosselies till after midday, and it was a long time before his troops cleared the village. They blocked the advance of D'Erlon, who had also been delayed by a false rumour of an advance against his left. It was not till half-past one that Reille, with Bachelu's division and two of Kellerman's regiments, reached Frasnes. When only half of Bachelu's infantry was in line, Ney proposed to advance on Quatre Bras. "There is hardly any one in the Bossu wood," he said, "We should clear it at once." Reille objected, "It will be perhaps like our battles in Spain," he said, "and the English will only show themselves when the time comes. It would be prudent to wait until all our troops are massed here before attacking." Ney made no reply, but he was influenced by Reille's advice, and did not give the order to advance until Bachelu's division was complete and Foy's had arrived. He had then some 10,000 infantry and eighteen guns in hand to attack the force in his front, which actually amounted at two o'clock to 7800 men (Dutch, Belgians, and Germans) under Perponcher, with fourteen guns. Brunswick's troops and Picton's British brigades were coming up, and relying on this support a wide front had been occupied. Ney, though he had taken some account of Reille's warning, persisted in the belief that there was a mere handful of men before him. It was strange that a soldier of such experience as his was so deluded. All the morning he had been in Frasnes. In his front the undulating ground, densely covered with high-standing crops of corn, ran up to a low swell, over which went the broad sun-baked ribbon of the dusty Brussels road. From the farms along the ridge shots had been fired at his advanced posts. On the higher ground beyond there was a glint of musket barrels among the trees on the green margin of the Bossu wood. The enemy was holding on to ground more than a mile in front of Quatre Bras, and had pushed his outposts forward at daybreak beyond the position they had held at nightfall. Surely this meant that he was strong and self-confident and intended to fight in earnest.

By two o'clock Ney had formed his infantry in a line of battalion columns: Bachelu to the right of the road, Foy on it and to the left. Piré's chasseurs were on the right flank, his lancers behind the centre; farther back on the road Lefèbvre-Desnouettes had massed the cavalry of the guard in a long column. To the left rear were two of Kellerman's cuirassier regiments. The guns unlimbered in the intervals between the infantry columns. The artillery opened fire upon the farms in

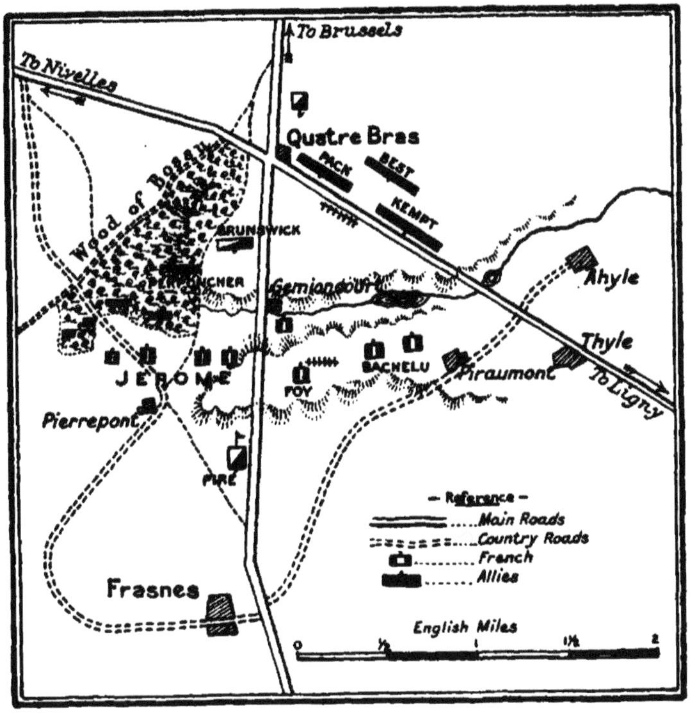

THE BATTLE OF QUATRE BRAS
(SITUATION ABOUT 3 P.M)

the enemy's front. Swarms of skirmishers pushed forward through the tall corn, and there was an exchange of musketry fire along the opposing fronts, then Ney sent Bachelu's infantry, and Piré's cavalry supported by one of Foy's brigades, against the long swell of rising ground to the east of the road. The Dutchmen who held this advanced position were not in force, and gave way after a short fight. Bachelu cleared the hamlet of Piraumont, Foy pushed across the ridge near the road, drove back a Nassau battalion, and, crossing the brook in the hollow beyond the height, dashed at the farm of Gemioncourt and routed a Dutch militia battalion posted there. Ney had ridden forward with the attack and had one of Mortier's horses killed under him. He brought up some of his guns to the ridge.

It was now three o'clock. From the right came the rumbling roar of a heavy cannonade. Napoleon had just begun his attack on Blücher's position at Ligny. Returning to his centre Ney found Jérôme Bonaparte's division marching through Frasnes and coming into line. He sent it towards Pierrepont, with orders to clear the farm and then attack the Bossu wood. Foy and Bachelu were to press on to Quatre Bras. Wellington had just ridden back to the cross-roads, after having paid a visit to Blücher, and had taken command of the defence.

Jérôme carried the farm of Pierrepont with a rush, and then sent one of his brigades against the south side of the wood, while he led the other forward between it and the road to attack its eastern side. Here he was charged by the famous Black Brunswickers with their Duke at their head. They were driven back, carrying with them Brunswick, mortally wounded. He died that evening at Quatre Bras. His father, the Brunswick of the Revolutionary Wars, had been mortally wounded nine years before at Auerstadt.

At the same time Piré's lancers had charged through the corn on the other side of the road, and were for a few minutes masters of a captured battery of eight guns, but they could not carry them off, and they were soon retaken. Foy and Bachelu had pushed on towards the Namur road east of Quatre Bras, but the whole face of the battle was now changing, and Ney's partial success had ended, for Picton had arrived and ranged his three brigades of redcoats and Highlanders in battle array along the Namur road and in the fields just to the south of it. They were almost hidden in the tall corn, and it was a surprise to the French when they were met by the heavy well-aimed musketry fire of the British at point-blank range. The attack collapsed, and the French fell back towards the hollow from which they had advanced.

Ney now realized that he had a serious business in hand. But D'Erlon, with the 1st Corps, 20,000 bayonets and six batteries, was marching up from Gosselies, and he counted on this reinforcement to decide the conflict. At four o'clock he had received an order from Soult, dated two hours earlier, telling him to push the enemy back vigorously and then fall on the right rear of the Prussians by the Namur road. He had been doing his best to clear the Quatre Bras position, but so far had not succeeded. Everything depended on D'Erlon's prompt arrival. But shortly after 4 p.m., when the head of his long column was still a mile from Frasnes, Colonel Forbin Janson of the Emperor's staff met the General and handed him a letter from Napoleon. The exact terms of it are disputed, but it was in effect an urgent order to march with all his corps and fall upon the right and right rear of Blücher. "You will save France and cover yourself with glory," wrote the Emperor. D'Erlon at once gave up the movement on Frasnes, and began to march towards the Ligny battlefield. Forbin Janson instead of going on to Ney to tell him of what was being done, returned to Napoleon's head-quarters. It was not till D'Erlon had gone some distance to the eastward that it occurred to him that Ney ought to be informed, and he sent off his chief of the staff, Colonel Delcambre, to the Marshal. Ney was puzzled by the non-appearance of D'Erlon. He was feeling every moment more and more the need of his presence, and he had just heard that the British were being further reinforced, when Delcambre arrived and told him the 1st Corps was far on the way to the other battle. He gave free expression to his angry disappointment. The round shot from an English battery were ploughing up the ground near him. "I wish one of these would kill me!" he exclaimed.

While he was still speaking another staff officer arrived with an order from Soult telling him to march at once against the right of the Prussians. "Their army is lost if you act vigorously," ran the message. If he had D'Erlon's corps he flattered himself that he could quickly storm the Quatre Bras position and then swing round against Blücher. He told Delcambre to ride back to the 1st Corps and tell D'Erlon he must march at once to Frasnes. Then he sent for Kellerman, and told him to charge with his cuirassiers. Speaking in an excited, hurried tone he said to him that the safety of France was at stake, he must make a great effort. Kellerman did not usually show any hesitation to obey such an order, but he now pointed out that there was little to be gained by hurling two regiments against a position held by more than 20,000 men. The other six had been left by Ney's orders at Liberchies. "No matter," said Ney, "Charge with what you have. Ride over them. I shall send the rest of the cavalry after you. Get on . . . get on at once."

Ney was indeed no longer the same man. In the old days of victory he was noted for his grim coolness in action. Now in his anger and excitement he had fairly lost his head. Kellerman thus urged put his two splendid regiments of steel-clad cavalry in movement at once. Before Piré could even receive the orders to support him, the cuirassiers were dashing through the trampled corn by the right side of the road. They broke through the first line and, fired on from three sides, some of them even struggled on till they were close to Quatre Bras. An officer who rode over the ground next day says he saw some of them lying dead close up to the cross-roads. But only the wreck of the regiments came back. As they returned Piré charged with his lancers. There was a confused fight in the long corn and they surprised one British regiment while forming square and brought back one of its colours. But the cavalry attack ended in failure. It had been broken on the British squares like a surf on a ridge of rocks, and as the beaten lancers rode back, Foy's infantry, disordered by their headlong rush, fell back with them in confusion.

Ney, who had just had another horse killed under him, was on foot watching the rally of Piré's squadrons and Foy's battalions, when up rode Colonel Baudus of Napoleon's staff.

He brought a note written in pencil by the Emperor himself: "It is absolutely necessary that the order given to Count D'Erlon shall be executed, whatever may be the present position of Marshal Ney. I do not attach great importance to what is happening to-day on his side. The affair is entirely where I am, for I want to make an end of the Prussian Army. As for the Prince of the Moskowa, if he can do no more, he must confine himself to merely holding the English Army."

Ney broke out into a new storm of angry words "with his face flushed and brandishing his sword like a madman," says Baudus. He said he would not obey the order. He had sent D'Erlon a message calling him back. He could not do without him. Baudus tried in vain to persuade him to send a counter-order. Ney turned on his heel and went off to rally Foy's men, and lead them against an advancing line of red-coats. Wellington was at last taking the offensive. When D'Erlon received the order of recall, conveyed by Delcambre, he was actually in sight of the battle round Ligny, where his intervention might have had important results. As he afterwards explained, he considered that Ney could not have told him to disregard a direct order of the Emperor, unless the Marshal was himself in the most desperate straits. Leaving therefore one division halted to observe the movements of the Prussian right, he turned back with the other three. When he arrived the fight was over. He had been marching all the afternoon without firing a shot, oscillating between two battlefields, on either of which his 20,000 bayonets might have made history.

After the repulse of the cavalry attack the British had pushed steadily forward gradually recovering all the ground lost in the first stage of the engagement. There was some hard fighting, but Jérôme was driven out of the Bossu wood, and Foy and Bachelu from the ground east of the Brussels road and the farms on the advanced ridge. As the firing died away towards sunset Ney held only the ground from which he had advanced at two o'clock. The battle had been lost. It was the last battle in which he held independent command and the delays, indecisions, and blunders of the day presented a pitiful contrast to his earlier victories.

It was not till next morning that the Emperor—a few

miles away—was informed of what had happened at Quatre Bras, and Ney heard of Napoleon's victory over Blücher at Ligny. It was on the morning of the 17th that Wellington also heard for the first time of the Prussian defeat. "Old Blücher has had a damned good licking," he said to his staff. "He has gone back to Wavre. As he has gone, we must go too. I suppose in England they will say we have been licked. I can't help that." But he was in no hurry to go, for the French under Ney in his front, and the main body under Napoleon away to the south-east, were strangely inactive. Once more the Emperor and his marshals were wasting valuable time. Napoleon had gone out to inspect the scene of his victory after dictating to Soult this letter to Ney :—

"The Emperor is sorry to find that you did not succeed yesterday. The divisions did not act together. Thus you have suffered loss. If the corps of Counts d'Erlon and Reille had acted together not one of the English, in the corps that attacked you, would have escaped. If Count d'Erlon had executed the movement ordered by the Emperor, the Prussian Army would have been totally destroyed and we would have made 30,000 prisoners. . . . The Emperor is going to the mill of Brye on the high road from Namur to Quatre Bras. It is not possible for the English Army to act against you. If it did the Emperor would march straight for it by the Quatre Bras road, while you would attack in front and it would be quickly destroyed. You will inform His Majesty of what is happening in your front. The intention of His Majesty is that you shall take up a position at Quatre Bras ; but if—though this is most unlikely—you cannot do so, report immediately with full details : and the Emperor will march there as I have said. If on the contrary there is only a rear-guard, attack it and occupy the position. To-day will have to be devoted to completing this operation, filling up ammunition, collecting stragglers, and bringing in detached parties."

When this letter was written, about eight o'clock, Napoleon was thinking only of massing his army along the Namur road, and advancing next day. But he soon changed his mind. The reports he had received seemed to point to a retreat of the Prussians to the north-east, leaving Wellington isolated. He would detach Grouchy to follow up Blücher, and with the rest of the army march on Quatre Bras, combining with Ney in an attack on Wellington if he stood, and hustling him back upon Brussels if he retired. He hoped that if vigorously attacked Wellington would eventually retreat towards the coast leaving the way to Brussels open. But he meant if possible to force a decisive battle.

Ney had taken no steps even to ascertain if Wellington still held Quatre Bras with more than a rear-guard. He was absolutely inactive until, between one and two o'clock, the Emperor began his advance on Quatre Bras. First came masses of cavalry, then Lobau's corps, followed by the Guard. The English were by this time retiring, Wellington leaving Lord Uxbridge's cavalry to hold on to the last about Quatre Bras, and cover the retreat. Ney had besides his divisional cavalry, and the light cavalry of the Guard, Kellerman's eight regiments of cuirassiers and dragoons, six of which had not yet been engaged, but he gave them no orders. It was only when the English began at last to withdraw their mounted rear-guard, that he put his troops in motion and rode forward to meet the Emperor. There was fighting in progress between Napoleon's cavalry and horse artillery and the squadrons and batteries of Lord Uxbridge, who was protecting the retreat by showing a bold front against Napoleon's advance along the Namur road. The Emperor had already met D'Erlon riding at the head of his corps. He asked him why he had not obeyed his order the day before. D'Erlon replied that he had been prevented by the counter-order of his immediate chief, the Marshal. The Emperor then told him to follow and support the cavalry advance by the Brussels road. It was just after this that Ney arrived. The Emperor was content with having expressed his opinion of his conduct the day before in the letter sent that morning, so he made no reference to the subject, but he asked the Marshal abruptly why he had not acted on the order sent at eight o'clock (six hours before) to occupy Quatre Bras. Ney answered that he had held his hand because he was sure he had in his front, not a rear-guard, but Wellington's army. Napoleon rode off without further discussion. For the rest of the afternoon he was well to the front of the advance, personally directing the hot pursuit of the retreating enemy, often under close fire, more than once himself giving orders to the horse batteries. The weather had suddenly changed. The intense heat had ended in a thunderstorm and a deluge of rain. At sunset Napoleon took up his quarters for the night at the farm of Caillou on the southern heights of the field of Waterloo, after issuing orders that the army should be concentrated for battle by 9 a.m. next day, Sunday 18 June. Ney, who had ridden all day with Reille's infantry behind D'Erlon's corps, spent the night at Genappe, riding forward in the early morning to the Emperor's head-quarters at Caillou.

He arrived there soon after eight o'clock after having taken a look at the enemy's position from the outposts. When he entered the house he found that Napoleon had just finished his breakfast and had spread his maps on a table, round which were Soult, Maret, Duke of Bassano, Drouot the commander of the Imperial Guard, and several other generals. As he came into the room he heard Napoleon say: "The enemy is 25 per cent stronger than we are, nevertheless we have ninety chances in a hundred in our favour". Ney had seen bodies of troops moving up the slope beyond the farm of La Haye Sainte, doubtless regiments that had halted lower down the night before, and were now taking up their battle positions, but he had misinterpreted what he had observed, and interrupting the Emperor said: "No doubt, Sir, if Wellington were simple enough to wait for you. But I can tell you that there are already marked signs of a retreat, and if you do not attack at once, the enemy will escape you." "You have not seen rightly," replied the Emperor. "The time for retreat is over. Wellington would only expose himself to certain loss. He has thrown the dice and they are for us."

Soult expressed his anxiety at two corps (33,000 men) being detached with Grouchy, and suggested that they should be recalled, leaving only the cavalry to keep touch with the Prussians. Napoleon scouted the idea. He was strong enough, he said, and turning to Soult he went on: "Because you have been beaten by Wellington you think him a great general. Well I tell you Wellington is a bad general, and the English are poor troops, and this will be a mere breakfast for us." "I hope so," said Soult. The head of the long column of the 2nd Corps was now passing Caillou, and Reille came in accompanied by Prince Jérôme. Asked his opinion by Napoleon Reille said it would be a tough piece of work to drive the British from their ground by a frontal attack. Napoleon did not like the turn the conference was taking, and abruptly broke it off.

The weather was now clearing up. Reille marched off to his position on the left, and Napoleon mounted with his staff to inspect his troops taking Ney with him. Now that the left column had rejoined the main body there was no reason for Ney holding any longer the separate command of Reille and D'Erlon's corps. During the ride Napoleon told him that in the coming battle he would give him the executive direction of the main attacks, which were to be launched against Wellington's centre.

There is no need to repeat the oft-told story of Waterloo. All that need be done is to note Ney's personal part in the great battle. It was near noon when after a long delay the fighting began on the French left. Shortly after eleven Napoleon dictated to Soult the order for Reille's corps to move against the British right at Hougomont, apparently with a view of misleading Wellington as to his real objective. The first shot was fired by one of Reille's batteries at 11·35 a.m., and then Jérôme's division was sent against Hougomont. Napoleon's order seemed to point to a mere demonstration on this side, but the movement became a persistent and fiercely pressed attack.

The cannonade begun on the left gradually extended along the French front. Ney was directed to prepare to attack in the centre with D'Erlon's corps, and some ninety guns were massed in front of La Belle Alliance to cover his advance. At half-past one the "Great Battery" opened fire. At two Ney gave the order to attack and himself led the advance with D'Erlon beside him. The four divisions of the 1st Corps, more than 20,000 bayonets, had been drawn up in four massive columns, each with the front of a battalion. These huge columns had come into fashion in the French Army in the later campaigns of the Empire. As the old veterans of the earlier wars disappeared, and the ranks began to be filled with young soldiers, it was found to be easier to move them under fire when they were thus packed together in solid masses, in which the men were as it were locked up, and as long as the formation held its compact lines even those who hesitated to advance had to go on. But it was a formation that diminished the firing front, and at the same time made a huge target for hostile artillery. Ney's order was that the advance should be in echelon of columns from the left—that is to say, Allix's division posted next to the Brussels road was to move first, its left against La Haye Sainte; then in succession Donzelot's, Marcognet's, and Durutte's columns were to march, an interval of about 400 yards separating them, so that the front of the whole attack was about a mile, Durutte's line of march being directed on the farm of Papelotte on Wellington's left. As the columns descended into the wide hollow in their front, the artillery fired over their heads, ceasing only as they went up the ridge held by the British. One of Allix's brigades cleared the orchard and garden of La Haye Sainte, but could make no impression on the buildings. The other brigade, flanked by a mass of cuirassiers, went up the slope. In front of Ney's left attack Bylandt's Dutch-Belgian division gave way, breaking and nearly throwing into confusion some of Picton's regiments at the back of the ridge. On the right Durutte carried Papelotte. The four columns were up to the crest of the English position, and it looked as if Ney was to win an easy victory. But then Picton made his counter-attack. Red-coats and Highlanders dashed at the French. Ponsonby's cavalry came charging into the dense masses. The household cavalry crashed into the cuirassiers. Ney, while trying to steady his left above La Haye Sainte, had his horse shot under him. He caught another and rode back amid the confused retreat of the broken columns, which were charged again and again by the British cavalry. These as they approached the French main position were in their turn charged and driven back by the French cavalry. The beaten infantry were disengaged and reformed, and the artillery duel began again. Round Hougomont, Reille's attack still raged furiously. It was now nearly four o'clock.

While Ney was leading D'Erlon's corps to the attack Napoleon was anxious about the appearance of troops to his right front, which proved to be Blücher's vanguard under Bülow. Lobau's corps was detached to guard this flank leaving Napoleon as his only reserve the Imperial Guard, and messages were sent, all too late, to recall Grouchy. The Emperor still hoped however to crush the British before the Prussians could give them effective support, and at the same time flattered himself that the approaching column was only a single corps detached by Blücher. It was the knowledge that Wellington would be reinforced before long that made Ney, to whom Napoleon had now left the actual direction of the attack, nervously anxious to force the British position at all hazards. While D'Erlon was reforming behind the guns the Marshal ordered one of Milhaud's cuirassier brigades to charge the British centre. The brigadier at first refused to act saying he could only take orders from General Milhaud. Ney settled the question by ordering Milhaud to charge with his whole division. It was thus that after four o'clock there began the series of cavalry onsets which lasted for some two hours, and in which division after division was thrown into action till hardly a squadron remained in reserve. Ney had begun his military career as a cavalry soldier. Now on his last battle-field he led charge after charge against the British squares. In the last great onset no less than seventy-seven squadrons were engaged. There is no need to tell again how

> "Dashed on every rocky square
> Their surging charges foamed themselves away."

Ney had more than once ridden up to the British bayonets. Two more horses were killed under him, and his clothes were torn with bullets, but he was unwounded. At times he seemed, as at Quatre Bras, like a madman. One of the officers who rode in the last cavalry attack tells how he saw Ney dismounted, standing beside one of the guns of a British battery, through which the charge had rolled on to close with the squares beyond. The Marshal stood sword in hand beside the piece, angrily beating the metal of the gun with the flat of his sword.

As the wreck of the last charge came back towards La Belle Alliance, Ney still hoped for victory. La Haye Sainte had been taken at last by the persistent attack of Allix's infantry supported by Bachelu. Along the ridge numbers of guns overturned by the cavalry in their charges were silent and abandoned. The British infantry were unseen behind the crest where they had been withdrawn from the fire of the French batteries, and numbers of wounded and unwounded stragglers passing over the ridge, and the dust clouds raised beyond it by retiring convoys of wounded, suggested that a partial retreat had begun, even though from the right came the thunder of the fight between Lobau and Bülow's Prussians, If he could only throw some fresh troops into the fight he might still break the dogged resistance of the British centre. He sent Colonel Heymès to Napoleon to ask for some infantry. "Where does he think I can find it? Does he suppose I can make it?" replied the Emperor. He had still fourteen battalions of the Guard in reserve, but these were his last stake in the game, and he hesitated to use it.

But after seven o'clock when the increasing din of the fight on his right told him that the Prussians were being rapidly reinforced, and when he must either abandon the field or try one more effort, he moved the Guard forward formed in three great columns, ordered Ney to lead it to the attack, and sent off gallopers to push forward what was left of D'Erlon's corps, and Bachelu's division. Ney led in person the final attack of the Guard, first on horseback, then on foot, sword in hand. When the onward march was stopped by the British fire he did all that despairing courage could attempt to steady the wavering ranks. As the columns were swept back before the counter attack of the British Guards he fought among the bayonets, and his sword was broken in his hand. D'Erlon, riding towards La Belle Alliance amid the rout, saw the Marshal standing by the road calling out to the beaten troops to rally again. Ney was hardly recognizable, his face black with powder, his uniform riddled with bullets, one epaulette hanging down torn by a sabre cut. When he saw D'Erlon he waved his broken sword and called out to him: "D'Erlon, if you and I escape from this we shall be hanged!" He did not want to escape. He was seeking death.

Amid the confused crowd on the rear of which the British cavalry were charging, he saw Brue's brigade of Durutte's division retiring with formed ranks, though reduced to half its strength. He forced his way towards them, halted, and faced them about. "Come and see how a Marshal of France can die," he said, as he led them against the enemy. But they broke and he found himself again without followers.

Near La Belle Alliance three squares of the Guard still stood like islands in the flood of fugitives. In one of these Ney found refuge for awhile, so exhausted that he was glad to rest by leaning on a soldier's arm. He remained with the square, while it slowly retired beating off more than one hostile charge. Then when it at last broke up he began to tramp in the darkness along the Genappe road, an unrecognized unit in the rout of Napoleon's last army.

CHAPTER XVIII

AFTER WATERLOO—THE COURT MARTIAL AND THE TRIAL BEFORE THE PEERS (1815)

NEY had been among the last to leave the field. He had exposed himself recklessly seeking death. Five horses had been killed under him. But he himself was untouched. So long as there was the remotest hope of rallying a rear-guard to cover the flight of the broken army he had fought on foot, sword in hand. When all was lost to remain longer on the battle-field would have been to become a prisoner of the Prussians. After he had gone some way on foot an Alsatian officer, Major Schmidt, gave him his horse and he rode off in the twilight in the hope of rejoining the Emperor.

He had more than one narrow escape before he reached the village of Marchienne at four o'clock in the morning of the 19th. Day had come again. He had for the moment outdistanced the pursuit, but he found at Marchienne only a crowd of beaten, demoralized men, with whom nothing could be done. He was told that the Emperor had passed through Charleroi. He rode on to Beaumont hoping to find there some portion of the army rallying for a stand on the frontier. But on the way he heard that parties of the Allied cavalry were already between him and Beaumont, and he turned and rode on to Avesnes, the Emperor's head-quarters, a few days before, on the eve of the march into Belgium.

In Avesnes all was confusion and disorder. He could get no news of Napoleon or of Marshal Soult, and he decided that the best course was to return at once to Paris, and report there to Davoût, the Minister of War. He secured a post-chaise and reached the capital on the morning of Wednesday, 21 June. As he changed horses at Le Bourget, the last stage before entering Paris, he heard that the Emperor had driven through the village about seven o'clock that morning.

He was weary with the overwhelming fatigues and disappointments of the last few days and had utterly lost heart. He had made up his mind that any further attempts at resistance were doomed to swift failure. They could not save the Empire and would only inflict useless miseries on France. For himself he thought only of taking refuge in some neutral country. He foresaw the speedy return of the Bourbons, and expected that he would receive no mercy for his defection.

His very first visit in Paris was to Fouché, the Minister of Police, who was now already arranging to secure his own interests by becoming the chief promoter of a royal restoration. He discussed with him the events of the campaign and the situation they had created, told him he intended to leave France at an early date and obtained from him two passports. The first was in his own name, "Michel Ney, Marshal of the Empire, Duke of Elchingen, Prince of the Moskowa and Peer of France". The second, intended to be used if a secret flight became necessary, and to enable him to take other refugees with him, was in the name of "Michel Theodore Neubourg, a merchant, travelling with his secretary Talmas, and his servants, Xavier, Serret, Bohnet and Maton". He then went to the Chamber of Peers.

In both houses the friends of Napoleon were making an effort to avert the rising demand for his abdication, to secure at least the succession of his son the King of Rome if he had to withdraw, and to induce the legislature to prolong the resistance if only for a few days in order to gain time for negotiations, that would not imply a complete submission to the victorious Allies. It was all important to show that an army was being rallied, that a fight could still be made, that the situation, though adverse, was not utterly desperate. Ney had hardly taken his seat when Carnot read a communication, just received from the frontier fortress of Rocroi, in which it was stated that on the 18th Grouchy had beaten the Prussians, and that he had repassed the Sambre with 60,000 men, whom he was bringing back to cover Paris. This (except for the exaggerated number) was true enough, but it was only part of the truth.

Ney sprang to his feet as soon as Carnot sat down. Carried away by the impulse of the moment he saw in the Rocroi dispatch, not a report of what had happened elsewhere (about Wavre) on the day of Waterloo, but an attempt to make out that the French arms were victorious all along the frontier. He broke out into an indignant denial. "The news," he said, "which the Minister of the Interior has just read, is false—false in every respect. The enemy is victorious at every point. I have witnessed the disaster, for I commanded the army under the Emperor. After the results of those days of disaster—the 16th and 18th—they dare to tell us that we ended by beating the enemy on the 18th, and that there are 60,000 men on the frontier. The statement is false. At the very most Marshal Grouchy has perhaps rallied 20,000 or 25,000 men. When they tell us that the Prussian army has been destroyed, it is not true. The greater part of that army has not been in action. In six or seven days the enemy will perhaps be in the midst of the capital. There is no other means for securing the public safety but to make proposals to the enemy at once."

An outburst like this went far to defeat the efforts that were being made by Napoleon and his brother Lucien, Davoût and Carnot to save something from the wreck. At the close of the sitting, as Ney went out, some of the Peers reproached him with having uttered such discouraging words at a moment when others were trying to rally France against the foreigner. "Well, gentlemen," replied Ney, "I spoke only in the interest of the country. Don't I know quite well that if Louis XVIII comes back, I shall be shot!"

And each hour that passed made it more certain that Louis XVIII would come back. It was abundantly clear that the Allied sovereigns would never accept half-measures, and even the majority of Frenchmen were now disillusioned by the double failure of Imperialism, longed for peace at any price, and were ready to welcome back the fugitive King. For the partisans of royalty Ney was a traitor. The Bonapartists showed an unworthy disposition to make him a scapegoat, and to cast upon him the chief responsibility for the collapse of their cause and the failures of the French Army in the field. On the morrow of his speech in the Chamber of Peers there began a series of virulent attacks upon him. He had brought upon the Emperor the defeat of Waterloo, said his enemies; he had been rash, incompetent—more than this he was perhaps a traitor to his old master. He had forced him to abdicate the year before, and he had now snatched victory from his grasp and placed him at the mercy of his enemies.

Ney, a soldier but no diplomatist, yielded to the impulse of the moment, and on the 26th wrote a long letter to Fouché, now the chief of the Provisional Government, in which he defended himself by attacking Napoleon. He gave his own version of the Waterloo campaign, and tried to show that he himself had done what was best and failed only because the Emperor did not support him, and he ended thus:—

"What is the source of those odious reports which have been suddenly spread abroad with startling rapidity? I could easily investigate this matter, but I fear almost as much to lay bare the truth as to remain in ignorance of it, so I would only say that there is every indication that I have been basely deceived, and that efforts are being made to cast the veil of alleged treason over the mistakes and extravagances of this campaign, mistakes that have been studiously concealed in the bulletins that have been issued."

There is here a plain insinuation that Napoleon was at the back of a campaign of calumny against the Marshal. Ney was desperate. He felt that both Royalists and Bonapartists were his enemies. And the proclamation issued by Louis XVIII from Cateau-Cambrésis on 25 June was a danger signal. The King promised to "reward the good and put the law into execution against the guilty," and in the eyes of the Bourbons none was more guilty than Ney after Bonaparte himself.

It was this proclamation, with its menacing language, that led Davoût as Minister of War and Commander-in-Chief of the army to insist that in the negotiations with the Allied generals for the evacuation of Paris and the withdrawal of the army to the Loire, there should be a clear agreement for an amnesty for all who had compromised themselves since Napoleon's return from Elba. This was the undoubted purpose of the 12th Article of the Convention of Paris, signed by the plenipotentiaries of both parties on 3 July. The 11th Article stipulated that public property and buildings should be safeguarded, and the 12th ran thus:—

> "Persons and private property shall be likewise respected. The inhabitants, and generally all individuals who are in the capital, shall continue to enjoy their rights and liberties without being disturbed or made the subject of inquiries of any kind regarding the functions they occupy or have occupied, and their conduct and political opinions."[1]

Bignon, one of the French delegates, proposed to add an article to the effect that those who wished to leave France would receive passports from the Allied generals and be given protection for their persons and property, but this was held to be unnecessary.

The extreme party of the Royalists had shown their delight at the threat conveyed by the King's proclamation. The Convention was hardly signed when they began to explain that it need not necessarily stand in the way of proceedings against "the traitors," for (they argued) Louis XVIII was not directly a party to it, and it concerned only the Allied generals. Ney's personal views as to his prospects seem to have varied from time to time during the anxious days he spent in Paris after Waterloo, but generally he was inclined to his first belief that his life would be in danger. He prepared for the worst, but he lost precious time through his hesitation to take a definite course while there was still a prospect of successful flight. Like Napoleon he thought of the United States of America as a possible refuge. New Orleans, so lately the capital of a French colony, and still to some extent a French city, was the place he had in mind as a residence for his years of exile. A friend of his, M. de Pontalba, gave him letters of introduction to M. Marigny a French merchant in that city. In one of these letters found in the Marshal's portfolio when he was arrested, Pontalba wrote:—

[1] The original text of the article is: "Seront pareillement respectées les personnes et les propriétés particulières. Les habitants et en général tous les individus qui se trouvent dans la capitale continueront à jouir de leurs droits et libertés, sans pouvoir être inquiétés ou recherchés en rien, relativement aux fonctions qu'ils occupent ou auraient occupées, à leur conduite et à leurs opinions politiques."

"When you know him you will see that he is a man of the most simple and modest character. If he notices that his presence causes you any embarrassment or involves you in extra expense on his account, he will go off to an inn. Receive him therefore with the greatest simplicity."

The Maréchale was anxious that he should start at once. One day she entreated him to go before it was too late, and in her anguish for his safety fell on her knees and begged him to lose no more time in Paris. Ney was in one of his fits of ill-humour and refused her with words that must have wounded her deeply. "It seems, Madame, that you are in a hurry to get rid of me."

He hoped for a while that the Provisional Government would call for his services, entrust him with a command, and thus give him a recognized position among those who restored the King. This would have been a pledge of future immunity. But Fouché and his colleagues gave no sign.

On 6 July—the eve of the occupation of Paris by the English and Prussian armies—Ney at last left the capital. He was in civilian dress, and he hoped to reach Switzerland. He arrived at Lyons on 9 July. There a commissary of police called upon him. The official was friendly, and when Ney talked of going to Switzerland told him that the roads in that direction were occupied by the Austrians, and suggested that he should either ask for a passport from them, or go to the baths of St. Alban near Roanne for a few days to watch events.

He remained at St. Alban till the last days of July. Notes, which he wrote in a pocket-book during his stay there, show that he was thinking of being able before long to return to his château of Coudreaux, for he jotted down memoranda of improvements to be made on the estate. At other times he was planning flight and concealment. On 23 July he went into Roanne and obtained from a friendly officer a military *feuille de route*, or travelling permit, in the name of Major Michel Reiset of the 3rd Hussars, under orders to proceed from Roanne to Toulouse.

Two days later he received a letter from his wife conveying serious news. On 24 July the King had signed two decrees. The first, countersigned by Talleyrand, deprived Ney and several others of their dignity of Peers of France. The second, countersigned by Fouché as Minister of Police, was a list of proscriptions. It was disguised as an act of grace, for the preamble set forth that its object was to define and *limit* the number of those, who, after incurring the guilt of a crime against the interests of the people, the security of the crown, and the peace of Europe, were to be dealt with according to law. The first article contained a list of twenty persons who were to be tried by court martial. Ney's name headed the list.

The extremists, the party of vengeance, had triumphed and the "White Terror" had begun. In her letter his wife suggested to him that he should hide for a while at the château of Madame de Bessonis, a relative of hers, who had a country house in an out of the way district on the borders of the hill country of the Cantal near Aurillac.

Travelling under the assumed name of Escaffre, Ney reached the Château on 29 July. At first he thought he was quite safe there, but within five days his place of concealment was discovered. The popular tradition, repeated in most biographies of Ney, is that his identity was betrayed by an accident. It will be remembered that Napoleon's gift to him on his marriage was a jewelled Turkish sabre, which he had brought from Egypt. The story goes that Ney left this splendid sword in the salon of the château and a visitor from Aurillac noticed it, and spoke of it to a friend, who at once exclaimed, "There are only two persons in Europe who have such a sabre—Ney and Murat". The prefect heard of this, searched the château and arrested the Marshal.

But Ney had left the famous Mameluke sabre at Coudreaux among his trophies. Neither this nor any other weapon is noted in the list of property in his possession drawn up by the *gendarmerie*, which mentions the smallest details of his personal effects on the day of his arrest. What really happened was this. On 2 August a zealous Royalist informed the prefect of the Cantal, Locard, that he thought the guest at Bessonis looked very like Ney. Locard at once sent for the Captain of the departmental *gendarmerie* who told him that he had heard that Ney had been recognized in Aurillac on 31 July, and had spent the night in the town, and that the château of Bessonis belonged to a relative of the Maréchale.

Early on 3 August the Captain went to Bessonis with fourteen of his men, posted sentries at all the gates, and entered the courtyard. Ney's room looked out upon the court. He heard the gendarmes marching into it and went to the window. He saw at once that further attempts at concealment were hopeless, and called out to the Captain. "Who are you looking for?" "Marshal Ney," was the reply. "Come up here," said Ney, "And I will show him to you." The gendarmes entered the house and reached the room. He met them at the door. "I am Marshal Ney," he said.

They seized his papers and luggage, and conveyed him to Aurillac, where he was confined in an improvised prison in the town hall, while awaiting orders from Paris as to his fate. He seemed quite resigned during the days he spent there. It was not till 15 August that the officers arrived who were to conduct him to Paris.

When the news of the arrest reached the capital there had been general rejoicing among the Royalist extremists. The time had come they said to make a great example. The King took another view of the matter. To Marmont he said: "Everything was done to favour his escape. The imprudence and folly of his conduct have ruined him," and he appeared to see in the arrest a source of embarrassment for his government. To another of the courtiers he even said openly: "He has done us more harm in getting himself arrested than he did on the day he betrayed us". On 13 September Madame Ney wrote a despairing letter to Fouché entreating his intervention on her husband's behalf, and sent him a copy of a petition she was forwarding to the King. She did not deny that her husband had been guilty of a grave offence against him, but she protested that it was an impulsive act without "premeditation or perfidy". She reminded Louis XVIII that at Fontainebleau the year before Ney had been foremost in pressing for the abdication of Napoleon, and had thus been the chief agent in averting civil war and securing the return of the Bourbons. During the Restoration he had held entirely aloof from political intrigue, living quietly in the country. Recalled to his command on the return of Napoleon he had protested his loyalty to the King:—

"He expressed with the vehemence that was characteristic of him his desire to do good service to your Majesty, and his language, in the midst of his family and among his most intimate friends, was the same as it was at the Tuileries. The frankness and loyalty of his whole career, his loquacity, the vehemence of his character—in a word all his good qualities, all his defects, concur in proving that he was sincere. . . . I will say even more, Sire. My husband could not have dissimulated in this respect even if he had had the infamous idea of so doing. His very nature would have made it impossible for him."

She pleaded that when the crisis came he found himself powerless in the midst of unreliable troops and was misled by information that made him to believe that all was lost for the royal cause and further resistance meant only purposeless bloodshed. Her husband, she said, was a man of splendid military courage, but without the same resolution in other affairs. He could grasp at one glance the combinations of the battle-field, but he was out of his element when chance forced him to play a part in politics. "He abandoned himself to a torrent which it seemed to him impossible to stop or to direct." She asked for mercy for him for the sake of her children. His Majesty, she said, had sent her a kindly message through Marshal Macdonald, promising that he would protect her sons, who were left almost without resources. She begged him to spare their father. They had been taught to be loyal to their King. She implored him to spare them from such a sorrow in the midst of the general joy of France.

No answer came to her letters. She asked for an audience with the King. It was granted, but Louis gave her no hope. Then she was told that her husband was on his way to Paris, and she went to meet him at one of the inns where horses were changed outside the southern barriers.

Captain Jomard of the Royal Guard with two of his lieutenants had gone to Aurillac on 15 August and taken over the prisoner from the custody of the local authorities. The Royalist captain, anxious to spare the great soldier humiliating precautions on the way, made him give his parole that he would not attempt to escape. Ney, Jomard, and the two lieutenants travelled in a post-chaise, preceded by Major Meyronnet, who rode on in advance to secure the horses required at the various stages, and followed by a few mounted gendarmes. Leaving Aurillac on the 16th they reached Clermont Ferrand on the 17th. Thence they drove through Moulins to Nevers. Here they found the Würtembergers occupying the town, and Jomard had lost or mislaid his passport, so there was a halt of two hours while another was procured from the local authorities. There was a disgraceful scene, a number of the foreign officers gathering round the carriage, pointing out Ney to each other and using offensive language about him in German and French. The same scene was repeated at the next post in the village of La Charité while Jomard was waiting for the German commandant to *visa* his passport. He protested against the insults to his prisoner, with the result that stones were thrown at him. After this at every halt hostile crowds gathered round the carriage, and Jomard was anxious for the Marshal's safety, not without reason, for a week before this Marshal Brune had been murdered by a Royalist mob at Avignon. He had an alarm of another kind when, at Fontainebleau, a party of Cossacks persisted in riding with the carriage, and could not be persuaded to depart until they had followed it for some miles along the Paris road. Ney himself more than once expected that he would be assassinated. Once on the way he had spoken with one true friend. While horses were being changed at Riom, he had stepped out of the chaise, and to his surprise a general in undress uniform pushed through the crowd of idlers looking on and grasped his hand. It was the famous cavalry leader Excelmans. He offered to arrange for Ney's escape during the next stage. "No," replied the Marshal, "I cannot. I have given my parole." At the last posthouse outside the barriers of Paris there was another meeting. Aglaé was waiting there for him. Jomard kindly allowed husband and wife to spend some time together alone in one of the rooms of the inn. As he parted with the Maréchale and came back to the carriage Ney was wiping away some tears. "You are surprised at seeing me weep," he said to the officers. "It is not for myself. It is for my wife and my four children."

It was the morning of 19 August. As Ney passed through the southern barriers Colonel Labedoyère was facing the firing party at his execution on the plain of Grenelle. The carriage drove to the Conciergerie,[1] where Ney was lodged in the cells of the gloomy prison that had been for so many thousands the antechamber of the scaffold.

He was allowed to take exercise in one of the courtyards. He found the long hours in the cell dreary, and asked to be given a flute with which to amuse himself. Flute playing was a German fashion, and he had learned to play a little in the days when he was a young general of the Army of the Rhine. Perhaps he was somewhat of a halting performer, for the jailers thought he was using the flute to signal with it to other prisoners. The cell of Lavalette was near to his. The flute was taken from him and he was removed to another room, a larger and better one.

On 20 August, the day after his arrival, the Prefect of Police came to interrogate him. At first he refused to say anything, but then he spoke freely enough. He admitted that he told the King that Bonaparte deserved to be brought to Paris in a cage. He outlined the same general defence that his wife had put forward in her letter to the King. He had been loyal till on the night between 13 and 14 March he was "swept away by the torrent". "Often since then," he said, "I have thought of blowing my brains out. I have not done so because I wished to justify myself. I know that honest folk will blame me. I blame myself. I did wrong; I reproach myself; but I am not a traitor. I was drawn on and misled." Throughout he refused to implicate others. To the last he kept secret the names of Napoleon's emissaries to Lons-le-Saulnier. He denied indignantly a story that when he saw the King he asked and received from him a large sum of money. He protested against this as a baseless calumny.

Two days later the Prefect came again and tried to make him confess that his treason was premeditated. Ney stood firm. "How can one explain such a sudden change of conduct?" he was asked. "It was like the breaking of a dyke before a flood," was his reply.

[1] The prison register gives the following *signalement* of the prisoner: "Age, 46; height, 1·73 metres (5 feet, 9 inches); hair, light chestnut; eyebrows, fair; eyes, blue; nose and mouth, medium; chin, full; face, long; complexion, clear.

Steps were being taken to convoke a "Council of War" or court martial for his trial. On the 21st his old comrade, Marshal Gouvion de St. Cyr, now Minister of War, ordered that it should be composed of a number of marshals under the Presidency of Marshal Moncey. Moncey refused the position. St. Cyr told him he must accept it or disobey the King. Then the old Marshal addressed to Louis XVIII, a letter which did more honour to the writer than all his military exploits:—

"Sire (he wrote) placed in the cruel dilemma of having to chose between disobeying Your Majesty or being false to my own conscience, I feel that I must explain myself to Your Majesty. I do not enter into the question of deciding whether Marshal Ney is innocent or guilty. . . . Ah! Sire, if those who direct Your Majesty's councils thought only of your welfare, they would tell you that the scaffold has never made friends. Do they imagine that death is so terrible for those who have so often braved it? Is it the Allies who require that France should immolate her most illustrious citizens? But, Sire, is there not a danger for your person and your dynasty in granting them this sacrifice? . . . The daggers that struck down Brune, Ramel, and so many others are glittering before my eyes. And am I by my presence to sanction an assassination? The throne of the Bourbons is endangered by its own allies, and am I to go to sap its foundations? No, Sire, and you yourself will not disapprove of my resolve. Twenty-five years of glorious services shall not be dimmed in one day. My hair grown grey under the helmet shall not become the mark of dishonour.

"My life, my fortune, all that is dearest to me, belongs to my country and to my King; but my honour is my own and no power on earth can wrest it from me; if I am to leave my children my name as their only inheritance, at least it shall not be tarnished.

"Is it for me to pronounce upon the fate of Marshal Ney? But, Sire, allow me to ask Your Majesty, where were his accusers while Ney was fighting on so many fields of battle? Did they follow him, did they accuse him during twenty years of toil and danger? If Russia and the Allies cannot pardon the conqueror of the Moskowa, can France forget the hero of the Beresina? At the crossing of the Beresina, Sire, in the midst of that awful catastrophe, it was Ney saved the remnant of the army. I had in it relatives, friends, and finally soldiers, who are the friends of their chiefs. And I am to send to death him to whom so many Frenchmen owe their lives, so many families their sons, their husbands, their relations! Excuse, Sire, the frankness of an old soldier, who always holding aloof from intrigues has known only his duty and his country. He believes that his voice, which spoke in disapproval of the wars of Spain and Russia may likewise speak the language of truth to the best of kings, to the father of his subjects. I do not disguise from myself that this might be a dangerous course with any other monarch. Nor do I fail to see that I may thus draw down upon myself the hatred of courtiers, but if, as I go down to the tomb, I can say with one of your own illustrious ancestors, 'All is lost but honour!' I shall die content."

The Government replied to Moncey's protest by expelling him from the Chamber of Peers and condemning him to a term of imprisonment in a fortress.

Marshal Jourdan, Ney's old comrade of the Rhine, was named President of the court martial on 30 August. The other members were Marshals Masséna, Augereau, and Mortier and Generals Vilatte, Claparède, and Gazan.

Ney had chosen for his legal advisers and advocates the two leading men of the Paris bar, Dupin and the elder Berryer. The younger Berryer assisted his father in preparing the defence. From the very day of his arrest he had protested against being tried by a "Council of War" or court martial, and declared that as a Marshal and Peer of France no such tribunal could judge him and he could only be arraigned before the Chamber of Peers. One would have thought that a soldier would rather trust his fate to his old comrades, than be tried before an assembly of politicians. But Ney believed that he had numerous enemies in the higher ranks of the army. "They would shoot me like a rabbit," he said. And on 14 September he formally protested against the competence of the court martial.

Masséna had tried to escape from any part in the coming trial by urging that as he had a quarrel with Ney in Portugal in 1811, he could not be regarded as an impartial judge of his conduct. His objection was overruled, his colleagues unanimously testifying that his high character made it impossible to suppose that he would be influenced against Ney by any personal incident in the past.

At last on 9 November the court martial held its first sitting in the great hall of the Palais de Justice. Ney was not present, and the whole sitting was taken up with the reading of various documents, including a mass of depositions. Ney's counsel put in two documents, long legal memoirs arguing that a Marshal or a Peer of France could not be tried by court martial, and that the tribunal was therefore incompetent to proceed further.

When the court met again next day there was a great display of military force, for Ney was to be present and there were rumours of an attempt to rescue him. But there was no disturbance. As soon as the marshals and generals had taken their places, Ney entered, escorted by a party of gendarmes. The guards presented arms as he passed. He was dressed in a general's uniform and wore the Grand Cordon of the Legion of Honour. It was remarked that he looked absolutely calm and impassive as he saluted the court and seated himself in the arm-chair that had been placed in front of the long table at which his judges sat. Jourdan, as President, formally asked him his name, age, place of abode, and profession. Ney took a paper handed to him by his counsel, opened it and in a firm clear voice read a protest against the competence of the court. He had he said no desire to show any disrespect to the marshals and generals of France, but he must refuse to be interrogated by a court martial or by any tribunal except that to which the law gave the right to judge him.

The lawyers then argued the point and at four o'clock the members of the court retired to consider their decision. Shortly after five they came back, and the President announced that by five votes against two they had judged that they had no jurisdiction. Ney returned smiling to his counsel. "Ah, Monsieur Berryer," he said, "what a service you have rendered me. Those fellows would have killed me like a rabbit!"

The Marshal's friends rejoiced. His enemies at court were furious. Ney was taken back to the Conciergerie, and now hoped that either further proceedings would be abandoned, or he would be saved by a favourable judgment of the Peers. In any case he had secured a respite of some weeks. Before he could be brought again to trial the whole procedure of the new tribunal would have to be settled.

On his return to his cell in the Conciergerie he asked for permission to see some of his relatives and friends and received their visits during the following days. They were Madame Ney and her four children, her sister Madame Gamot, his aide-de-camp Colonel Heymès, and his notary M. Batardy.

But the party of vengeance did not mean to lose their prey. On the news of the collapse of the prosecution by court martial there was an outcry in the court and in the salons. Among those who expressed their disappointment most freely were noble ladies, who in those days of the "White Terror," seemed to have forgotten the gentleness of their sex like the *tricoteuses* of the "Red Terror". The Government, however, needed no urging on. The court martial had given its decision on 10 November. On Saturday the 11th the Duke de Richelieu, President of the Council and Minister of Foreign Affairs, rose in the Chamber of Peers to move a resolution for the trial of Marshal Ney by that assembly. During the Empire Richelieu had been in the service of Russia and he was known to be a valued friend of the Czar. This gave a new force to his words when he told the Peers that it was not only in name of the King and in the name of France but "*in the name of Europe* that the ministry conjured and required them to pass judgment on Marshal Ney".

Richelieu suggested that the Chamber might adopt the same procedure as regulated its ordinary debates and decisions, but in the discussion which followed the feeling was expressed that this would hardly be sufficient. The Peers would have to sit as a high court of justice with special rules and methods of procedure. Though the next day was Sunday the Procureur General was put to work to draw up a new royal ordinance setting forth what this procedure was to be. It was issued on the 13th, and on the same day it was decided that a fresh set of depositions should be prepared for the new tribunal.

There was presented to each of the Peers, a copy of a memoir jointly addressed by the Marshal and the Maréchale Ney to the ambassadors of Great Britain, Russia, Austria, and Prussia. There was something of an apology for this appeal to the Allies, but it was justified by the action of Richelieu in making the proceedings against Ney an international question, and by the nature of the arguments embodied in the memoir. For it was an appeal to the faith of treaties, to the agreement set forth in Article 12 of the capitulation of Paris, that no one should suffer for his opinions or his actions during the Hundred Days.

The paper, though signed by Madame Ney and represented

as her petition, was of course drawn up by the lawyers. But the poor wife was active in supporting the plea thus put forward for amnesty to her husband. Her visits to the gloomy Conciergerie were devoted to consultations as to what could be done. She haunted the offices of Dupin and Berryer. At home she was busy with endless letters claiming for her husband the pardon and immunity which the convention of Paris seemed to guarantee to all. She wrote to the ambassadors, to Wellington, to the Prince Regent of England. To all her touching appeals came the same cold official answers. Lord Liverpool instructed Sir Charles Stewart, the British ambassador, in Paris, to say that His Royal Highness the Prince Regent could not interfere in a matter of internal French policy—in which by the way His Royal Highness's Government had been interfering most effectually on a score of occasions. Wellington answered that he could not see that the Convention applied to Ney's case and must regretfully decline to take any action. He sent the same answer to a personal appeal from Ney, assuring the Marshal that he had "the honour to remain his obedient servant, Wellington". He would have done himself more honour if he had exerted himself to save the life of his gallant and unfortunate adversary. The ambassadors all replied that the Convention of Paris only concerned the action of the Allied generals towards Frenchmen, but could not be taken to limit the rights of the King in dealing with his own subjects. But no one ever supposed that it was anything but a pledge of political amnesty when it was signed, and the King was undoubtedly bound by the act of his Allies. Yet this strained interpretation of the Convention and the subsequent Treaty of Paris of 20 November, was insisted upon, because Ney was already doomed in advance, and this loophole for escape must be closed against him at all costs.

Meanwhile the legal proceedings were in progress. The Chamber had resolved that during the actual trial Ney should be confined in an improvised prison in the palace of the Luxembourg, where it held its sittings, so as to minimize the chance of rescue by avoiding having to escort the prisoner backwards and forwards from the Conciergerie. There were constant rumours of plots of old soldiers to deliver the Marshal, and precautions of all kinds were multiplied for his safe keeping. On 20 November all preliminaries had been completed and on the 21st the trial at last began.

When places had been provided for the Peers, the lawyers and officials, and the witnesses, there was little room left in the great hall of the Luxembourg for the public. It was noted that those who crowded the narrow tribunes of the spectators were largely foreign visitors to Paris. Metternich was there, and the Prince Royal of Würtemberg and several British and Russian officers in uniform. The President of the Chamber, the Chancellor Dambray, opened the proceedings with a brief address, in which he called on the Peers to dismiss all prejudice from their minds and give the prisoner the "most ample latitude for his defence". The course of the trial showed that even Dambray himself was not prepared to act on this advice Ney entered escorted by four gendarmes. He had been brought from the Conciergerie with a display of force inspired by the current rumours of a rescue. He wore the undress uniform of a general with both the Legion of Honour and the Cross of St. Louis on his breast. He was quite calm and self-possessed, and gravely saluted the court before taking his seat near his counsel. He looked paler than when he appeared before the court martial. His prolonged imprisonment was telling upon him.

The roll of the Peers was called, and then an officer of the court read the long "act of accusation" drawn up by the Procureur Bellart. It was a combination of an indictment and a speech for the prosecution. It was couched in language bitterly hostile to the accused. The prosecution endeavoured to show that Ney had from the first intended a treacherous defection; that he had declared for Napoleon at a time when his troops were still willing to follow him against the "usurper"; and that his treason had been a chief cause of the collapse of the Royalist resistance to Napoleon, and thus led to the disastrous events that followed. Desertion to the enemy, levying of war against the sovereign, and promotion of armed strife between the citizens of France were the crimes charged against the Marshal, and attention was called to the clauses of the penal code that punished such crimes with death.

Asked by the President if he had any defence, and assured that the court would give him a favourable hearing, mindful of the glorious memories attached to his name, Ney rose and saluted and then read from a paper handed to him by his counsel protesting against various details of the procedure of the court. Then came a prolonged argument on these points between Bellart on the one side and Dupin and Berryer on the other. This went on till the court adjourned. At the second sitting on the 23rd, the defence, besides arguing several legal points, pleaded for a further adjournment of several days on the ground that the accused had not been fully informed of the nature of the indictment, and must have time to obtain evidence to refute certain matters alleged against him. He was especially anxious to show that he had not contemplated defection up to the night of 13 March. Bellart, eager to avoid further delays, offered to grant this, though with such a concession all the theory of a treasonable plot must fall to the ground. But the Procureur believed he could secure a condemnation even without this. Dupin rejected the offer. He wanted no concessions; he would solemnly prove that in this Ney was falsely accused. Finally the court agreed to give the prisoner until 4 December further to prepare his case. Ney was taken back to the Conciergerie, more hopeful than the facts warranted.

On 4 December he was again arraigned before the Peers at the Luxembourg. Before replying to the questions of the President, Dambray, Ney declared that he reserved the right of his defenders to plead the protection of Article 12 of the Paris Convention of 3 July and its virtual confirmation in the Treaty of Peace of 20 November.

In relating his parting interview with the King, Ney tried at first to show that he had not used the unfortunate phrase about bringing Napoleon back in an iron cage, but on being pressed on the point he practically admitted it. Throughout he insisted that up to the morning of 14 March he had loyally done his best for the royal cause, and only abandoned it at the last moment when further efforts were impossible.

Then the hearing of the witnesses began. The testimony

as to his conduct up to 14 March was on the whole very favourable to him. The dramatic moment of the day arrived when General de Bourmont was called to give his evidence. He had been an Emigré and a Royalist soldier of La Vendée before he made his peace with the Empire. He and General Lecourbe had been Ney's lieutenants during the crisis at Lons-le-Saulnier. It would be difficult to clear him of a very large complicity in Ney's overt acts of treason. But on the march from Lons-le-Saulnier he slipped away from the column, reached Paris, and reported to the King that he had been a reluctant spectator of the Marshal's defection. After the flight of Louis he remained hidden in Paris, and then, having seen how events would develop, he rejoined Napoleon. He obtained a command of a brigade in Gérard's corps, but during the actual advance to cross the frontier he deserted to the Prussian outposts, and rejoined the exiled King at Ghent, posing once more as a pronounced Royalist.

Lecourbe had died a few weeks before the trial at the Luxembourg. De Bourmont had therefore no reason to fear that he would be confronted with his colleague of Lons-le-Saulnier when he appeared to testify to the treason of Ney, regardless of his own record of frequent changes of sides, culminating in desertion to the enemy while the troops he abandoned were actually marching to battle.[1]

De Bourmont deposed that when, in the early morning of 14 March, Ney showed to him and to Lecourbe the Emperor's proclamation, told them that further opposition to him was useless, that the cause of the King was lost and there was nothing left for them but to declare for the Emperor and lead the troops to join him, he and Lecourbe had both persistently opposed the proposal. Asked why he had after this gone with Ney to the parade, he replied that he had done so only to

[1] It is of interest to note the contrast between the fates of Ney and De Bourmont. The former was sent to execution. The latter, after all his changes from side to side, had a remarkable and a successful career. He commanded a corps in the French intervention in Spain in 1823, won the victory of Sanlucar, and took Seville. For these services he was made a Peer of France. He was Minister of War in the Polignac Cabinet in 1829, and in 1830 was given the command of the army embarked for the conquest of Algiers. He captured the city on 5 July, and was rewarded with the rank of Marshal of France.

watch what would happen. Then he added a statement which, if true, would have told heavily against Ney's whole line of defence, as tending to show that he had started on the campaign prepared for an act of treason. "Marshal Ney," said De Bourmont, "was so thoroughly resolved beforehand to take the side of Bonaparte, that half an hour after reading the proclamation he was wearing the Grand Eagle of the Legion of Honour with the effigy of the usurper." This was absolutely false, as was proved at the next sitting of the court, when M. Cailsoué, the Marshal's jeweller produced his books and swore that it was not till 25 March at Paris that he handed him his decorations bearing the insignia of the Empire.

Ney had been more than once on the point of interrupting De Bourmont. When he told the story of the decoration the Marshal lost patience and sprang to his feet. "Monsieur de Bourmont," he exclaimed, "accuses me to clear his own conduct. It seems that he prepared his denunciation of me months ago at Lille. He flattered himself perhaps that we would never meet again face to face. He thought I would have short shrift like Labedoyère. I have no oratorical talent, but I come direct to the fact. It is unfortunate for me that General Lecourbe is no longer living. But I call him to witness in another place." Then pointing upwards with his right hand he went on. "Against these depositions I appeal to a higher tribunal, to God who hears us all, to God who will judge us—you and me, Monsieur de Bourmont!" Then turning to the President he added. "Here Monsieur de Bourmont is beating me down. There we shall be judged—both of us."

De Bourmont glanced round at the audience, pale and agitated. The Peers, the lawyers, the crowd in the tribunes, were all visibly impressed for the moment, and neither the President nor the opposing counsel interrupted Ney as he continued, and gave his own account of the debate at Lons-le-Saulnier. "There I was," he said, "with my face bent over that fatal proclamation, while they stood opposite me with their backs to the fire-place. I called on General Bourmont as a man of honour to tell me what he thought. Bourmont, without any preliminary remark, took the proclamation, read it, said he quite agreed with it, passed it to Lecourbe. Lecourbe read it and handed it back to him without a word. Lecourbe did not protest. Bourmont thought we might read the proclamation to the troops. Neither said to me: 'Where are you going? You are going to risk your honour and your reputation for a fatal cause.'" Then turning to De Bourmont: "I had no need, Monsieur de Bourmont of your opinion as to the responsibility with which I alone was charged. But I was asking for light, for advice, from men who I believed had enough of old affection, enough of energy, to say to me 'You are wrong'. Instead of this you drew me on and flung me over the precipice!" Turning again to the court Ney said: "It was Bourmont who assembled the troops to hear the proclamation. He had two hours for reflection. If he considered my conduct criminal, why did he not arrest me? I had not one man with me, and not even a saddle horse to escape with."

The President saw the force of Ney's last argument. He asked De Bourmont: "Who gave the order for the troops to parade?" "It was I," replied the witness, "on the verbal order of the Marshal." "He assembled them," interrupted Ney, "after he had been shown the proclamation." "How came it," asked Dambray, "that after disapproving of the Marshal's conduct you followed him to the parade ground, knowing what he meant to do there?" "I wanted to see the effect produced by the proclamation," was the answer. Then he explained that he wanted to see if there were any signs of opposition to the Marshal among the troops. The President asked him if he had taken any steps to evoke such opposition. De Bourmont was now very uneasy. Ney's counter-attack had almost changed his position from that of a witness to a defendant. "I had no time," he said. "I could do nothing unless I had killed the Marshal." Ney interrupted again in his deep sonorous voice: "You would have done me a great service, and perhaps it was your duty!"

De Bourmont had tried to show that the troops were loyal till Ney addressed them. Now he went on to say that he feared arrest, that he was anxious to get back to Paris and inform the King after seeing all that happened. He reminded the court that on 18 March he actually reported to the King. He did not add that a few days later he took service with Napoleon and then deserted him on the frontier. Ney struck in again with a fresh protest against the story that he had the decoration of the Imperial Legion of Honour with him, ready to display it on his breast when the moment came. "Do you take me for a miserable wretch," he asked indignantly. "You want to make out I brought it from Paris with the set purpose of betraying the King. I am angry at an intelligent man using such false and such base methods against me. He must be in a strange state of mind to testify to such theories as this." Bellart was becoming anxious at the effect produced by Ney's words. He asked the President to put to the Marshal the question whether there was not some personal cause of quarrel between him and the witness. "None whatever," replied Ney emphatically.

So far his counsel had not intervened. Berryer now rose and asked De Bourmont whether it was also out of mere curiosity that he went to the banquet on the evening of 14 March at Lons-le-Saulnier. The witness replied that he did so to prevent Ney suspecting him, and to avoid a possible arrest. "I arrested no one. I left every one free," interposed Ney. "Neither you nor anyone else objected. You held an important command. You could have had me arrested and you would have done well. The officers of rank came to dine with me. I was dull enough. Monsieur de Bourmont was there, and if he tells the truth he will tell you that the party was a gay one. That is the truth."

Dambray asked the witness what force Napoleon had at Lyons on the eve of the revolt at Lons-le-Saulnier. "Five thousand men," was the reply. "Why deceive us as to the number," asked Ney. "Every one knows that he was at the head of 14,000 men, without counting the soldiers who were coming in from all sides and a crowd of half-pay officers." "Then," he added, "I saw already that civil war was inevitable. One would have had to march over 60,000 French corpses." Dambray put this point to the witness, "Do you believe that the Marshal could have made any resistance to the troops of Napoleon?" "Everything depended on the first step," replied

De Bourmont. "If he had taken a carbine and fired the first shot, no doubt his example would have been decisive, for no man had a greater empire over the minds of the soldiers. Nevertheless I dare not affirm that he would have been victorious." Dupin put in a question: "Had De Bourmont taken any steps to prevent the effect of the proclamation?" "There was no time." "Well, then," insisted Dupin, "how can you know that the troops were inclined to support the King?" "I could not answer for that," said the witness. "What," asked Berryer, "was the effect of the reading of the proclamation?" De Bourmont answered that the men cried, "*Vive l'Empereur!*" the officers looked stupefied. "Will the President ask Monsieur de Bourmont whether he cried '*Vive le Roi*'?" suggested Berryer. De Bourmont looked miserable, and the attack was clearly telling against him. Two of the Peers came to his help. One protested that Berryer's question was quite uncalled for, another begged the court to stop these "personalities". Bellart rose and declared that time was being wasted on irrelevant details. De Bourmont was allowed to retire, and an officer of the court read the statement of Lecourbe taken by a magistrate shortly before his death.

It was on the whole favourable to Ney. He told how the Marshal had shown the proclamation to him and to De Bourmont, and they had "made some remarks on his changed attitude," and then he had tried to persuade them that it was all an arranged affair and nothing could prevent Napoleon reaching Paris. The magistrate had then asked Lecourbe if he thought Ney could offer any effective opposition to Bonaparte with his troops. Lecourbe replied, "No". Why had he gone to the parade? He could hardly avoid it, he said, the troops were so excited that it would have been dangerous to stay away. Would they have remained faithful to the King if Ney had not read the proclamation? "I do not believe they would," replied Lecourbe, "for we were so near Lyons, that the troops could not but know what had happened there. Some of the officers and even some few of the troops might have held out for a while against the torrent, but the moment they were brought into contact with other troops who had sided with Bonaparte, they, too, would have been swept away." "Who were opposed to

Ney and what line of conduct did they take?" asked the magistrate. "*There was no opposition*," answered Lecourbe.

Other witnesses were called, civilian officials and Royalist officers who had met Ney during the march to Lons-le-Saulnier, or had witnessed the scene on the parade ground. The net result of their testimony was to show that before the 14th he had been zealous for the King, and that on that day there had been no opposition to the declaration for Napoleon. The Marquess de Vaulchier, the Prefect of the Jura, declared that after the proclamation Ney told him to preserve order and not to disturb anyone on account of his opinions. He said Ney was wearing the Napoleonic decoration of the Legion. "You did not see rightly, Sir," interposed the Marshal.

At the close of the sitting Ney was conducted to the improvised prison in an upper story of the Luxembourg. He was closely watched by soldiers wearing the uniform of grenadiers of the National Guard. But they were mostly nobles of the Royal Guard who had volunteered for the service, and assumed this disguise. Some of them were posted in his room, others in the corridors and the garden below the windows. He was calm and even cheerful. He ate his dinner with a good appetite and then had a consultation with his counsel.

The court met again at half-past ten on the morning of the 5th. The first witnesses gave evidence that had no bearing on the case and ought to have been excluded. They were officers who told how Ney had spoken strongly against the Bourbons during his tour of inspection of the northern fortresses, after Napoleon was again in power at Paris. Cailsoué, the jeweller, deposed that Ney had only the Royal and not the Imperial decorations with him until he returned to Paris after Napoleon's arrival there. Other witnesses, civilians, and soldiers, spoke of the language he had held before 14 March and showed that he had till then been loyal in his utterances, and even hostile to the Emperor personally.

At last the three witnesses were called on whose evidence the defence mainly relied. These were Marshal Davoût, Minister of War during the Hundred Days and under the Provisional Government, and two of the envoys who, acting under his instructions, had signed the Convention of Paris on

3 July, namely his chief of the staff, General Guilleminot, and the ex-Prefect of the Seine, the Count de Bondy. Davoût came first. The President Dambray was questioning him about his personal knowledge of the accused, when Berryer rose and asked that the evidence as to the Convention and its 12th Article should be taken at once. Bellart opposed this. Berryer pressed his request, and then Bellart said that, "to show with what generosity the prosecution was acting," he would not further object. Then Berryer asked Davoût to make a statement as to the Convention.

Davoût replied: "In the night between 2 and 3 July all was ready for a battle, when the Provisional Government ordered me to treat with the Allies. The first shots had been fired. I sent to the outposts to prevent the effusion of blood. The Government had given me a draft of the Convention. I added to it the words referring to the line of demarcation between the armies, and I also added the articles relating to the safety of persons and property, and I specially charged the envoys to break off the negotiations if these articles were not ratified.

Berryer asked him if in that case he would have been in a position to offer serious resistance to the Allied armies. "I would have fought a battle," replied Davoût, "I had 60,000 infantry, 25,000 cavalry, and four or five hundred cannon. I had all the hopes of success, which a general can have who commands Frenchmen."

Then Berryer put to Davoût the all-important question. "I ask the Prince of Eckmuhl," he said, "to state what was the sense that he and the Provisional Government attached to Article 12?"

Bellart, for the prosecution, protested against the question. If there was to be a discussion on the Convention what had the Prince of Eckmuhl's opinions to do with it? "The act exists as it exists, and his declarations cannot change it." But the very eagerness of Bellart to prevent Davoût from stating the object he had in view, when he insisted on this provision, and was ready to fight a battle rather than forgo a pledge of immunity for his old comrades, surely showed plainly enough that he foresaw that if Davoût was allowed to explain he would give evidence of the utmost value for the defence. Berryer pressed his point, but the President Dambray, who at the opening sitting of the court in November had declared that "the utmost latitude" must be given to the defence, now weakly yielded to the prosecution, and ruled that Article 12 must be interpreted according to its terms, without any evidence being taken as to the views of those who embodied it in the Convention. During the discussion Ney had again interposed. "The Convention," he said, "is such a protection, that it was upon it that I relied. Otherwise do you not see that I would have preferred to die sword in hand? I was arrested in contradiction to that capitulation. It was because I put faith in it that I remained in France."

After the President's ruling Davoût withdrew, and the two other witnesses gave very brief evidence. The Count de Bondy said: "The chief object of the Convention was the public tranquillity, the safety of Paris, and respect for persons and property. It was with this view that it was drawn up and proposed to Generals Wellington and Blücher. There was some discussion, but no difficulty was raised as to Article 12. It was accepted in a way that was most reassuring to those to whom it applied." General Guilleminot deposed: "As chief of the staff (to Marshal Davoût) I was directed to stipulate for an amnesty in favour of all persons, whatever were their opinions, their functions, or their conduct. This point was granted without any objection. I had been ordered to break off all negotiations if this was refused to me. The army was ready to attack. It was this article that made it lay down its arms." In answer to Dupin, he said that the presence of both military and civil representatives on the French side showed that the Convention applied both to military and civilian individuals.

This closed the evidence. Bellart then made his speech for the prosecution, a fierce protest against any mercy being shown to Ney. The President then called on Berryer and Dupin to reply. They asked to be allowed further time to consider their defence and the court adjourned. On 6 December the court assembled for the final session. It was evident that the main argument of the defence would be that

Ney's case was covered by the Capitulation or Convention of Paris. The prosecution had taken measures to prevent this point being raised. Before the public session of the court was opened Dambray read a notice of motion that had been handed to him by one of the ultra-Royalist Peers, the Comte de Tascher. The document ran thus:—

"The Comte de Tascher has the honour to ask M. le President to be pleased to obtain from the Chamber authority to forbid the defenders of Marshal Ney to speak of the Convention of Paris in their pleadings, seeing that this Convention in no way concerns the Chamber of Peers and lies beyond their attributions. The Chamber is charged by the King to judge the Marshal on the indictment which has been laid against him by His Majesty's Ministers. The question whether the Treaty of 3 July applies to the Marshal, and whether or not he is included under Article 12, concerns only the Government, and it is to the Minister of Foreign Affairs that the accused was and is bound to address himself. I demand that the trial shall proceed without objections being admitted.

"DE TASCHER.

"*Nota.*—It was irregular to hear three witnesses yesterday on a subject thus lying outside the indictment.

"6 December, 1815."

Dambray declared that he agreed with De Tascher. There was a brief debate. Molé, Keeper of the Seals under Napoleon, and now more Royalist than the Royalists themselves, argued that if the Convention had limited His Majesty's right to judge his subjects, Ney would never have been accused by the King's Ministers. A vote was taken, and the Chamber decided that the Convention must not be pleaded as a bar to its jurisdiction.

The public sitting then opened and Dambray called on the counsel for the defence. Berryer rose. He reminded the court that at Fontainebleau in 1814 Ney had been foremost in securing the abdication of Napoleon. He appealed to the evidence of the witnesses to show that he had been horrified at the news of his return from Elba, that day after day he had manifested the utmost repugnance for Bonaparte's enterprise and a loyal zeal for the King's service. How then had there come such a sudden change in his conduct? Then he traced the situation in France after Napoleon's return, the rapid progress of his little army, the general outburst of enthusiasm for his cause, the failure of every attempt to oppose him. Ney found himself in an impossible position. He was told that the King had already left Paris. The Princes had failed to hold Lyons. The proclamation placed in his hands was not his composition. The style, the date, the very form of the signature proved this. Whether he read it to the troops or not mattered little. Many of them had already copies in their hands. What was it but "a gazette giving the most recent news of the actual state of affairs"? If Ney tried to suppress it, tried to lead his troops against the invader, what could he foresee but civil war? It appeared to him that France had declared for the Empire once more. He was a simple soldier, and no politician. He had seen many changes of Government, and in each change he had recognized only the will of the people. Behind each varying form of government he saw the fatherland, and gave it his allegiance. His Lieutenants, Lecourbe and De Bourmont, had been shown the proclamation, informed of the state of affairs, and they, too, saw no possible course but to accept the logic of facts and accompany Ney to the parade ground. He insisted that throughout his brilliant career Ney had thought only of the interests of the country. "This," he said, "was the constant object with him of a religious devotion. This incontestable truth, which was demonstrated by so many splendid exploits, ought to sweep away all ideas of criminal conduct on the part of the Marshal. Once more we must attribute the act with which the Marshal is charged entirely to his ardent desire to avoid the shedding of French blood by the hands of Frenchmen." Then he argued that when the Powers engaged themselves to depose Bonaparte by force of arms, the Vienna pact of 25 March, 1815, made them the Allies of the King of France. They defeated the "usurper" at Waterloo, and their armies arrived before Paris, but their acts were all part of the common accord to which the King was a party.

Bellart saw what was coming and protested against any argument being based on the Convention of Paris, and read a formal demand from the Ministry insisting that the Court should confine itself to the indictment. Dupin rose to put in an objection that seemed singularly ill-timed, but was meant to give Ney an opening for his protest. He called the attention of the court to the fact that, by the Treaty signed on 20 November,

Saarlouis was no longer French territory. Marshal Ney was no longer a French subject though he remained French at heart. Up sprang the Marshal: "Yes," he exclaimed, "I am French, I shall die French!" Then reading from the note given him by Dupin which he had placed inside his hat, he went on: "So far my defence has seemed to be free. I now perceive that it is to be fettered. I thank my generous defenders for what they have done, and for what they are still prepared to do. But I beg them to desist altogether from defending me rather than defend me imperfectly. I would rather not be defended at all than have a sham defence. I am accused in defiance of the faith of treaties and I am to be forbidden to appeal to them! I do like Moreau. I appeal from you to Europe and to posterity." Then he handed the paper to Dupin. "To you I confide it," he said. The last two phrases were his own, added on the impulse of the moment.

"It is a lawyer's trick," said one of the Peers. Berryer sprang up to speak, but Ney stopped him by saying: "You can see very well that it is all settled in advance. I would rather not be defended at all than have my defence regulated by my accusers." Bellart intervened and asked the court to decide according to the demand of the ministers. "Defenders," said Dambray, "continue your defence, confining yourselves to the facts of the case." But turning to his counsel Ney said again: "I forbid you to speak unless you are allowed to speak freely".

Then Bellart told the court that "since the Marshal insisted on closing the discussion" the prosecution would say no more, and would leave certain points in M. Berryer's speech unchallenged. He simply asked the court to apply to the case of the accused the provisions of the Penal Code against treason and attacks on the safety of the state. "Accused," asked the President, "have you anything to say against the application of the penalty?" "Nothing whatever, Monseigneur," replied Ney. Then came the formal order of the President, "The accused, the witnesses, and the public will leave the court". It was just five o'clock. The darkness had come and the lamps had been lighted. The court was cleared, and the long process of taking the votes of the Peers began.

The President announced that a vote would be taken on three separate questions of fact:—

"1. Did Marshal Ney receive certain emissaries on the night between 13 and 14 March?

"2. Did Marshal Ney read a proclamation on the *place publique* of Lons-le-Saulnier on 14 March, inviting the troops to rebellion and defection?

"3. Has the Marshal been guilty of an attempt against the safety of the State?"

Each Peer was called upon by name to give his vote. On the first question 111 voted affirmatively and 47 negatively. Of the minority three Peers, the Marquess D'Aligre and Counts Lanjuinais and Nicolaï protested that they could not in conscience condemn the accused, as he had not been allowed the right to speak on the question of the Convention of Paris in its relation to his case. On the second question 158 voted "Yes," and the three who had made the protest voted "No".

On the third question 157 voted "Yes". Four dissented in various ways. Of this minority two, D'Aligre and Richebourg, replied "Yes," but added an appeal to the clemency of their colleagues. Lanjuinais voted "Yes" but added that the case was "covered by the capitulation of Paris". The Duke Victor de Broglie alone voted "No," and explained his vote by adding, "There is no crime unless there is a criminal intention, no treason without premeditation. One does not commit treason on a first impulse. I do not see in the facts justly alleged against Marshal Ney either premeditation or a design to betray."

Marshal Ney was thus declared guilty by majorities of the Peers. Then came the question of the sentence. Dambray announced that two votes would be taken in case the first scrutiny decided for the capital sentence. This was to give the Peers an opportunity of taking a more merciful decision on second thoughts. Each Peer was called in turn to give his opinion. Thirteen voted for deportation beyond the frontiers, 142 for death by military execution. One only was base enough to vote for death by the guillotine. I am sorry that he bore an Irish name. It was Count Lynch who had headed the Royalist revolt of Bordeaux in 1814. Then came the second vote. One hundred and thirty-seven Peers persisted in decreeing the death of the Marshal, seventeen voted for deportation, five abstained from voting and proposed an appeal to the clemency of the King. Among the five were De Nicolaï and D'Aligre. Among the seventeen who gave the merciful vote for deportation were the Duke de Broglie, Ney's old comrade General Colaud, and another soldier General Gouvion. But amongst those who twice voted for his death were a crowd of distinguished soldiers who had once been proud to be the comrades of the "bravest of the brave". Five marshals were among them, Kellerman (the old Duke of Valmy), Marmont, Sérurier, Pérignon, and Victor, and fourteen generals, among them Dupont (the *capitulard* of Baylen), Maison, Lauriston, and La Tour-Maubourg. Side by side with Royalists of the emigration, old Imperialists who owed the positions they had held under the Empire to Ney's victories joined in the cry for blood.

The President drafted the judgment and sentence. It was to be pronounced in the absence of the accused and afterwards communicated to him. It was half-past eleven when Dambray told the ushers to call in the counsel for the prisoner. But neither Dupin nor Berryer appeared. They knew too well what was coming and had gone to attend Ney in his prison.

It was midnight. The tired audience left the tribunes and hurried out to tell the waiting crowds what they had heard. The police prevented anyone lingering about the Luxembourg. But the proceedings were not yet over. The Peers were required to sign the judgment. It was written out by one of the secretaries, and then on page after page the Peers were called in turn to sign the record. There was a story that as soon as the public withdrew the Peers had been invited to a banquet in one of the halls of the palace. The only foundation for this report was the fact that in an adjoining corridor those who wished could go to a buffet on which were soup, bread, and some light wine. De Broglie noted that as they snatched this supper no one spoke. The crowd in the hall of judgment gradually dwindled as the weary judges signed in turn and went away. It was after 2 a.m. on the 7th that Count Lynch signed the last of all.

There had been some talk of obtaining the clemency of the King, but it was too late. While the Peers were still signing the record, the preparations were being made for the execution that very morning. The party of vengeance did not mean to lose its prey.

CHAPTER XIX

THE TRAGEDY OF THE LUXEMBOURG (1815)

WHEN the last of the Peers signed the record Ney had been some time sleeping soundly. At five in the evening, when the court was cleared for the voting, he had been escorted back to his room, where four sentries were posted one in each corner. The two Berryers and Dupin joined him there almost immediately. His dinner had been brought in, and while talking to them he ate heartily. "I am sure," he said, "that Monsieur Bellart will not dine with as good an appetite." He was much more cheerful and self-possessed than the lawyers.

After dinner they sat and talked together by the fire. Something was said of an appeal to the King's mercy, but Ney had no illusions. He told his friends he had only a few days, perhaps a few hours, to live. He asked them to arrange for him to see his wife and children, his sister-in-law Madame Gamot and his notary M. Batardy. When they left him he said it might be the final parting. It was he who had to console them. He embraced old Berryer and said to him, "Adieu, my dear defender, we shall see each other again above". He warmly thanked Dupin and the younger Berryer as he bade them farewell. He wrote for a while at the table—his last instructions for M. Batardy. Then the four sentinels saw him take a bundle of papers from his desk, and sit by the fire looking over them and tearing and burning them. It was a bitterly cold night and outside in the gardens of the Luxembourg snow was falling. That night, three years ago, he had slept wrapped in his cloak in the deep snow, east of Wilna with the starved ragged soldiers of the Grand Army keeping guard and the Cossacks prowling around in the darkness. Did he think of it now, or of old days in the cooperage at Saarlouis, and the dull time in the lawyer's office, and the time he spent in mines and ironworks and then the barracks at Metz when he was a trooper of hussars, and the swift rise to honours and fortune and his hundred battle-fields from the cannonade by the mill of Valmy to battles on the Rhine, the glories of Hohenlinden, Elchingen, Jena, Friedland, and the Moskowa, the terrible Russian retreat, the last struggles of the Empire, and only a few weeks ago the thundering charges of Waterloo, the desperate advance at the head of the Old Guard, the utter ruin of the hopeless rout? His aged father still lived. His wife and children would soon come to bid him a last farewell. This man of iron nerve, who looked so calmly at the death he had so often faced, had wept at the thought of their sorrows, but to-night, before the men who watched him so jealously, he showed no sign of weakness. Whatever his career had been, and there had been none more brilliant in that age of great soldiers, it was all over now, shrivelled up like the last scrap of paper he cast upon the blazing logs, as just before midnight he rose and threw himself, all dressed as he was, on the bed and fell asleep.

In the hall below the death sentence had just been read. Bellart had proclaimed his "dishonour," the Peers were waiting to sign the sentence. The audience was dispersing, carrying the news to crowds outside, driving off through the scattering flakes of snow to convey the tidings to cafés on the Boulevards and the hotels and *salons*, where so many were eagerly waiting for their message. Paris was at its gayest that December. The uniforms of officers of the Allied armies brightened the social gatherings that were held each night in scores of great houses. At some of these, just after midnight, the dancing stopped and players put down their hands at the card tables, as the word went round that Marshal Ney had been found guilty and condemned to be shot. Men said he had got his deserts —men who had fought against him or beside him. Women, sad to say, were found to express their delight. In the cafés old veterans of the Empire spoke in fierce fury, debated if rescue were not still possible, felt a pleasure in hurling challenges to deadly duels at those who, not knowing their company, showed their pleasure at the news. When would they kill the "bravest of the brave"? It would be on the Plaine de

Grenelle where Labedoyère had died. They would go there in the morning, and each morning, in the wild hope that something might be attempted.

In one great house in the Rue de Bourbon where, not so long ago, some of those who had voted for the Marshal's death had been proud to be his guests Aglaé, Princesse de la Moskowa, had been waiting through the evening for news. Ominous messages came from Berryer. At last after midnight her sister, Madame Gamot, arrived, and she knew the worst. She said she must see him. After awhile Madame Gamot yielded to her entreaties. The children were awakened and dressed, the carriage was sent for and the two women and the boys drove through the darkness to the Luxembourg. There were lights in the palace windows, mounted gendarmes on the move in the neighbouring streets, troops under arms in the garden. An officer came and told Madame Ney she could not be admitted till morning. She had better return then. But she refused to go, and with her sister she waited in the carriage for the time when the doors would be opened to her, while the tired children slept.

Many carriages came up and presently drove away, as the Peers quitted the building after a long session of sixteen hours. It was three o'clock. Ney woke from his dreams, for some one had entered the room. He sat up on the bed. The sentries were standing to attention in a group around a quiet little periwigged civilian who held a paper in his hand. It was M. Cauchy, the Secretary of the Chamber of Peers.

"What is it?" asked Ney. "I have a very painful duty," began Cauchy. "Well, that can't be helped. Every one must do his duty," said the Marshal encouragingly. "Tell me what it is."

The Secretary began to read the judgment of the Peers. He was rolling out the Marshal's titles, when Ney interrupted him. "Come to the point. Don't mind all those formalities." Cauchy read on. When he came to the mention of the Article of the Penal Code, which denounced the penalty of death against whoever tried to change the succession to the throne, Ney remarked quietly that this law had been enacted to maintain the Bonaparte family on the throne. Then, as the official went on, he interrupted again, "Come to the conclusion," he said. As he heard the sentence, he remarked. "They might have said in soldier phrase, make him bite the dust." This was perhaps the origin of the theatrical expression attributed to him in some narratives of his last hours, "Say, Michel Ney, soon to be a little dust".

He was then told that the Ministers had decided that he should be executed at nine o'clock that morning, and he said only, "When they wish. I am ready." Colonel de Montigny, the commandant of the Luxembourg, had come in. Ney asked him to arrange for his wife to see him at seven. The Colonel promised this. He did not then know that she was already waiting outside the palace. Ney was then told that the Abbé de Pierre, Curé of St. Sulpice, was in attendance to offer him the consolations of religion. He replied that he would think about it and send for him if he required his help. Cauchy then informed him that, if he wished, he could choose some other confessor. For the first time Ney showed impatience. "You are worrying me with your priests," he said, "I shall appear before God as I have appeared before men. I have no fear." Cauchy went away disappointed and saddened.

The Ministers had meanwhile ordered General de l'Espinois, military governor of Paris, to carry out the execution, and sent him written instructions on the precautions to be taken. He sent an aide-de-camp to wake up one of his officers, General Count Victor de Rochechouart, to whom he entrusted this terrible duty. He had made a good choice, for De Rochechouart, the son of an old Royalist family, had served under the Duc de Richelieu as a Russian officer in the days when the Duke was Governor of Odessa. Then he had fought against the French armies in the campaigns of Russia and Germany. He had perhaps been actually opposed in battle by the great soldier whom he was now to put to death.

He drove to the Luxembourg and took command there soon after three o'clock. Cauchy's visit had hardly ended when, accompanied by Colonel de Montigny, the General went to the prisoner's room. He told Ney that he was authorized to see his wife and children, his notary, and his confessor. "I shall first see the notary," said Ney. "He is probably in the palace.

Then I shall see my wife and children. As for the confessor, don't trouble me about him."

As he said this one of the guards on duty in the room, an old soldier belonging to the company of veteran non-commissioned officers, approached, saluted him respectfully, and said, "You are wrong, Marshal." Then pointing to the chevrons on his sleeve he went on, "I am not as brave as you, but I am as old in the service. Well, I have never gone under fire so boldly as when I had first of all recommended my soul to God." The Marshal seemed to be suddenly impressed. Using the familiar and friendly "*tu*," he replied: "Perhaps you are right, my brave friend. That is good advice you have given me." Then he turned to Colonel de Montigny and asked: "What priest can I send for?" Montigny named the Abbé de Pierre, without saying that he had already come to the palace. "He is," he added, "in every way one of the most distinguished of ecclesiastics." "Ask him to come. I will see him after I have seen my wife," was Ney's answer. Then the officers left him, after telling him that the first of his visitors would arrive about six o'clock. It was then four and the Marshal again lay down and slept soundly for two hours.

At six he rose, put on a civilian dress with a long dark blue coat, black knee breeches, silk stockings and a white cravat. Then the notary Batardy arrived. He was an old friend as well as his man of business. The interview was brief, for Ney had, the evening before, written down his last instructions as to his affiairs, and was able to hand the paper to him. At half-past six the notary went away, and Colonel de Montigny entered and ordered the guards to leave the room. In the passage outside Madame Ney and her four boys were waiting with Madame Gamot. The Colonel came out, and leaving the children in the corridor he re-entered with Ney's wife and her sister.

Poor Aglaé was exhausted with the weary waiting and with the terrible mental strain. As she saw her husband she gave a loud cry of agonized grief and fell fainting to the ground. De Montigny caught her as she fell, carried her to the Marshal, placing her in his arms. Her sister knelt beside him. Then Montigny left them.

Aglaé soon revived. In voices broken with fits of weeping the two women talked for a while with the Marshal who bore up well, and did his best to console and encourage them. Then Madame Gamot came out to bring in the children, the eldest a handsome boy of twelve, the future General and Prince of the Moskowa in the days of the Second Empire, the youngest a child of three years, who, yet unable to understand what was happening, cried bitterly at the grief of his mother. Ney kissed them and told them always to love her, and turning to his wife said that perhaps after all he was leaving them an honoured name, and she would teach them to do further honour to it. Aglaé spoke of appealing personally to the King. She would go to the Tuileries. Marmont, Duke of Ragusa, was their friend. He would obtain her an audience. She would yet save her husband. She did not know that Marmont had twice voted for his death. Ney had no hope whatever, but to end the painful interview and give her the momentary consolation of this last effort; he agreed that she should make the attempt to see the King. Then the sad farewells were spoken, and Madame Ney left the room supported by her sister. The three elder boys came out with their heads bent down, leading their little brother who was crying aloud. In the long corridors Madame Ney had more than once to stop and rest on her way to her carriage.

It was a few minutes after seven o'clock. Aglaé drove to the Tuileries, alighted there and sent Madame Gamot home with the boys. At the Tuileries the officers of the Guard and the ushers told the Maréchale that it was quite impossible for anyone to see the King at that early hour. She insisted on entering and sent her name to the chamberlain on duty. He told her that no audience was possible till later. The King had not yet risen. She said she would wait; she must see him at the earliest possible moment. Madame Gamot, returning to the palace, found her sitting in an ante-room weeping and praying. There she waited for two hours hoping against despair.

As soon as she left her husband, he had asked Colonel de Montigny to bring in the priest and the Abbé de St. Pierre entered. He had a record of courageous devotion to duty under conditions even more trying than those amid which Ney had won his name of the "bravest of the brave". Before the Revolution the Abbé had been one of the Sulpician community. In the days of the Terror he had remained hidden in Paris. He had said Mass in garrets and cellars for little groups of the faithful. He had gone disguised to the bedsides of the sick and dying. He had ventured to the very steps of the guillotine to give the last blessing and absolution to Catholics on their way to death. For months he had carried his life in his hands, and after the Concordat, refusing a higher position, he had become Curé of St. Sulpice and re-organized the great parish. He was the right man to help Ney in his last moments. The soldier and the priest were together for more than an hour. Then the Abbé left him, promising to return and be with him to the last.

Meanwhile General de Rochechouart had completed his arrangements. The firing party paraded, twelve veterans of the corps of old non-commissioned officers who formed the guard of the Luxembourg. They were commanded by Major de St. Bias, a Piedmontese. An escort of grenadiers and gendarmes commanded by Colonel Auguste de Larochejacquelein was waiting in the great court of the palace. At half-past eight a closed carriage was called from a cab-stand on the neighbouring Boulevard. The Abbé de Pierre went into the Marshal's room to tell him that the time was come. Before he could speak a word Ney had risen and said with a smile:" "Ah, Monsieur le Curé, I understand. I am ready." They went out into the corridor, where De Montigny grasped his prisoner's hand and bade him farewell. Then escorted by two lieutenants of gendarmes the priest and the Marshal went down to the entrance that opens on the court. The priest was greatly agitated, Ney perfectly calm. As he stepped out into the courtyard he said, "It's a wretched day". The snow had ceased to fall, but a drizzling rain was descending from a cloudy sky.

The carriage was waiting between two rows of soldiers with bayonets fixed. The Curé stood aside for the Marshal to enter it first, but Ney, smiling again, said to him: "Get in, Monsieur le Curé. I shall be going before you presently."

The Marshal, the priest, and the two lieutenants seated themselves in the carriage. The grenadiers and the gendarmes formed closely round it. De Rochechouart and De Larochejacquelein mounted and rode behind it. Then came a company of veterans, St. Bias with the firing party, and a company of the National Guard. The General gave the order to march, and the procession moved on out of the courtyard and southwards across the garden and down the Avenue de l'Observatoire.

The Park of the Luxembourg is now smaller than it was then. In 1815 its southern end extended over all the ground in the triangle between the Rue d'Assas and the Boulevard St Michel. Much of this ground has since been built over. Where now stand the School of Mines, the Colonial School and the School of Pharmacy and the houses about the Rue Herschell there was then a broad stretch of grassy lawns and rows of trees. All that is left of this part of the garden is the wide double avenue of the Observatory. At the southern end of the Avenue, but still within the iron railings of the garden, there was an open space—the Place de l'Observatoire. On one side of it there was a dead wall. At the open space the carriage stopped, and an officer opened its door. "What! arrived already!" exclaimed the Marshal. He thought that he was to be taken to the Plaine de Grenelle, the great parade ground outside the south-western barriers where Labedoyère had been shot. Crowds had gathered on the plain that morning in the same expectation, among them half-pay officers and veterans of the ranks of the Grand Army, some of them with arms concealed under their overcoats, in the wild hope of taking part in a rescue. The Government was anxious to risk nothing. Hence the place of execution had been selected in this corner of the Luxembourg gardens.

The troops moved up to the railings and sent out parties to block the openings of the neighbouring streets. Beyond their lines a crowd was gathering. There were also a few spectators in the garden itself, and a group of horsemen, among them a Russian general in uniform. When the Czar heard that he had thus gone to see Ney shot, he struck the general's name off the roll of the Russian Army.

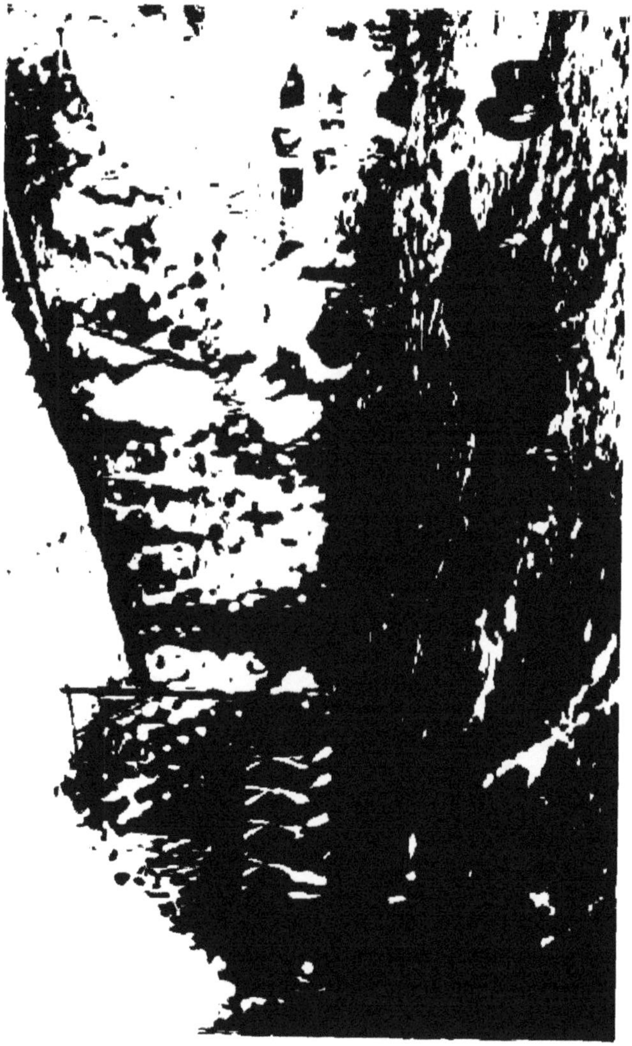

Ney got out of the carriage, followed by the Abbé de Pierre and the officers. He spoke for a minute with the priest, bowed his head as he received the last absolution, and then handed him a gold snuff-box, telling him to give it to Madame Ney as a keepsake. He pulled out his purse. There were a few gold louis in it. He gave these also to the Curé, telling him they were for the poor of St. Sulpice. The priest embraced him, and then knelt on the wet ground at a spot where Ney could still see him, when he took his place in front of the wall. Three lines of troops formed the sides of a square with the wall for the fourth. St. Bias marched in his twelve veterans, and gave them the order to load. According to the instructions he had received the Major wanted to blindfold the prisoner and make him kneel. He refused. "Don't you know, Sir," he said, "that a soldier does not fear death." He would meet it standing and open eyed.

De Rochechouart in his narrative of the tragedy tells how, sitting on his horse outside the square, he had a full view of the Marshal, and was struck by his calm and noble attitude. As Major de St. Bias walked back to his men to give them the order to fire, Ney strode forward four paces towards the levelled muskets, took off his hat, and said in a loud clear voice: "Frenchmen, I protest against my condemnation. My honour . . ." St. Bias gave the word "Feu!" and the volley crashed out before Ney could utter another word. The kneeling priest raised his hand in blessing as the smoke rolled over him. Ney had fallen dead on his face on the muddy ground, his hat rolling away to near his feet. Six bullets had struck him in the chest, three in the head, one had gone through his neck, another broken his right arm. One of the twelve bullets hit the wall high up bringing down a shower of plaster. There was one of the veterans who had refused to fire upon the "bravest of the brave".

There was a roll of the drums, a cry of "*Vive le Roi!*" from some of the soldiers and the spectators. Then the troops formed fours, and marched off the ground, only a few of the gendarmes remaining. De Rochechouart had turned to Larochejacquelein as Ney fell and said to him: "This, my friend, is a great lesson to teach one how to die well". Hostile as he was to Ney, he had yielded to the spell of his matchless courage in the face of death.

It was nine o'clock. Madame Ney was still waiting in the ante-room of the Tuileries, happily ignorant of the hour that had been fixed for her husband's death. Shortly after nine the Duke de Duras came to her. He was deeply touched by her grief, and when she told him she was waiting to see the King he said to her: "Madame, the audience you have asked for with the King would now be useless". He had not to say any more. She understood, and broke out into a wild burst of weeping. Madame Gamot took her back to her home more dead than alive.

The body of Ney was left lying where he fell for a quarter of an hour. Curious onlookers gathered round. Some were full of grief, and an old soldier dipped his handkerchief in the pool of blood as if to keep a relic of his former chief. Others openly expressed their delight at the accomplishment of this act of vengeance. One rider trotted his horse across the ground and leaped it over the prostrate body. The story ran that he was an Englishman. One hopes that this was not true, and that even in the strange crowd of adventurers of all nations that had been drawn to Paris, there was no Englishman base enough thus to insult a brave enemy.

Among the crowd, heedless of sympathy or insults the Abbé de Pierre remained kneeling in prayer. At last a bearer-party arrived with a stretcher and an escort of the National Guard. The body was taken up and conveyed to a neighbouring hospital, the Curé walking at the head of the little procession.

The Sisters of Charity who served the hospital paid the last honours to the dead hero. The body lay in state in one of the halls of the building, with flowers strewn upon the bed and long candles burning around it while the nuns came in turn to watch and pray beside it during the day and night. In the afternoon some hundreds of Parisians and foreigners were allowed to pass through the room. In the early morning of the 8th the body was coffined, and conveyed to the cemetery of Père la Chaise. The time and place of the funeral had been kept secret by order of the Government. As the hearse passed along the streets few knew that it was the corpse of Ney that was being taken to the grave, and there was only a small group of friends present when the Abbé de Pierre read the burial service. The grave marked only by a plain stone with the one word "NEY" is at the junction of two paths on the east side of the famous cemetery. Ney's monument is not there. It is the statue by the sculptor Rude in the Carrefour de l'Observatoire close to the spot where he fell.

The erection of this statue was part of a national act of reparation. After long years of agitation for the cancelling of his sentence, a movement in which his eldest son took a prominent part, the Provisional Government after the Revolution of 1848, decreed that his trial and sentence should be declared irregular, that his name should be restored to the roll of the Legion of Honour, and that a statue should be erected to his memory on the place of his execution. The work was not completed till after the inauguration of the Second Empire. It was on 7 December, 1853, the 38th anniversary of the execution that the statue was solemnly unveiled. Marshal St. Arnaud, the Minister of War presided at the ceremony. A great square was formed round the place by detachments of the Imperial Guard and the garrison of Paris. Batteries of artillery were unlimbered under the trees of the neighbouring garden. On one side of the veiled statue were grouped a crowd of generals, admirals, and officers of state; on the other Cardinal Morlot the Archbishop of Paris and his clergy. In front of the monument a deputation of the people of Saarlouis, and a group of his surviving friends and relatives. Dupin was there and the younger Berryer, and with them the aged widow of the great Marshal, and three of her sons, General Joseph Napoleon Ney, Prince of the Moskowa; General Michel Ney, Duke of Elchingen, and his two sons; and Colonel Edgar Ney. There was a short religious ceremony. Then St. Arnaud standing by the veiled statue delivered an address in which he spoke of the "act of national reparation" that was being accomplished, and referred to the services of Ney to France. He wished, he said, that he could dismiss from his mind the memory of those internal discords that in 1814 and 1815 had done more evil to France than the armies of the Allies. It was in that time of disunion that Ney's judgment failed him, as had been the case in earlier times of civil strife with Condé and Turenne. Like them he had erred. Unlike them he had expiated his error. So posterity would forget his passing weakness and remember only his greatness and the glories of his career. The veil dropped from the statue. The artillery roared out its salute, and with bands playing and the eagles displayed, that Ney had so often led to victory, the troops marched past the statue, saluting with lowered colours and waving swords.

Long before that "act of reparation," the public opinion of the civilized world had seen in his condemnation less of an act of justice than a deed of vengeance. Moncey's warning had been verified. The political trial, the sentence passed in defiance of solemn treaties, the refusal of all mercy, and the hurried execution had helped to sap the throne of the Bourbons. Ney's error had been forgotten in pity for his tragic fate and in admiration for his career as a soldier of France. When we repeat his name, we think, not of the parade at Lons-le-Saulnier, but of those long days and nights of unflinching endurance and dauntless courage amid the snows of Russia, when Ney won his title of the "bravest of the brave," from the greatest soldier that the world has ever seen.

INDEX

Lightning Source UK Ltd.
Milton Keynes UK
UKHW022150291119
354463UK00007B/1021/P

9 780469 521377